Economic Efficiency in Law and Economics

NEW HORIZONS IN LAW AND ECONOMICS

The application of economic ideas and theories to the law and the explanation of markets and public economics from a legal point of view is recognized as one of the most exciting developments in both economics and the law. This important series is designed to make a significant contribution to the development of law and economics.

The main emphasis is on the development and application of new ideas. The series provides a forum for original research in areas such as criminal law, civil law, labour law, corporate law, family law, regulation and privatization, tax, risk and insurance and competition law. International in its approach it includes some of the best theoretical and empirical work from both well-established researchers and the new generation of scholars.

Titles in the series include:

Inflation and the Enforcement of Contracts
Shirley Renner

Law and Economics and the Labour Market
Edited by Gerrit De Geest, Jacques Siegers and Roger Van den Bergh

Economic Efficiency in Law and Economics
Richard O. Zerbe Jr.

Economic Efficiency in Law and Economics

Richard O. Zerbe Jr.,

Professor of Public Affairs, Daniel J. Evans School of Public Affairs and Adjunct Professor, Law School, University of Washington, USA

NEW HORIZONS IN LAW AND ECONOMICS

Edward Elgar

Cheltenham, UK • Northampton, MA, USA

Published by
Edward Elgar Publishing Limited
Glensanda House
Montpellier Parade
Cheltenham
Glos GL50 1UA
UK

Edward Elgar Publishing, Inc.
136 West Street
Suite 202
Northampton
Massachusetts 01060
USA

A catalogue record for this book
is available from the British Library

Library of Congress Cataloguing in Publication Data

Zerbe, Richard O.
Economic efficiency in law and economics / Richard O. Zerbe, Jr.
— (New horizons in law and economics)
Includes bibliographical references and index.
1. Law and economics. 2. Economics—Philosophy. I. Title. II. New horizons in law and economics series.

K487.E3 Z47 2001
330—dc21

00–047645

ISBN 1 84064 301 3 (cased)

Typeset by Manton Typesetters, Louth, Lincolnshire, UK.
Printed and bound in Great Britain by Bookcraft (Bath) Ltd.

Contents

This book is dedicated to my wife, Diane, for her support and encouragement and to Ronald H. Coase in great appreciation.

I would like to thank Steve Vinyard and Robin Boadway.

1. History of the concept of economic efficiency

1.1 INTRODUCTION

James Buchanan won the Nobel Prize by proving that the process by which elected officials enact policy in a decentralized polity, such as the United States, leads to spending patterns that are inevitably inefficient. Ronald Coase won the prize for showing that traditional concepts of efficiency fail to account for costs that affect every trade and government action: the costs of transactions. Both Coase and Buchanan showed how institutional arrangements affect efficiency, and how changes in these arrangements can be either efficient or inefficient.[1]

If the concept of efficiency is to serve a useful role, it needs to rest on a firm foundation. To create such a foundation is the aim of this book. Practical people need practical measures of economic efficiency. Theorists want measures that are theoretically sound. Still others want measures that are ethically satisfying. No current measure of efficiency satisfies all of these requirements. The weight of moral and technical criticism promises to undermine the authority of the current efficiency criteria (Zerbe 'Three Rules' 1998b). Indeed, criticisms of legal and economic thinking about efficiency has reached the popular press (see, for example, Purdy 1988).

The purpose of this book is to meet the critics' challenges. Its purpose is *not* to argue, or to determine, whether or not their charges are true, but rather to provide a version of normative analysis, the foundation and use of which are robust with respect to these sort of charges. In this book, I will produce a definition of efficiency that is workable in practice, theoretically sound, and ethical.

To accomplish this task, I will suggest criteria for defining efficiency, and demonstrate how they can be used to judge one of the most concrete expressions of collective will: the creation of law. I will strip the current concept of efficiency to expose its moral and ethical basis. Then, I will build up a similar concept, which differs in small – but crucial – ways from the traditional concept. To accomplish this task, I suggest seven axioms to use in forming a definition or criterion of efficiency, and I demonstrate the power of the criterion through several applications, particularly in that most practical arena, the law.[2] The aim of this book, then, is to suggest measures of efficiency that are practical, that are reasonably well motivated theoretically, and that are logical extensions and modifications of the existing measures, namely the Kaldor–Hicks (henceforth KH) measures of economic efficiency.[3] I refer to my definition of efficiency as KHZ.

In the course of doing these things, I will demonstrate that the Scitovsky paradox does not occur for our welfare measure and, indeed, is irrelevant for benefit–cost analysis in its usual and customary applications. I will further explain why the sum of compensating variations is both a necessary and sufficient condition for KHZ efficiency. I will show that the incorporation of distributional considerations – and the facts about whether or not compensation actually occurs – are a logical part of any welfare measure built on traditional grounds, so that the present exclusion of such considerations is unnecessary and damaging.

I will show that current ethical criticisms of normative economics generally do not apply when the theory is correctly understood, and clearly do not apply when the modest modifications to the definition of efficiency I suggest are adopted. I will show that the alleged 'status quo bias' that occurs when considering welfare changes is not a bias, but is well founded. Further, I will demonstrate that the problem of indeterminacy in assigning an previous unassigned right that Posner (and others) say arises does not in fact exist when the problem is approached correctly. Incidental to this, I will show that the Coase theorem – even the efficiency part of the Coase theorem – is wrong, even if we accept the assumption that transactions costs are zero, in that there is a loss of efficiency if the right is assigned to the wrong person. I will show that Baker's (1980) objections to the application of efficiency analysis to legal issues are incorrect and that Hovenkamp's (1991) suggestion for measuring the value of changes is not well grounded. Then, I will show the general form of the efficiency equation to apply to the assignments of rights in dispute. In the last two chapters, I present a theory of common law efficiency and indeed inefficiency. Finally, and most importantly, I provide numerous examples from the law of the application of the criteria developed here.

But what are the current measures of economic efficiency, and how did they arise? To understand the foundation for KHZ, it is useful to understand the foundation for the traditional KH measures. The history given here is hardly definitive, as the material on KH is voluminous. Rather, the history here is meant primarily to provide a context for the practical measure suggested.

1.2 CURRENT MEASURES OF ECONOMIC EFFICIENCY

Pareto Efficiency

The most prominent notion of welfare criteria, a Pareto optimum, was introduced by Vilfredo Pareto (1896). A Pareto optimum is a state of affairs such that no one can be made better off without making someone else worse off.[4] A change in the economy is said to represent a Pareto improvement if at least one person is made better off as a result of the change and no person is made worse off. The obvious limitation of this criterion is that it is not applicable to most changes; few policies indeed have no losers.[5] This limitation was recognized early on, resulting in a search for a more applicable measure of welfare that continues to this day.

The attraction of the Pareto notion of efficiency is that it seems to eliminate interpersonal comparisons of welfare. Many economists feel that the inescapable conclusion is that if one precludes interpersonal comparisons of welfare the only logically consistent foundation analysis is the Pareto principle (Slesnick 1998; Arrow 1951). Yet even the Pareto principle makes interpersonal comparisons in an important sense. A choice rule that is identical with the Pareto principle is that any loss of welfare to even one person is sufficient to offset or to veto any possible gains to others, regardless of how large the gains are. This gives infinite weight to losses as a basis of making interpersonal comparisons.[6] In this sense, then, the Pareto principle not only makes interpersonal comparisons, it does so in a manner that is unlikely to be widely acceptable.

An early approach, lasting until the 1930s, rested, according to Hammond (1985, p. 406), on the notion that interpersonal comparisons of utility could be made on a more or less objective basis. The basic assumption was that every individual had an 'equal capacity for enjoyment' and that therefore gains or losses among different individuals could be directly compared (Mishan 1981, pp. 120–121). As Hicks (1939, p. 640) noted, '[D]uring the nineteenth century, it was generally considered to be the business of an economist ... to lay down principles of economic policy, to say what policies are likely to be conducive to social welfare, and what policies are likely to lead to waste and impoverishment.' During the nineteenth century, economists believed that the marginal utility of income (the satisfaction associated with an additional dollar of income) decreased with total income, and, largely on this basis, they supposed that an optimal distribution of income was an equal distribution.[7] Although Robbins (1932) objected that this assumption about the marginal utility of income was unscientific, the issue remained unsettled.

For example, even in the late 1930s, Harrod (1938) continued to argue that the net benefit from a policy could be established, if the aggregate changes in income were positive, on the assumption that the individuals affected were equal in their capacity to enjoy income.[8] Harrod (1938) used this reasoning to justify the 1846 repeal of the English Corn Laws, a classic test case for British economists. In response, Robbins (1938, p. 640) pointed out that interpersonal comparisons of utility cannot rest on a scientific foundation since utility cannot be measured, and that the justification for such comparisons is more ethical than scientific.[9] Harrod (1938, pp. 396–397) then complained that, in the absence of comparability of utility of different individuals, 'the economist as an advisor is completely stultified'.[10] Thus, by the late 1930s, leading British economists, including the future Nobel prize winner Hicks (1939), were raising questions about such policy prescriptions because they were seen to rest on interpersonal comparisons of utility. Harrod's complaint about stultification was echoed elsewhere, creating a sort of temporary professional depression among economists, who feared the loss of their ability to pronounce judgments with respect to normative policy. Normative economic analysis remained in this state until the Kaldor–Hicks criteria were introduced.

Kaldor–Hicks

The origin of the Kaldor-Hicks criteria

The Kaldor–Hicks (KH) efficiency criteria have now existed for over sixty years. Both the legal and the economic literatures consider the validity of the KH criteria to be an important issue. For example, a computerized search of law reviews and legal journals finds a total of 1933 citations to Kaldor–Hicks or its synonyms.[11] The criteria arose out of discussions among prominent British economists during the late 1930s.[12] The goal was to develop a welfare measure that was more broadly applicable than Pareto efficiency and that avoided interpersonal comparisons. Kaldor (1939, pp. 549–550) acknowledged Robbins' point about the inability to make interpersonal utility comparisons, but suggested its irrelevance. He suggested that where a policy led to an increase in aggregate real income:

> the economist's case for the policy is quite unaffected by the question of the comparability of individual satisfaction, since in all such cases it is possible to make everybody better off than before, or at any rate to make some people better off without making anybody worse off.

Kaldor goes on to note (1939, p. 550) that whether such compensation should take place 'is a political question on which the economist, qua economist, could hardly pronounce an opinion'. Kaldor's (1939) suggestion was later formalized by other economists, such as Boadway and Bruce (1984, p. 96) as the proposition that:

> state *a* is preferable to another state if, in state *a*, it is hypothetically possible to undertake costless (lump-sum) redistribution and achieve an allocation that is superior to the other state according to the Pareto criterion.

Hicks (1939) agreed with Kaldor's potential compensation approach and suggested a test similar to Kaldor's, which is formally stated as

> state *a* is preferable to another state if, in the other state, it is not possible, hypothetically, to carry out lump-sum redistribution so that everyone could be made as well off as in state *a*. (see Boadway and Bruce 1984, p. 97)

In less formal language, the Kaldor test is passed if in the new state, redistributions are possible that would create a state Pareto superior to the original state. The Hicks test is that there exist no redistributions in the original state that would produce a situation Pareto superior to the new state. These two tests are generally known as the Kaldor–Hicks compensation tests[13] or, alternatively, as the potential compensation – or potential Pareto – tests.[14] They represent what economists and lawyers generally mean, or think they mean, when they speak of economic efficiency.[15] Posner (1985a, pp. 86–89; 1986, pp. 12–13; 1987a, p. 16) has indicated that a term of his creation, 'wealth maximization,' is identical with KH. Although this identity has not been borne out in his actual uses of the term, this identity will be assumed here, except as otherwise indicated.[16]

1.3 THE SEPARATION OF EFFICIENCY AND DISTRIBUTION

The Origin of the Separation

The approach adopted by Kaldor, and then by Hicks, attempted to separate economic efficiency from issues of the distribution of income. It was generally thought that by separating distributional considerations from aggregate gains a value-free measure would be obtained (Kaldor 1939; Hicks 1939; Chipman and Moore 1978, p. 578).[17] The change in aggregate gains was to be the measure of efficiency, so that there was a separation of effects into those of efficiency and distribution. The eagerness of economists to separate considerations of efficiency from those of distribution arose from a desire to put economics on a firm base as a policy instrument. Kaldor (1939, p. 551) argued that the economist cannot be concerned with distributional questions, and then endorsed the procedure adopted by Pigou (1932), which Kaldor describes as 'dividing welfare effects into two parts: the first relating to production, and the second to distribution.' With respect to the second part,

Kaldor (1939, p. 551) suggests, 'the economists should not be concerned with prescriptions at all ... For, it is quite impossible to decide on economic grounds what particular pattern of income-distribution maximizes social welfare.'

Hicks (1939, p. 712) agreed with this separation and noted that 'if measures making for efficiency are to have a fair chance, it is extremely desirable that they should be freed from distributive complication as much as possible.' To Hicks (p. 696) it would be 'rather a dreadful thing' to have to accept the view that welfare analysis was unscientific. If it were, its conclusions would

> depend on the scale of social values held by a particular investigator. Such conclusions can possess no validity ... one's welfare economics will inevitably be different according as one is a liberal, or a socialist, a nationalist or an internationalist, a christian [sic] or a pagan.

This separation of efficiency and equity has remained the standard analysis of economists to this day. From this period in the late 1930s, then, this dichotomy between efficiency and distribution has been, in the main, accepted by the economics profession as necessary to avoid interpersonal comparisons of utility.[18] Notwithstanding this rationale the major criticism of the KH compensation tests, by critics of benefit–cost analysis, is that the tests ignore income distribution effects (see, for example, Anderson 1993, p. 191).

Earlier, before the advent of the KH tests, Pigou (1932) had suggested a dual test, and proposed that greater equality in income was a good thing. Under Pigou's test, a new position was better than an old one if, for an unchanged KH efficiency, it showed an increase in the equality of distribution. Later, Little (1957) correctly pointed out that any criteria, whether KH or not, rested on value judgments. Value judgments are inescapable in normative economics. The important thing is to make the judgments clear so that the decision maker knows what he is getting into. Little proposed that there also be a distributional test in addition to the hypothetical compensation test. Thus, a change in policy that causes a movement from position A to position B is desirable if (1) it passes a compensation test and (2) position B is distributionally superior to position A. Little did not, however, suggest what the distribution test might be. And this failure probably explains Little's lack of influence, aside from bringing attention to the issue of distribution of income. Although Little, unlike Pigou, did not suggest a distribution test, his work ushered in an outpouring of literature about distribution tests for judging economic policy.

1.4 COMPENSATING AND EQUIVALENT VARIATIONS

In 1943, Hicks proposed the compensating variations (CV) and equivalent variations (EV) tests as money measures of changes between different welfare positions. Hicks adopted these measures to make welfare change measurable and to furnish measures to use in KH tests. They are money measures of welfare change (sometimes called 'exact utility indicators') that order choices for individuals. The CV measures the value of a change at the prices holding in the new situation, the EV measures the value of a change at the original prices. The CV assumes the original utility level as the status quo; the EV assumes the final utility level as the status quo. For both of these tests, if the money measure of value for a move from position A to position B is positive for an individual, it is assumed that the individual will prefer position B to position A. To use the EV measure for a welfare gain implicitly assumes that one has a right to that gain. To use the CV measure assumes no such right. For a negative change, the CV assumes a right to the status quo, so that one has a right to avoid the loss; the EV assumes no right to avoid the negative change (for an elaboration, see Zerbe and Dively 1994, pp. 74–80 or Boadway and Bruce 1984).

The advantages of the CV and EV values were, first, that they were measurable and, second, that they appeared to have intuitive meaning, in terms of the willingness to pay (WTP) and the willingness to accept payment (WTA). The WTA reflects the price that someone who has the good would accept to sell it. The WTA is also the minimum amount of money one would accept to forgo some good or to bear some harm. The CV measure (for consumers) is the sum of the WTPs for a beneficial change plus the sum of the WTAs for a negative change. The EV measure (for consumers) is the sum of the WTAs for a positive change plus the sum of the WTPs for a negative change. The CV measure is associated with the Kaldor compensation test, and has generally been the standard for benefit–cost analysis, on the grounds that a change should be made only when the potential losers of a good could potentially be compensated on the basis of their values, as reflected by their willingness to sell that good.[19] For a normal good, the WTA is greater than the WTP, for reasons that I will discuss later. Therefore, it was thought that the use of the CV ensured that potential compensation of losses was possible. We shall see in Chapter 3 that the relationship among the WTP and the WTA, and the EV and the CV and potential compensation tests is more complex than usually indicated.

For the economists of the late 1930s and early 1940s, the critical question became whether or not a policy could pass a Kaldor or a Hicks compensation test, in terms of whether the sum of the compensating or equivalent variations was positive. In the case of the Corn Laws, the question was, then, whether or not the gainers from the laws' repeal could, in principle, compensate the losers (the landlords), and still have something left over for themselves. These tests were then to be regarded as 'objective test[s] of economic efficiency; prescriptions based on it were thought to have a scientific status and to be free from value judgments' (Mishan 1981, p. 303).[20]

1.5 CRITICISMS OF KALDOR–HICKS

Moral Criticisms[21]

Many critics of benefit–cost analysis have said that it ignores issues of income distribution and actual compensation, so that it approves a project that hurts those who should be helped, and benefits those who do not need it (Fried 1978). The critics say that normative economic analysis is missing values such as personal integrity, so that it condemns a person who uses resources to keep a promise to a dead friend when the friend can no longer benefit from the kept promise, resulting in a waste of resources (Kelman 1981; Smart and Williams 1973). Critics say that benefit–cost analysis rests on faulty moral grounds, because it does not tell us the right thing to do, as when it fails to condemn slavery, rape, or abortion (Dworkin 1980; Meeks 1990). Further, critics say that normative economic analysis embodies defective moral principles, because it does not count the well-being of future generations as heavily as that of the present generation. For example, critics say that the use of a discount rate to discount benefits or harm to future generations is unethical (Parfit 1992, 1994). Other critics say that benefit–cost analysis rests on utilitarianism, so that it weighs pleasure deriving from bad acts – as when a sadistic person derives pleasure from beating another – equally with the pleasure that more generous people derive from good acts – such as helping others (Kelman 1981; Posner 1981a; Sen 1982).

Technical Criticisms

Reversibility and status quo bias

In addition to these moral or ethical criticisms, there are technical ones. Scitovsky raised two objections to the KH criteria: the status quo bias and preference reversals. On the status quo bias, he noted with respect to the Kaldor criterion 'the objection to using this criterion by itself [Kaldor?] is that it … attributes undue importance to the particular distribution of welfare obtaining before the contemplated change' (Scitovsky 1941, p. 88).[22] This objection arises because using the Kaldor or the Hicks tests to compare positions A and B, the criteria can suggest either that A is better or that B is better, depending on which is the starting point. The starting point determines the result.[23] That is, status quo bias exists because the KH criteria would generally lead to the decision to take no action when there was uncertainty from application of the criteria (Mishan 1981; Zerbe and Dively 1994).

Scitovsky's second objection to KH has received more attention: he pointed out that the use of one of the KH tests, but not the other, can result in a circularity when two second-best states are compared. That is, the CV (or EV) test can first suggest that a move from state A to state B is desirable. Then, having moved from A to B, the same test can suggest that a move from state B to state A is desirable. Scitovsky suggested a solution to the reversal paradox. The Scitovsky test would require that both the CV test and the EV test be passed to justify a movement from one state of the world, A, to another state of the world, B. This eliminates the possibility of reversals, since they can occur only when one test is passed and the other failed. This means that there is what might be called a status quo bias attached to the Scitovsky test, in that no change is suggested for projects which pass one test but not the other one.

Compensation tests

Boadway and Bruce noted that the KH criteria themselves may not satisfy the potential compensation tests on which they are said to rest. That is, the relationship between compensating tests and the sum of the compensating and equivalent variations is more complex, and less satisfactory, than economists originally believed. To obtain a positive sum of individual CVs is a necessary but not a sufficient condition for a Kaldor (weak) compensation test to be passed (1984, p. 271). (A weak compensation test is one carried out in terms of purchasing power rather than in terms of goods. A strong compensation test is carried out in terms of goods. That is, the weak test allows the aggregate bundle of good produced to change as redistribution occurs in a manner consistent with the production possibilities in the original state (Kaldor), or consistent with the production possibilities in the final state (Hicks). A strong test limits the hypothetical distribution to a reallocation of the goods available in the original (Kaldor) state or the final (Hicks) state.)

That is, if a sum of CVs is not positive, we can say that a Kaldor compensation *is not* passed. But, if the sum is positive, we cannot be certain that a Kaldor compensation test is passed. A positive value for the sum of EVs is, however, sufficient to pass a Hicks (weak) compensation test, but it is not a necessary condition. That is, if the sum of EVs is positive, we can be confident that a compensation test is passed, but if the sum of EVs is *not* positive, it still may be the case that a Hicks (weak) compensation test is passed.

Clearly, no problem exists for those projects that pass an EV test. Such projects should, on the basis of a potential compensation principle, be adopted.

Similarly, no problem arises for those projects that fail a CV test. They should be rejected as failing to pass a compensation test. The problem arises for those projects that pass a CV test but do not pass an EV test. We cannot know whether they pass or fail a compensation test. We do not know how common these projects might be. We do not know if they are likely only for projects involving expensive or unique goods.[24]

The difficulties do not end here, however. If there are distortions in the economy, such as those created by taxes, so that some people face different prices for goods than others, the aggregate CVs are not even a necessary condition for a compensation test to be passed (Boadway and Bruce 1984, p. 271). For at least small projects, however, use of the compensating variation does provide a necessary and sufficient condition for a Kaldor compensation test, when a weighted average of prices is used (ibid., p. 271; Bruce and Harris 1982).

Gorman (1953) derived the condition under which it is possible to say that a positive aggregate sum of the CVs or EVs, such as is performed in the KH tests, results in an actual welfare improvement. The required condition is constant and identical marginal utility of income with respect to changes in income, but not prices, across individuals. That is, the marginal utility could change with price changes, but not with income changes (for a brief elaboration of the Gorman form, see Zerbe and Dively 1994, p. 99). Few will accept this condition as a reasonable assumption. Boadway and Bruce (1984, p. 271) conclude that 'the use of the un-weighted sum of household compensating or equivalent variations as a necessary and sufficient indicator of potential Pareto improvement is rife with difficulties. At best, such measures can be used as a preliminary attempt to rank social states.'

Another major objection to the KH theory of efficiency was raised by Coase in a series of papers (see, for example, Coase 1960, 1988). Coase points out that the theoretical analysis proceeds without considering transactions costs and that a consideration of transactions costs changes important welfare propositions. This failure to consider transactions costs is thought to result in activities, such as giving gifts at Christmas, which are labeled as inefficient when, in fact, no improvement exists that could be efficiently made (Waldfogel 1993; Coase 1960, 1988; Zerbe and McCurdy 1999).

These moral and technical objections to KH are telling criticisms. The claims of those who criticize benefit–cost analysis are sweeping. The proponents of KH respond to these criticisms with puzzling and unclear statements, which only serve to further undermine its value. For example, when analysts claim that slavery is efficient, or that abortion is inefficient, what do they mean? Can they be correct? When economists suggest that Christmas giving is inefficient, are they being silly or are they making an important point? When proponents of KH claim that the common law is generally efficient, but are unable to explain why this should be the case, is this a statement about the common law on which we can reasonably rely?

The standard modern approach to questions of economic welfare is to adopt a 'Social Welfare Function.' This is nothing more than a decision rule for welfare changes. We are still left with justifiying any such decision rule. This book then is about a particular social welfare function, its justification, and its use in practice.

1.6 CONCLUSION

The KH criteria arose from the need for a practical measure that would allow economists to say something objective about the desirability of different projects. A number of ethical and technical criticisms have been leveled against the criteria. The weight of these has reached the point where the criteria lack moral authority (for example, see the 1980 issues of the *Hofstra Law Review*).

Chipman and Moore (1978, p. 548), in their useful survey of post-1939 welfare economics, conclude that 'judged in relation to its basic objective of enabling economists to make welfare prescriptions without having to make value judgments and, in particular interpersonal comparisons of utility, the New Welfare Economics must be considered a failure.' However, this failure was inevitable because the objective was impossible. The question remains: what objective is possible? To this question we now turn.

NOTES

1. Coase's (for example 1960) and Buchanan's (for example 1974) works also address a variety of other issues.
2. The major applications include analyses of slavery, of segregation, of trespass, of the law of dueling, of theft, of abortion, of rape, of benefit–cost analyses of dam removal to preserve salmon, of Christmas giving, of the Lorenzen case, and of the efficiency of the common law.
3. The Kaldor–Hicks measures are loosely defined as being satisfied when the winners from a policy gain more than the losers lose. More precise definitions are given below.
4. In its strong form, Pareto efficiency claims that state A is preferred to state B when state A is ranked higher than state B for one person and all other persons rank A at least as high as B. If the utility (well-being) of each individual is higher in state A, then state A is preferred according to the weak form of Pareto efficiency (Boadway and Bruce 1984, p. 62).
5. I challenge the reader to recommend one. Even a voluntary sale of a good by one person to another is probably not Pareto efficient, since even though both the seller and the buyer are better off as a product of the sale, other members of the community may suffer, at least marginally, since the sale might drive the market price up (harming consumers) or down (harming suppliers) (Posner 1984, p. 13). Of course, the probable harm to potential buyers and sellers is low, approaching zero, but any potential harm defeats Pareto efficiency.

6. In this, the Pareto principle is similar to, but significantly more demanding than, Rawls's (1971) proposal that, subject to basic freedoms and liberties, no project should harm the least well off. Rawls's suggestion has generally been rejected in practice as too demanding and the Pareto principle as a practical approach has been similarly rejected (Black 1969).
7. Hammond (1985) notes that it was also assumed that individuals had the same marginal utility of income schedules. However, Lerner (1944) had by the mid 1940s shown that equal incomes maximized expected utility even if their schedules were different, provided that there was diminishing marginal utility of income.
8. That is, an improvement can be assumed by looking at changes in income as long as, in modern terminology, the marginal utility of income with respect to income changes is the same for all individuals.
9. Robbins (1938, p. 635) believed it politically expedient to treat all people as if they had the same marginal utility of income, but was concerned that this be seen to rest on an ethical not a scientific principle. In fact, he says, '*But I do not believe that, in most cases, political calculations which do not treat them [men] as if they were equal are morally revolting*' (emphasis added).
10. This debate about whether or not prescriptions of economics were scientific is paralleled by the 1980s debate, mostly in the legal literature, about the normative foundations of wealth maximization. For example, see the *Hofstra Law Review*, 1980, volume 8, numbers 3 and 4. The 1980s debate was haunted, and confounded, by the issues that I consider in this book.
11. I found 425 references to 'Kaldor–Hicks' directly; 92 more are found under the rubric 'potential Pareto,' and 1,416 cites are to some form of 'wealth maximization.' The numbers reported here were generated by three Westlaw searches on 29 October 1997, all of which were conducted using the *Journals of Law Reviews* database.
12. These are, in the main, those already mentioned: Robbins, Hicks, Kaldor, and Harrod, all writing in the *Economic Journal*.
13. Chipman (1987, p. 524) suggests that the compensation principle may be traced back to Dupuit in 1844, and, later, to Marshall (1890). Marshall used the concept of consumer surplus to compare losses of consumers to gains to the government. Lerner (1944) invoked a potential compensation principle in measuring monopoly power. Hotelling (1938) anticipated the KH test by suggesting that a new public investment is justified, given its benefits, if its costs could – in theory – be distributed so as to make everyone better off. Anticipating issues of distribution, Hotelling noted that where extreme hardship resulted from a policy, actual compensation was needed.
14. The term 'Kaldor–Hicks' was used, at least as early as 1951, by Arrow (1951, p. 928), and, in 1952, by Mishan (1952, p. 312).
15. The other concept, of course, is that of Pareto optimality, but this is a concept ill suited to discussion of economic changes and is, therefore, of limited practical application.
16. Posner sometimes uses wealth maximization to mean KH but at other times seems to use it to mean an increase in GDP or the maximization of monetary wealth. In this regard, Posner uses it to support his tastes in favor of a work ethic and the importance of production as compared with consumption (see Posner 1987a, pp. 19–20). This is, however, a different meaning from KH. The fact that economic efficiency is not the same as national income was shown by Harberger (1971, p. 785). Economic efficiency is the opposite of common but narrow concepts such as workplace efficiency, in which people are to be managed as machines (Kanigel 1997).
17. Certainly Mishan (1952, p. 312) was aware that questions of distribution belonged to welfare economics and recognized that the separation was useful, since there was less agreement about the income distribution issues.
18. I will note some rather random examples from reputable sources. Boardman *et al.* (1996, p. 412) note that, 'Strict use of the Kaldor–Hicks test means that information on how benefits and costs are distributed among groups is ignored in decision making.' Friedman (1984, p. 170) notes, 'Some analysts would like to ignore equity altogether and use the compensation test as the decisive analytic test ... [A] second rationale for relying on the

compensation test is the belief that concern for equity is simply unfounded.' Posner (1992b, p. 13) notes that wealth maximization is simply the Kaldor–Hicks tests and that wealth maximization ignores distributional effects (Posner 1984, pp. 132–133). McCloskey (1982, p. 229) incorrectly contends that the consumer surplus measure of social happiness is the same as the national income measure. Of course, the national income measure contains no measure of income distribution.

19. The CV measure is generally the standard for benefit–cost analysis.
20. For a discussion of the historical development of the theory of compensation principles, see Chipman (1987).
21. See Zerbe (1998b).
22. In this 1941 article, Scitovsky is listed as Scitovzsky but the simpler spelling was used thereafter and is generally used.
23. This result arises only in comparing first-best states. A first-best state is an efficient state in which two conditions are satisfied. First, no more of any good can be produced without reducing the amount of some other good. Second, the marginal rate at which one good can be transferred into another in production is the same marginal rate at which the two goods are valued.
24. The problem of reversals arises from the difference between the CV and EV. If there is no difference, there can be no reversals. The greater the difference the more likely are reversals (see generally Mishan 1981, Chapter 7).

2. The foundation: A new measure for economic efficiency

2.1 WHY A NEW MEASURE IS NEEDED

In Chapter 1, I suggested that criticisms of normative economic analysis have eroded its use and particularly its moral authority. In this chapter I offer a set of seven axioms to address these shortcomings, based on considerations of usefulness and acceptance, on which a new normative criteria can rest. These axioms are then the social welfare function promised in Chapter 1.

2.2 CRITERIA FOR A NEW MEASURE OF EFFICIENCY

Sen (1995, p. 11) notes that it is difficult to agree upon a rule for measuring social welfare because of the disparate considerations that pull us in different directions when we attempt to evaluate policies or welfare procedures. The goal I set for myself here is ambitious; it is to suggest a set of principles and accompanying procedures which will provide an ethical basis for benefit–cost analysis.[1]

The failure of 'the New Welfare Economics noted in Chapter 1 was guaranteed, as its objective was the unattainable one of a value-free measure' (Chipman and Moore 1978, p. 581). Both the undesirability and impossibility of such value-free measures are now well recognized (ibid.; Sen 1995; Hammond 1985). Criteria that are used to determine what is 'good,' or 'better,' or 'best' must encompass a definition of 'good,' or 'better,' or 'best.' Determining what is 'good' cannot, by definition, be a value-free process. Who would wish it to be value free, since values are the foundation for determining what is good?

The Pareto criterion itself is not value free, because it embodies preferences based on choice, or what Hammond (1985, p. 408) calls 'consumer sovereignty.' In addition, an ethically superior position may not, and usually will not, be one that is also Pareto superior.[2] More important, the choice to confine oneself to such a limited choice device as Pareto superiority is itself clearly an ethical one. Indeed, the adoption of a Pareto-superior rule to the exclusion of other rules gives veto power to anyone harmed, regardless of the gains of others.[3] And, from a practical standpoint unanimity is not a very workable voting rule (Black 1969).

It is equally misguided to suggest that any meaningful choice criterion that affects more than one individual can avoid interpersonal comparisons (Sen 1995, p. 8). Such a notion does not survive its statement. Even if utility were measurable, a choice must be made as to how to weigh the utility of different individuals. A decision to maximize unweighted utility is an ethical decision, one to which, for example, Zerbe (1998b, pp. 427–429) and Posner (1985a, p. 97) object. After all, there is such a thing as bad utility. For example, consider the utility some receive from committing bad acts (Sen 1982; Zerbe 1998b, pp. 427f). We might not wish to give the same weight to utility that arises from the pleasure of hurting others, as to utility that arises from doing good works. Posner (1985a, pp. 97–98) suggests that wealth maximization avoids this issue, but he does not indicate why. If, as he says, by 'wealth maximization' he means the same thing as KH (Posner 1986, pp. 12–13), and if, as he says (Posner 1987a, p. 18), 'wealth' is essentially 'utility' as used by economists, then he does not avoid the issue and is mistaken to think that he does.[4] How is the issue of bad utility to be resolved? How do we decide what utility is bad and what is not? These facts and questions about the ethical basis for normative rules are not, or at least should not, be at issue.

The upshot of the criticisms of welfare criteria laid out in Chapter 1 is that modern economists have abandoned the search for a perfectly scientific welfare criterion, and have recognized that the justification for any criterion must encompass both moral and technical considerations. Such a criterion is now called, fancily, a social welfare function. The reader should understand that no matter how such a function is derived – and no matter how sophisticated the mathematics are that were used to derive it – its justification as a practical measure must lie in practical considerations, and its justification as an ethical measure must lie in ethics.

The criteria I propose here constitute a social welfare function. The criteria are not value free, nor do they seek to avoid interpersonal comparisons. Rather, they embrace values and confront interpersonal comparisons. Additionally, I agree with Sen's (1995, p. 12) discussion of the undesirability of a consequence-independent system of ethics. So I seek a measure that embraces social values, that makes interpersonal comparisons, that considers practical consequences, and that confronts the problem of bad utility.

There is a trade-off between the theoretical strength of a measure and the extent of its applicability. The Pareto measure suffers from few technical criticisms but it is of little practical use. It is virtually free from ambiguity and is theoretically and ethically appealing where it applies, but it applies to almost no real-world cases. What complicates the problem is that at this time we do not have the empirical data to know how much we give up or gain as we move from more restrictive measures to less restrictive ones, except in a quite general sense. We can suggest that the KH measures are unlikely to be subject to reversals or to fail to meet compensation tests where projects are small, involve goods that are not unique, and have relatively small income effects. But KH does not provide the analytical tools we need to know, in a particular case, whether a project that passes the KH tests may, nonetheless, be socially undesirable because of reversal difficulties, or because actual compensation is impossible.

The measure to be sought, then, is not one that is perfect but the one that is the most useful. The goal I adopt is to seek a measure of economic efficiency that provides useful information on which to base decisions, not one that necessarily provides the answer or the decision in itself. An acceptable rule for project analysis, then, does not have to be perfect. It only needs to be better than nothing and also better than alternative rules. Here, I propose and introduce a justification for a variant of benefit–cost analysis, which I call KHZ. I suggest that a measure of economic efficiency should meet three tests, and that KHZ is acceptable according to these three criteria: (1) it should provide useful information, (2) it should be widely accepted or widely acceptable both to professional analysts and to the public at large, and (3) there should be no other rule that is superior to the chosen rule, with respect to the first two criteria. These tests ground my suggested measure in the sentiments of society. This grounding is both the strength and the weakness of the measure. *For the purpose of the criteria is not to tell us the right thing to do but rather to provide useful information in a form that promotes consensus building* (Zerbe 1998b, p. 421). This suggests further that the purpose of normative economic criteria is *to provide useful information to the decision maker, and not to furnish the decision itself* (Zerbe and Dively 1994, p. 2; Lesser and Zerbe 1998, p. 221; Zerbe 1998b, p. 421). This approach is suggested in a statement of principles by a panel of experts (Arrow *et al.* 1996). They note:

> Benefit–cost analysis should be used to help decision-makers reach a decision. Contrary to the views of some, benefit–cost analysis is neither necessary nor sufficient for designing sensible public policy decision … . agency heads should not be bound by a strict benefit–cost test. Instead, they should be required to consider available benefit–cost analyses and to justify the reasons for their decisions in the event that the expected costs of a regulation far exceed the expected benefits.

In discussing the problem of defining a good income distribution, Hammond (1985, p. 427) notes that 'it seems a reasonable degree of consensus can be achieved even among laymen.' I would say, instead, that consensus among laymen is the crucial ingredient for social welfare criteria.

The purpose of the KHZ criteria, then, is simply to provide better information about what the public wants. These criteria recognize that the ethical value of a measure based on such criteria will not rise above the value of the sentiments of the people to whom the measure applies. Of course, the sentiments of society may not meet some set of ethical standards. The use of a normative economic standard developed on the basis of the criteria suggested here is then vulnerable to criticisms of social values that are embodied by the standard. This is as it should be. If this is a weakness, it is also the strength of a measure so grounded. A rule for decision making that does not command a reasonable degree of consensus is useless. Moreover, social values evolve and grow, and this evolution will be reflected by a change in the benefit–cost outcome.

2.3 A NEW MEASURE FOR NORMATIVE ECONOMIC ANALYSIS

To put normative economics on a firm basis, I have suggested the use of the KHZ criteria, defined by seven axioms. The tests I have suggested for an evaluation of KHZ are that the criteria be useful and socially acceptable and that the proposed criteria be better than alternative criteria, including no criteria. To apply this test, I compare the KH and the KHZ criteria in analyzing a number of difficult problems of efficiency. The KHZ criteria rest on the following seven axioms:

1. KH: an adjusted Kaldor–Hicks measure
   The measure is the same as the traditional KH measures, with the addition of the following six requirements.
2. Use
   The purpose of the criteria is to furnish information to the decision maker and not to determine the right thing to do.
3. Psychology: psychological nature of benefits and costs
   Gains and losses are calculated from status quo positions and are inherently subjective.
4. Information
   (a) *Available information*: an efficiency measure should not require information that would never be available.
   (b) *Better information*: decisions made with better information are preferable to those made with less.
   (c) *No utility*: since utility cannot be measured, it is unavailable information. Our measure will not rest on utility.
5. The costs of change

   (a) *Transactions costs*: transactions costs are to be included in evaluating an economic change or in determining economic efficiency. These costs include the costs of enforcing a suggested rule.
   (b) *Rule changes*: the costs of enacting a rule change are not to be included in determining whether or not a new rule is efficient.
   (c) *Compensation test costs*: costs (that is administrative costs) of hypothetical distributional changes required for compensation test are not to be counted.
6. Values
   (a) *Definition of a good*: values or goods to be included in the measure are any for which there is a willingness to pay.
   (b) *Missing values*: values that appear to be missing in benefit–cost analysis are not in fact missing when the definition of a good used here, axiom 5(a), is applied.
      (i) *income distribution*: income distribution is an economic good.
      (ii) *compensation*: the fact of compensation (or its absence) is also an economic good.
      (iii) *the regard for others*: the regard for others is an economic good and is an important part of value
7. Rights
   The measure should recognize the effect that the law has on economic efficiency, since the law determines the pattern of existing rights.

Using these axioms allows an economist to answer a number of thorny criticisms and to solve current dilemmas. Among these are the problems of (1) the ethics of the discount rate and other missing value puzzles; (2) the relationship of economic efficiency to income distribution, compensation for harm, and other equity issues; (3) how to value goods in the hands of a thief; (4) whether or not harm occurs when it is unknown; (5) whether or not benefit–cost analysis tells us the right thing to do; and (6) whether or not benefit–cost analysis and wealth maximization are ethically grounded standards. This book is, in large part, concerned with the development of the fifth and sixth axioms, those concerned with missing values and legal rights. These axioms, I will argue, do a better job of meeting the ethical criteria of usefulness and acceptability than do the KH criteria. We will explore the basis and implications of these assumptions more fully in later chapters. I offer here the following brief notes on the assumptions I make in the course of explaining the axioms.

2.4 THE AXIOMS EXPLAINED

KH: An Adjusted Kaldor–Hicks Measure

By the KHZ tests, I mean a set of tests in which a project is evaluated by willingness to pay (WTP) measures for gains and by willingness to accept (WTA) measures for losses. I will show that these are not equal to the sum of either the compensating CVs or the compensating EVs but rather to some combination of them. Unlike the CV or EV measures alone, I will show further that these measures satisfy a Kaldor compensation test.

By building on the KH measures we help to ensure that our new criteria will meet the proposed tests of acceptability and usefulness. The KH measures have been the practical standard for project analysis since they were introduced in the 1930s. They have persisted as the standards of practical art despite voluminous technical economic criticism, trenchant ethical criticisms, and overly extravagant claims by some of their supporters.[5] Thus they represent a good starting point for a measure attempting to be acceptable and useful.

The KH measures, however, have rested on using either a CV measure or an EV measure. Yet, as Chapter 1 noted, some projects which have a positive sum of CVs may not meet the Kaldor potential compensation test.

The KHZ measure requires no potential compensation test rationale. The revolutionary aspect of the KHZ approach to benefit–cost analysis is that it abandons the traditional potential compensation test, yet it retains the essential features of the Kaldor–Hicks criteria. To abandon the potential compensation test is to jettison the baggage of the efficiency–equity dualism that, as we have seen, has been a part of normative economic analysis since the 1930s. Yet the proposed test for economic efficiency remains true to the essence of the KH criteria in its reliance on the sum of compensating and equivalent variations.

Use

Many criticisms of benefit–cost analysis are result driven: for example, someone complains that the use of a discount rate is immoral in its treatment of future generations. Regardless of the merits of these criticisms (though the criticisms often have little merit), by assuming that the purpose of benefit–cost analysis is to provide information to decision makers, I can get benefit–cost analysis 'off of the hook' whenever its use leads to a result that is unappealing for ethical reasons. Moreover, my statement of the purpose of benefit–cost analysis accords with reality. Benefit–cost analysis itself is not capable of implementing a decision: only individuals can make decisions. At most, benefit–cost analysis can help an individual make an informed decision. There is probably no evidence that the public would want decision makers to be wholly constrained by the results of a benefit–cost analysis. In part, this may reflect an understanding that not all considerations are likely to be captured by a benefit–cost analysis. No benefit–cost analysis will be perfect.

Because benefit–cost analysis performed according to the KHZ criteria rests on existing social sentiments, its ethical value depends on the ethical value of those sentiments. If one argues that the 'right thing to do' should be determined without considering the current sentiments of a society, benefit–cost analysis does not provide the relevant framework to respond to that argument. For example, a study might conclude that it would be KHZ efficient to legalize narcotics, if there was evidence that the sentiments against the use of narcotics had declined or had disappeared. However, a person who felt that the use of narcotics was immoral – regardless of whether or not society was opposed to narcotics – would not find the study persuasive.

Psychological Nature of Benefits and Costs

There is a distinct tendency in economics and decision theory to view material assets as the main carriers of utility (Kahneman and Varey 1991, p. 130). As important as material assets may be, however, choices are not well explained without considering the psychological aspects of choice and of well-being (Kahneman and Tversky 1979). Economic analyses that incorporate regret (Loomes and Sugden 1983), that recognize loss aversion (Kahneman and Tversky 1979), and that recognize framing and positional considerations (ibid.) have improved predictability of decisions (Thaler 1991).

We seek a measure of value that tries to determine whether or not people will be better off as a result of a new rule or project and which determines which people are likely to be better off. Such a measure must then incorporate information about psychological states and subjective value. We will say then that the correct economic measure of value is one that best measures well-being and that this measure is a psychological measure (Knetsch 1997, p. 509). The psychological reference point is the correct one because benefit–cost analysis rests – and has always been thought to rest – on the preferences of individuals (Kahneman and Varey 1991).[6] This reference point represents what I will call 'psychological ownership.' Both losses and gains are subjective. Both are felt psychological states (ibid.). Moreover, the measure of a loss is different from that of a gain because it is frequently felt differently psychologically (Kahneman, Knetsch, and Thaler 1991). The economic theory, then, is clear: one should use willingness to pay (WTP) for gains and willingness to accept (WTA) for losses. A loss is determined by what one has to lose. A psychological reference point determines whether a positive change is a gain or a loss restored, or whether a negative change is a loss or a gain forestalled.

Information

Available information

The KH measures rest on the compensating or equivalent variations, which are measurable, or on consumer and producer surpluses, which are also measurable estimates of the CV or the EV. The fact that the proposed criteria rest on measurable data and on information that can be gathered (even if imperfectly) is, of course, a major reason for their usefulness and success. The KHZ measure suggests expanding the range of goods or values that must to be represented and, to this extent, imposes greater information requirements. These requirements do not, however, go beyond the possible and are justified by the gain in usefulness of the criteria.

Better information

This aspect of the axiom has implications for situations in which different preferences arise from different information. The choice one makes quickly may, for example, differ from the one that would have been made after greater reflection. This assumption allows us to include the more reflective decision in the benefit–cost analysis, where this can be determined. I do not say, however, that more information is always worth the costs.

No utility

In economics the clearest and most trouble-free use of the term 'utility,' is that which represents 'preferences' and not 'good' (Broome 1991, p. 10).[7] Utility in economics is a concept that is convenient for modeling choice decisions. It need be nothing more. It need not be a measure of hedonistic pleasure, or a measure of satisfaction, or of happiness, nor should it. Even when using utility as an argument in modeling the economics of normative decisions, economists should not define utility as a hedonistic measure. Why should the profession have a measure of something that cannot be measured? To claim such a measure is both unscientific and unnecessary, as well as false.

There is something unscientific about using, as a measure of welfare, a term such as 'utility,' which cannot be measured. Economists must feel ambiguity about retaining the notion of utility at least in their more secret moments. Like the old 'ether' of physics, the concept of utility does little work for us. The convenience in its use is now outweighed by the confusion it causes. Most approaches to normative economics rest on utility-based formulations (Hammond 1985). I drop that approach here. *The KHZ criteria approach to determining preferences is to determine the purchase or sale price of anything that people care about.*

Costs of Change

Transactions costs

A fundamental insight of Coase was that in determining inefficiency economists compare a world without transactions costs with the real world. This leads to absurd results but more important it also taints the usefulness of KH efficiency. When transactions costs are ignored every transaction is inefficient as compared to a transaction in a hypothetical world in which transactions are costless. When transactions costs are ignored, externalities are ubiquitous as Zerbe and McCurdy (1999) have shown.

There is now a large, not to say enormous, literature on this issue that suggests that it is appropriate to include transactions costs in the determination of what is efficient (e.g. Allen 1991; Coase 1960, 1964, 1974, 1988; Eggertsson 1990; Barzel 1985; Baumol 1979; Randall 1983; Nelson 1987; Medema and Zerbe 1999a, 1999b; Zerbe and McCurdy 1999). The seminal source is Ronald Coase (1960). As Coase has pointed out, little can be learned from the study of theoretical optimal systems (Coase 1964, p. 195).[8] Analysts who become enamored of 'blackboard economics,' in which equations are substituted for underpinnings, produce concepts that bear little correspondence to the actual social system. The world portrayed is one that exists only on the blackboard: 'the analysis is carried out with great ingenuity, but it floats in the air' (Coase 1988, p. 10).

This assumption addresses the criticisms quite properly raised by Coase that a welfare analysis is improper that ignores transactions costs. Coase (1960) has shown that in practical matters the exclusion of transactions costs in one's analysis can lead to absurd results. The absence of transactions costs is the source of the 'failure of market failure' (Zerbe and McCurdy 1999) and the alleged 'inefficiency of Christmas giving.' Economists or lawyers may speak of a particular change in the state of the world as being efficient when what they mean is that the state of the world would be efficient if transactions costs were zero.[9] This practice, which is endemic throughout the legal and the economics literature, has led to considerable misunderstanding (Coase 1960; Zerbe and McCurdy 1999; Medema and Zerbe 1999a, 1999b) and to the development of concepts of market failure that are at worst incoherent and at best poorly thought out (Zerbe and McCurdy 1999).

A welfare measure will be more accurate, and therefore better, if it includes the property transactions costs associated with the change contemplated, in accord with Coasean welfare economics.[10] The KH tests were devised to be practical measures that would be applied to changes in the real world, not to an ideal world in which transactions costs are zero. Not to include the costs of change is to ignore a component of transactions costs. Ignoring the costs of change has, in fact, opened the door for confusing comparisons that ignore various other components of transactions costs (Zerbe and McCurdy 1999).[11] When two states of the world are compared and the analysis of the changed world does not include the costs of making the change, one cannot reasonably say that a change is desirable. Thus, anyone who ignores the property transactions costs of a proposed change itself cannot say that a change is 'efficient' if they mean to imply that a change is desirable. The failure to use the term 'efficiency' more precisely creates ambiguity about whether or not one is speaking of efficiency in a zero transactions cost world or not.

I wish to distinguish between the transactions of economic exchange and the transactions costs of making rule changes. The first, what I here call property costs, are the costs of making exchanges and protecting property given the legal regime (Allen 1991). These I define broadly to include search and information costs as well as the costs of registering ownership, negotiation over price and quality, and, in general, the whole panoply of property right maintenance costs and exchange costs. The second sort of transactions costs, that I call rule change costs, are the costs of changing the legal regime. The proposal here is that property transactions costs should be included in evaluating economic inefficiency.

Rule changes

At the same time I do not purpose to include rule change costs in the KHZ measure of efficiency. To do so would make the world tautologically efficient. For if the all costs associated with a rule change, including the costs of enacting the rule, are to be included, then in some sense this rule should already be in effect. That it is not in effect must be due to some (unspecified) costs. Thus when an economist or lawyer says that some new rule is efficient, or that some existing rule is inefficient, he or she will be taken to mean that the rule would be efficient or inefficient aside from the costs of enacting or eliminating a rule itself.

Compensation test costs

The hypothetical cost of administering a system of compensation should not be considered, unless the decision maker actually intends to compensate those harmed by a change. The purpose of KHZ is to furnish information about gains and losses from an actual change. To include costs that are not incurred would reduce the informational value (usefulness) of the KHZ measure.

Values

Definition of a good

Axiom 6 (values) appears straightforward and perhaps innocuous. It is neither. Its formal adoption has substantial, perhaps profound, implications for normative economic analysis.

The axiom is, however, within the spirit of KH. Even for the KH criteria, no well-founded reason has been suggested for limiting the goods to be covered by the criteria. Consider the following description of the KH process suggested by Talbot Page (1992, p. 102):

> You are asked to compare two worlds. The first is the status quo: the world the way it is now. The second is identical with the status quo except for a change brought about by the project. In the comparison, you take into account the ramifications of the project, differences in income to you and others, differences in habitat, and so on; but except for the changes brought on by the project, the two worlds are the same.
>
> Suppose that you value the first world more highly than the second. Then you are asked what is the minimum you need to be compensated so that you would value the change (with the compensation) just as much as the status quo. If you value the world with the project more than the status quo, then you are asked how big a payment you could make in the changed world (with the project) so that you would just value equally the status quo … The economic criterion says that if the sum of all the compensations (to those who would lose by the project) is less than the sum of the equilibrating payments (from the gains from the project), then the change from the status quo is worth making.

Somewhat more technically, in the opening remarks of their well-known book on welfare economics, Boadway and Bruce (1984, p. 1) note:

> A social ordering permits one to compare all states of the world and rank each one as 'better than,' 'worse than,' or 'equally good as' every other. Ideally we would like the (social) ordering to be complete (so that all states could be ranked or ordered) and transitive … The term 'state of the world' can be interpreted as a complete description of a possible state of an economy including economic characteristics, political conditions such as freedom of speech and non-discrimination, physical characteristics such as the weather, and so on.

What is common to the statements of Page (1992) and Boadway and Bruce (1984) is that a 'good' is implicitly defined by what is of value.[12] A 'good' in economic analysis is – or at least should be – defined by what people care about. This goes well beyond just physical attributes.[13] People care about the fairness and efficiency of rules,[14] for example, so that we can also call the fairness of a rule or a project a 'good.' Because people care about fairness, they will often not just care about the cost of a project but about who pays for it, about whether or not the project is an efficient one, and about whether or not the beneficiaries are deserving. They care about who pays for a good even when they do not expect to pay nor to be paid. Similarly, they may feel more strongly about being uncompensated for a loss when they consider compensation fair than when they feel otherwise. And, aside from specific compensation for harm, they often care about the equity implications of income distribution itself, so that the income distribution is itself a good.

Missing values

The economic literature, including very recent literature, has many examples in which goods that meet the test proposed here are, apparently arbitrarily, omitted in attempting to determine economic efficiency. The goods which are ignored include, for example, the ethical value attached to actions, the value associated with income distribution itself, sentimental value, and demoralization costs. These sorts of omissions reduce the acceptability of the KH criteria and should be avoided when using the KHZ criteria.

Income distribution Most of the criticisms of KH rest on its omission of income-distribution considerations in determining efficiency. Income distribution did not traditionally qualify under KH. However, income distribution does qualify as a good under KHZ, because people other than those directly affected nevertheless care about income distribution.[15] In Chapter 1, I explained the historical decoupling of distributional equity and efficiency. This decoupling did not, however, achieve the value-free criteria that were desired. Other more recent reasons given for the decoupling are (1) that there is less agreement about income distribution questions than about traditional efficiency (Posner 1985a, p. 104) and (2) that as a practical matter it is better to separate the equity and the KH efficiency issues (Posner 1985a, pp. 104–105; Polinsky 1983, pp. 105–113).[16] As a matter of fact, it is unclear whether there is less agreement about distributional matters than about traditional efficiency questions. But unanimous agreement is not required for KHZ analysis. Under KHZ analysis the purpose is to furnish useful information to the decision maker. Information about equity can be useful to the decision maker, as I will show. Whether it is practical to ignore equity and focus on traditional efficiency is a question of usefulness – a test for the acceptance of KHZ criteria. In Chapter 5 I will show when such separation is desirable and will show that in these cases such separation is consistent with KHZ.

I suggest adopting a criterion proposed by Harberger (1978) for valuing changes in income distribution. This criterion would allow a choice between different distributional states. Mishan (1981, pp. 365–367) has shown that where a choice between first-best states cannot be made on KH or hypothetical compensation grounds, the only remaining considerations in making a choice are distributional. By including a method of evaluating distributional choices, I increase the ability to make a choice between first-best states.

Compensation Because people who are not directly affected by a project will care about the fact of compensation or the fact that there is no compensation, the presence or absence of compensation is a relevant good. The issue of compensation will receive particular treatment here. The presence or absence of compensation is part of the regard for others.

The regard for others The omission of important goods from most normative economic analyses arises from their failure to consider the regard for others.[17] Economic efficiency should be defined with respect to all states of the world that people care about. According to Ernst Mayr (1997),[18] people care about others, including the welfare of people to whom they are not related. As Sen (1995, p. 15) notes, Adam Smith himself hardly saw an individual as the narrowly focused 'economic man.' Smith examined the role of 'sympathy,' 'generosity,' 'and 'public spirit'. I claim that people will care about a social change even when they themselves are not otherwise directly affected by it. They will care about fairness, about waste, and about income distribution. I will speak of 'the regard for others' and about the 'kindness of strangers.' By these terms, I mean the concern of some for what they regard as fair outcomes for others, whether or not the regarding parties are themselves directly affected. So, one expression of the regard for others is when we are concerned about the appropriate application of principles of justice in situations in which we ourselves are not directly affected. The failure of traditional KH analysis to consider the regard for others is particularly ironic, since under the logic of KH there is no reason to ignore it.[19]

One reason why people care about rules which are applied to others is that they believe those rules may also be applied to them. A second reason is that some people will be truly 'other-regarding' or altruistic; they care about the fairness of justice of rules and outcomes applied to others even when they do not expect to be subject to the rules or outcomes. I call this 'ethical' or 'altruistic regard for others.'[20] Mayr maintains that genuine altruism (as opposed to reciprocal or kinship altruism) and ethics have evolved in humans because they have survival value for the relevant genes through group selection. He notes that 'as history has repeatedly illustrated, those behaviors will be preserved and those behavioral norms will have the longest survival that contribute the most to the well-being of the cultural group as a whole' (1997, p. 254). In other words, ethical behavior for humans is adaptive.[21] Both the regard for others that arises from self-regard and the regard for others which is truly altruistic are part of our felt experience.[22]

Rights

Critics of benefit–cost analysis sometimes assert that it will inevitably ignore legal and moral rights (Lothrop 1986).[23] This is profoundly wrong (Sen 1995; Zerbe 1998b). Admittedly, as Sen noted, 'the violation or fulfillment of basic rights and liberties tends to be ignored in utilitarian welfare economics … particularly because of its "welfarism" whereby states of affairs are judged exclusively by the utilities generated.' To ignore rights is, however, incorrect even by 'welfarism's' standards, since the psychological consideration of value mentioned previously shows that rights affect one's valuation of goods. More to the point, my approach is not one of 'welfarism.'

The fact that a person has a recognized legal right to a good is some evidence that it is efficient to allow that person to possess the good. Similarly, the fact that a person does not have a legal right to a good is some evidence that it would be inefficient to allow that person to take the good from its lawful owner without permission. Although all values that may be measured by the WTP and the WTA should be considered, some goods and some individuals have been excluded from the judge's implicit benefit–cost analysis because those individuals have no legal right to those goods. The decision to deny a legal right to possess a good is itself frequently the product of a prior benefit–cost test. The interrelation between rights and benefit–cost analysis is a major theme of this book, which I explore in depth in the following chapters. The recognition of property rights, for example, may be held to rest also on a previous KHZ test that such recognition is desirable. No rule for normative decision making can be widely acceptable if it does not recognize as a starting point the existing pattern of rights. This is as it should be. How could it be otherwise? Why would one want it to be different? Judges recognize rights in making decisions. Should they not? As Heyne (1988, p. 56) notes, 'economic theory takes for granted, far more extensively than economists seem generally to recognize, the normative force of established rights and obligations.' This is even true of attempts to predict. Heyne goes on to say, 'economists who want to predict the effects of agricultural price supports must assume, *inter alia*, that the existing property rights of farmers will be respected, that public servants will carry out the provisions of the law, and that taxpayers will provide the amounts which they are assessed to subsidize the program' (1988, p. 56).

2.5 JUSTIFICATION FOR KHZ

The traditional moral justification for KH has been the potential compensation test. However, such a test does not provide a satisfying moral justification for the use of KH. The fact that a project could – in principle but not in fact – be converted into one in which no one loses does not explain why it is acceptable to implement such a project which *actually* harms some people. Economists have justified the potential compensation test by arguing that it is necessary to separate efficiency and distributional justice. Economists reasoned that decision makers should decide distributional matters and that economic science required a consistent measure. Others have questioned this justification on technical grounds (Boadway and Bruce 1984, pp. 267f) or on moral grounds (Coleman 1980, pp. 531f). But I will show later that this separation is unnecessary to gain a consistent measure so that the efficiency–distribution dichotomy is not necessary to have a consistent measure. The justification for KH and for KHZ rests on grounds other than the traditional sort of potential compensation test.[24]

If the government uses KH or KHZ as general criteria for evaluating all of its decisions *instead of using some other criteria* it has the best chance of making *all* of the people in a society better off 'at the end of the day'. Every year most governments undertake several projects which help some people but hurt others. A particular person is better off 'at the end of the day' if his gains from the projects that help him outweigh his losses from the projects that hurt him. If the government uses KHZ to evaluate each project, and only approves projects that are KHZ efficient, the net social gain will be higher than it would be if the government used any other basis for evaluating each project. This is a tautology because KHZ incorporates every value that society cares about. In the absence of a systematic bias against any class of people, a criterion that leads to the highest net social gain will also have the best chance of ensuring that any particular person in the society is actually better of at the end of the day. We might imagine comparing KHZ to some alternative system – call it the 'Moral Veto System' (MVS) – that allows anyone to veto a project when it violates their sense of moral rightness. It seems likely that everyone (or almost everyone) would prefer KHZ to MVS because they would prefer a society with flaws but lots of useful projects to one to which no one had any moral objections – except that there were practically no useful projects.

One might think that the best way to ensure that everybody is better off at the end of the day would be to use the Pareto criterion. However, that is not true. Using the Pareto criterion would be the best way of ensuring that nobody is *worse* off; but it would actually do a very poor job of ensuring that the government makes most people *better* off, since it would foreclose most (indeed, virtually all) opportunities for net gains. Now of course KHZ is inferior for any one person to a rule that particularly favors that person. The question, however, is whether KHZ would be chosen in an initial or original position or for the sort of consent that is envisioned in social contract theory.[25]

However, if we justify KH and KHZ on the grounds that they do the best job of ensuring that *everybody* is better off at the end of the day, it is necessary to ensure that no group is consistently on the losing side of KH efficient projects. The way to achieve this outcome is to include considerations of just compensation into the KH tests and to recognize value in distributional effects, as KHZ does. Otherwise there is a potential for a sort of cyclical downgrading of poorer groups so that they would have a tendency to fall into the loser group. Consider a project to place an undesirable public project such as a jail into a neighborhood. The most efficient location, if we ignore distributional effects and the regard for others, is likely to be in the poorest neighborhood – the land is cheaper and the WTA of its residents is likely to be less than that of other neighborhoods. However, if we place the undesirable project into the poorest neighborhood without compensating its residents we will further degrade the neighborhood. As a result, the next time a project is considered, which will have undesirable neighborhood effects, the poorest neighborhood will – a fortiori – be the preferred choice. If using KHZ leads to a cycle of making poor people worse off and rich people better off simply because the poor literally have less to lose, than KHZ probably would not have much moral appeal to most people.

KHZ's solution to this dilemma is to incorporate the regard for others. If we consider the regard for others, then we cannot assume that it is more efficient to place the jail in the poorest neighborhood, since society might suffer a loss if it felt that it was unfair to degrade a poor neighborhood in that fashion. If the regard for others was opposed to degrading the poor neighborhood further, it might not be efficient to build a jail there, or it might only be efficient to build the jail there if the neighborhood was directly compensated for it (and not just by a vague promise that the poor neighborhood will be better off at the end of the day).

Alternatively, we might be concerned that some people will be consistently harmed by government projects because that group of people is socially unpopular. It is true that KHZ's use of the regard for others may lead to systematically injuring people who are condemned by society. This is why I say that KHZ does not tell us 'the right thing to do' in a transcendent moral or spiritual sense. However, the fact that KHZ may lead to consistently injuring people is not necessarily morally problematic. Put bluntly, some groups may deserve to be unpopular: thieves and rapists are unpopular and government attempts to suppress theft and rape are almost certainly efficient, and most people would probably argue that the government should not compensate rapists and thieves for the losses flowing from the laws against rape and theft. Of course, historically some groups have been unpopular for reasons that seem absurd and unjust today, and future generations will probably be horrified by at least a few of the current generation's prejudices. However, when an economist feels that a society's sentiments and prejudices are unjust, the solution is to attempt to combat the prejudices, not to pretend that an action is inefficient when it is actually efficient.

Similarly, we might be concerned that the government will ignore the interests of people who have trouble forming political coalitions, and so we cannot assume that people who have trouble forming political coalitions will be better off 'at the end of the day.' However, the regard for others incorporates the values of all people with a WTP or WTA, not just those people who are effective in lobbying efforts. If the government consistently ignores the values of people who are unable to effectively form political coalitions, then the government is not *using* KHZ, and so KHZ cannot be criticized if the government is acting in ways that seem unfair.

KHZ and the Social Contract

The argument for KHZ may be expressed as a sort of social contract argument. Although KHZ is supportable by a social contract justification, one may ask what is the validity of a social contract justification as compared to some other moral criterion. My response is simply consistent with the basis for KHZ itself – it rests on existing sentiments and many endorse a social contract justification.These arguments are well known and well made (Talbott 2000).

Thus, I do not attempt to provide a full social contract analysis here. Rather I will simply say that since the purpose of KHZ is to provide decision makers (namely, governments) with useful information, the use of KHZ is morally justified if it helps governments behave in ethical ways. It is generally agreed that the moral justification for government action is that there is an implied social contract between a government and its citizens, in which the citizens give the government the exclusive right to use coercive power in return for a promise that that power will be used in a way that is consistent with the citizens' wishes.

Therefore, the use of KHZ is ethically justified if it helps governments fulfill their citizens' wishes. It is probably safe to assume that most people want their government to give *some* consideration to two factors when deciding whether or not to implement a project. First, the project should increase the net wealth of the society. Second, the project should distribute wealth in a reasonably fair way. KHZ provides the government with important information, since it helps the government determine whether a project is likely to actually increase the net wealth of the society and whether a project is reasonably consistent with distributive justice.

In contrast, the Pareto criterion assumes that the only relevant questions in benefit–cost analysis are whether a project harms nobody and helps at least one person. In practice, that is not a realistic assumption, and it is an assumption that would prevent the economist from discovering and conveying useful information. Most governments want to consider a project even if it harms some people, so long as the costs are outweighed by the benefits, and the costs are not apportioned in a grossly unfair way.

On the other hand, the KH criteria assume that the only relevant question is whether a project results in a net gain. This is not a realistic assumption, either, since a project with a net gain may be unacceptable to the citizens of a nation if the citizens believe that the project distributes benefits or costs unfairly. Furthermore, KH tends to ignore certain types of benefits and costs (such as the regard for others and transactions costs) and therefore its predictions about whether or not a project will result in a net social gain are unreliable as well.

Unlike the KH and Pareto criteria, KHZ assumes that a wide variety of factors are relevant in deciding whether or not a project is efficient. KHZ assumes that all goods that people care about are relevant to economic analysis, including a society's concern for a fair distribution of benefits and costs. Therefore, KHZ is able to provide useful information to governments and other decision makers that the KH and Pareto criteria do not provide. As a result, KHZ does a better job of helping governments comply with their implied social contracts.

2.6 CONCLUSION

This chapter introduced the axioms that form the KHZ criteria. It provides a brief justification for each axiom. The underlying values which justify the use of KHZ are usefulness and acceptability. A rule that tells us 'the right thing to do,' in a morally transcendent sense, will not necessarily be acceptable or useful. Thus, one assumption is that the purpose of the KHZ criteria is not to tell us the right thing to do in an objective sense, but rather to furnish useful information that is acceptable and useful to a decision maker. The axioms aim to increase the utility of benefit–cost analysis by ensuring that an economist's analysis provides more realistic and acceptable information. More information is furnished by a benefit–cost standard, the KHZ standard, that includes the costs of change, that expands the concept of goods, and that grounds the analysis in the recognition of the reality of rights.

NOTES

1. Richard Posner has also attempted to put wealth maximization or benefit–cost analysis on a firm basis (Posner 1980, 1984, 1985a, 1986, 1987a, 1992a and b). In my view, Posner's attempt was unsuccessful.
2. See Zerbe and Dively's (1994, p. 274) discussion of the former practice in India of allowing condemned criminals to hire substitutes to be executed in their stead (see also Chapter 7 of this book).
3. For example, if only Pareto-superior changes were allowed, it would have been impossible to eliminate slavery in America in the nineteenth century. Eliminating slavery harmed slave owners, so the Pareto criteria would have given veto power to the slave owners.
4. In other writings Posner (for example 1981a, p. 60) is at pains to disassociate wealth maximization from utility maximization.
5. Chapter 1 mentions some of the extravagant claims made by economists. In addition, some lawyers and economists have either stated that KH efficiency is value free, or have spoken as if KH efficiency was the only important value.
6. Kahneman and Varey (1991) point out that preferences may be poorly informed and changed by experience. The issue of whether or not valuation should reflect transitory preferences or experience preferences is not considered further here.
7. Broome and I came to this conclusion independently. I discovered his valuable article as this book was being finished. I thank Fauska for bringing it to my attention. Broome (1991, p. 1) points out that the original meaning of 'utility' by Benthan and others was usefulness.
8. In a similar vein, Coase argues that 'generalizations are not likely to be helpful unless they are derived from studies of how such activities are actually carried out within different institutional frameworks. Such studies would enable us to discover which factors are important and which are not in determining the outcome and would lead to generalizations which have a solid base. They are also likely to serve another purpose, by showing us the richness of the social alternatives between which we can choose' (Coase 1974; p. 375).
9. This statement is true for almost any proposition regarding economic efficiency. For example, see Posner (1986, pp. 254–259) on the issue of efficiency consequences of monopoly.
10. Kuznets (1948) pointed out an apparent circularity in the KH criteria.
11. The usual reason given for the failure to reach a first-best situation is the existence of externalities, that is effects outside the decision process. The failure to consider these external effects, however, arises because the costs of considering the effects are too great. That is, production costs, in the guise of transactions costs, limit, as costs always do, output, as Howard McCurdy and I (1999) and others have pointed out. From this perspective the so-called second-best situations are not in fact second best but are in fact first best, and the reversal paradox disappears leaving only the status quo bias.
12. Posner (1985a, pp. 86–89) points out that in economics 'wealth' is not just monetary wealth.
13. The remarks of Hewins (1911, pp. 898, 900) are instructive: 'The concept of the standard of life involves also some estimate of the efforts of and the sacrifices that people are prepared to make to obtain it; of their ideals and character, of the relative strength of the different motives which usually determine their conduct.' For an elaboration, see Zerbe and Medema (1997).
14. This, however, is not to say that 'fairness' and 'efficiency' are independent concepts. Indeed, this book advances a definition of efficiency which incorporates a standard of fairness.
15. Posner (1992b, p. 264) echoes a common theme, that 'efficiency and redistribution are antithetical.' Far from being antithetical, they are in fact the same thing. Elsewhere, however, Posner (1985a, p. 99) recognizes this.
16. Posner (1984, p. 133) suggests that courts should ignore income distribution issues because

'courts cannot do anything about the distribution of wealth.' This seems disingenuous. Courts can certainly affect the distribution narrowly. Posner (1985a, p. 104) also says, 'Given the absence of anything approaching a consensus on the optimum distribution of wealth, however, it is very hard to see how courts could adopt a redistributive ethic to guide their decisions.' A consensus on the optimum distribution of wealth is unnecessary to justify a redistributive ethic. All that is required is agreement that, at the margin, gains to the poor are worth a modest extra consideration. This seems best applied however in benefit–cost analysis proper or, as Posner (1985a, pp. 104–105) notes, in actions by the legislature and not by the courts. Polinsky (1989, p. 122) notes that it is usually not possible for courts to redistribute income in contract or product liability disputes, whereas legal rules can always redistribute income in disputes between strangers.

17. The importance of the issue of the regard for others and in particular the distribution of resources in the context of differences between native Americans and other Americans is discussed by Malloy (1992, pp. 1624f).
18. E. O. Wilson (1998) appears to have recently adopted this view as well.
19. Had this been recognized earlier, Stigler's (1982, p. 13) lament might have been unnecessary:

    > I come to the error of my ways, and indeed of economists' ways generally. We expect the society eventually to believe our case for free trade ... The disapproval [of these policies] by economists, however, is uninformed. It is uninformed with respect to the reason that the disapproved policies are adopted – uninformed with respect to what the operative political desires of the community are. Clever economists have displayed an obtuseness in this matter that is difficult to believe. They will say, not year after year but generation after generation: 'Parliament, do you not realize that free trade will increase the national income.' As if the Parliament did not know this.

20. Economists usually discuss altruism as a positive interdependent utility function. Posner (1992b, p. 464) notes that 'the major cost of poverty is the disutility it imposes on affluent altruists.'
21. The regard for others may, of course, reflect negative emotions as well. For example, it may involve envy (Posner 1992b, pp. 264, 461n, 467). One might argue that the extent of positive regard for others is, in fact, one of the desirable qualities of civilization and, in part, can be a consequence of growth in income.
22. See also David Cheal (1988), Carol Rose (1992), and Richard Titmuss (1971), for evidence of altruistic behavior.
23. Lothrop (1986, p. 535) notes that 'cost–benefit analysis is generally blind to legal rights'.
24. First, the traditional KH tests ignore transactions costs and transfer costs. Therefore, even if a project passes the KH tests, it might not be possible to compensate the losers and retain a net benefit. Second, in many cases the government may not even attempt to compensate all of the parties who are harmed by the project. The fact that the government *could* compensate the injured people is unlikely to make them feel better if the government refuses to compensate them.
25. Posner has advanced a consent justification for wealth maximization, but since he proposes what is not the case, namely actual consent, his justification serves merely to invite easily made attacks (for example, Coleman 1980).

3. The nature of economic efficiency

3.1 INTRODUCTION

Chapter 2 outlined the axioms for KHZ efficiency. In a formal sense some of these are redundant. Here I pare down the axioms of Chapter 2 into the three essential axioms required to generate the results in the following chapters. I define an action or decision as efficient if (1) there is a positive sum for the willingness to pay (WTP) for gains and the willingness to accept (WTA) payment for losses; (2) gains and losses are measured from psychological reference points (Kahneman and Tversky 1979); (3) the transaction costs of operating in states of the world are included in costs for purposes of determining efficiency, but the transactions costs of changing to a new state of the world are not included. (To require economists to include the costs of persuasion in their pronouncements of what is efficient would be stupefying at best.) I call an approach based on these axioms KHZ.

KHZ efficiency has the following characteristics: (1) it is not subject to preference reversals (Zerbe 2001); (2) it satisfies a compensation criterion (Zerbe 2001); (3) it defines all goods for which there is a WTP as economic goods (Zerbe 1998b); (4) it includes the income distribution, as well as the fact of compensation or its lack, as an economic good, so that a project that provides compensation may be valued differently in efficiency from one that does not (Zerbe 1998); (5) it obviates other important ethical objections that have been made to KH (Zerbe 1998b, 2001); (6) it eliminates the practice of finding market failure or inefficiency in situations in which in fact there is no superior alternative (Zerbe and McCurdy 1999).

3.2 MEASUREMENT OF BENEFITS AND COSTS WITH THE WTP AND WTA

Benefits and costs are measured, respectively, by the willingness to pay (WTP) and by the willingness to accept (WTA) (Zerbe and Dively 1994). The WTP reflects the amount that someone who does not have a good would be willing to pay to buy it; it is the maximum amount of money one would give up to buy some good or service, or would pay to avoid harm.[1] The WTA reflects the amount that someone who has the good would accept to sell it; it is the minimum amount of money one would accept to forgo some good, or to bear some harm. Benefits and costs are determined by the WTPs and WTAs of the affected parties. The benefits from a project may be either gains (WTP) or losses restored (WTA). The costs of a project may be either a gain forgone (WTP) or a loss (WTA). Both the benefits and the costs are the sum of the appropriate WTP and WTA measures. Thus, the relation of benefits and costs to the WTP and the WTA may be measured in the following manner:

Benefits: *The sum of the WTPs for changes that are seen as gains and of the WTAs for changes that are seen as restoration of losses.*

Costs: *The sum of the WTAs for changes that are seen as losses and of the WTPs for changes that are seen as foregone gains.*

The measurements are summarized in Table 3.1 below.[2] Note that whether a change is a benefit or cost is a different question from whether it is a gain or

Table 3.1 The measurement of benefits and costs in terms of gains and losses

	Gain	**Loss**
Benefits	**consumers** WTP – the sum of CVs for a positive change – is finite.	**consumers** WTA – the sum of EVs for a positive change–could be infinite.
	producers WTP – the sum of EVs for a positive change – is finite	**producers** WTA – the sum of CVs for a positive change – could be infinite.
	Gain forgone	**Loss restored**
Costs	**consumers** WTP – the sum of EVs for a negative change – is finite	**consumers** WTA–the sum of CVs for a negative change – could be infinite.
	producers WTP – the sum of CVs for a negative change – is finite	**producers** WTA – the sum of EVs for a negative change – is finite

a loss. Benefits can be either a gain or a loss restored, and costs can be either a loss or a gain forgone. *The important point here is that benefits are not measured exclusively by the WTP, nor costs exclusively by the WTA. Benefits are measured by the WTA, where benefits include losses restored, and costs are measured by the WTP, where they include gains forgone.*

3.3 GAINS AND LOSSES AND CV AND EV

The CV or compensating variation measure of a welfare change for consumers uses the WTP to measure the benefit associated with price decreases and the WTA to measure the cost associated with price increases. However, it does not follow that the CV measure will correctly measure the effect of price increases or decreases on consumers. This is because a price change is a good like any other, in that a consumer may or may not have psychological ownership of the right to a price decrease or the right to avoid a price increase. If a social change raises prices but consumers do not believe that they have the right to avoid price increases, the value of the price increase should be measured by the WTP of consumers, not their WTA. Similarly, if a social change decreases prices and consumers believe that they have the right to lower prices, the value of the price decrease should be measured by the WTA of consumers, not their WTP.

The situation is somewhat different for producers or suppliers. A supplier may value a good as a purely commercial good, a good whose value is just the present value of its income stream and thus for which there is no divergence between the WTP and the WTA. I shall call the supplier of a purely commercial good a producer. In this case, the relevant indifference curve is a straight line. In other cases, a supplier, as for example with a worker who supplies labor, may have a typical convex indifference curve and have a divergence between the WTP and the WTA. I will call the supplier of a non-commercial good a supplier rather than a producer. In either case the difference in expenditure M^* represents WTP and WTA just as for consumers.

For producers there is no difference between WTP and WTA, since producers view the items as commercial goods. Therefore, there is no difference between using EV and CV to measure the value of a price change to a producer.

For a supplier, EV uses WTP to measure a producer's benefit from price increases and WTA to measure a producer's cost from price decreases. However, as was the case with a supplier, whether WTA or WTP should be used to measure a price change depends on whether the supplier has psychological ownership of the price change, not on whether the change is a price increase or a price decrease. Therefore the use of EV would be appropriate to measure the value of a price increase to a supplier if the supplier did not believe that he had the right to a price increase, but it would be appropriate to use CV if the supplier did have psychological ownership of a price increase.

It is sometimes thought that the CV measure of a welfare change is a harder test than the EV test, and on this basis the CV measure is thought to be the more conservative and therefore the best measure of welfare change. This is only true, however, as long as we confine ourselves to studying the effect of a social change on consumers and ignore producers. For consumers, CV for a welfare gain is the WTP and for a welfare loss it is the WTA. For a consumer, the WTP for a normal good will be less than the WTA for the same good. Thus the measure of gains for the CV is said to be the sum of the WTP for the gainers and the sum of the WTA for the losers. The measure for the EV is the sum of the WTA for the gainers and the sum of the WTP for the losers. Since for each person the WTP < WTA, it is said that CV will be less than the EV. This is all true as long as we consider that a price decrease is good for all or that a price increase is bad for all. That is, this is true for consumers. It is, however, in general not true for all. Producers may benefit from price increases and lose from price decreases. For producers it is the case that for a gain the CV > EV and for a loss that the CV < EV (Just *et al.* 1982, pp. 123–124). Thus a price decrease will produce measures of welfare gain for consumers for which we can say that the aggregate CV < EV. It will, however, also produce a welfare decrease for producers for which it is the case that (the absolute value of) aggregate CV > EV. It is thus possible that the aggregate CV measure for both gains and losses will be greater than the aggregate EV. The fact is that the CV measure and EV measure do not produce in a simple way an identification with the intuition of the WTP and the WTA concepts.

Furthermore, it is worth remembering that the goal of benefit–cost analysis is to use the most accurate measure of a social change, not the most conservative one. We might be tempted to use a conservative welfare test to indirectly recognize transactions costs, but it would be better to use the right welfare test and then attempt to measure transactions costs directly. Therefore, even though it is true that CV is a more conservative test from the perspective of consumers, CV might not be the most accurate measure of the effects of a price change on consumers. The CV and EV terminology should be abandoned.

3.4 PSYCHOLOGICAL OWNERSHIP AND THE DETERMINATION OF GAINS AND LOSSES

The Psychological Nature of Gains and Losses

Benefits and costs are subjective and psychological. The older generation of economists say that those writing before the 1940s well recognized the complexity of the notion of a standard of living, of measuring economic value. Hewins, for example, providing a description of economics for the classic 1911 edition of *Encyclopedia Britannica*, notes:

> The concept of the standard of life involves also some estimate of the efforts and sacrifices people are prepared to make to obtain it; of their ideas and character; of the relative strength of the different motives which usually determine their conduct … [I]it is doubtful whether the most complete investigation in terms of money (q.v.) would ever enable us to include all the elements of the standard of life in a money estimate. (p. 900)

Much of the subsequent history of welfare economics, however, has associated value with material goods. Some thoughtful economists, such as Hewins, were quite aware, however, that both gains and losses were also psychological concepts. In the 1970s, economists were confronted with the unpleasant fact that many of their predictions about human behavior under uncertainty were incorrect. It was eventually recognized that it was necessary to make the connection between gains and losses as psychological concepts and gains and losses as measures of economic value (Kahneman and Tversky 1979). The psychological issues they addressed in the 1970s were not ones of individual idiosyncrasies, but rather concerned the way *most* people actually thought, valued, and made decisions.[3]

Efficiency and the Psychological Reference Point

In KHZ efficiency gains are measured by the willingness to pay (WTP) for them, while losses are measured by the willingness to accept payment (WTA) as compensation for these losses (Zerbe and Dively 1994, Chapters 5 and 6; Knetsch 1995; Thaler 1991).[4] WTP is the correct measure of gains, and WTA is the correct measure of losses (Knetsch 1995; Levy and Friedman 1994; Thaler 1991). Gains and losses are to be measured from a psychological reference point, which stems from one's beliefs about ownership (Kahneman and Tversky 1979; Knetsch 1997; Thaler 1991). The WTP measure assumes that one does not have psychological ownership of the good, and asks how much one would pay to obtain it. The WTA measure assumes that one believes one owns the good, and asks how much one would accept to sell it

(Levy and Friedman 1994). A psychological owner of a good will have the value of a loss of the good properly measured by the WTA. Anyone who buys or acquires a good will experience a gain, which is properly measured by their WTP.

Now a price change is a good 'like any other.' What I mean is that it is theoretically possible for an individual to have psychological ownership of the right to a 'better' price (or to avoid a 'worse' price) and that, as with any other good, the WTA should be used whenever a party has psychological ownership of a price change (or no price change).

For some goods, the WTP and WTA may not differ by much. But in other circumstances the WTP and WTA will differ greatly (Kahneman, Knetsch and Thaler 1991). They can differ because of income effects, substitution effects, and loss aversion (Lesser and Zerbe 1988). That is, the difference will be great when the good is expensive, or when it is unique, or when there is a psychological attachment to it. First, when one owns an expensive good, one's wealth is greater, so that the money measure of the value of the good is also greater (income effects). That is, one values money less, relative to an additional amount of the good. Second, when one owns a unique good, there are no substitutes for it, so that one may have a great reluctance to part with it that materially exceeds what one could pay. Thus, the Sierra Club might require a large amount to sell the Grand Canyon if it owned it, but could pay only a much smaller amount to gain it if it did not own it. Third, psychological attachment exists for most goods, so that even for quite ordinary goods a difference can arise (loss aversion). Losses, then, are felt more than gains, so that the value function, which reflects the value of changes from the psychological reference point, is steeper for losses than for gains (Kahneman and Tversky 1979).[5]

KH recognizes the potential relevance of both the WTP and the WTA measures, but it does not provide a methodology for *choosing* between WTA and WTP in measuring an individual's interest in a good. Mishan (1982, p. 183) noted that an economist might as well flip a coin when trying to decide between using the CV measure (which uses the WTA for benefits and the WTP for costs) and the EV measure (which uses the WTP for benefits and the WTA for costs). Mishan attempts to resolve the ambiguity by advocating the exclusive use of CV, even though this creates a status quo bias. Mishan (1982, p. 183) argues that status quo bias is appropriate, since any change will involve some transactions costs, even if the economist is not measuring them directly. By using CV, an economist can indirectly give effect to transactions costs.

However, if an economist wants to give effect to transactions costs, he or she should do so directly, by estimating their actual value. CV should not be used simply to approximate transactions costs. Furthermore, KHZ provides a rational basis for choosing between WTA and WTP in measuring the value of a good (and therefore provides a basis for choosing between EV and CV).[6] KHZ recognizes that gains and losses should be measured from a psychological reference point – what one believes one has. An improvement from this state is said to be a gain, while a deterioration from this state is said to be a loss. An exchange or a project is KHZ efficient if the sum of the gainers' WTP exceeds the sum of the losers' WTA, even if the losers are not in fact compensated.

3.5 LEGAL RIGHTS AND PSYCHOLOGICAL VALUES

Ownership, then, is both legal and psychological. From a legal perspective, the use of the WTA to measure losses and the WTP to measure gains rests on a normative decision to recognize ownership. Where psychological and legal ownership correspond, the situation is clear: ownership establishes a reference point, from which losses are to be calculated by the WTA, and gains by the WTP. In a sense, this has long been noted, as Atiyah (1979) pointed out.

Hume and Adam Smith, for example, both said that expectations arising out of rights of property deserved greater protection than expectations with regard to something that had never been possessed. To deprive somebody of something which he merely expects to receive is a less serious wrong, deserving of less protection, than to deprive somebody of the expectation of continuing to hold something which he already possesses (Atiyah 1979).

The law has long recognized that it is more serious to stop an owner from conducting an ongoing activity than to prohibit the owner from undertaking the same activity if he has not yet begun it. The currently fashionable expression of this may be found in Justice Brennan's phrase in *Penn. Central Trans. Co.* v. *City of New York*,[7] that a restriction is more likely to cause a taking if it destroys 'investment backed expectations.'

One's sense of psychological ownership will usually conform to one's knowledge of legal ownership. Most people feel that they have a moral right to what they legally own, and do not feel that they have the moral right to something they do not own. For most cases, then, the law will determine whether or not the WTP or WTA will be used. The common assumption is that a choice based on assigned legal entitlements will usually be correct, but it is correct because of the correspondence between the legal and psychological states; it is not correct as a matter of principle, and it is incorrect in important cases. Levy and Friedman (1994, p. 509) incorrectly assert that 'the determination of the conceptually appropriate form of CV query is a matter of property rights, not economics or psychology.'[8] It is, of course, true that the law will be the major determinant of psychological reference points.

This is very different from saying, as Levy and Friedman (1994) imply, that in the event of a conflict between the law and a psychological reference point, the law ought to govern. The reverse is true

3.6 WHY THE CHOICE OF WTP OR WTA MAKES A DIFFERENCE

The traditional decision is to use the WTP for gains and the WTA for losses. The correct motivation for this lies in the recognition of the economic significance of psychological ownership, and the pattern of legal rights. Gains and losses are psychological; they represent changes from some psychological reference point. In many cases, this point is determined by legal ownership. Ownership implies a right to have what one owns measured by the willingness to sell it – that is, by the WTA. In other cases, a person may feel a moral entitlement based on reasonable expectations that may engender psychological ownership, even where legal ownership is lacking.

Until recently, it was thought that the choice between WTP and WTA made little difference, aside from exceptional cases, and that the source of the difference was solely income effects (Willig 1976, p. 589). Now it is recognized that the choice can make a great difference (see Levy and Friedman 1994 and Coursey, Hovis and Schulze 1987, pp. 679–690). Researchers have demonstrated repeatedly that WTA questionnaires generate values from three to nineteen times greater than those elicited by WTP questionnaires (Levy and Friedman 1994, pp. 493, 495, n. 6; see also Coursey, Hovis and Schulze 1987). These differences are not found just in questionnaires, but also in experiments using a wide array of methods, and they are found, as well, in many cases of real decisions (see, for example, Knetsch 1997). Nor are these differences only empirically driven; they are based on the psychology of valuation.

There are three reasons for the difference: income effects; substitution possibilities; and loss aversion, or the endowment effect, as it is sometimes called. The latter two reasons have been appreciated only in recent years.

Income Effects

The income effect arises from the fact that the value of additional income relative to some good is less when you have more income. Suppose an indigent wins a Mercedes in a contest, and that the rest of the indigent's assets, combined, are worth $5. The indigent's WTP for the car is (at most) $5, since that is his total wealth, not counting the car.[9] The indigent's WTA is almost certainly more than $5, and presumably would be equal to the market value of a new Mercedes. This is an example of the most extreme form of income effect – a buying constraint.

However, income effects can exist without buying constraints. Suppose Al has $1,000 of disposable income, and owns a new coat, for which his WTA is $1,000. If Bob offered to buy the coat for $1,000, Al would accept, by definition. However, if Al's coat was stolen, and he later found it for sale in a pawnshop for $1,000, undamaged, he might not buy it. When Al loses his coat, his perspective changes. He is $1,000 poorer, and proportionately less willing to spend his money on expensive coats. Al might prefer to buy a $500 coat, and spend his other $500 on other things.

Figure 3.1 below shows the operation of income effects, in creating a divergence between the WTP and the WTA. U_0 and U_1 are indifference curves that represent two goods that are perfect substitutes for each other. Let us call them fame and money. Income is shown on the vertical axis, and fame on the horizontal axis. U_1 has a steeper slope than U_0 at every quantity of fame, indicating that fame is more valuable at a higher level of income. The initial level of income is at I_0 at point A on the indifference curve U_0, so that the initial amount of fame is q_0. The consumer gains more fame in moving to position q_1. To gain fame as presented by position q_1, the consumer is willing to give up in income $(I_0 - I_a)$ to arrive at point C, which is just as satisfying a position as point A, the initial point. This difference in income $I_0 - I_a$ is the WTP. The WTA is shown by also beginning with income I_0, but at point B on

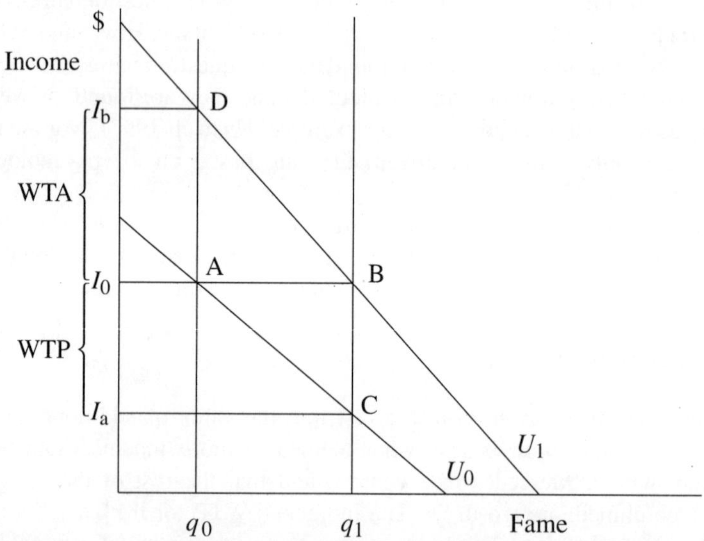

Figure 3.1 The income effect

indifference curve U_1 representing a higher level of satisfaction corresponding with having greater fame available. The consumer would be willing to accept less available fame if he gained income sufficient to put him at point D, a point that is equally satisfying as B. This income is $I_b - I_0$, and is the WTA. The WTA will exceed the WTP, since U_1 is steeper than U_0.

Both the WTP and the WTA measure the effect of a change.[10] The WTA presumes greater wealth than the WTP does; the greater wealth consists of possessing, in a psychological sense, the very good in question. This greater wealth means that the money measure of a positive change is larger for a normal good than when the same person has lower wealth. Whether or not the higher measure (which includes the greater wealth) is the better measure depends on whether that person possesses psychological ownership of the good being considered. The WTA measures the change from the perspective of one who claims the good.

Substitution Possibilities

Recently, Hanneman (1991, pp. 635f) showed that the poorer the substitutes for the good, the greater the divergence between the WTP and the WTA. Put another way, the more unique the good, the greater the divergence. The substantial divergence between WTP and WTA for environmental goods arises, in part, from the fact that many of these goods have no close substitutes. In general then, the divergence between the WTA and the WTP can be any positive value for normal goods.[11]

This can be shown by the following diagram. In Figure 3.2 the initial income is I_0. The WTP for a move from position A on U_1 to position C also on U_1 leaves the consumer with less income, but more time. The consumer is indifferent about income, since the loss of income does not affect his welfare. Starting from position A, the consumer moving to position C would be willing to pay either zero, or at most, $I_0 - I_a$, because any income greater than I_a is worthless to the consumer without more time. This is the WTP. Starting at position A′, the consumer would be willing to pay zero. The reader needs to realize the strangeness of the situation here. Because the loss of income is the loss of a worthless good, we can say that the WTP for income is either zero, or at most $I_0 - I_a$. A consumer who begins at position B, also with income I_0, but on the higher indifference curve U_2, will be unwilling to accept any amount of money in exchange for giving up time, since additional money is of no value to him without additional time. His WTA for time is infinite.[12] Since the WTP is finite and the WTA is infinite, the difference is also infinite.

The substitution effect does not, however, operate independently from the existence of the income effect. In Figure 3.2, the income effect is positive,

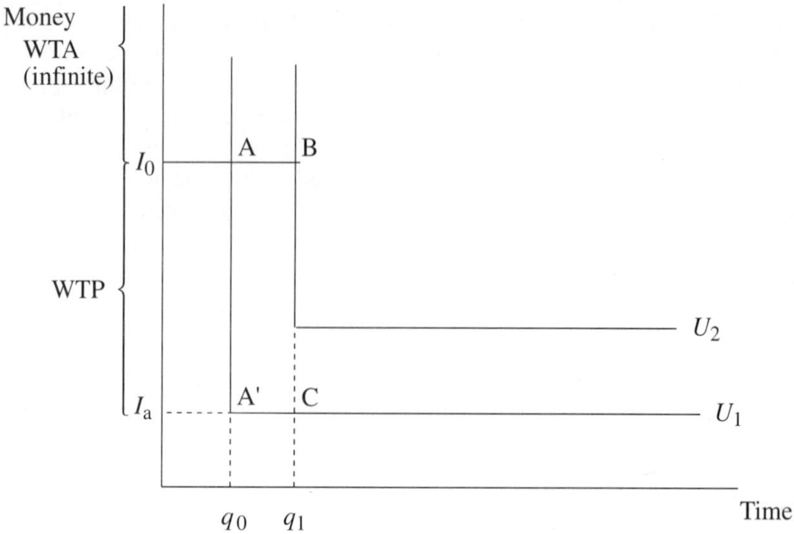

Figure 3.2 Pure substitution effect: divergence between WTA and WTA can be infinite

since a parallel shift in a budget line to the right will increase the amount of time purchased.

Suppose, instead, that there is no positive income effect, as in figure 3.3. In this case, the indifference curve, U_2, will have its vertical axis lying on U_1, but its horizontal axis lying above the horizontal axis, on U_1. Here, an increase in income (a shift to the right on the budget line, which is not shown) will not increase the purchase of time. In this situation, the WTA will be the same as the WTP, and no divergence exists.

The WTP for a move from A or A′ to C would be either zero, or, at most, $I_0 - I_a$, as before. The WTA for a move from B to A will be zero, or, at most, $I_0 – I_a$, for a move from C to A′. There is no divergence between the WTP and WTA. That is, *some* income effect is necessary for the substitution effect to drive the wedge between WTP and WTA.

Loss Aversion or the Endowment Effect

The essence of the endowment effect is found in an asymmetrical value function.[13] This function reflects the consequences of living in a state in which individuals value losses more highly than they value gains. Empirically, individuals appear to place a significantly higher value on a unit of a good that they already have, and might lose or have to give up, than they

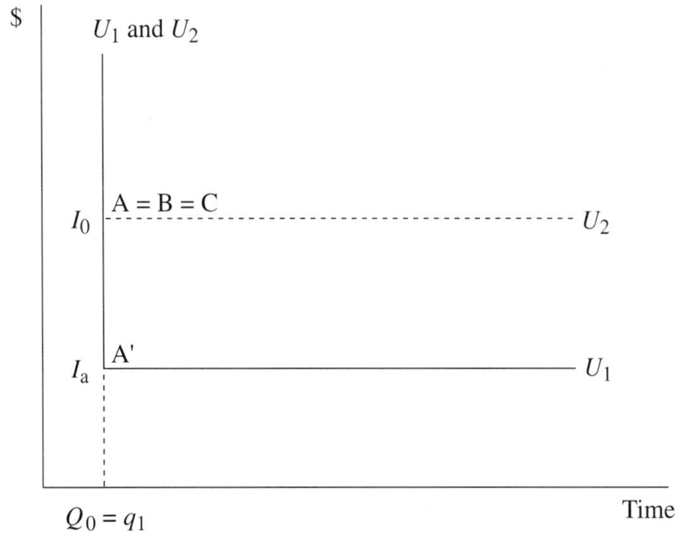

Figure 3.3

would place on acquiring a unit of the same good, if they did not own any. The standard benefit–cost approach, in which losses are valued according to the WTA and gains according to the WTP, is consistent with the empirically derived asymmetrical value function (Kahneman and Tversky 1979).

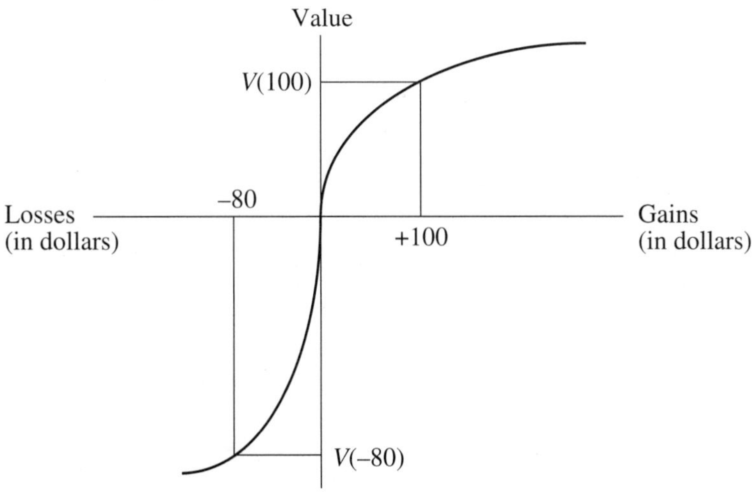

Figure 3.4 Value function

Among other things, this function, as shown in Figure 3.4, suggests that losses have a greater value than equivalent gains, and that the way in which goods are packaged will affect their value. For example, the value of two smaller gains is greater than the value of one equivalent gain – so that, as Thaler (1991) admonished, one should not put all of one's presents in one package.[14]

3.7 COMMERCIAL GOODS

A commercial good is one that is valued by its owner (or potential owner) purely because of the stream of income it produces. For commercial goods, WTA and WTP will not differ. Therefore, it is safe to use WTP to measure the value of a commercial good. Commercial goods help explain the existence of middle men, because if a middle man purchases and resells a good, he does not experience a loss arising from the divergence between the WTA and WTA. An owner *never* acquires psychological ownership of a commercial good, since the owner plans on selling the item for profit from the moment he or she acquires it. The WTA and WTP of a commercial good are both determined by the discounted value of the gross profit the item produces, minus all other costs the owner will face in selling or using the commercial good. The owner of a commercial good will not usually suffer from income effects, and will never suffer from substitution effects or loss aversion.

The reason why the owner of a commercial good will not usually suffer from income effects is that an owner of a commercial good who loses it can replace it by borrowing money against the future earnings from it, without drawing on his current wealth. And, unless there is an imperfect capital market, a non-owner who can expect to make a profit from a good can borrow money to purchase that good, even if his present resources are insufficient to purchase it. Thus, even small businesses with low total assets will not suffer *income effects* if their most valuable commercial goods are improperly taken from them, since they can replace the commercial goods by taking out a loan.

Of course, a small business that loses its most valuable commercial goods will suffer a significant decrease in wealth, but that decrease in wealth will be the same, no matter whether it is measured in WTA or in WTP terms. Even if the small business is impacted so severely that it must decrease its output, or go out of business altogether, its loss will be the same, whether it is viewed in WTA or in WTP terms. However, in imperfect capital markets, owners of commercial goods might have a divergence between WTA and WTP, since they might not be able to replace an asset if they could not borrow against future earnings. For example, if they could not convince a lender that their future earnings would be sufficient to repay the loan. For most purposes, it is probably safe to assume that the capital market is *sufficiently* perfect, so that low cash reserves do not lead to income effects.

The owner of a commercial good will never suffer substitution effects. This is true even though a commercial good may be unique. A good is 'unique,' in an economic sense if no substitutes good for it exists.[15] Of course, if the proper owner of a commercial good is deprived of a unique good, he or she will suffer a decrease in wealth, and the negative change in wealth will be magnified by the fact that no reasonable substitutes for the good exist. However, the fact that a commercial good is unique affects its WTA and WTP equally. Therefore, there is no substitution effect.

Consider a widget company, *X*, that can make its widgets only if it uses Acme brand spokes. *W* sells the widgets for $12. To make each widget, *X* needs one spoke ($5), various other parts ($1/widget) and labor ($1/widget). If Acme suddenly discontinued spoke production, and no other company made spokes that *X* could incorporate into its widgets, the remaining spokes might be relatively unique goods. Suppose *X* planned to make 1,000 widgets, and that the only alternative to making widgets is investing its cash at a 10 percent interest rate. In this hypothetical example, the spokes are relatively unique, since they allow a much higher net profit than the second-best alternative. If *X* managed to buy 1,000 spokes before Acme discontinued production, and a competitor, *Y*, wanted to buy the spokes from *X*, *X*'s WTA would be $10/spoke (the gross profit on the widget, $12, minus $2 parts and labor), less the interest that could have been made by investing both the proceeds of the sale and the money that would have gone into parts and labor, or roughly $8.90/spoke. If W had not managed to buy any spokes from Acme, and it learned that *Y* had 1,000 Acme brand spokes and was willing to sell them, *X*'s WTP would be $10/spoke ($12 minus $2), less the interest that it could have made by investing its cash, or roughly $8.90/spoke, as in the WTA case.

If the spokes were not unique, and comparable or identical spokes could be bought at $5, then *X*'s WTA and its WTP for the spokes would be $5. If *X* tried to buy spokes from *Y* instead of Acme, *X* would never spend more than $5/spoke, since that is the most that *X* would have to pay Acme. If *X* wanted to sell the spokes to *Y*, they would not insist on much more than $5/spoke, since at that price *X* can sell the spokes to *Y*, and buy replacements from Acme, and receive a net profit. For example, if *X* sold a spoke to *Y* at $5.01, *X* could buy a replacement from Acme for $5.00, and have $0.01 left over as profit. The fact that a commercial good is unique increases its value to an individual, but it increases the individual's WTP and his WTA by an equal amount.

Finally, the owner of a commercial good will not be loss averse, so loss aversion will not cause WTA and WTP to diverge. If a good is a commercial good, the owner attaches value to the good only because of the income it produces. To be loss averse, the owner would have to attach value to the fact of possession as well as to the expected income. Put another way, if it is true that a good is valued only because of its expected stream of income, an owner is indifferent to being deprived of the good at a different time than he had planned, so long as he receives the full expected profit for the good.

For example, suppose *X* owns 1,000 widgets, which are commercial goods with an expected profit of $12. Suppose that an average widget company loses 1 percent of its widgets to thieves every year, and that *X* has no reason to think that it will have fewer than average thefts this year, so it will most likely lose ten widgets. The most that *X* would spend to protect its widgets is $12 per stolen widget (or $120), which means that *X*'s WTA for each widget is $12.

It is worth noting that a good which a business purchases primarily for use in its business may not be a pure commercial good. Business people may attach value to their business' assets for reasons unrelated to the expected stream of income, such as the satisfaction of running a successful business, or the pride of beating a competitor by making a better product, or the achievement of a larger market share. Therefore, not all business assets are commercial goods. In fact, there is some empirical evidence that *most* business people are at least somewhat loss averse, in the sense that they will accept reductions in their net profits in order to avoid reducing their output (Levmore 1992, p. 334). If that is true, then it may be that relatively few business assets are pure commercial goods. However, most business assets are *almost* pure commercial goods, so it is safe for most purposes of economic analysis to assume that a business asset is a pure commercial good.

Finally, it is important to note that the rule of thumb that one person's WTA is higher than another person's WTP for a normal good assumes that the two parties intend to put the good to similar uses. When two parties intend to put an asset to completely different uses (particularly when one views an asset as a commercial good and the other views it as a consumer good) it is *not* safe to assume, *even as a general matter*, that the owner's WTA for the good is higher than the prospective buyer's WTP for a good. A commercial good can be safely measured by the WTP, since an individual's WTP and WTA for the good are likely to be virtually identical, but the individual's WTP and WTA for the good might both be extremely high, and might be far higher than the owner's WTA.

3.8 AN EXAMPLE OF THE IMPORTANCE OF SPECIFYING THE PSYCHOLOGICAL REFERENCE POINT IN LEGAL ANALYSIS

Consider the following example, the classic case of *Vincent* v. *Lake Erie Transportation Co.*[16] A dock owner refused to allow a ship to remain docked beyond the period of time set forth by the terms of its contract, and ordered it to leave. The captain refused to move his ship, because a storm was impending and the ship would likely have been lost at sea. The ship remained, the storm came, and the ship inflicted $500 of damage to the dock. The court held that it was reasonable for the captain to refuse to leave, because the damage to the dock was probably less than what would have been done to the ship had he risked the storm. The court held, further, that the captain secured the ship to the dock with the proper equipment and used the proper techniques. Nonetheless, it held that the dock owner was owed compensation for whatever damages resulted from the captain's decision to stay moored to the dock.

Jules Coleman (1980, pp. 509–551) cites the outcome in *Vincent* as an example of a Pareto improvement, but one to which the parties had not consented. His statement is confusing. If the two parties to a dispute are behaving rationally, they will never fail to consent to a proposed Pareto improvement. Furthermore, in order to say that a decision is a Pareto improvement, one must specify the status quo, and then compare it to a supposedly Pareto superior alternative. It is also necessary to specify the status quo to determine if a change is KH or KHZ efficient. Here, Coleman does not specify the status quo.

Why did the parties in *Vincent* fail to reach an agreement? In other words, why didn't the dock owner agree to let the captain tie his ship to the dock during the storm, so long as the captain agreed to reimburse the dock owner for any damage he inflicted? The most plausible answer is that the captain and the dock owner disagreed about their respective legal rights. In other words, the captain may have believed that he had the right to remain tied to the dock, and that he was not liable for the damages he inflicted on the dock owner. From the captain's perspective, he would be suffering a loss if he agreed to reimburse the dock owner. The dock owner may have believed that the captain would not have to reimburse him for any damage that the captain inflicted on his dock. However, the dock owner may have believed that the captain did *not* have the right to tie his ship to the dock in the first place.

Given the parties' different psychological reference points, it is not surprising that they did not reach an agreement in which the dock owner let the captain tie his ship dock in return for a promise to pay damages. From the dock owner's perspective, he would suffer a loss if he let the captain tie his ship to the dock, unless the captain agreed to compensate him. From the captain's perspective, he would suffer a loss if he agreed to compensate the dock owner, since he already had the right to tie his ship to the dock under the common law. In other words, any agreement between the captain and the dock owner would make at least one party worse off, without making the other party any better off.

Because the parties had different psychological reference points, the decision in *Vincent* was not a Pareto superior change. A Pareto superior decision must make at least one party better off, without making any party worse off. *Vincent* made the ship owner worse off, from his perspective. In fact, given the parties' different psychological reference points, no Pareto superior move was available to the court.

Coleman (1980) might have meant that the decision in *Vincent* was Pareto superior to a state of the world in which the ship was *actually* lost at sea during the storm, and in which the *dock owner* owed damages to the *captain* (or the captain's surviving relatives) for the loss of the ship. However, it is important to note that the dock owner almost certainly did not believe that he would be liable to the captain for the loss of the ship if the ship was lost at sea. If the dock owner believed that he would be liable in that situation, it would have been in his own interest to let the captain tie his ship to the dock, since suffering $500 in uncompensated damages is better than having to pay for the lost ship. Since there is no reason to assume that the dock owner was irrational, we should assume that the dock owner did not believe that he would be liable to the captain if the ship was lost. Therefore, Coleman is suggesting a status quo which is inconsistent with *both* parties' psychological reference points.

Although *Vincent* was not Pareto efficient, it was probably KHZ efficient compared to any other decision the judges could have reached. If *Vincent* held that the captain had the right to tie his ship to the dock and that the dock owner was not entitled to damages, that outcome might have been inconsistent with the regard for others, since society might feel that it is unfair for the captain to be able to damage the dock owner's property for his own benefit without compensating the dock owner. Furthermore, in the future dock owners will be more likely to voluntarily allow ships to dock if they know that they will be compensated for the damages that the ships cause. Conversely, if dock owners know that they will *not* be compensated, they might spend money to ensure that ships are *actually* prevented from docking during storms. For example, if a dock owner suspected that a ship would inflict $500 of damage to his dock during a storm, and the dock owner knew that a court would not compensate him for this loss, he might be willing to pay a sneaky individual $450 to untie the ship when the captain was not looking. The dock owner would save $50 but would inflict a much larger loss on the ship owner, and therefore there would be a net social loss.

For the determination of a Pareto improvement, as well as the determination of KH or KHZ efficiency, an understanding of the concept of psychological reference points is needed. Further, an understanding of the psychological nature of benefits and costs is essential to the Coase theorem, and to efficiency analysis when rights are uncertain or in dispute, as Chapter 4 will show.

3.9 THE KALDOR–HICKS CRITERIA AND THE WTP AND WTA

KHZ is defined in terms of the WTP and WTA. The KHZ test is passed when the aggregation of gains and losses as measured by the WTP and WTA are positive. When this occurs, I shall say that there are net benefits from the project. This test meets the essential requirement: any one person who has net benefits over a set of projects, can be said unequivocally to have gained. Incidentally, it also meets two other requirements that were thought to be important for KH: it meets a potential compensation test, and is subject to neither Scitovsky reversals nor status quo bias.

The essential test that positive net benefits exist over a set of projects for an individual is met whether or not there is path dependence. The path dependence issue is the following: suppose an individual, over a set of two projects, loses \$9 on the first and gains \$10 on the second. Is this the same result as if the individual gained \$10 on the first and lost \$9 on the second so that in either case there is a gain of \$1 over all. When the order makes no difference, then there is said to be path independence. When there is no path dependence, then many projects can be treated as one so that the overall net benefit KHZ test gives the correct answer. When there is path dependence, KHZ will also give the right answer by following the correct path.

Path Independence

In modern economics, the measure of welfare change is normally the expenditure function. The function $M^*(p_1,U_0)$ is the minimum cost or expenditure of achieving utility level U_0 at price p_1. M^* represents the expenditure level that is the solution to the problem of minimizing cost or expenditure. Changes in the value of the expenditure function show the change in expenditures to attend a given utility level as prices change.

Consider a price change from p_0 to p_1. Let U_0 represent the psychological reference point before the change. Then the difference in expenditures M_c occasioned by the price change is

$$M_c^*(p_0, U_0) - M_c^*(p_1, U_0) \tag{3.1}$$

This measure of welfare change is path independent so that all projects affecting a particular individual may be treated as one project for that individual.

Path Dependence

The literature on the psychological nature of gains and losses, however, suggests that gains and losses are in fact path dependent. In general, KHZ notes that the correct measure of gains and losses must take into account the psychological underpinnings or value. Thus the recognition of path dependence does not affect the fact that an individual with net gains over a set of separate projects can be said to be better off. Rather, KHZ corrects for the measure of gain and loss to determine net benefits.

Suppose, for example, that the government proposes a project that will raise the price of electricity to consumer A but that to undertake it they also need to buy land from consumer A and the income from the sale of the land will more than offset the higher electricity cost. Consider two ways to value this project. It could be regarded as two different projects, one involving the sale of land and the other an increase in electricity prices, or as one project. When it is evaluated as two separate projects, this assumes that the consumer values the higher price as a loss to be measured by the WTA. If the consumer were to regard the project as just one project with a gain, the KHZ measure would be the WTP and the measure of gain for the overall project would be larger than when valued as two separate projects. Thaler (1985) reports an experiment in which the following questions were asked. Who should be happier: A who wins $100 in the state lottery but the same day drops a bottle of ink and does $80 worth of damage to his living room rug; or B, who wins $20 in the lottery? Of a large sample of subjects 70 percent responded B, 25 percent said A, and 5 percent said the two should be equally happy. Since KHZ recognizes the psychological nature of gains and losses, it recognizes this path dependence. Thus, KHZ in general would not treat the $20 net gain from the lottery as the same as the $100 gain with the $80 loss.

In its emphasis on WTP and WTA measuring gains and losses, KHZ differs from the KH criteria. The KH criteria are potential compensation tests. KHZ is defined rather in terms of aggregate WTP and WTA. The usual measure of welfare changes through the EV and CV are not quite the same as potential compensation tests (Boadway and Bruce 1984). The KHZ measure is consistent with the practice, roughly derived from KH, of expressing benefit–cost analysis in terms of WTP and WTA.

3.10 DO TECHNICAL OBJECTIONS TO KH APPLY TO KHZ?

Four technical objections have been made to the use of KH efficiency calculations. These are (1) circularity, (2) compensation test failure, (3) indeterminacy, and (4) status quo bias. These issues arise partly out of a basic confusion that exists about the relationship between the KH compensation tests, the CV and EV measures of welfare change, and the concepts of WTP and WTA. I propose to show that none of these criticisms applies to KHZ. All of the technical objections to KH arise from measurement problems: if perfect measurement of welfare states were possible the objections would disappear. In defining KHZ, I do not mean to imply that measurement problems do not remain. Clearly in some cases the measurement of WTP or WTA will be imperfect or will imperfectly reflect actual preferences. This empirical problem is a matter for another sort of discussion than this one.

Compensation tests

The first requirement is met because, under KHZ, the measurement of the value of gains is always less than the (absolute value) of the measurement of equivalent losses by definition. So, the potential compensation tests are met by definition. (An extended discussion of compensation and circularity issues is provided in the appendix to this chapter.)

Circularity

Coleman (1980) cites the Scitovsky reversal problem as a major issue of the use of KH. There are fundamental errors in his analysis as is shown in Appendix 3. But there is no circularity issue for KHZ. For in using KHZ and thus the WTP and WTA net benefit test to gauge the value of a move from I to II and from II to I, it is quite impossible to approve a move from I to II and then back again, as is required for the Scitovsky test, when gains are valued less than or equal to equivalent losses. This is because if one gains from a move from I to II, one will lose even more in a move back. And, if one loses from a move from I to II, one will gain less from a move back.[17]

Status quo bias

As Chapter 5 shows and as is well known, it is possible for the results of a KH or KHZ test to favor the status quo as between A and B, whichever position is the status quo. So, if society is in position A, it will not pay to move to B, and if society is in B it will not pay to move to A. This is not a bias, however, but arises naturally from the divergence of WTP for gains and WTA for losses. That is, the KHZ measure correctly reflects the power of the existing property rights and the fact that a move from the current legal/

psychological position will inflict losses that are felt more than equivalent gains.

Indeterminacy
Similarly, it is shown in Chapter 5, that the indeterminacy problem disappears with use of KHZ. Under KHZ welfare is maximized by selling the right to the highest bidder (see Chapter 5).

APPENDIX 3

3.1A Circularity (Reversibility) and Compensation Tests

Scitovsky reversals do not occur for KHZ. In short, this is because if the income distribution is an economic good, than community indifference curves do not cross. Elsewhere I consider this formally (Zerbe 2001). The reasoning is this: in comparing two positions on two different community indifference curves that cross, the choice may be reduced to one of income distribution (Mishan 1981). KHZ requires that the income distribution is an economic good and provides a method of choosing between distributions. Thus we may define a KHZ community indifference curve that includes the income distribution as an economic good. KHZ community indifference curves will not cross and preference reversals will therefore not occur.

Even for KH discussions of reversibility as a problem are unpersuasive. Coleman (1980, p. 519) supposes that the rationale for KH is utilitarian and rejects KH on the grounds that no interpersonal comparisons of utility can be made and that the KH tests lead to 'inconsistent preferences over social states' – i.e. Scitovsky reversals. Coleman's example of reversibility falls apart upon a fuller analysis. More generally, this sort of reversibility occurs only when second-best states are being compared but the relevant comparison should be for first-best states.

Coleman uses the following example to argue that the KH tests are not useful criteria for evaluating projects: Mr. A has two units of *X*, and Ms. B has one unit of *Y*. A prefers one unit of *X* and one of *Y* to two units of *X*, and B would prefer one unit of *Y* and one unit of *X* to two units of *Y*. The government is considering a project which will allow B to have two units of *Y*, but which will lead A to have only one unit of *X*. The results are summarized in table 3.1A.

The project passes the Kaldor test. If Ms. B gave one unit of *Y* to Mr. A, she would be no worse off than she was before the project, and Mr. A would be better off, since he would rather have one unit of *X* and one unit of *Y* than have two units of *X*. However, the project fails the Hicks test. If Mr. A gave

Table 3.1A

	Status quo		Proposed rule	
	X	*Y*	*X*	*Y*
Mr. A	2	0	1	0
Ms. B	0	1	0	2

Ms. B one unit of *X* in return for *not* receiving the benefits of the project, Mr. A would be no worse off than the project made him, while Ms. B would be better off, since she would rather have one unit of *X* and one of *Y* than have two units of *Y*. Passing the Kaldor test and failing the Hicks test means that Coleman's example is an instance of the classic problem of the Scitovsky paradox: the dilemma facing economists about what to do when a project passes the Kaldor test but fails the Hicks test.

The Scitovsky paradox is said to create a problem of 'reversibility' for the following reason: to fail the Hicks test, in considering a move from the status quo to a new position, means that the reverse move, from the new position to the original status quo, will pass a Kaldor test. That is, if we used Kaldor to evaluate both a proposed change and the repeal of that change, we would face a dilemma of always wanting to reverse whatever decision we had made before. For example, suppose a law passes the Kaldor test but fails the Hicks test. One might justify the new law on the grounds that it passes the Kaldor test. However, if the law was passed, one could also show that repealing the statute would be efficient, since *repealing* it would satisfy the Kaldor test. If both the Kaldor and Hicks tests were used to test a decision to pass a law or a decision to repeal the law, we would face no problem of reversibility, but it might be argued that we had a problem of status quo bias. Coleman argues that the Scitovsky paradox shows that the Kaldor and Hicks tests are not useful bases for decision making.

This example appears compelling. But it fails, first, because it is incomplete. In addition, it fails as a criticism of KHZ because it is does not consider the WTP or the WTA. As a first step note that the example supposes that one of A's two units of *X* can be transformed into one unit of *Y*, or, starting from the proposed rule, that one unit of *Y* can be transformed back into one unit of *X*. But we are told by Coleman that A prefers one unit of *X* plus one of *Y* to two units of *X*. And we are told that Ms. B prefers one unit of *X* and one of *Y* to two of *Y*. So we must ask: why has the transformation not taken place? Starting from the status quo state, Mr. A would be better off and Ms. B no worse off by the transformation so the transformation is a Pareto superior move. Perhaps, though, A needs the help of Ms. B to complete the transformation. In this case, Mr. A transfers some small amount of *X* to Ms. B to help with the transformation and both Mr. A and Ms. B are better off. A similar result is obtained if we take the proposed rule as the starting point. Ms. B could improve her position either unilaterally or with the help of A.

Consider the following example, depicted in Table 3.2A, based on Coleman's example. A is a wheat farmer with two acres of wheat, while B is a cotton farmer with one acre of cotton. A would prefer having one acre of wheat and one acre of cotton to having two acres of wheat or cotton and B would also prefer having one acre of wheat and one acre of cotton to having two acres of wheat or cotton. B asks for a legal decision which will give her one acre of A's land, but which will only allow her to grow cotton there.

Table 3.2A

	Status quo		Proposed rule	
	Wheat	Cotton	Wheat	Cotton
Mr. A	2	0	1	0
Ms. B	0	1	0	2

Just as in Coleman's example, we have a project which passes the Kaldor test (since A would prefer having one acre of cotton and one acre of wheat to having two acres of wheat) but which fails the Hicks test (since B would prefer having one acre of each crop to having two acres of cotton).

Clearly, we are comparing second-best states. If A really preferred growing one acre of wheat and one acre of cotton to growing two acres of wheat (after transactions costs), A would *already* be growing one acre of each crop – he would not wait for a court to give an acre of his land to B, let B turn it into a cotton patch, and then try to convince B to give the land back to him. Similarly, if B really prefers growing one acre of each crop to growing two acres of wheat, she would not sue for the right to grow *cotton* on one of B's acres of land, she would sue for the right to grow *wheat* there. Indeed, since A is already using the land to grow wheat, B would not even have to spend money to convert the land into a wheat farm.

Therefore, we are really choosing between four projects, not two. The four possibilities are outlined in Table 3.3A.[18]

Possibility 3 is identical to a situation in which the rule was passed and B *actually* compensated A. Similarly, possibility 4 is identical to a situation in which the rule was not passed and A actually compensated B in return for not

Table 3.3A

	Possibility 1		Possibility 2		Possibility 3		Possibility 4	
	Wheat	Cotton	Wheat	Cotton	Wheat	Cotton	Wheat	Cotton
A	2	0	1	0	1	1	1	0
B	0	1	0	2	0	1	1	1

getting the benefits of the rule. Possibility 3 Pareto dominates possibility 1 and possibility 4 Pareto dominates situation 2. Thus situations 1 and 2 are, by definition, second-best states. Therefore, one way of restating the Kaldor (strong) test is that a proposed rule (possibility 2) is better than the status quo (possibility 1) if *possibility 3* is better than the status quo. Similarly, the Hicks (strong) test can be restated as saying that the proposed rule is *not* better than the status quo if *possibility 4* is better than the proposed rule.

To compare the four possibilities in terms of KHZ, we need to know the WTA and WTP of A and B for wheat and cotton, and we need to know A and B's relative senses of psychological ownership. Coleman's example does not give us enough information to compare even the two states he presents, let alone the four states that are relevant. All we know from Coleman's example is that A's WTA and WTP for cotton is higher than A's WTA and WTP for wheat, and that B's WTA and WTP for wheat is higher than B's WTA and WTP for cotton. Based on Coleman's example, we know that possibility 3 is better than possibility 1, since B is equally well off in 1 and 3 while A is better off in 3. Similarly, we know that possibility 4 is better than possibility 2, since A is equally well off in 2 and 4 and B is better off in 4. Therefore, the first-best states are possibilities 3 and 4. Therefore, possibilities 1 and 2 are second-best states. Once we specify WTAs, WTPs, and senses of psychological ownership for the two parties and the two goods, it will be possible to determine the most efficient distribution of the goods.

First, consider a set of numbers which would make possibility 3 the best distribution of goods. For simplicity we assume that these are commercial goods, so there is no divergence between the WTA and the WTP as outlined in Table 3.4A.

These numbers are consistent with Coleman's example, since A prefers one acre of cotton to a second acre of wheat and B prefers an acre of wheat to a second acre of cotton.

The reader will discern that if these numbers are used no reversibility is possible. The WTP to move from state 1 to 2 becomes just the WTA to move from state 2 to 1. Similarly, the WTA to move from state 1 to 2 becomes the

Table 3.4A

	A WTP = WTA	B WTP = WTA
Retain 2nd acre of wheat	$10	
Acquire 1st acre of cotton	$20	
Acquire 1st acre of wheat		$20
Acquire 2nd acre of cotton		$5

WTP to move from 2 to 1. So if the sum of the WTP and the WTA to move from 1 to 2 is positive (negative) it will be negative (positive) for the reverse move.

3.2A First-Best States Unavailable

What does it mean to compare second-best states and why would we want to do it? Suppose that possibilities 3 and 4 are not available as choices for some reason. Perhaps A and B live in a society in which it is illegal for one person to grow both wheat and cotton, and A and B are unwilling to violate the law. Then the status quo and the proposed rule change are not really 'second-best states,' since they are the only states that are available.

But if possibilities 1 and 2 are first-best states in the sense that states 3 and 4 are unavailable, then the nature of the compensation test must change. Coleman's assumptions about values are incorrect if it is true that the third and fourth choices are unavailable. In other words, if A cannot grow cotton, then it is not true that A would prefer having one acre of cotton and one acre of wheat to having two acres of wheat. An acre of cotton would not necessarily be worthless to A, since he might be able to convert it back into a wheat farm or use it in some other way. Presumably, though, his WTA and WTP to retain his second acre of wheat would be at least as high as his WTA and WTP for putting the acre to some other use. After all, if a better use of his second acre of wheat was available to him and was more valuable to him, he would already be using it for something other than growing wheat. He would not experience a benefit if he lost his acre of wheat to B, allowed it to be turned into a cotton farm, re-acquired it from B, and then turned it back into a wheat farm, since such a scenario would lead to a ludicrous series of transactions costs. For exactly the same reasons, B would not prefer an acre of wheat to a second acre of cotton if B was not allowed to grow wheat.

In addition, if we must choose between the status quo and the proposed rule change, we should not use the Kaldor and Hicks (strong) tests. After all, the logic of the Kaldor test is that the proposed rule is better than the status quo if possibility 3 is better than the status quo. For one thing, I have shown that that prediction is incorrect. Furthermore, the silliness of using the Kaldor (strong) test is even more obvious if we remember that the possibility 3 is not really possible at all. If B is legally forbidden to compensate A by giving him an acre of cotton, it is not possible, even in theory, for B to compensate A by giving him an acre of cotton in return for his acre of wheat, because A does not prefer cotton to wheat if he is not allowed to grow cotton.

However, KHZ can help us determine whether the proposed rule is better than the status quo, by assigning a WTA and WTP to A and B for wheat and cotton. The rule would be inefficient if A's WTA and WTP to retain his second unit of wheat was greater than B's WTA and WTP to acquire a second unit of cotton. Similarly, the rule would be efficient if B's WTA and WTP for cotton was greater than A's WTA and WTP for wheat.

A diagrammatic treatment

The reversibility issue can also be illustrated diagrammatically. Figure 3.1A shows utility frontier curves for two individuals A and B. Scitovsky reversals occur when they cross as shown. Utility frontiers show the trade utility trade-offs between individuals 1 and 2 for different production regimes A and B.

The utility of individual 1 is shown on the vertical axis and the utility of individual 2 is shown on the horizontal axis. The lines U_A and U_B show the

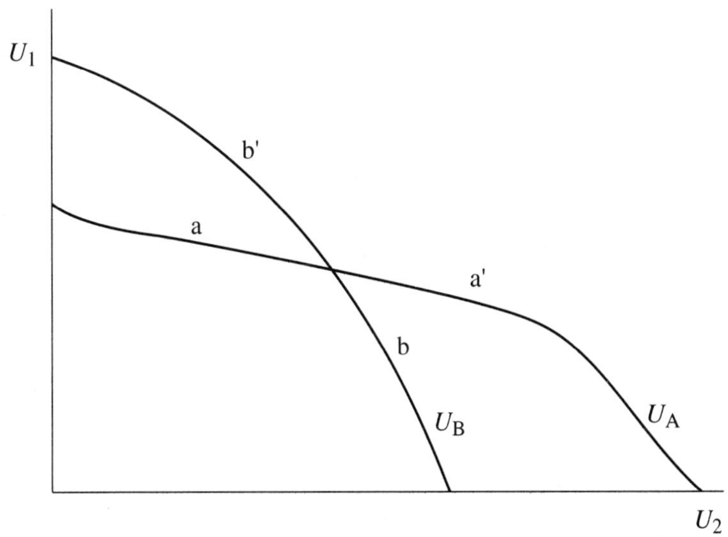

Figure 3.1A

the utility frontiers for individuals 1 and 2. The two different utility frontier lines are drawn for different outputs. The utility frontier lines U_A and U_B show the utility for individuals 1 and 2 that result from the contract curve associated with two different outputs, A and B, respectively (see Mishan 1981 for further exposition). The key is, of course, the fact that the utility lines can cross. If they do not cross, no reversal is possible. Consider a move from a to b. The Kaldor test is passed, since along U_B we can consider moving up from b to b′, which is Pareto superior to a. If, now, on the basis of this test, we move to b, we find a difficulty. Starting from b, a move to point a is potentially superior because, having arrived at a, we could move along U_A to a′ which would be Pareto superior to b. Again, however, why should a and b be comparable points? Since there are points that are Pareto superior to both of these, namely a′ and b′, should not the comparison be between a′ and b′? If so, status quo bias may exist, but not reversal. The obvious question is: 'Why doesn't a society in a second-best situation move to a better first-best situation?' That is, why not just move directly from $U_{A(a)}$ to $U_{B(b')}$, or from $U_{B(b)}$ to $U_{A(a')}$?

Samuelson reversals

Paul Samuelson (1950) suggested a more generalized form for the Scitovsky paradox. In the Scitovsky reversal, the utility frontier lines, U_A and U_B, must cross between the choices being compared. These lines may, however, not

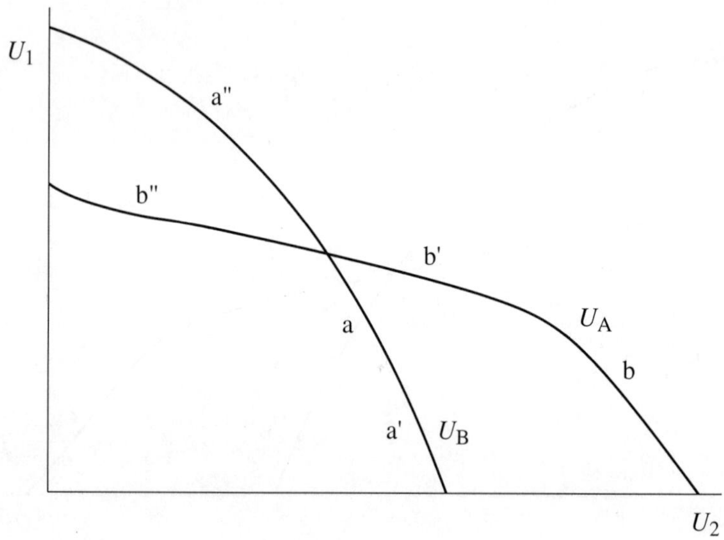

Figure 3.2A

cross within this space, but cross elsewhere – outside the points being compared. In Figure 3.2A this is the case.

Situation b is clearly superior to a by a Kaldor compensation test. There is no Scitovsky reversal. From b, a redistribution may be made to b′, and b′ is clearly Pareto superior to a. And a move from b to a finds no redistribution along U_A that is superior to b. Samuelson pointed out, however, that there is a point a″ that is superior to b″, and that b′ is a redistribution of the goods available at b. Samuelson suggests that position b be regarded as superior to position a only if the utility frontier curves do not cross. To say this another way, Samuelson suggests that the state of the world 2 would be called superior to state 1 only if for *any* distributional arrangement of the state 1 goods there is a Pareto superior arrangement in state 2. This is often called the Samuelson test or condition (Mishan 1981, pp. 313–314). Scitovsky actually noted the possibility discussed by Samuelson, but believed that comparisons should involve the positions being actually considered. The Samuelson criterion in some cases is more restrictive than KH, and its use would entail a greater status quo bias. In fact, Samuelson is even more restrictive than Pareto. Not only does Samuelson object to moving from a to b and then to b′, but he would apparently object to moving *directly* from a to b′, even though a direct move to b′ is Pareto efficient, since a″ is Pareto superior to b″. Thus all projects that fail the Scitovsky test would also fail the Samuelson test, but in addition, there would be others that would fail only the Samuelson test.

For an example that would pass Samuelson, imagine two utility frontier curves that do not cross. One might compare two positions on these different curves, neither of which is Pareto superior to the other. However, Samuelson's criterion would allow the selection of the position on the higher of the two utility frontier curves, even though in moving from one position to another some are worse off. Thus Samuelson does not allow some moves, even though they are Pareto efficient, but his test does allow some moves that are not Pareto efficient.

Under KHZ, we assume that all efficient changes which are possible under a legal regime have already been made; therefore, we should only compare points which are first-best positions.

The example provided by Table 3.4A at hand is additionally instructive. Note that even though the Kaldor (strong) test is passed, the EV and the CV tests and the KHZ net benefits test are all failed. (Possibility 1 has KHZ net benefits of zero; the status quo always has an efficiency of zero, and is the best state only if every other regime would result in a net loss.) Possibility 2 has KHZ net benefits of –5, since A would have a cost of 10 if he lost one of his acres of wheat, while B would only gain 5 if she acquired a second acre of cotton.

Possibility 3 shows us that the net benefit test and the CV and the EV tests can be passed even though the Hicks (strong) test failed. Possibility 3 has an EV and a CV and KHZ net benefits of +20. B undergoes no change, and A has a benefit of 20 when he acquires a new acre of cotton.

Possibility 4 has an EV and a CV of –1, since A has a cost of 10 when he loses his second acre of wheat and B only has a benefit of 9 when she acquires an acre of wheat. Note that possibility 4 is better than possibility 2, because it results in a lower net loss than possibility 2 does, but that the status quo is actually better than possibility 4.

However, possibility 4 can also be the best state, if we plug in different numbers, which are also consistent with Coleman's example. See Table 3.5A.

Table 3.5A

	A WTP = WTA	B WTP = WTA
Retain 2nd acre of wheat	$5	
Acquire 1st acre of cotton	$9	
Acquire 1st acre of wheat		$20
Acquire 2nd acre of cotton		$10

Possibility 2 has an efficiency of +5, since B has a benefit of 10 and A has a cost of 5. Possibility 3 has an efficiency of +4, since A has a benefit of 4 (or, if you prefer, A has both a benefit of 9 and a cost of 5), and B has no change in wealth. Possibility 4 has an efficiency of +15, since B has a benefit of 20 and A has a cost of 5. Again, we see that possibility 3 is better than possibility 1, and possibility 4 is better than possibility 2.[19] Among other things, this discussion shows that saying that a pair of states are the first-best states does *not* necessarily mean that both of them are better than any one of the other states; it simply means that one of the pair will always be the *best* state possible.

This sort of result helps explain why KHZ does not embrace the Kaldor and Hicks tests, although the examples refer only to the strong test. The logic of the Kaldor (strong) test is that a proposed rule is better than the status quo if *possibility 3* is better than the status quo. However, in Table 3.4A I have shown that it is possible for the proposed rule change (possibility 2) to be worse than the status quo (possibility 1) even if possibility 3 is better than the status quo. This means that even if a rule *would* be Pareto superior to the status quo *after* compensation, it might be less efficient than the status quo *before* compensation. Of course, since possibility 3 is the best choice of all, in a sense it does not matter whether possibility 1 is better than possibility 2. However, it is noteworthy that the prediction of the Kaldor (strong) test is incorrect.

The logic of the Hicks (strong) test is that a proposed rule is *not* better than the status quo if *possibility 4* is better than proposed rule change. However, in Table 3.5A I have shown that *possibility 4* is better than the status quo and the proposed rule change, but the proposed rule change (possibility 2) is more efficient than the status quo (possibility 1). Therefore, the Hicks (strong) test makes a prediction which is incorrect.

This appendix has shown that the possibility of preference reversal is only possible when comparing second-best states and is also only possible when using the KH potential compensation tests. It is not, however, possible when using the KHZ net benefits test. Even if a project is subject to Scitovsky reversal, this does not present a dilemma or paradox for KHZ, since WTP and WTA evaluation will unambiguously rank one regime over all of the others.

This issue is also related to the one of choosing among first-best positions and of choosing between a first-best and a second-best position. As Mishan (1981, pp. 359–376) has shown, however, the choice between these sorts of positions (or indeed between second-best positions) can be reduced to a choice of income distribution. This income distribution is a good in KHZ analysis. In so far, then, as KHZ provides a method of choosing between different distributions, it offers a method of choice without contradiction.

NOTES

I would like to thank Robin Boadway, Neil Bruce and Gene Silberberg for comments on parts of this chapter. Any errors are my own.

1. These are non-technical definitions and, as such, are not wholly accurate. The compensating variation (CV) is the sum of money that can be taken away or given to leave one as well off as one was *before* the economic change. The equivalent variation (EV) is money taken or given that leaves one as well off as *after* the economic change. See Zerbe and Dively (1994, Chapter 5), for a derivation of these concepts in terms of indifference curves.
2. The difference between benefits and costs is simply their sign: positive for benefits and negative for costs. Thus, without loss of accuracy, costs can be counted as negative benefits and benefits can be counted as negative costs.
3. Their work raised at least the following questions relevant for benefit-cost analysis:

    1. Should gains be treated differently (asymmetrically) from losses?
    2. Should expert opinion about risk be used when it differs from that of the public?
    3. Should the more reflective, longer considered values of people be used, or their less reflective values?

    The first question is answered affirmatively in this chapter. The second and third questions are ultimately questions about economic standing. I discuss economic standing in Chapter 4, and show the relationship between standing and expert opinion and reflective values.

4. The other sort of efficiency used in economics is Pareto efficiency. A change in ownership is Pareto efficient if the buyer's WTP exceeds the seller's WTA, assuming no other parties are affected. A trade or project is Pareto efficient when at least one person gains from it and no one loses from it (Zerbe and Dively 1994, pp. 12–13).
5. There is some complexity here that is being passed over. It will be efficient to assign the right to the right person initially, of course, as this may save transactions costs. In Chapter 4, I argue that this means, in effect, holding an auction. But in our static world, the efficient rule for assigning rights would already be in place. For more detail, see Frank (2000, p. 256).
6. In some cases, two individuals may both have some sense of psychological ownership, but the sense of ownership may be less than 100 percent. EV and CV assume that one person has complete psychological ownership and that another person has no psychological ownership. When both parties have partial psychological ownership, KHZ advocates the use of a weighted average of EV and CV. I discuss cases of partial psychological ownership in Chapter 5.
7. *Penn. Central Trans. Co.* v. *City of New York*, 438 U.S. 104 (1978). I would like to thank William B. Stoebuck for this reference.
8. The authors use the term 'CV query' in reference to questionnaire studies. 'CV' here stands for 'contingent valuation.'
9. In a perfect capital market, an indigent who had a chance to buy a new Mercedes Benz for less than the market price (even if it was, for example, $20,000) would be able to do so by taking out a loan, buying the car, selling it at the market price, and repaying the loan. In practice, it is hard to imagine any lender being willing to loan an indigent $20,000.
10. For a diagrammatical treatment, see Zerbe (1998b).
11. Normal goods are those that become more desirable when income increases, all other things being equal (see, for example, Pashigian 1995, p. 93).
12. In order for the WTA not to be infinite, U_2 would need to cross the vertical line extending upward from q_0.
13. Hanneman's (1991) analysis is independent of the endowment effect, as he notes.
14. Thaler (1991) mentions many other implications not discussed here.
15. Unlike the traditional watchdogs of good English, economists deem it allowable to speak of 'uniqueness' as something that exists to a greater or lesser degree: the poorer the closest market substitute for a good is, the more unique the good is. Of course, 'more unique' is an oxymoron, from the perspective of the pernickety guardians of proper English.
16. *Vincent v. Lake Erie Transportation Co.*, 109 Minn. 456, 124 N.W. 221 (1910).
17. Mishan (1982) demonstrates this result.
18. Of course, there are possibilities other than these, such as the possibility of A receiving all three acres of land, or of A and B each having 1½ acres of land. There are, in fact, an infinite number of ways that A and B could share and use the three acres of land. For the sake of simplicity, I will assume that the land cannot be partitioned without destroying its value (that is, one acre is the minimum commercially feasible area to grow either cotton or wheat) and that it would be inefficient to give A or B all three acres of land since A and B each value their *first* acre of land more than the other one would value a *third* acre of land, regardless of whether the third acre is used to grow wheat or cotton.
19. Ironically, possibility 2 is actually better than possibility 3, but that is irrelevant since possibility 4 is the best choice.

4. The nature of inefficiency

4.1 THE DEFINITION OF INEFFICIENCY

I will say that economic inefficiency occurs when there is some hypothetical new rule that would pass a KHZ efficiency test, not counting the costs of changing the rule, but counting other transactions costs.[1] By not counting the costs of changing a rule, the economic analyst is saved the difficult job of estimating the political costs associated with rule change. I call this efficiency or economic efficiency. With this definition a paradox arises in so far as an economist may then label some rule inefficient, when the costs of enacting the rule are sufficiently great that society would lose were the rule to be enacted. If, however, to define efficiency to include the costs rule change then every society is always completely efficient as a tautology. I will call this sort of efficiency tautological efficiency. Inefficiency incurs then because transactions costs are higher than they need to be, or because property rights do not correspond to psychological rights. By this definition, inefficiency lies solely within institutions with rule-making authority. That is, given rational, wealth-maximizing behavior on the part of individuals, inefficiency arises only from inefficient rules, which arise from institutions. Here, I view the role of institutions as setting rules of property and liability, by which I mean rules of transactions. That is, inefficiency occurs only when an efficient rule is known but not in force.

4.2 THE DEFINITION OF EFFICIENCY

I will say that an economy is efficient when all efficient trades take place for which the following conditions hold: the willingness to purchase a good of one party exceeds the willingness to accept payment by the owner, by an amount greater than the transactions costs, or

$$WTP_i^m > WTA_j^m + T \tag{4.1}$$

for persons i and j and for good m, and for transactions costs T. T represents the costs of transacting given the rule. T_g represents the cost of changing a rule.

Now the rules of trade and of property are themselves goods. From (4.1) we can say then that an efficient society requires that all rules are enacted for which the following condition holds

$$\sum WTP_i^r > \sum WTA_j^r + Te \tag{4.2}$$

where *Te* represents the enforcement cost of the rule.

Consider a society that is economically efficient and that is static in the sense that there is no change in sentiments, knowledge, or technology. How could economic inefficiency arise? The answer is that it could not. That is we have the following proposition.

Proposition 4.1: inefficiency arises only from change; a static society is always efficient.[2]

By a change in conditions, I mean a change in sentiments, in technology, or in knowledge. Since pointing out an inefficiency represents new knowledge, conditions have changed.

What is of interest now is how inefficiency arises. A useful definition of inefficiency requires for a new rule to be noted that would improve efficiency, but not counting the transactions costs of changing the rule. This is what economists sometimes mean, and what they should mean, when they declare a rule inefficient.

Inefficiency arises only in a nonstatic society – that is, a dynamic society. When conditions change a different, new rule may lower transactions costs or create new property for which rights need to be assigned, or a change in conditions may create an inefficient divergence between psychological and legal ownership (see Chapter 5).

Suppose that it was originally efficient to assign liability to B rather than to A, as B was the low-cost accident avoider. But, over time, costs change due to a change in technology, so that conditions change, and A is now the low-cost avoider. If this fall in costs is unobserved, I will say that the society is still efficient, as no assertion of inefficiency can be asserted until it is discovered. Suppose it is discovered by an economist. This is an assertion of new knowledge. Now the society has become inefficient. To call a new action, rule, or decision efficient – or an old one inefficient – is to assert new knowledge, so that by definition conditions have changed. I turn now to examples to illustrate the nature of inefficiency.

4.3 EXAMPLE ONE: EFFICIENCY AND CHANGES IN KNOWLEDGE

For example, imagine a society in which all the above conditions for efficiency are met, considered from the community level. The community is entirely dependent on the stocks of salmon in a nearby lake for its food supply. Suppose, further, that the society believes – incorrectly – that the supply of salmon is infinite: that it will regrow faster than it could possibly be depleted. In such a community there would be no rule which limited the number of fish that could be caught each day. Indeed, the community's rules might encourage each member to catch as many fish as possible, to ensure a readily available food supply.

It would *not* be efficient, before the community encounters a fish shortage, for the community to pass a new rule limiting fishing, because nobody in the community knows that the number of fish is limited, and everybody in the community would regard the rule as foolish and unfair. This is true even though a rule limiting fishing will benefit the group – objectively – whether they know of the impending shortage or not. But the objective view assumes that the community has somehow acquired new knowledge, in violation of the requirement that conditions (including knowledge) do not change. In hindsight, the community will presumably realize that the existence value of a healthy stock of salmon to that community was so great that a rule protecting the stock would have been efficient, since the cost of losing the salmon could be the extinction of the entire community through starvation (assuming they could not find an alternative food source in time). That is, in hindsight the tribe will wish that it had reduced its catch.[3] The reason for this counterintuitive result is that efficiency can only be measured from the standpoint of an *observer* who is conducting an economic analysis (Zerbe 1991).[4]

In other words, efficiency requires a perspective. Whittington and MacRae (1986) define economic standing, which determines whether or not one's values are to count in an economic analysis. Zerbe (1991) has argued, for example, that the thief's valuation of his stolen goods is not to count, on the basis that theft is illegal, unless the issue is the legality of thievery itself. Standing, according to Zerbe (1991) is something that is determined according to the regard for others and the law of the community; it represents a prior decision about how efficiency is to be measured.

The related issue in the salmon example is whether or not an outside, expert observer has been given standing to have his assessment of the valuation of the community's costs and benefits with regard to salmon counted. Questions have been raised about how to count values where the expert's opinion differs from the opinions of those directly affected (Portney 1992), and as to whether harm can occur when it is unknown (Dunford, Johnson and West 1997). These issues are considered in Chapter 5.[5]

In our static community hypothesis, there is no way that any observer who was part of the static community could become aware of the potential salmon shortage, since that would require the observer to acquire new knowledge.

Suppose, however, that a naturalist from a nearby, *dynamic* community observes that the salmon stock is on the brink of a shortage.[6] If we introduce an observer who *is* aware of the salmon shortage, does the efficiency of a rule limiting fishing change? In order to answer this question, we have to decide whether the naturalist – or, more to the point, his or her knowledge – has standing. The static community might decide to grant the naturalist's information standing, and if it did so, it would decide that it would be efficient to change the fishing rule, even though a rule change would upset older rules and norms. However, if the static community granted the naturalist's knowledge standing, it would, in effect, be increasing its *own* knowledge, so that it would no longer be a static community.

Alternatively, we might ask whether it would be efficient for the world to impose fishing limits on the static community. For example, the dynamic community that the naturalist belongs to might have the power to force the static community to change its rule,[7] or it might have sufficient wealth to 'bribe' the static community to change its rule voluntarily.[8] If we conclude that the static community should listen to the naturalist, and grant him or her standing, then the formerly static community has changed into a dynamic one. If we conclude that the naturalist's community should impose a change (forcefully or peacefully), then the static community *itself* remains static (since its rule is changing but its norms, knowledge, and technology are not), but *we* are adopting the perspective of the naturalist's dynamic community in making this judgment. The important point is that there is no way for the naturalist's new knowledge to matter, economically speaking, unless one adopts the perspective of a dynamic world.

This hypothetical situation shows that whether or not an economist counts gains or losses that the community is not aware of can make a profound difference in the economist's recommendations. If the community welcomes new knowledge (provided that the knowledge is reliable), the economist's new knowledge has standing within that community, and the economist should count gains and losses that the community is not aware of (Zerbe 1991). If the economist considered only gains and losses that the community knows about, the economist might encourage a community to do something which he or she knows to be inefficient, or even self-destructive. This hypothetical situation also shows that although it is efficient for a static community to pass laws that are consistent with its norms, even when its laws and norms are based on incomplete knowledge, it is *not* necessarily efficient to *be* a static community in the first place. To put this another way, it is never efficient for a static community to adopt a rule which is inconsistent with its settled norms, even when its norms are grounded in ignorance, but it may be efficient for a static world to become dynamic.[9] Indeed, in this hypothetical situation, the fact that the fishing community is static prevents it from acquiring knowledge that is necessary to ensure its survival.

4.4 EXAMPLE TWO: FALSE EFFICIENCY

In *Lorenzen* v. *Employees Retirement Plan of the Sperry & Hutchinson Co.*, a widow, Delvina Lorenzen, sued her husband's employer, Sperry & Hutchinson (S & H), alleging that S & H had violated two of its fiduciary duties, by failing to provide her and her husband with necessary information about the terms and conditions of his retirement benefit plan.[10] Under the Employee Retirement Income Security Act (ERISA), an employer has two fiduciary duties which are relevant to this case.[11] First, the employer must clearly explain the terms and conditions of eligibility for retirement benefits to the employee.[12] Second, whenever an employee's spouse's consent is required to select a retirement plan option, the spousal consent form must explain the effect of the consent.[13] On a social level, an efficient rule would require employers to take additional steps to warn employees who delay retirement, if the benefits of additional warnings to all beneficiaries under ERISA plans would outweigh the cost to employers of providing additional warnings to their employees.[14]

However, even assuming that the efficient rule is that S & H should have provided additional warnings to the Lorenzens, Mrs. Lorenzen would not be entitled to recovery if S & H could prove that the Lorenzens had *actual* knowledge of the risk Mr. Lorenzen was taking by delaying retirement. This is because Mrs. Lorenzen would not have standing to sue unless S & H's failure to warn the Lorenzens actually caused her harm.

Although Judge Evans, the district judge, granted summary judgment to Mrs. Lorenzen,[15] Judge Posner reversed, setting the damages at a level that was favorable to S & H.[16] Posner assumed that Mr. Lorenzen knew what the terms and conditions of his retirement plan were, since Posner believed that the language of the retirement plan was clear, and concluded that Evans had found for Mrs. Lorenzen out of sympathy for a poor widow.[17] Several of my colleagues have mentioned the *Lorenzen* case to me, as one in which efficiency was used to arrive at a judicial decision. Some have mentioned the decision with approval, while others point to it as an example of inherent deficiencies in efficiency analysis.[18] It is, however, an example of neither. In *Lorenzen*, the language of efficiency is used, but without the necessary analysis to determine the efficient outcome.[19] Many who discuss the *Lorenzen* case assume that the only issues it raises are ones of distributional justice. In fact, *Lorenzen* raises – or should have raised – important issues about information costs and about who is the low-cost information provider. The heart of the plaintiff's argument in *Lorenzen* is that her husband's employer failed to disclose the necessary information to her and her husband, not that she is a poor widow who is being oppressed by a greedy company.[20]

Warren Lorenzen, a sales manager and a long-time employee of S & H, was eligible to retire on 1 February 1987, having turned 65.[21] S & H asked Lorenzen to stay on because he was in the midst of managing a company project. He agreed, and this extended his retirement date to 1 July 1987. At this time (February) he decided, with the written consent of his wife, that when he retired he would take his retirement as a lump sum benefit, rather than as a series of monthly payments.[22]

On June 15, two weeks before the newly scheduled retirement date, Mr. Lorenzen suffered cardiac arrest and was hospitalized in a grave condition. On June 27, three days before retirement, he suffered a further cardiac arrest and needed a life support machine. His physicians believed his case to be hopeless, and advised Mrs. Lorenzen to ask that the life support machine be disconnected. She did so, it was disconnected, and Mr. Lorenzen died on June 27.[23]

Had Mr. Lorenzen retired as planned, he would have received the entire lump sum.[24] However, under S & H's plan, when employees died before retiring, their spouses were entitled only to 40 percent of what the lump sum would have been (if the lump sum was selected) or to 50 percent of the monthly annuity payments (if the '50 percent joint-and-survivor' plan was selected).[25] Mrs. Lorenzen sued the plan program for a violation of fiduciary duties to her husband and herself.[26] She claimed that S & H did not adequately appraise her husband of the risks of his electing to keep on working rather than to retire at the earliest opportunity. Specifically, S & H did not warn him that delaying retirement would cut his retirement benefits in half if he died before retirement.[27] Furthermore, the spousal consent form, which she signed, did not warn her that she would not receive the full lump sum if her husband died before retiring.[28]

S & H claimed that they had fully complied with their duty of disclosing the terms and conditions to Mr. and Mrs. Lorenzen.[29] S & H claimed that they had satisfied their duty to Mr. Lorenzen, since the language of the retirement plan itself clearly indicated that his beneficiary would not receive the full retirement benefits unless he lived to retire. The plan summary says:

> If you should die either before retirement or after retirement but before benefits begin … your spouse or other beneficiary will receive a benefit … If you die after

> age 55 and your legal spouse is your beneficiary, this benefit will be the larger of 40% of the lump sum equivalent of the benefits you have earned under the plan or the amount he or she [the legal spouse] would receive if you retired on the day before your death under the 50% joint-and-survivor option.[30]

S & H argued that they had satisfied their duty to inform Mrs. Lorenzen, by establishing a toll-free number, which she could have called to find out whether she would receive the full lump sum if she removed her husband's life support prior to his retirement.[31]

Evans found that S & H had not satisfied their duty to inform either Mr. Lorenzen or Mrs. Lorenzen.[32] S & H's duty to Mrs. Lorenzen was to inform her on the consent form itself, not by creating a toll-free number, which placed the burden on her to ask what her rights were. The consent form said nothing about the consequences of selecting lump-sum or monthly payments, if her husband should die before retiring.

However, Evans concluded that S & H's failure to inform Mrs. Lorenzen did not cause her any significant harm.[33] Its duty was to inform her about the consequences of her decision to *sign the consent form*, not the consequences of her husband's decision to *continue working* – since her husband did not need her permission to continue working. If she had refused to sign the form once she learned that she would get only 40 percent of the lump sum if he died before retiring, she still would not have received her husband's full retirement benefits.[34] Failing to sign the form simply would have meant that she would receive 50 percent of her husband's earned monthly payments instead of 40 percent of his earned lump sum.[35] There is no evidence that the reduced monthly payments would have been better than the reduced lump sum, so the failure to inform *her* did not cause her damages.

Evans also found that S & H had not satisfied its duty to warn Mr. Lorenzen of the danger of delaying his retirement.[36] Evans cited three factors which suggested that the language in the summary plan was not as clear as it appeared. First, S & H itself apparently did not understand its own retirement plan.[37] Second, S & H's plan summary, its retirement plan, and ERISA's legal requirements contradicted each other, on some fairly important points. Therefore, even seemingly clear language in the plan summary is not necessarily clear, since the retirement plan and ERISA contradicted it. Third, S & H required Mr. Lorenzen to consult an accountant about the tax consequences of electing a lump sum, which suggests that it knew that a layman could not understand the consequences of the retirement plan. Therefore, Evans argues, S & H should have informed Mr. Lorenzen about the legal consequences of continuing to work past his original retirement date, since those legal consequences would also confuse a layman.

Unlike the failure to inform Mrs. Lorenzen about the difference between lump-sum and monthly payment plans, the failure to warn Mr. Lorenzen of the danger of working past his original retirement date was *not* harmless – had he retired at the normal time, because of the danger of jeopardizing his wife's entitlement to his full retirement benefits, Mrs. Lorenzen would have received $191,730.10, not $88,561.26.[38] Therefore, Evans granted summary judgment in her favor, awarding her $191,730.10.[39]

S & H appealed to the 7th Circuit, where Posner gave the opinion for the majority.[40] Posner reversed and remanded, directing Evans to calculate damages as 40 percent of the lump sum, plus prejudgment interest.[41] Both Posner's majority opinion and Judge Cudahy's dissent assume that Evans was driven by his concern for distributional justice: that he saw it as a dispute between a poor widow and a rich employer.[42] Although it is true that Evans expressed concern for Mrs. Lorenzen, the essence of his opinion is not distributional justice, but S & H's failure to meet its fiduciary duty to warn Mr. Lorenzen of the risk of delaying retirement.[43] Posner gives the issue of whether S & H met its fiduciary duty short shrift, while Cudahy flatly states that 'benefit–cost analysis' is of no help in this case.[44] My argument is not that Posner's resolution of this issue (or the case) is wrong or right, but rather that it cannot be said that efficiency demands the outcome Posner reached. And, contrary to Cudahy, I will show that a properly conducted benefit–cost analysis of the problem of who is the low-cost provider of information can contribute much to the discussion of how to resolve this case.

Posner characterizes Mr. Lorenzen's decision to delay retirement as a 'gamble,' in which he wagered that he would live to retire (and retire with marginally higher benefits, since he worked for an extra few months), while the company wagered that he would die before retiring (allowing it to escape paying half of his earned benefits). It seems unlikely that Mr. Lorenzen was consciously making a gamble of this sort; for that matter, it is unlikely that S & H was making this sort of gamble, either. Mr. Lorenzen does not appear to have been 'gambling,' he appears to have been trying to do his employer a favor. S & H's only 'gamble' is that Mr. Lorenzen's contribution to the project would be more valuable than his salary, not that his death would deprive his widow of half of his retirement benefits.

However, if we jettison the metaphor of 'gambling,' the essence of Posner's argument is valid, at least in part. Posner's point is that it is efficient to hold people to the terms of their contracts – even if the contracts turn out to be less advantageous than they had hoped, provided that the contracts were made voluntarily, and that the terms of the contracts were reasonably clear. That statement is correct, if we define 'reasonably clear' to mean the efficient level of clarity, that is, the point at which any additional warnings would cost more than they are worth.

However, Posner goes on to assume that Mr. Lorenzen had *actual* knowledge of the risk he was taking, because the language of the plan was unmistakably clear.[45] Posner's assumption that Mr. Lorenzen had *actual* knowledge seems unfounded, and directly contradicts Evans' finding that there was no basis for concluding that Mr. Lorenzen knew about the risk he was taking.[46] Similarly, Posner's conclusion that the plan's language was unmistakably clear[47] rests on shaky evidence. Evans cited a number of reasons which suggested that the language of the plan was not as clear as it appeared to be, and which suggested that it would have been fair to require the company to make a better effort to warn Mr. Lorenzen.[48] Posner does not respond, even implicitly, to *any* of Evans's points.[49]

Underlying Posner's assumption that the plan's language was clear is the belief that it is common sense that one must be alive in order to retire. Contrary to Posner, we might argue that most laymen (and some lawyers and judges) would assume that somebody who is *eligible* to retire, but who dies *before* retiring, is entitled to the *same* benefits as somebody who has formally retired.

Although Posner does discuss whether it would be efficient to require S & H to provide additional warnings to the Lorenzens, his discussion is somewhat superficial. Posner sets up the straw man of whether S & H breached its fiduciary duty by failing to 'advise participants of the consequences of finding themselves on life support machinery shortly before the scheduled date of retirement,' since it would not serve anybody's interests (employer or employee) to clutter a retirement plan with warnings about 'every possible idiosyncratic contingency' that might affect the parties' rights. However, the question is not whether S & H should have warned the Lorenzens of the risk of the *specific* tragedy that befell them, but whether S & H should have warned them that Mr. Lorenzen's decision to continue to work past his retirement date might lead to forfeiting half of his benefits. Had he known this, he might have chosen to retire on his original eligibility date and then work for S & H as a consultant on that particular project.

Whether or not we agree with Posner's conclusion that Mr. Lorenzen knew what he was getting into, his assumption that Mr. Lorenzen had actual knowledge would not be demanded by economic analysis (unless an economist had a slavish devotion to the simplifying assumption that all actors make decisions with perfect knowledge). To the extent that Posner's decision was driven by his conclusion that Mr. Lorenzen had actual knowledge, one can disagree with Posner's decision without rejecting the validity of economic analysis of retirement law.

In contrast, Posner's conclusion that it would not be efficient to require S & H to provide additional warnings rests on an economic argument that requiring additional warnings would cost more than they are worth. However, Posner does not provide us with the information we need to evaluate the validity of this economic argument. Posner compares the costs and benefits of not requiring S & H to provide any additional warnings with the costs and benefits of forcing S & H to mention 'every possible idiosyncratic contingency.' The proper comparison, however, is the benefits versus the costs of requiring S & H to warn an employee about the risk of dying before retirement – a risk that S & H created in the first place by asking Mr. Lorenzen to delay his retirement. Posner's decision cannot be said to be supported by economics until the proper comparison is made.

From the record, it is not possible to determine what the efficient rule would be regarding a company's duty to inform an employee of the risk of delaying retirement. Judge Posner sets up a straw man and destroys it, but does not consider more reasonable alternatives. Unfortunately, Evans did not specify a solution, either.[50] He simply states, with unconcealed exasperation, 'Surely *something* could be plainer' than the plan's language. Evans's decision might have led to inefficiency, if it had not been reversed, because it condemns S & H's actions without suggesting a reasonable alternative.[51] Employers might have responded to the decision by making excessive efforts to inform employees – they might have peppered their plans with the sort of endless list of 'idiosyncratic contingencies' that Posner rightly condemns.[52]

Therefore, however unappealing one may find Posner's decision, in order to say that his decision was inefficient it is necessary to specify an alternative rule that would benefit employees and their spouses more than it would cost employers. Since neither Posner nor Evans specifies – or even hints at – such a rule, I will propose one: When a company asks employees to delay retirement, and the employees' pre-retirement death benefits are lower than their retirement benefits, the company must have them sign an additional document, which clearly warns them that if they die before retiring, their spouse will receive only a fraction of their earned benefits.

Although she reaches the opposite conclusion from Posner, Cudahy's approach to this problem is equally troubling.[53] She says

> Fate claimed Mr. Lorenzen in a period when he was doing his employer a favor. And fate pressed on Mrs. Lorenzen a tragic choice which, quite by chance from her point of view, resulted in losing half her pension benefit. Judge Evans thought these fortuities too cruel and decided the case in favor of the widow. Judge Evans, I believe, stepped back from the remorseless logic of the law with respect ... to the merits.[54]

Cudahy makes the mistake of treating the tragedy that befell the Lorezens as inevitable. In fact, while Mr. Lorenzen's *heart attack* may have been unavoidable, the *financial consequences* of the heart attack were not. Even though Mr. Lorenzen could not have predicted the heart attack, he might have acted differently if he had understood that delaying his retirement ran the risk of depriving his widow of half of the benefits. As I noted, he could have retired as planned, and worked as a consultant on the project. Or he might not have chosen to do his employer a 'favor,' if he had known that a potential cost of this generosity was a significant injury to his wife. If S & H had provided him with additional information, he might have avoided the financial tragedy. If this information could have been provided by S & H at a much lower cost than it would have cost Mr. Lorenzen to uncover it – an assumption which is not unreasonable – efficiency might favor requiring S & H to provide a more complete warning to Mr. Lorenzen than it had.[55]

Furthermore, the law is not as 'remorseless' as Cudahy implies. In fact, the law places a burden on employers to make the terms and conditions of benefit plans clear to their employees.[56] If a company fails to comply with its legal duty to adequately warn employees, and the employees and their beneficiaries suffer losses as a result of this breach of legal duty, the law is not 'remorseless.'[57] Rather, the law demands that the company compensate its employees and their beneficiaries.

Perhaps most important, Cudahy is wrong to conclude that 'cost–benefit analysis is beside the point.'[58] Whenever the law requires one party to take 'reasonable efforts' to protect another party's interests, cost–benefit analysis, particularly KHZ analysis, is a powerful tool for determining what degree of protectiveness is 'reasonable,' by quantifying the advantages and disadvantages of extra protective procedures.

Another question posed by *Lorenzen* is whether the case encourages 'beneficiaries' in Mrs. Lorenzen's position to artificially keep their spouses on life support.[59] Although Evans and the parties themselves apparently assumed that Mrs. Lorenzen would have received her husband's entire lump sum if he had remained on artificial life support for another three days, it is not clear whether Posner adopted that rule. Instead, Posner appears to decide that this question is irrelevant, since the cost of maintaining life support, and the 'human' cost of keeping one's spouse in a vegetative state, are so high that they would swamp any gains from receiving higher retirement benefits. It is likely true that the benefits of artificial life support would outweigh the costs to the beneficiaries in many situations, and it is probably true that few private parties would elect to keep a spouse in a vegetative state in order to receive higher retirement benefits. However, there are probably at least a few marriages in which a spouse would choose to maintain life artificially in order to receive more retirement benefits, especially if the financial cost of life support costs were borne by medical insurance. Since it is now stare decisis in the 7th Circuit that a widow in Mrs. Lorenzen's position cannot receive the full lump sum in this situation, an enterprising plaintiff might try to maintain life support, and then sue for its cost (or accept the cost as a loss which is offset by the higher retirement benefits). Just as the most efficient tax law is the one that does not distort people's choices, it is probably true that the most efficient retirement benefit law is one that does not distort choices. It is hard to imagine a more wasteful expenditure than artificial life support which is maintained purely to increase retirement benefits.

The *Lorenzen* case is not, as my colleagues have suggested, one in which KH efficiency analysis was applied. Or, rather, it is one in which it was not applied well. I have tried to show that a more careful application of KH analysis could certainly have improved the language of the decision, and possibly the result as well. There might have been room in the case, also, for a fuller consideration of fairness and distributional justice, but I will resist the temptation to discuss that issue.

4.5 EXAMPLE THREE: A CHRISTMAS CAROL ABOUT THE EFFICIENCY OF CHRISTMAS GIVING

As I stated at the beginning of this chapter, KHZ efficiency explicitly requires (1) a recognition that benefits and costs are psychological and subjective, (2) the inclusion of the value of all goods for which there is a WTP or WTA in determining inefficiency (which inclusion follows from the recognition that benefits and costs are psychological), (3) the inclusion of the transactions costs of operating the rule or practice as a part of the determination of efficiency, and (4) the recognition that one must point to a superior rule or practice to say that some existing rule or practice is inefficient. I end with the application of these requirements to an example from the economics literature.

Sentimental Values are Psychological Values

Sentimental values are apparently psychological ones. According to KHZ then they should be included in efficiency analysis. Yet some studies fail to consider sentimental values in determining efficiency.

Waldfogel (1993, p. 1328) suggests that gift-giving may in general create inefficiency ('a deadweight loss'), as 'the gifts may be mismatched with the recipients' preferences.' He estimates (1993, p. 1328) that 'holiday gift-giving destroys between 10% and a third of the value of gifts.' To determine the value of gifts, Waldfogel and others (Solnick and Hemenway 1996; List and Shogren 1998) conducted surveys which asked the recipients to estimate the WTA and WTP for the gifts. Waldfogel's survey instructed the survey recipients to exclude the 'sentimental value' of the gifts, but it did not define the term 'sentimental value.' Waldfogel uses the term 'material value' to describe the value of a good aside from its sentimental value. If we recognize that all values are psychological, we will realize that Waldfogel's attempt to separate sentimental and material value is a false dichotomy.

There is a WTP or WTA for Sentimental Value

Chapter 5 presents a survey that shows clearly that there is a WTP and a WTA for sentimental values. Moreover, this survey – and the work of others – shows that this value is substantial.

Because Waldfogel does not consider sentimental value in determining dead-weight loss (inefficiency), he clearly violates one of KHZ's requirements for determining inefficiency. But, equally important, he also fails to determine a superior alternative practice, and thus violates another requirement of KHZ.

The Costs of Economic Change

A defender of Waldfogel offers the following support:

> that welfare gains from gift giving are likely to be positive does not undermine Waldfogel's basic point that there is a deadweight loss involved in gift giving if the cost of the gift is less than the material value of to [sic] to the recipient ... Another way to see this is to state that if there is a welfare loss from gift giving [due to the giver's choice of a gift, the cost of which is less than the recipient's assessment of the gift's cost], this loss would persist and would be reflected in a shortfall in *actual* total welfare gain [including sentimental value from either the gift giver or the recipient] from gift giving relative to *potential* total welfare gain from gift giving. *The difference between actual and potential is deadweight loss.* (emphasis added)[60]

The quote represents a common defense of this sort of work, and is a defense that violates several of KHZ's axioms for determining efficiency. I shall argue that it is necessary to observe KHZ's axioms in order to properly determine efficiency, and by doing so I will show that this attempted defense of Waldfogel's work is not coherent.

There is now a large, not to say enormous, literature on this issue that suggests the propriety of including transactions costs in the determination of what is efficient (Allen 1991; Coase 1960, 1964, 1974, 1988; Eggertsson 1990; Barzel 1985; Baumol 1979; Randall 1983; Nelson 1987; Medema and Zerbe 1999a, 1999b; Zerbe and McCurdy 1999). The seminal source is Coase (1960). As Coase (1964, p. 195) has pointed out, there is little that can be learned from the study of theoretical optimal systems.[61] Analysts who become enamored of 'blackboard economics,' where equations are substituted for underpinnings, produce concepts that bear little correspondence to the actual social system. The world portrayed is one that exists only on the blackboard: 'the analysis is carried out with great ingenuity, but it floats in the air' (Coase 1988, p. 10).

The difficulty with ignoring transactions costs is that doing so leads to absurd results. When transactions costs are ignored, every transaction in the real world is inefficient when compared to a world in which transactions are costless (Zerbe and McCurdy 1999). When transactions costs are ignored, externalities are ubiquitous, as Zerbe and McCurdy have shown.

To include transactions costs in our definition of efficiency, however, might seem to subject us to the criticism that such a definition asserts we live in the best of all possible worlds. Or, more formally, the definition leads to the tautological proposition that every static position is a first-best welfare position in the sense that there does not exist an attainable position that is Pareto superior to it. For, if there are no costs to attaining a Pareto superior position, then it has been attained. The logical criticism of this approach is presumably that this is the best of all possible worlds – where, of course, no discussion of welfare is possible. But the world is not static.

The mistake arises in assuming that acceptance of this proposition means that nothing further need be done, which is far from the case. That is, the criticism of this approach is presumably that this is the best of all possible worlds where, of course, no discussion of welfare improvements is required. In a non-static world, the optimum is continually changing and must be continually re-determined. That is, more formally:

> A potentially Pareto superior alternative to the status quo is created only when conditions change. A situation in which conditions change may justify a transitional state of movement towards the new Pareto superior position.

That is, when one says that a change is efficient, it is an assertion of superior knowledge, or a plea for a new understanding that will then result in the proposed efficient change. When an economist says that a tax on pollution emissions is more efficient than command and control for pollution abatement, the transactions costs may consist simply of the costs of persuading the relevant decision makers of the virtues of her proposal. She must mean that if these transactions costs are sufficiently low her proposal is efficient. Economists or lawyers may speak of a particular change in the state of the world as being efficient when what they mean is that the state of the world would be efficient if transactions costs or some portion of transactions costs were zero.[62] This is what economists and lawyers mean, or should mean, when they propose a change on grounds of efficiency.

One might correctly say, then, that a change will be desirable if the costs of bringing it about are not too high. The failure to use the term 'efficiency' more precisely creates ambiguity about whether or not one is speaking of efficiency in a zero transactions costs world or not.

What are the transactions costs relevant to operating a new, more efficient regime of Christmas giving? First, imagine the possible range of transactions costs: (1) Perhaps it would be efficient if we generally gave gifts of cash. If so, it would be correct to say that Christmas giving is inefficient. But, my empirical evidence suggests that cash gifts usually destroy sentimental value, so a regime of giving gifts of cash is unlikely to be efficient. (2) Perhaps gift givers could preserve sentimental and material value by simply asking the potential recipient what he or she wants. But the results of my survey suggest that asking, in many cases, destroys sentimental value, so that this method, too, is unlikely to be efficient. (3) Perhaps, though, it would be efficient for givers to double the time they spend on searching for the right gifts; they might increase material value, without detracting from sentimental value (in fact, sentimental value might be increased as well). But we have no proof that an increased search would justify its increased transactions costs by the increase in material or sentimental value. Even if it did, and givers knew this, having been informed by economic analysis, givers might be unwilling to incur the costs, as they might not fully reap the benefits. So, we can still not say that the current regime of Christmas giving is inefficient.[63]

To argue, in any real sense, that Christmas gift-giving is inefficient requires one to show that the transactions costs, as shown in the alternative regimes (1) through (3), are low enough that a change to a different giving regime is warranted. Such an argument is not made by Waldfogel, and the argument would be difficult to make. If people in general really did prefer cash, or prefer to be asked what they want, those practices would likely be the custom, since it would be easy for gift recipients to tell gift givers that they had those preferences. Similarly, no evidence exists that, in general, people should spend more time on gift selection, or hire gift advisers. The fact that none of the above practices are customary suggests that no solution is available that is more efficient than the status quo. This does not mean that knowing that the material yield is fractional is worthless knowledge (though it may be), since such knowledge may be useful in prompting one to come up with a more efficient solution. The objection I raise, which is also the one Coase raised, is that it is inappropriate to call a practice inefficient when no apparent change would improve the situation.

That is, when one says that a change is efficient, it should be either an assertion of superior knowledge or a plea for a new understanding that will then result in the proposed change becoming efficient. When an economist says that a tax on pollution emissions is more efficient than command and control for pollution abatement, the transactions costs may be simply the costs of persuading the relevant decision maker of the virtues of the economist's proposal. The economist should mean that in actual operation, a tax scheme would be better than a command and control regime. The economist does not count the costs of affecting the relevant change in the law, since with KHZ one can assert inefficiency without counting the costs, T_g, of affecting the change. This is what economists and lawyers mean, or should mean, when they propose a change on grounds of efficiency.

One might correctly say, then, that a change will be desirable provided that the costs of bringing it about are not too high. The failure to use the term 'efficiency' more precisely creates ambiguity about whether or not one is speaking of efficiency in a zero-transactions cost world or not.

4.6 CONCLUSION

In this chapter, I discussed the implications that KHZ has for measuring the benefits and costs of a proposed social change. Although traditional KH analysis assumes that the WTA and the WTP measures of the value of a good will almost never differ, and will only differ by small amounts if they differ at all, I have shown that the WTA and the WTP measures will frequently differ by significant amounts. The difference between WTA and WTP stems from income effects, substitution effects, and loss aversion. However, the owner of a commercial good does not experience income effects, substitution effects, or loss aversion, and so the WTA and WTP measures of a commercial good will generally be identical.

Furthermore, while traditional KH analysis recognizes the existence of WTA and WTP, and recognizes that in theory they could differ, KH does not offer any means of deciding whether it is appropriate to use WTA or WTP to measure an individual's interest in a good. Since KH offers no means of determining whether WTP or WTA is appropriate, it also cannot offer any means of determining whether CV or EV is appropriate. Most economists have resolved this dilemma by relying on CV, because CV is more 'conservative' and gives indirect effect to transactions costs. However, it is better to incorporate transactions costs directly, and form a more sensible methodology for picking between CV and EV when they differ.

In contrast, KHZ explains that the difference between WTA and WTP is one of a psychological perspective, or reference point. Therefore, an economist should use the measure (WTA or WTP) which corresponds to a person's sense of psychological ownership. In many cases, it is safe to assume that a person's psychological ownership corresponds to the person's legal rights. However, where the law and the person's sense of psychological ownership differ, the person's psychological reference point should be used.

NOTES

1. In most, or certainly in many, cases a new rule that is KH efficient would also be KHZ efficient.
2. It does not follow that it is inefficient for a society to change. Rather, a rule which was ever efficient will only become inefficient if conditions change. If a social change renders some of a society's laws inefficient, but allows its members to acquire greater wealth, the change is efficient if the extra wealth is greater than the cost of altering its laws.
3. Of course, passing a rule which reduces the catch after the lake has run out of fish will be too late to do either the salmon or the tribe any good.
4. Although it is tempting to speak of efficiency as if it existed in the abstract, whether a change is efficient is a question that can only be answered from a particular standpoint. For more information on the concept of economic standing in general, see Whittington and MacRae (1986).
5. The use of the concept of standing can help to resolve these issues (Zerbe 1991).
6. Of course, our hypothetical 'naturalist' may also be an economist.
7. Whether it would it be efficient for the naturalist's community to force the static community to change the rule is a complex question. First of all, we would have to decide whether the naturalist's community attaches a positive existence value to the salmon, the static community, or both. Second, we would have to consider whether the dynamic community's regard for others attached value to allowing other cultures the right of self-determination, and whether even good-intentioned interference is justified. Third, we would have to consider the extraordinary transaction costs involved in forcing another culture to do anything, since this sort of outside interference could trigger a war.
8. Whether it would be efficient to 'bribe' the static culture involves the same sort of difficult calculations: a bribe would probably involve lower transaction costs than a war, and be a less obvious interference with a culture's self-determination, but would still involve some interference and some transaction costs.
9. This point is discussed in greater detail in Chapter 8.
10. See *Lorenzen* v. *Employees Retirement Plan of the Sperry & Hutchinson Co.*, 699 F. Supp. 1367 (E.D. Wis. 1988), rev'd 896 F.2d 228 (7th Cir. 1990).
11. See *Lorenzen*, 896 F.2d at 235 (stating that the employer must clearly explain the terms and conditions of the retirement benefit plan to the employee). See *Lorenzen*, 699 F. Supp. at 1369 (stating that the spousal consent form must inform spouse of effect of consent).
12. See *Lorenzen*, 896 F.2d at 235.
13. See *Lorenzen*, 699 F. Supp. at 1369.
14. The benefits to employees and their spouses should be considered in WTA terms, since the ERISA statute explicitly states that employees have the right to have the terms and conditions of their plans made clear to them. The costs to employers should be measured by their WTP. The benefits plan is most likely a commercial good (or a commercial 'bad') to employers. It most likely is not a commercial good to employees, since there is considerable psychological attachment to being able to retire in comfort after having spent years in hard work.
15. See *Lorenzen*, 699 F. Supp. at 1371.
16. See *Lorenzen*, 896 F.2d at 237.
17. See ibid. at 234, 236.
18. The limitations of economic analysis has been well discussed by Armitage (1985) who points out a number of cases in which the issues are unlikely to be illuminated much by economic analysis This argument applies relatively easily to such issues as to what extent free speech should be balanced against considerations of libel. See Armitage (1985).
19. See *Lorensen*, 896 F.2d at 234, 236. I benefited from discussions of this case with Louis Wolcher.
20. See *Lorenzen*, 699 F. Supp. at 1368.
21. See ibid. at 1368.
22. See ibid. at 1368, 1369.

23. Ibid.
24. Ibid.
25. See *Lorenzen*, 896 F.2d at 235.
26. See *Lorenzen*, 699 F. Supp. at 1368.
27. See ibid. at 1370.
28. See ibid. at 1369.
29. See ibid. at 1370.
30. See *Lorenzen*, 896 F.2d at 235.
31. See *Lorenzen*, 699 F. Supp. at 1370.
32. See ibid. at 1370, 1371.
33. See ibid. at 1369.
34. See *Lorenzen*, 896 F.2d at 235.
35. See *Lorenzen*, 699 F. Supp. at 1369.
36. See ibid. at 1370, 1371.
37. Ibid. Originally, S & H's retirement plan administrator wrote to Mrs. Lorenzen, telling her she could select either $90,421.05 or 50 percent of the monthly payments. A few days later, the administrator wrote to inform her that he had miscalculated, and she was entitled only to $88,561.26 (with no reference to monthly payments). Although the difference between $90,421.05 and $88,561.26 is relatively small, it shows that even a professional who worked exclusively with S & H's retirement plans did not understand how to calculate the benefits.
38. See ibid. at 1368.
39. See ibid. at 1371.
40. See *Lorenzen*, 896 F.2d 228.
41. See ibid. at 237.
42. See ibid. at 234, 238
43. See *Lorenzen*, 699 F. Supp. 1370. Judge Evans did mention that it seemed 'very unfortunate' that Mrs. Lorenzen was not able to receive her husband's full retirement benefits, and he characterized some of S & H's arguments as 'cold hearted,' but these stray remarks are not the essence of his opinion. The fact that a judge expresses sympathy for a party does not undermine the legitimacy of the entire opinion.
44. See *Lorenzen*, 896 F.2d at 234–238.
45. See ibid. at 235.
46. Compare *Lorenzen*, 699 F. Supp. at 1370, with *Lorenzen*, 896 F.2d at 235.
47. See *Lorenzen*, 896 F.2d at 235.
48. See *Lorenzen*, 699 F. Supp. at 1370, 1371.
49. See *Lorenzen*, 896 F.2d at 234–237.
50. See *Lorenzen*, 699 F. Supp. at 1370.
51. Ibid. Of course, it would not be reasonable to expect Judge Evans to speculate about reasonable alternatives to S & H's actions if neither party argued this issue at trial. Judges are usually reluctant to speculate about such matters, in the absence of a developed trial record.
52. See *Lorenzen*, 896 F.2d at 236. Of course, Judge Evans' decision would not have been binding precedent in any event, as a trial court opinion, but it certainly might have been viewed as a 'warning' by employers, and could have 'set a precedent' in a business sense.
53. Note that the primary – if not sole – basis for Cudahy's dissent is her disagreement with Posner on the procedural question of whether S & H's appeal was timely. Cudahy is clearly troubled by the tone of Posner's analysis of the economics of the situation, but it is not clear whether this would have led her to dissent had she felt that the appeal had been timely. See ibid. at 238.
54. See ibid. at 239.
55. See *Lorenzen*, 699 F. Supp. at 1368–1371.
56. *Lorenzen*, 896 F.2d at 239.
57. See *Lorenzen*, 699 F. Supp. at 1371.
58. See *Lorenzen*, 896 F.2d at 239. In fairness, the statement that 'cost–benefit analysis is beside the point' seems to have been made in the context of whether Mrs. Lorenzen should

have kept Mr. Lorenzen on life support. However, from the tone of Cudahy's opinion, it seems likely that she would also view cost-benefit analysis as 'beside the point' on the question of whether S & H had adequately warned Mr. and Mrs. Lorenzen.

59. See ibid. at 234.
60. This quote is taken from a referee's report when an earlier version of this article was submitted to the American Economic Review.
61. In a similar vein, Coase (1974, p. 375)argues that 'generalizations are not likely to be helpful unless they are derived from studies of how such activities are actually carried out within different institutional frameworks. Such studies would enable us to discover which factors are important and which are not in determining the outcome and would lead to generalizations which have a solid base. They are also likely to serve another purpose, by showing us the richness of the social alternatives between which we can choose.'
62. This statement is true for just about any proposition regarding economic efficiency. For example, see Posner (1986, pp. 254–259) on the issue of the efficiency consequences of monopoly.
63. A similar argument may be made about using a professional gift chooser.

5. Rights and the relationship of law to efficiency

5.1 THE LAW AND EFFICIENCY

This chapter considers efficient rules for the assignment of rights. The law influences these rules in two ways. First, the law affects issues of economic standing, which determines whose values are to be counted, and what goods are legitimate and should be counted. Second, the law determines how values are to be counted: whether a WTP or a WTA should be used. In large part, these are questions of legal ownership. The law affects the psychological reference points, which determine felt ownership. One cannot lose what one does not have, nor gain what one already has a right to. Yet ownership also affects the choice of the measure of value, since what one is willing to accept to bear a loss of a good may be different than what one would pay to obtain it.

I will show, first, that even the efficiency part of the Coase Theorem applies only to commercial goods, and that otherwise it is both technically wrong and misspecified, since it fails to take into account the divergence between WTP and WTA. I will show that where no psychological ownership exists, rights should be assigned to the highest bidder, subject to the regard for others. The regard for others, however, may lead society to experience a loss unless the right is given to a person who is not the highest bidder – in which case it would *not* be efficient to give the right to the highest bidder.

Then, I consider the situation in which rights are in dispute and in which psychological ownership is uncertain or incomplete. First, I show that Baker's objection to the use of potential compensation tests, as a guide to settling the assignment of rights in dispute, fails to consider the right argument and that his objection can be removed. Baker notes that when psychological expectations of ownership are greater than 100 percent of the value of the right or good in question, it would be impossible to satisfy a potential compensation test. This is true but not relevant. The question instead, even in a KH context, is whether or not the use of a KH measure rather than some other measures, can satisfy a potential compensation test with respect to the other measures. Next I show further that where rights are partly but incompletely specified, both the WTP and the WTA should be considered in the assignment of rights and that the weight that they should be given depends on the degree of psychological ownership of the parties.

In this chapter I also introduce and illustrate the important issue of economic standing – who should have their values counted in a benefit–cost context. Examples are found in the criminal law of theft, in abortion rights, and in determining whether harm can occur when it is unknown by those injured. The analysis of abortion rights illustrates particularly the important role that the regard for others often plays in determining efficiency. The case examples from the law involve efficiency in recovering sentimental value as part of the law of remedies and in the law of trespass.

5.2 THE COASE THEOREM

The Coase Theorem has engaged and perplexed scholars now for forty years. The Theorem is held to have two parts, an efficiency claim and an invariance claim. These claims are variously expressed. One expression of the efficiency claim by Calabresi (1968, p. 68) states: 'if one assumes rationality, no transactions costs, and no legal impediments to bargaining *all* misallocations of resources would be fully cured in the market by bargains.' The invariance claim, which is the claim that the production outcome is invariant to legal rules, has also been variously expressed. Regan (1972, p. 427) states it thus: 'in a world of perfect competition, perfect information and zero transactions costs, the allocation of resources in the economy will be ... unaffected by legal rules regarding the initial impact costs resulting from externalities.'[1] The literature on the Coase Theorem is simply enormous (Medema and Zerbe 1999b). Most of it concerns the nature of a zero transactions cost world. The arguments concern whether or not efficiency and/or invariance is guaranteed by a zero transactions costs assumption.

A fundamental insight of Coase was to realize that in traditional welfare analysis the determination of inefficiency was based on the comparison of a situation in a zero transactions costs world, with the situation in the real world. Not surprisingly, KH inefficiency is then found to exist everywhere (see Chapter 6).

The criticisms of the Theorem, in general, have the following structure: an externality is pointed out, whose existence depends, say, on imperfect or asymmetrical information or on search costs or on exclusion costs. It is then said that the Coase Theorem does not hold, since the presence of the external effect indicates inefficiency. The defenders of the Theorem then argue that zero transactions costs include perfect information or zero search costs, and so forth, so that the Theorem is then said to hold. The discussion is wholly semantic and academic, since transactions costs are ubiquitous in the real world.

Perhaps the best-known example is from the classic article by Starrett (1972) on non-convexities in the production or consumption set of externality victims. This article was long considered the final nail in the coffin of both the invariance and the efficiency claims of the Theorem. The sort of example Starrett had in mind considers a situation in which there is over-pollution but there are no initial gains to be had from the reduction of pollution. There is a Pareto-better point available, but the non-convexity means that the bargaining parties will fail to reach it, because the immediate marginal adjustments are not Pareto better. The victim will not be able to spend $20 for a change that will make him or her $30 better off, because the first step along this path would involve spending a dollar, with no resulting gain (Medema and Zerbe 1999b, p. 10). The editors of the *Journal of Economic Theory* contended that Starrett's non-convexity argument 'destroy[s] the validity of the Coase Theorem' (Starrett 1972, p. 222). Medema and Zerbe (1999b, p. 10), however, point out that the victim would take the first welfare-reducing steps if he was certain that he would be better off in the end. The issue is one of information. If information costs are considered part of transactions costs, Starrett's argument does not point to the incorrectness of the Theorem. Similar statements may be, and have been, made (Medema and Zerbe 1999b) about the whole range of objections to the Coase Theorem.

This semantic stew has been created by the continuing, implicit insistence in welfare economics on using an unattainable optimum as the standard one attainable only if transactions costs were zero. The results are different in a KHZ world. First, I wish to show that the Coase Theorem is incorrect even in a world of zero transactions costs, for reasons that are irrelevant to transactions costs. Second, I will show that an efficiency theorem applies equally well to the real world of transactions costs. Third, I will show that the Theorem does not apply, however, in a world where conditions change. It is change that produces inefficiency, and not transactions costs.

5.3 THE ASSIGNMENT OF RIGHTS UNDER CERTAINTY

The Assignment of an Unowned Right or Good

Proposition 5.1: KH and KHZ welfare require that a legally and psychologically unowned right should be given or sold to the party with the highest WTP for it, regardless of transactions costs (unless the right is a commercial good and transactions costs are also zero).

That is, efficiency is *not* indifferent to whom is assigned the right, whether or not transactions costs are zero, contrary to the Coase Theorem. It is usually assumed, from the Coase Theorem, that in zero transactions costs' worlds efficiency does not depend on whom is initially assigned the right. This is because a right incorrectly assigned to B will be sold to A without incurring transactions costs, so that the outcome and the net efficiency is the same as it would be if the right was given to A initially. However, I will show that in some instances if the right is given to B, B will not sell it to A, while if the right is given to A, A will not sell it to B. In those cases, the outcome is different, depending on whether A or B is given the right. Furthermore, if the good is incorrectly given to A (or B) then the net efficiency will be lower, even if the good ends up in the 'right' party's hands.

Consider two parties, A and B. There is a valuable right and neither A nor B have psychological or legal ownership of it. The government will be defined as the institution that sets rules, so that the government is the only possible source of inefficiency. In what follows, I will assume that some right or good is to be sold or given away by the government. I will assume that the government's WTA and WTP for the good are both zero. Party A has a WTP_a to purchase the right. Party A also has a WTA_a for the right, which is the price at which she would sell it if she owned it. Party B, similarly, has a WTP_b and a WTA_b. I assume that the good is a normal good, so that, for each party, the WTA is greater than the WTP. Suppose, for simplicity that A's WTP_a is greater than B's WTA_b. It follows that A's WTP_a is greater than B's WTP_b. In short, we have the assumptions:

(I) $WTA_a > WTP_a$

(II) $WTA_b > WTP_b$

(If I and II are both true, then the good is not a commercial good to A or B.)

(III) $WTP_a > WTP_b$

(IV) Transactions costs are T and $T \geq 0$.

(V) Rationality: worthwhile trades will be made (that is, all trades for which $WTP_i > WTA_j$ for the good will be made).

(VI) Property rights are fully specified, except for the right in question, and correspond to psychological ownership.

(VII) The world is static: which means that technology, sentiments and knowledge do not change.

(VIII) There are only two parties with a WTP or a WTA.

Therefore it follows that:

1. If A has the right, she will not sell, since $WTA_a > WTP_b$.

2. The gain from giving the right to A is A's WTP for the right.
3. The gain from giving the right to B, before he sells it, will be WTP_b.
4. If B has the right, he may sell to A if $WTP_a > WTA_b + T$,
5. The KH or KHZ gain from the sale is $WTP_a - WTA_b - \mathrm{T}$.

Then, the net social gain (NSG_a), or the difference from giving the right initially to A rather than to B, will be the difference between the gain to A and the gain to B. This gain will be different in the case where B will sell the right to A were B to receive the right, and in the case where B will not sell the right. If B will not sell the right, this means either that transactions costs are too high or that $WTP_a < WTA_b$. The net gains from assigning the right to A are either

$$\begin{aligned} &NSG_a \text{ (where right } \textbf{will} \text{ be sold by B)} \\ &= WTP_a - [WTP_b + (WTP_a - WTA_b) - T] \\ &= NSG_a = WTA_b - WTP_b + T \end{aligned} \tag{5.1}$$

or

$$\begin{aligned} &NSG_a \text{ (where right } \textbf{will not} \text{ be sold by B)} \\ &= NSG_a = WTP_b - WTP_b \end{aligned} \tag{5.2}$$

Even if transactions costs are zero, the net gain from giving or selling the right to A rather than to B will be

$$NSG_a = WTA_b - WTP_b \tag{5.3}$$

The net social gain if the right is given to A rather than B will always be positive, whether or not B will sell the right to A if the right is given to B. The fact that the net social gain is positive in (5.3) shows that it is inefficient to sell or give the right to B even in the absence of transactions costs, in violation of the Coase Theorem. This is the difference between B's willingness to sell and his willingness to pay for the right. The initial assignment of the good will affect the total KH welfare gain unless it is a commercial good, contrary to the Coase Theorem. The advantage of giving the right to A initially in a world with transactions costs is, a fortiori, greater than in the zero transaction cost world, by the amount T.

What happens is that value is lost by sending the product to A by way of B. This loss of value arises from the divergence of the WTP and the WTA. This means that if B bought the good, he would suffer income effects, substitution effects, and/or loss aversion if he sold it to A. In short, the usual expression of the Coase Theorem is wrong, since the total KH welfare gain will be higher if the good is initially assigned to A rather than B.

To make this more clear, let us assume the figures in Table 5.1 apply.

Table 5.1

	WTA	WTP
A	100	90
B	80	50

In addition, I assume that all transactions occur at no cost (that is, $T = 0$). If the government sold the right to A for \$90, there would be a net social gain of \$90, since A and B would have no gain and the government would gain \$90. If the government sold the right to B for \$50 and B sold the right to A for \$90, B would gain only \$10, the difference between what A paid (\$90), and the price that B is willing to accept (\$80). If the government gave the right to B and B sold it to A, the net social gain would be B's gain of \$10 plus the government's gain of \$50, for a total of just \$60. The loss from giving the right initially to B instead of A is the difference between \$90 and \$60, or \$30, which is also the difference between B's WTA and B's WTP. B's assumption of psychological ownership upon receiving the good causes a reduction in values to be obtained of \$30.[2]

What we have established is that the right should go to the highest bidder, regardless of transactions costs, where there is a difference between WTP and WTA, if there is no psychological ownership and no regard for others. That is, the right or good should go to A when:

$$WTP_a - WTP_b \tag{5.4}$$

This rule is at slight variance from the one suggested by Posner. Posner (1972, p. 18) suggests it is efficient 'when the law: (1) assigns the right to the party who would buy it from the other party were transactions costs zero'; Posner's rule is mute, as mine is not, when neither party would buy it from the other when transactions costs are zero. This case arises when each party's WTP is less than the other party's WTA.

It has long been known that the assignment of a right may determine its final resting place, and that this may be the case whether the entitlement is assigned to A or to B. The person who possesses the right will have a WTA measure of value that is greater than the WTP for the person who wishes to gain the right. Since this is the case regardless of who owns the right, whoever owns it keeps it. Figure 5.1 shows the situation. Starting at A_0 and moving to the right, shows A's marginal WTP or WTA for increasing amounts of the property. Similarly for B starting at B_0.

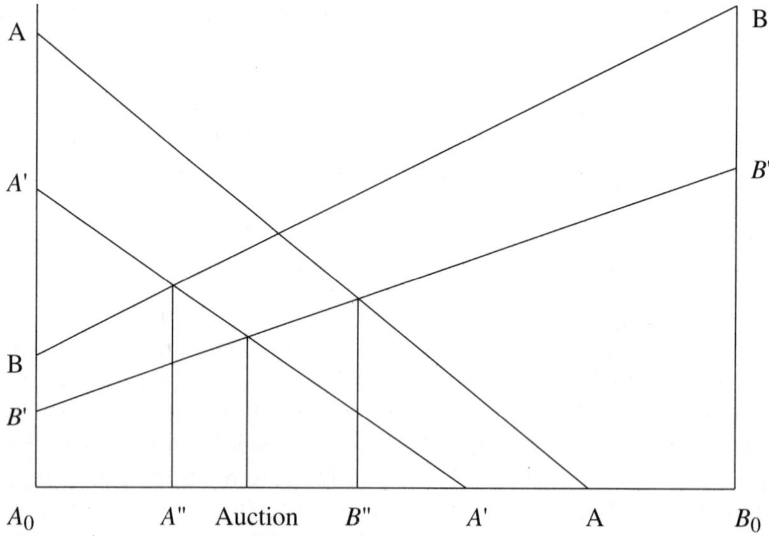

Figure 5.1

There is some right or property that is to be allocated between A and B by use of KHZ. If the property belongs to A, he will sell the amount $B_0 - B''$ to B, and retain $A_0 - B''$. The reason is that is the WTP of B exceeds A's WTA for this portion of the property or the right. If the property belongs to B, he will sell the amount $A_0 - A''$ to A and retain the amount $B_0 - A''$. Thus, regardless of who is the original owner, A will have at least $A_0 - A''$ and B will have at least $B_0 - B''$. If property rights are already assigned, this initial allocation will determine who owns the portion between A'' and B''. This already established ownership is efficient, in the sense that a change in ownership does not pass the KH test.

The case of no ownership, where the WTA of each party exceeds the WTP of the other party, is widely seen as rendering the KH criteria useless, or at least indeterminate.[3] For example, Posner (1985a, p. 92) says in the case of no ownership, in which the initial allocation determines the outcome, 'I don't know how to solve this particular problem.' He goes on to say that, 'cases of this kind – where wealth maximization provides no guidance to the initial assignment of property rights … are rare; they reveal a limitation to an ethics of wealth maximization.'[4] I show that such cases have a solution and do not indicate a limitation to wealth maximization and shall argue that such cases are not rare.

Such cases, however, do not reveal a limitation to the ethics of wealth maximization, nor are they rare. When two parties seek a good and neither has (psychological) ownership of it, any allocation of the good represents a net gain, for no owner needs to be compensated. But the fact that there is a net gain whether the government gives the good to A or to B does not mean that our economic analysis is indeterminate in such cases. If there is a greater net social gain when the good is given to A (or to B), then it is more efficient to give the good to A. The correct psychological measure of a gain is the WTP when the party receiving the good has no psychological ownership. The good will then be worth more – in a KH sense – to whomever is willing to pay the most for it. This may be derived from equation (5.4).[5]

The WTP measure is also consistent with KH in cases where the good would be traded, since in assigning the good to whoever has the highest WTP, there is a saving in transactions costs (assuming that A's and B's transactions costs are the same).

Note that if the government assigns a right through a public auction, it will end up selling the good to the party with the highest WTP. The WTP measure has a particular attraction in allocating a productive asset since it tends to ensure that it goes to whoever will use it in the most productive way, which is also KHZ efficient. In the case of a good to which no prior right is attached – for example, a license to operate a taxicab, or to broadcast a radio or a television signal – allocation by auction is the appropriate device.

Posner (1985, p. 94) suggests also that such cases 'are rare,' and that 'with natural resources, the initial assignment of property rights is not critical, because, presumably, whoever gets the rights will sell or rent them to those who can get the most value out of them.'[6] It is for just such important goods, however, with poor substitutes and with a sense of public ownership, that the divergences between the WTA and WTP are largest, and for which, contrary to Posner, the initial assignment is critical. That such cases are not rare may be seen immediately by considering virtually any important natural resource, such as Glacier National Park, the Grand Canyon, the Elwha River, or the redwoods in the Headwaters Grove. For those who care about the environment, the divergence between the WTP and WTA for these sorts of goods is very large.

The results here are also at variance with those of Hovenkamp (1991, pp. 225, 229–234), who suggests that whether or not an entitlement is currently owned, wealth is maximized when the entitlement goes to the person who has the highest WTA. He (1991, p. 229) asserts, for example, that 'if for any given entitlement, WA^* is significantly greater than WP^*, then wealth is maximized only when the entitlement is held by the person who has WA^*' (by WA^* and WP^*, Hovenkamp means what we have called WTA and WTP). This cannot be correct, however, if we assume with Posner (1985a, pp. 88–89, 1986, pp. 12–13, 1987a, p. 16, 1992b) that by wealth maximization we mean application of the KH criteria. The reason is that a rule based on the

WTA does not meet KHZ or KH efficiency. In KH terms such a rule may not insure that a potential compensation test is passed. For example, if an entitlement to a piece of land is taken from Ronald and given to Richard, on the grounds that Richard has the higher WTA, no compensation test is passed, since the value of the gain to Richard must be measured by his WTP, which may be lower than Ronald's WTA. In KHZ terms, the use of the WTA alone cannot be justified on efficiency grounds as the rule does not recognize the fact rooted in human psychology that gains and losses are different.

Hovenkamp (1991, p. 229), however, essentially defines wealth maximization as the attainment of the higher of WTP or WTA. Since for normal goods the WTA will be higher than the WTP, Hovenkamp's propositions supporting the use of WTA are essentially tautologies, not proofs. The criterion of maximizing WTA may or may not be desirable,[7] but maximizing WTA is not what the KH criteria dictate. In addition, no one has yet provided a compelling ethical or economic basis for a pure WTA standard. As we shall see, the matter is both more complex and more interesting than Hovenkamp suggests.

If we include transactions costs, the argument that it is efficient to assign the goods to the party with the higher WTP is strengthened, but the existence of transactions costs is not necessary to the argument that the goods should be assigned to that party. If the party with the lower WTP is given the goods, the transactions costs may prevent the party with the higher WTP from buying them. When an initial assignment of goods makes it impossible for the party with the highest WTP to acquire the goods, the net social gain is lower, by definition. If the transactions costs are sufficiently low that the party with the higher WTP will buy the goods from the party with the lower WTP, assigning the goods to the party with the lower WTP will still reduce the NSG, since there will be additional transactions costs.[8]

Commercial Goods

The initial assignment of the right may not affect KHZ welfare. This is the case where there is what I have elsewhere called a commercial good (Zerbe and Graham 1999). Note that if assumptions I and II are correct, the right cannot be a commercial good to either party.[9] A commercial good is one that is valued purely for the stream of income that it can produce – for example, by selling it to another person for a net profit.[10] Because the owner of a commercial good values it solely for the profits, the owner of a commercial good will not suffer income effects, substitution effects, or loss aversion for the loss of the right, so $WTA = WTP$. In this case we have proposition 5.2:

Proposition 5.2: If the good is a commercial good, the Coase Theorem holds.

In the above example, the gain from selling the good to A is WTP_a, as in equation (5.1), but now, since $WTA_b - WTP_b$ is zero, there is no advantage to initially assigning the good to A.

Another way to look at this is that the 'owner' of a commercial good never takes psychological possession of the good; he or she buys it expecting to sell it. If B views the right as a commercial good, the KH welfare gains are not affected by whether the right is given to A or to B. This provides one important reason for the existence of specialized sellers, whose ownership of the good rests on a purely commercial basis. Note that even with commercial goods, assigning the goods to the party with the higher WTP may allow the parties to economize on transactions costs. The only way to explain specialized sellers, then, is that the transactions costs of the various parties are not equal. For example, a specialized seller might be able to buy a good from the government at a transactions cost of $5 and sell it to a competitor at a transactions cost of $2, while his competitor's transactions costs of dealing with the government might be $10, such that it is actually cheaper to have two transactions rather than one. Since specialized buyers and sellers are common in most markets, we can conclude that the phenomenon of unequal transactions costs is a common one.

To make this clearer, let us assume that transactions costs are zero, and that the figures in Table 5.2 apply:

Table 5.2

	WTA	WTP
A	100	90
B	50	50

Now, suppose B buys the right from the government for $50, and sells it to A for $90. The total KH welfare gain will be B's profit of $40, plus the government's gain of $50, or $90. If, instead, the government sold the good originally to A for $90, then the KH welfare gain would also be $90, with the government receiving all of the gains, while A simply breaks even. Therefore, the net social gain is the same whether the good is given to A or B, when transactions costs are zero and the good is a commercial good to the parties. Note that the Coase Theorem is correct whenever the good is a commercial good to the party with the lower WTP (B), even if the good is not a commercial good to the party with the higher WTP. In this example, the good is *not* a commercial good to A, and yet the Coase Theorem is correct.

Proposition 5.3: It is, in general, efficient to assign a right to the party with psychological ownership, where the WTA figures are not known.

Suppose that A has psychological ownership to the right, but that B does not. In this case, the welfare change from assigning the right to A rather than to B is

$$NSG_b = WTA_a - WTP_b \tag{5.5}$$

This will be positive, on the average. That is, if we cannot distinguish A and B in terms of their WTAs, then the expected value is greater from assigning the right to A since, in general, WTA will exceed WTP.

For example, assume that transactions costs are zero, and that the figures in Table 5.3 apply:

Table 5.3

	WTA	WTP
A	100	50
B	140	90

Suppose that A believes he owns the right and that B also believes that A owns the right or good. If the court assigns the right to B, the welfare change is WTA_a – WTP_b. If a court picked up a copy of this book and only read propositions 5.1 and 5.2, it might assign the right to B, since B's WTP is higher than A's WTP. This would be a mistake because in this case assumption V does not hold. Assigning the right to B would be inefficient, as the value of the right to B is measured by his WTP, but the value of the right to A is measured by his WTA, which is higher than B's WTP. The loss from this assignment would be WTA_b – WTP_a, which will usually be positive, as in the above example.

But what about the case in which B would be willing to buy the good from A, if it was assigned to A? That is, suppose A has psychological ownership, but WTP_b is higher than WTA_a. In this case, assuming zero transactions costs and no regard for others, there is no difference in net efficiency between assigning the right to A or B.

For example, imagine A has psychological ownership, that transactions costs are zero, and that the numbers in Table 5.4 apply. If the government assigns the right to A at no cost, neither A nor B will experience a gain or a loss. A will not experience a gain if the good is given to him because A

Table 5.4

	WTA	WTP
A	80	50
B	110	100

believed that he already owned the right, and B will not experience a loss because B never believed that the right was his. Once A receives the right, he will sell the good to B at some price between $80 (A's minimum sale price) and $100 (B's maximum purchase price). If A sells it to B at $100, A will receive a gain of $20, while B will break even. There will be a net social gain of $20. On the other hand, if the government assigns the right to B at no cost, A will suffer a loss of $80, while B will experience a gain of $100, for a net social gain of $20. A will not buy the right from B, since A is not willing to pay B's minimum price. Therefore, the net social gain is the same, whether the right is initially assigned to A or to B.

The argument for assigning the right to B initially is that transactions costs would be saved since no sale need take place. Indeed, I noted above that it is generally efficient to assign a good to the party with the higher WTP when no party has psychological ownership. However, this case is different, as one party has psychological ownership. To understand why the right should go to A even though this necessitates a sale, we need to consider the consequences to the legal system of assigning it to B.

If both A and B believe that the good is A's, it will most often be the case that the good *legally* belongs to A. In other words, at some point in the past the government assigned the right to A, at least in the sense that the government created a system of acquiring property rights. Therefore, B's suit is simply an attempt to circumvent the established rules of acquiring property rights, which will itself create transactions costs. Of course, A and B may both be mistaken about the law, but this will not be the typical situation.

Therefore, the correct comparison is *not* between the transactions costs of the government assigning the good to B and the transactions costs of the government assigning the good to A, plus the costs of A and B negotiating a sale privately. By making that comparison, we are assuming that B's suit (which may be legally frivolous) is inevitable while the private sale is an unnecessary, additional transaction. However, this is an absurd assumption in a capitalistic society, particularly when *all* of the parties believe that one party is the legitimate owner.

It is more sensible to compare the transactions costs of A and B privately negotiating a sale with the transactions costs of B suing A for the good in court, plus the costs of A and B negotiating a sale (assuming that the court assigns the good to A). Anybody with any experience of the American legal system will immediately recognize the absurdity of assuming that it is more efficient for B to file a claim to a good he does not believe he owns than for him to buy it from the owner, on the grounds that he avoids transactions costs by suing the owner. Moreover, if courts routinely assigned a good to parties in B's situation, it would encourage much greater use of lawsuits to acquire property than is the case today. It is not efficient, in any meaningful sense of the word, to encourage frivolous lawsuits.

Where the Psychological and Legal Measures Differ

But what if the psychological expectations and the legal rules differ? I offer the following proposition:

Proposition 5.4: It is efficient that the law should conform to the psychological reference point.[11]

A heuristic proof of this can be made by imagining that the condition for efficiency is not met. Imagine that Ronald believes (with 100 percent certainty) that he owns a right or a property B, and that Richard also believes (with 100 percent certainty) that Ronald owns property B. They discover that the law, however, holds that Richard, not Ronald, owns B. Ronald suffers a loss of B psychologically, while Richard gains B. Since losses are, on average, worth more than equivalent gains (as a result of income effects, substitution effects, and loss aversion), on average Richard will gain less than Ronald loses, and assigning the right to Richard will *never* result in a net social gain, unless it allows the parties to avoid transactions costs or is consistent with the regard for others. This is perfectly general. The application of the law to effect a legal ownership that is different from psychological ownership must, on average, impose net losses, provided Ronald and Richard may be regarded as equivalents (provided, that is, that, on average, one does not have a greater income than the other or does not differ in some other relevant characteristic).

More formally, the proof is simply the proof already offered for the case in which the sense of psychological ownership resides with just one party. The right should always go to the party, A, with the sense of psychological ownership, ignoring the regard for others, when the following condition is satisfied

$$WTA_a > WTP_b$$

Even when $WTA_a < WTP_b$, there will be no social gain if the right is assigned to B (assuming, again, that we ignore transactions costs and the regard for others).[12]

This equation expresses the condition that B has to be willing to pay more than A will accept before a change of ownership should occur, and *even then* it must be shown that the regard for others or transactions costs favor assigning the right to B. Since, other things being equal, the WTA will be greater than the WTP for normal goods and, since psychological ownership usually corresponds to the regard for others, it is efficient for the party with the sense of psychological ownership to gain the good as a general rule. If, for example, one class of claimant psychologically possesses property so that its removal would be felt as a psychological loss, and a rival claimant has a lesser psychological claim or no claim, efficiency requires that the law grant the right to the psychological possessor. The common law doctrine of adverse possession codifies just such a scenario (Cohen and Knetsch 1992).

Ellickson (1991) studied a change in the law in Shasta County, California. In one half of the county, ranchers were liable for straying cattle; in the other half, farmers bore any damage under the law. In fact, however, this change did not alter the time-honored custom enforced by social norms, by which ranchers were liable for damage caused by their cattle. The psychological reference point was one of liability by ranchers for their straying cattle. Thus, in Shasta County, efficiency would suggest a change in the law, to place liability on the owners of straying cattle. In a sense, this has long been recognized. This does not necessarily mean that the law should be changed so that ranchers are liable, though it suggests it; liability rules are not ownership rules. It is possible that the efficient rule is for the farmer to bear the costs of the damage from straying cattle, but the psychological reference point of rancher liability makes this conclusion unlikely, since a change imposes a loss properly measured by the WTA on farmers. In considering whether or not to change the liability rule, the calculation of gains and losses of the change should reflect the psychological reference point.

The law attempts to conform to – or to recognize – the discrepancy between measures of value for benefits and costs.[13] In this respect, the law is correct in recognizing the primacy of the psychological basis for valuation. Cohen and Knetsch (1992) point to six classes of legal rules that are consistent with recognizing the valuation disparity between gains and losses.[14] Evidence suggests that restoration of environmental health following an environmental injury is viewed at times as the restoration of a loss, whereas monetary compensation for the same injury is viewed as a gain. Under the common law measure of natural resource damage, as well as some new environmental statutes, there is implicit recognition of the asymmetry between gains and losses, in the sense that restoration of environmental health following environmental harm is given a different status from market measures of damages. The generally accepted common law measure of damages is the lesser of either the cost of restoration of the natural resource or the diminution in market value attributable to the injury to the resource. This is not an *absolute* rule, however. The law in some cases recognizes restoration as an appropriate measure of damage if the cost of restoration is reasonable in comparison to the diminution in the value of the land.[15] Since restoration costs may be recognized as reasonable that are greater by 50 percent or more than the diminution in market value, restoration clearly may be afforded special status. Recently a number of environmental statutes have been interpreted by the courts or by regulatory agencies to state a preference for restoration costs – including variation of replacement, rehabilitation, and the acquisition of equivalent resources – over diminution of economic value.[16] Regulations first adopted by the US Department of the Interior (DOI), in response to the Comprehensive Environmental Response, Compensation and Liability Act (CERCLA), held that the public trustee was required to select the lesser of either restoration costs or diminution of value of the resources at issue. New parallel regulations giving greater weight to restoration were, however, adopted by both the DOI and the National Oceanographic and Atmospheric Administration (NOAA) in response to the State of Ohio.

There are also a number of areas in which some sorts of public rights to ownership are recognized in the law. For example, the concept of public rights in federal land remains basic common law today in non-environmental cases and is not irrelevant in environmental law (Levy and Friedman 1994, pp. 517–519).

5.4 THE ASSIGNMENT OF RIGHTS WHEN LEGAL RIGHTS ARE UNCLEAR OR UNCERTAIN

Conflicts in Ownership

The meat of much of the law concerns cases in which ownership or entitlement in some form is asserted by more than one party. A psychological sense of ownership may exist for the same good by different people. Both Ronald and Richard may, for example, assert ownership to the same piece of land. Both may have legitimate expectations of ownership. In a contest at law, one will lose. This will be felt as a psychological loss.

How to Choose between WTA and WTP under Uncertainty, Using KHZ

Uncertain ownership: a simple example

The simplest case of uncertain ownership is one in which both parties believe they own the right. This case has been used by Baker (1980, p. 939) to attack the use of the potential compensation justification for the KH tests. He points out that compensation is not possible when starting points are considered, because the sum of expectations of parties in dispute will exceed the total to be gained. This is correct, as far as it goes, but it does not prove that the KH tests or KHZ are worthless. Suppose the property in dispute is valued at \$120 by Mr. A, and at \$100 by Ms. B (for now, let the WTA and WTP for any one party be the same). Both parties, A and B, believe with 80 percent probability that the property is morally and legally theirs. Their combined valuation is, thus, 80 percent of the total of \$220, or \$176. If A wins the property, he cannot compensate both himself and B. If A compensates B with \$80, her expected value, A receives only \$40, which is less than his expected value of \$96. If B wins the property but fully compensates A with \$96, B is left with only \$4, far below her expected value of \$80. This difficulty will be compounded if we take into account the difference in value as between a gain and a loss. Thus, the KH and KHZ compensation tests cannot be passed – *in this manner* – regardless of who wins.

Baker (1980) goes on, however, to use this sort of analysis to dismiss the use of Pareto or of the KH criteria in legal disputes. In this he is incorrect. He makes the wrong comparison. The issue, for the use of benefit–cost analysis to settle disputes, is not whether A could compensate B (or whether B could compensate A) but whether, in a move from a system of legal allocation that is not KH efficient to one that is, the parties could be compensated; that is, whether or not such a move is efficient. But any non-KH-efficient system, by definition, will produce a smaller surplus, or a larger deficit, than a KH-efficient system, so that the move to a KH-efficient system will produce a surplus that could, in principle, compensate the losers. For example, suppose the non-KH-efficient system is one in which the right is assigned on a random basis. A will receive the property one-half of the time, and B will receive the property one-half of the time. The resulting surpluses, using the earlier example, will be –\$56 and –\$76, so the average surplus is –\$66. Under KH, A will always receive the property, and the average surplus will be –\$56. There will be a positive surplus of \$10 in moving from the random system to the KH-efficient system. By definition of KH, there will be a greater surplus under KH than with any other system, so that a move from any system to a KH-efficient system passes the KH compensation test. So, Baker's argument against using KH as a practical guide to legal decisions is not a valid one, if one uses efficiency as the criterion.

Now this same argument applies to the choice of KHZ over KH. KHZ has more scope than KH as it considers a greater variety of goods than KH as well as transactions costs, so it is more efficient in a WTP and WTA sense. Thus, the argument for KHZ rather than KH is the same argument as for KH rather than other (non-KHZ) rules.

A more interesting example

Let us complicate the example now by allowing WTA and WTP to differ. Even here we can say that a system of property allocation that allocated the property to the person to whom it is worth the most is KH efficient, as compared with any other system of allocation.

Consider Mr. A and Ms. B, in our previous example, who both believe they have a right to the property. Table 5.5 shows their valuations. A has a WTP for the property of $120 and a WTA of $150. B has a WTP of $100 and a WTA of $200. Since A believes with 0.8 probability that he has the right to the property, he will feel a loss of 0.8 × $150, or $120, if he loses the property. B will lose $160 if she fails to get the property. If the property is given to A, as a result of court action, she will gain only the difference between $120 and $96, or $24.[17] B will, however, lose $160, so that the loss exceeds the gain by $136. If the property is gained by B, however, the gain is $20 and A's loss is $120, so the net loss is $100. In either case, there is a net loss, which is Baker's point. Where KH is used, however, there is a smaller net loss. Thus, in moving from any non-KH-efficient allocation system to a KH-efficient system, there will be a net gain, so that the winners under the non-KH-efficient system can be 'bribed' to move. The move from a non-KH-allocation system to a KH-allocation system is itself KH efficient, which is my point. As in the simpler example, it is KH efficient to use a system of allocation in which the right is granted to the party to whom it is worth the most. This approach is generalized and formalized below.

Table 5.5 With WTP and WTA values for A and B

	Person A		Person B	
Measures of value	WTP_a	WTA_a	WTP_b	WTA_b
Values	$120	$150	$100	$200
Subjective probability of ownership	0.8	0.8	0.8	0.8
Value of ownership	$96	$120	$80	$160

Using KHZ to allocate entitlements when ownership is uncertain or in dispute

Suppose that both parties A and B have a sense of psychological ownership with respect to some property. This sense of ownership may be less than 100 percent. One may be uncertain about one's moral or legal claim. Let P_a and P_b represent the subjective sense of psychological ownership by A and B, respectively – that is, the 80 percent certainty in the previous example. The entitlement should go to the party to whom it is worth the most, which is correctly determined by considering both the WTP and WTA. The gains to A and B are measured by the WTP, and their losses are measured by the WTA (but it should be understood that the regard for others offers a definitive WTA_c in favor of recognizing the legal owner). Ignoring the regard for others, the right should go to A when the following condition is satisfied

$$WTP_a(1-P_a) - WTA_b(P_b) > WTP_b(1-P_b) - WTA_a(P_a) \qquad (5.6)$$

where P_a and P_b represent the subjective probability of ownership by A and by B. The gain to A is A's WTP, weighted by the extent to which A does not have psychological ownership. Similarly for B. The loss to B is B's WTA, weighted by the extent to which she does have psychological ownership. The right goes to A when the gain to A from having the right is greater than the loss to B from being deprived of her expected right.

Equation (5.6) can be expressed as

$$WTP_a + P_a(WTA_a - WTP_a) > WTP_b + P_b(WTA_b - WTP_b) \qquad (5.7)$$

This is an interesting result, because it says that the *divergence* between the WTA and WTP is relevant to the decision concerning whom should receive the entitlement. Consider a contest between two parties over an entitlement, in which the first is willing to pay more than the second, but the second is willing to fight to the death for it. Equation (5.4) suggests that the one who is willing to fight harder should get it.[18]

In a famous anecdote King Solomon, called on to decree which of two women should have ownership of the baby both of them claimed, proposed that the baby be cut in half. His proposal may be regarded as a clever device for determining their respective WTAs. The false claimant readily assented to the plan, but the real mother of the baby agreed to give it up so that it might live. The baby, then, went to the person who loved it the most (with love being defined as the person who attached the highest existence value to the baby).

Suppose that Richard and Ronald each believe – with a probability of 50 percent – that they own the same piece of land along the Elwha river. Richard has a WTP of \$200,000 and a WTA of \$680,000. Ronald has a WTP of \$300,000 and a WTA of \$325,000. In this case, the value to Richard of receiving good title is his WTP of \$200,000, plus 50 percent of the divergence between his WTA of \$680,000 and his WTP, for a total of \$440,000.[19] The value to Ronald of receiving good title is his WTP of \$300,000, plus 50 percent of the divergence between his WTA of \$325,000 and his WTP, for a total of only \$312,500. So, even though Ronald is willing to pay more for the title, it should go to Richard.[20] Efficiency suggests that the land should go to Richard, and in this case the WTA figure dominates. If, however, each believes with a probability of only 10 percent that he owns the land, then the value to Richard is \$248,000 and to Ronald is \$302,500, so that the land should go to Ronald. Contrary to Hovenkamp, the outcome should not be dominated by the WTA. Rather, both the WTA and the WTP should play a role.

Consider the Headwaters Grove in Northern California, which is the last major privately owned stand of ancient redwoods. For about ten years, the Pacific Lumber Company has been trying to cut the trees, filing logging plans with the California Forestry Board. The value of these trees as timber has been estimated at between \$100 and \$500 million.[21] The company's efforts have been thwarted by environmental groups. This seems to be an example in which the WTP of the environmental groups is less than the WTA of the timber company, but in which the WTA of the environmental groups is much higher than Pacific Lumber's WTA, so that the divergence between the environmental groups' WTA and WTP is also much higher. The probability that the WTA is a better measure of the psychological effect of the loss of the redwoods to environmental groups (and to others) suggests that some recognition of property rights on their behalf is appropriate, and that, as shown by their ability to delay the cutting of this timber, the courts have recognized this.

Equation (5.7) reduces to (5.4), to yield the previous result of assigning the right to the highest bidder when there is no psychological ownership, as P_a and P_b are zero.

When the psychological ownerships of A and B are equal, and are both 100 percent, then the above condition reduces to the suggestion of both Hovenkamp and Minkler, that the WTA determine ownership, if we leave out the regard for others. The terms $(1–P_a)$ and $(1–P_b)$ are zero and, thus, the WTP terms drop out, so that the condition represented by equation (5.7) then becomes

$$WTA_a > WTA_b \tag{5.8}$$

which says that the right should go to the party that values it the most, in a WTA sense. In general, as P_a and P_b increase, more weight will be given to the WTA. Note that the use of the WTA exclusively is a special case, and not the general case as Hovenkamp and Minkler suggest.

When A has a sense of ownership less than 100 percent, and B has no sense of ownership, but the ownership is nevertheless in dispute, the condition for granting the right to A is

$$WTP_a + P_a(WTA_b - WTP_a) > WTA_b \qquad (5.9)$$

In general, as one party's sense of ownership is greater, the likelihood is greater that that party should receive the right. When A has a 100 percent sense of ownership and B has none, it is never *more* efficient to give the right to B (assuming transactions costs and the regard for others are both zero), and it will be more efficient to give the object to A when

$$WTA_a > WTP_b \qquad (5.10)$$

which is simply the condition that B has to be willing to pay more than A will accept before a change of ownership should occur. Note that in the real world, if A and B have a legal dispute over a good, and A has 100 percent ownership and B has zero, the court should be skeptical of B's claim that his WTP is higher than A's WTA, since if this were true we would expect A to voluntarily sell the good to B.

Different customs and legal regimes will result in different expectations of ownership. Consider the issue of whether or not public use of a path across private property establishes a right of way. In Britain, public use for a period of 20 years establishes a public right of way.

In Cornwall, England near the village of Magwan, there has been a dispute between Mr. Jed Trewin and Sir Ferers Vyvyan over use of a path across Vyvyan's property.[22] Mr. Trewin believes that public use has established a right of public use. Sir Ferers believes that no such right exists as he has always closed the path for six months each year. Suppose that each believes with 100 percent probability that he has the right – to use the path in Mr. Trewin's case, and to close it in Sir Ferers's case. In this situation, the KH criteria suggest that the right should be allocated solely on the basis of the WTA.

Suppose that no such right of public right of way existed. Then Mr. Trewin would have no expectation that he had a right, and thus the KH criteria would compare the WTP of Mr. Trewin with the WTA of Sir Ferers. Clearly, the understanding of the law and custom itself will determine in many cases the sense of ownership.

For many goods – environmental goods, for example – the sense of psychological ownership may be diffuse, unformed, or uninformed. Public debate, discussion, and political leadership can help to fix the reference point. This is just the sort of discussion commended by Sagoff (1988), and to which benefit–cost analysis (that is the application of the KH criteria) can contribute. Thus, with respect to a question such as whether or not the dams on the Elwha River should be removed, the discussion here suggests that to the extent that a sense of public entitlement to a free-flowing Elwha exists, both the WTP and the WTA are relevant to an allocation decision. The WTA would be the correct measure to the extent that restoration of the Elwha may be viewed as the restoration of a previous loss rather than as a gain.[23] A benefit–cost analysis might reasonably calculate benefits, using both WTP and WTA measures. A public discussion could allow the analyst to determine where psychological ownership lies, and therefore determine what the efficient legal rule for ownership would be.

Public opinion may be unreliable and misguided; it may be caused by sensationalism in news accounts, or formed on the basis of poor or inaccurate information. Again, the analysis and the analyst can contribute information to the debate, but, even if there is no debate, there is no basis in benefit–cost analysis for disregarding public values. The reliability of psychological reference points is a matter of public process; their unreliability should properly and explicitly increase the uncertainty of guidance provided by benefit–cost analysis.

5.5 ABORTION: AN EXAMPLE WHEN RIGHTS ARE UNCERTAIN

Meeks (1990, p. 126) uses an econometric benefit–cost approach to persuade us that 'banning abortion of human beings would in general be efficient.' Meeks (1990) compares the consumer surplus that women derive from access to abortion with the expected loss of earning that would have accrued to the aborted conceptuses. The consumer surplus is estimated from a demand equation for abortion. Meeks finds that the expected loss of earnings would be greater than the women's loss of consumer surplus, that this result is 'robust' (1990) to different specifications, and that, therefore, a ban is efficient. There are a number of technical and conceptual difficulties with Meeks' work, which have been ably pointed out by Nelson (1993). Yet the dominant conceptual error by the participants in this debate is that efficiency is not correctly defined. Two errors are made. One is that the relevant parties are incorrectly defined; that is, the regard of others is ignored. The second is that WTP measures alone are used, when WTA measures are relevant as well.

To define efficiency for the abortion case, we need to define the psychological status quo. The status quo is clearly one of conflicting expectations. If we regard this matter as one in which both sides to the debate have some sense of psychological ownership then the relevant equation is (5.4) which is

$$WTP_a + P_a(WTA_a - WTP_a) > WTP_b + P_b(WTA_b - WTP_b) \qquad (5.11)$$

Let us say that the persons designated by *a* in equation (5.4) are the parties A, in favor of a ban, and that *b* represents parties B, who are opposed. Meeks would then have to show not only that the WTP of party A was greater than the WTP of party B, but that the divergence between their WTA and WTP was also greater. If both parties have complete psychological ownership instead of a partial sense of ownership, the correct equation is (5.6), which is

$$WTA_a > WTA_b \qquad (5.12)$$

That is, with complete psychological ownership by both parties, Meeks would need to show that A's WTA is greater than B's. This neither he nor Nelson attempts.

To do a proper economic analysis, parties A and B must include not only the women who demand abortion and the conceptuses that might be born; A and B must include all people whose feelings about abortion are sufficiently strong that they are willing to pay or to accept to have abortion legal, on the one hand, or banned, on the other. Whether or not the conceptuses' WTP or WTA should be included is, in the terms of the KH perspective, a matter of standing, and one which clearly has not been decided. Posner (1992a), in a more sophisticated discussion, also attempts to use economic efficiency to favor a ban. He makes, however, the same two conceptual errors as Meeks. Thus, we cannot say that either a ban on abortion or the legality of abortion is efficient. We can say, however, that this is an issue in which the language of economic efficiency is not the best suited to the discussion.

In this case, there are indisputably a number of people on both sides of the abortion dispute with some degree of psychological ownership and whose WTAs would be infinite. Some people would not allow a woman to be forced to give birth, no matter how much they were 'bribed' to vote for an anti-abortion law, and other people would not allow a fetus to be destroyed, no matter how much they were 'bribed' to allow the abortion to occur. Indeed, many if not all people with a strong stance on abortion would find the question of what sort of 'bribe' would convince them to change sides highly offensive. Where there are parties on both sides with infinite WTAs, and where there is some sense of psychological ownership on both sides, KHZ is unlikely to contribute clarity to the discussion.

5.6 RIGHTS AND THE REGARD FOR OTHERS

The Effect of Incorporating the Regard for Others on the Previous Rules

The incorporation of the regard for others into the analysis generally serves to strengthen the previous conclusions. We have treated the world so far as if it were a two-person world with a government. We now consider adding other parties. I will let party C represent all other parties with some concern for the rights of A and B. We are assuming that C has no chance and no interest in receiving the good herself. C's role is to care about whether A or B receives the right. By considering C's interests, we incorporate what I have called the regard for others.

C will also have a WTP or WTA for the assignment of the right. As with other rights, whether it is C's WTP or her WTA that is relevant, is determined by her legal standing, or legal ownership. Where C has ownership of the right in question, it is the WTA that is used; otherwise it is the WTP. In general I shall assume that C's interest is rather like that of an observer, and that C's interest is in rules that maximize KHZ efficiency for society, that is, for A, B, and C.

Of course, this assumption generally just strengthens the case for the allocation rules we have previously developed. Accounting for the regard for others simply adds a term, WTP_c or WTA_c, that is to be included in the previous equations. For example, if we assume that the correct measure for C is C's WTP for the assignment to A or to B of a previously unassigned right, then equation (5.1) would now be

$$NSG_a = WTA_b + WTP_c + T - WTP_b \tag{5.1'}$$

and similar adjustments would be made to the other equations. Thus the previous conclusions generally hold, a fortiori. If we factor in the regard for others, the case for selling the right to the highest bidder, and giving or assigning the right to the party with psychological ownership, is all the stronger, provided C is a party who cares about the efficiency with which the system works, rather than about A and B as people.

The role of the regard for others is more complex when C cares about A and B as particular people. As a general rule, however, we can assume that C will side with the party with psychological ownership. This is because C's regard for others, and A's and B's notions of psychological ownership, are all determined, in large part, by their cultural upbringing,[24] and A, B, and C are most likely products of the same social culture, if they belong to the same legal community. One of the most basic values in most cultures is that people should not take something that does not belong to them unless they pay for it. It is also probably the case that C cares about distributional justice between A and B, and would be upset if B were able to gain at A's expense, if A was not compensated. Of course, if A and B are highly unusual people, or belong to a different subculture than C, they may have very different values, and their psychological ownership may not correspond to C's regard for others. To return to the example in which B is suing A for a good that A and B both believe belongs to A, it is probably clear that C is much more likely to side with A than with B.

Therefore, the general rule that the court should side with the party with psychological ownership is most often strengthened rather than weakened by including the regard for others, since in most cases the society's regard for others will be consistent with the parties' notions of psychological ownership, and with society's notions of distributional justice. In practice, the regard for others is usually incorporated through the notion of economic standing.

Of course, judges who are considering whether a good or a right should belong to A rather than to B will consider more than simply the value of the good to A and to B. The general equation for there to be no change in the law is equation (4.2) from chapter 4

$$\sum_{i=1} WTA_j^r + Te > \sum_{i=1} WTP_i^r \tag{5.13}$$

which expresses the view that the status quo prevails as long as its WTA value for all parties with standing is greater than the WTP of those who wish to have it changed and who have standing.

Even in a case in which both parties had some psychological ownership of a good, in practice most judges would probably try to determine which party had the stronger claim and would dismiss as irrelevant the fact that the party with less psychological ownership had a higher WTP or WTA. For example, suppose a widow and her greedy nephew both claim ownership of the widow's home. The nephew has a contract which purports to give him ownership of the home, but its enforceability is questionable. The nephew is not certain whether the contract is enforceable, so he has some psychological ownership but much less than 100 percent – say 10 percent. On the other hand, the widow's psychological ownership is 80 percent, since she suspects that the nephew's contract is not enforceable but harbors some doubts. The widow has few assets aside from the home, so her WTP is only $40,000, while her WTA is $200,000. The nephew is a land developer, and knows that if the house is demolished he can build a highly profitable shopping mall on the cite, so the house is a commercial good to him. His WTP and WTA are both $250,000.

The value of giving the land to the widow is \$40,000 + 80% (\$200,000 – \$40,000), or \$168,000. The value of giving the land to the nephew is \$250,000 + 10% (\$250,000 – \$250,000), or \$250,000. Ignoring transactions costs and the regard for others, efficiency would favor giving the home to the nephew. In practice, it is highly unlikely that a judge would award the house to the nephew, unless the nephew and the widow were both mistaken about their legal rights (in other words, the nephew's contract claim was stronger than either he or the widow realized). The regard for others would likely be very strongly in favor of the widow, and would outweigh the \$82,000 NSG that would otherwise be gained by awarding the house to the nephew. Perhaps more important, transactions costs would be much higher, in the long run, if nephews could win lawsuits in these circumstances, since that would invite additional lawsuits. Put another way, we want a society of law, not a society in which people with weak contract claims file suits. In this example, if the nephew attempted to buy the house from the widow rather than go to court with his contract claim, the two of them could presumably find an acceptable price between \$200,000 (her WTA) and \$250,000 (his WTP), and the transactions costs of their private negotiations would almost certainly be lower than the transactions costs of a trial.

Standing and the Regard for Others

The thief

While working as a consultant for the Federal Trade Commission (FTC), I faced the following issue as part of a non-public investigation. A large nationwide company offering a regular service billed one month in advance. When customers quit the service they were often owed credit balances. The company did not return these balances unless customers asked for them; often they did not ask. As part of a settlement agreement, the company agreed to return credit balances in the future. The issue that remained for the FTC to decide was whether or not the company should return past balances. The average past balance was approximately \$15. The cost of locating a typical customer and of sending them a check was estimated to be \$2. The benefit–cost calculation suggested was, then, that there would be a loss of \$15 to the company, a resource cost of \$2, and a gain to the consumer of \$15, for a net KH loss of \$2. The FTC did not order past credit balances returned. What was the correct calculation of benefits and costs?[25]

The definition of standing

'Standing' is a term for a short-hand approach to incorporating the regard for others into the analysis. 'Economic standing' concerns who shall have their values counted (Whittington and MacRae 1990).[26] It also concerns, or should concern, what values are to be counted. There are two main economic criteria for standing. First, individuals must be able to rank choices: they must be able to say that one choice is better than, equal to, or less than another (completeness). The implication of the completeness criterion is that individuals have sufficient knowledge of the choices to know which makes the greater contribution to their utility. Second, the individuals must be rational (reflective and transitive).[27] In general, the economist would grant standing to all who are rational, and who have sufficient knowledge to make choices.

The company as a thief

However, a rational party who is able to make choices should still be denied standing in some circumstances. In the context of a KHZ analysis, a party should be denied standing when it is efficient to do so.[28] It is efficient to deny people standing whenever it is safe to *assume* that it is inefficient to give them the right. If it would be expensive to undertake a complete cost–benefit analysis of a dispute, and if we are confident that a complete cost–benefit analysis would conclude that the person should not receive the right, we can reduce transactions costs by denying standing instead of conducting an expensive inquiry. If a court denies standing to a class of people, the court only has to inquire whether a given person fits the class – which is usually a simpler process than applying KHZ's seven axioms to all the relevant parties in a dispute. When the law denies a class of people standing, we can *usually* take this as a reasonable conclusion by the legislature or the judge that if a complete benefit–cost study was conducted then it would conclude that it was inefficient to give people in that class the good in question.

However, it is only efficient to deny a class a class of people standing if it is safe to assume that a full benefit–cost analysis of any particular dispute would almost always conclude that it is inefficient to give the good to a member of that class. Furthermore, because we live in a dynamic world, a decision to deny standing that had once been efficient may become inefficient, if changing social conditions undermine the reliability of the assumption. For example, if the decision to deny standing is based on the assumption that the regard for others would be opposed to giving a good to a class of people, and subsequently the regard for others towards that class of people changed, it may no longer be efficient to deny standing to that class.

We should count the value of the goods to the thief only if we wish to address the question of whether or not theft should be illegal. If we lived in a nation of thieves who obtained sufficient pleasure from theft, a benefit–cost analysis would suggest lower penalties for theft, and might even suggest that theft should be legal.

Every KHZ question thus involves two issues: (1) the value of the action being contemplated – whether or not to build a sports arena, or to tear one down, and so forth – and (2) whose values are to count in addressing the first question. The realization that more than one thing is being valued clarifies the nexus between the legal system and benefit–cost analysis. The question of standing is thus part of the more basic and fundamental question of the pattern of rights that are assumed to be extant when performing a benefit–cost analysis. The analyst takes the current law against theft as a prior determination that, were a study to be undertaken to address the issue of whether the value of the goods to the thief should be counted, its answer would be in the negative. The determination of prior rights may then be taken as a reasonable conditional finding about the results, were everyone to be surveyed. This sort of approach is consistent with counting preferences where they lie, but it takes into account missing values. For if the analyst does count the value of the goods to the thief, he or she fails to account for the (negative) value placed on theft by others.

Of course, we may provide a benefit-cost analysis of the law itself. In this situation, it is not appropriate to assume that it is efficient to deny economic standing to a person simply because the law denies them legal standing. For example, we might wish to consider whether or not theft should be legal. In this case, there is no a priori justification that a prior analysis has determined that the value of goods to the thief should be counted as zero. For this question, then, standing should be given to the thieves.

The rights that establish standing are not different from those that establish the WTP or WTA themselves. The WTP will depend, in part, on income and wealth, which are sanctioned by the legal system. Whether an action that results in a positive change is felt as a loss restored or as a gain is in large part a matter of established property rights. Courts and policy analysts routinely assume well-settled rules of property rights in conducting their analyses. Who would have them do otherwise (see Heyne 1988, pp. 53, 57)? Thus, the correct calculation of benefits and costs for the FTC, in the case of the greedy utility company, would have been that the benefits to consumers were $15, and resource costs to the company were $2, for a net gain of $13.[29] These kinds of issues arise not only in considering questions of theft but also environmental harms, how to treat foreigners in policy evaluations, and in other areas. Consider the area of expert opinion.

The book thief[30]

Derek sues Amartya for stealing his book. He asks for the return of the book and costs. Derek is poor and Amartya is rich. Derek loves the book, but Amartya cares only a little for it. Derek would have been willing to pay $10 for the book, or would have sold the book to Amartya for $15. Amartya would pay $20 for it, but would sell it for $22.50. A benefit–cost analyst hired by Amartya testifies at trial that the value of the book is greater for Amartya than for Derek, in the sense that Amartya's WTP exceeds Derek's WTA. So, the benefit–cost analyst suggests that wealth will be maximized if the book goes to Amartya. The court finds, however, that since Amartya stole the book, it belongs to Derek, the benefit–cost analysis notwithstanding.

Regarding the theft of Derek's book by Amartya, we should ask: Why not count the value of the stolen book to Amartya, since no questions of completeness or rationality were raised? The explanation is that to count the value of the stolen goods to the thief, or to consider the value of the book to anyone other than Derek, examines only one question, when there are instead two to be considered. One question concerns the value of returning the book; the other question concerns the value of holding theft itself to be illegal – that is, deeming that the goods count for nothing in the hands of the thief. The presence of these different questions may explain why some studies consider the value of the goods to the thief, and others do not.[31]

Every benefit–cost question thus involves two issues: the value of the action being contemplated – whether or not to build a dam, or to tear one down, and so forth – and whose values are to count in addressing the first question. The realization that more than one thing is being valued clarifies the nexus between the legal system and benefit–cost analysis. The question of standing is thus part of the more basic and fundamental question of the pattern of rights that are assumed extant in performing a benefit–cost analysis (Zerbe 1991, pp. 97f). It is usually neither feasible, nor cost effective, for the analyst testifying in the sort of case represented by *Derek* v. *Amartya* to perform the meta-contingent valuation study required to undertake a full benefits–cost analysis. Instead, the analyst should take the current law against theft as a prior determination that, were such a study to be undertaken to address the issue of whether the value of the goods to the thief should be counted, its answer would be in the negative. The determination of prior rights may then be taken as a reasonable conditional finding about the results, were everyone to be surveyed.

Of course, we may provide a benefit–cost analysis of the law itself. For example, we might wish to consider whether or not drugs should be legalized. In this case, standing should be given to illegal drug users.

The foreigner

Benefit–cost analyses are usually done from a point of view: for a client, as it were. An analysis done for New York City will not often consider the effect on the residents of New York (except as effects on them may affect New York City residents); an analysis done for the State of Illinois will not usually consider the effects on the residents of Iowa; an analysis done for the US Department of the Interior will not normally consider effects on residents of another nation. Again, there are actually two goods involved. One is the action to be taken; the other is the issue of whether the foreigner should have standing. The existence of these city, state, or national jurisdictions may reasonably be taken as evidence of a prior decision (a benefit–cost decision) that foreign parties have no legal standing to complain.[32]

Standing and trespassers: an in-depth analysis of standing

Another example of courts denying economic standing can be found in the law of premises liability. This is also an example of common law efficiency and of the regard for others. The law of premises liability determines the circumstances in which a landowner is liable to visitors (wanted or unwanted) who are injured by a dangerous condition on the land, such as unattended machinery. Somewhat arbitrarily, I will draw on Washington state's premises liability law.[33]

Guests (invitees and licensees) with an express or implied invitation to be on the landowner's premises, who are injured by dangerous conditions, have economic standing: they are entitled to compensation if the landowner failed to take reasonable efforts to protect them (for example, by warning them of the danger).[34] Trespassers who are injured by a dangerous condition lack standing in most circumstances: an adult trespasser is entitled to damages only if the landowner deliberately or wantonly injured him. A trespasser who has been injured by a dangerous condition on property has undoubtedly suffered 'real' losses (such as physical injury, pain and suffering, and lost wages), but the losses do not 'count,' because the law has determined that trespassers are not entitled to compensation.[35]

The denial of economic standing to injured trespassers is a social judgment, which includes a 'short-hand' analysis that the costs of granting standing outweigh the costs of denying standing. To the extent that the short-hand analysis is correct, the denial of standing is efficient (by definition). The costs of granting standing to trespassers are said to outweigh the benefits of granting it for two reasons. First, the trespasser's injury is offset by the injury to the legal order that is caused by his or her unlawful intrusion on to land.[36] Second, the trespasser is usually the least-cost avoider of dangerous conditions on other people's land, while an owner is frequently the least-cost avoider of injury to a guest.[37] A trespasser can avoid injury by not trespassing in the first place. A landowner would have to undergo considerable expense to protect trespassers from dangerous conditions on his land, since a landowner cannot predict who will trespass, when they will trespass, or what they will do while trespassing.[38] On the other hand, an owner can provide warnings to guests at less expense, since the owner has, after all, invited them there, and probably set a date for their arrival.[39]

However, Washington state courts have recognized that the 'short-hand' analysis that denying standing to injured trespassers is efficient is not always correct, and have carved out three exceptions to the law: intentional injuries to trespassers, attractive nuisance, and child trespassers 'of tender years.' Although courts do not always justify the exceptions in economic terms, the exceptions are economically efficient, for two reasons. First, in each case the disruption to the legal order that is caused by the trespass is itself outweighed by society's regard for others. Second, for each of the exceptions, the trespasser is *not* the least-cost avoider of the injury.[40]

Trespassers *do* have standing against an owner who deliberately or wantonly injures them.[41] An owner who deliberately injures a trespasser has created an even greater disruption to the legal order than the trespasser, since the legal proscriptions against intentionally injuring another person are stronger than the owner's property interest in exclusive possession.[42] While society has little regard for trespassers, it has enough to be troubled by an owner who deliberately harms one. Furthermore, an owner cannot persuasively say that it would be unreasonably expensive for him to avoid deliberately injuring a trespasser.[43]

Second, an owner may be liable to a child trespasser, under the doctrine of attractive nuisance. Attractive nuisance is a narrow doctrine, and applies only when five elements are proven.[44] Society's regard for the safety and welfare of children outweighs the disruptive effect that child trespassers have on the legal order.[45] Furthermore, unlike adult trespassers, child trespassers are not necessarily the least-cost avoiders, because children frequently do not understand either the legal significance of trespassing, or the dangerousness of a condition.[46] Where the child does understand the significance of trespassing and the dangerousness of his actions, he would be the least-cost avoider, and courts do not impose damages.[47] Courts also inquire whether the least-cost avoider is the child's parents.[48]

Finally, an owner may be liable to a child trespasser under the 'tender years' doctrine. The tender years doctrine holds that certain children are so young that they are incapable of being 'true' trespassers.[49] Unlike attractive nuisance, the tender years doctrine does not require a plaintiff to show that the condition was inherently dangerous or attractive to children.[50] The efficiency of the tender years doctrine is unclear, since it applies even where the least-cost avoider would appear to be the child's parents.[51] The legal strength of the tender years doctrine is also questionable, and it is rarely enforced.[52]

The interesting point of the law of premises liability is that both the general rule which denies economic standing to trespassers and the exceptions to the general rule which grant economic standing appear to be finely tuned to promote efficiency.

Access to sunlight and the law of nuisance: standing and changing social values

The issue of denial of economic standing in the case of thieves is straightforward. The legal and the economic arguments rooted in the laws against theft are clear, but not all cases are so easy. *Prah* v. *Maretti* involved a dispute about whether the defendant committed a nuisance when he obstructed the plaintiff's access to sunlight.[53] The plaintiff, Prah, had built a system that used solar collectors to provide his house with heat and hot water. The defendant, Maretti, then purchased property adjacent to Prah's, and he began to build a home there.[54] Prah argued that Maretti's construction would prevent him from receiving enough sunlight to get adequate use from his solar collectors, and that Maretti committed a nuisance by interfering with his access to sunlight. Maretti argued that, under Wisconsin law, one could not commit a nuisance simply by obstructing his neighbor's access to sunlight.[55] That is, in essence, Maraetti argued that Wisconsin denied standing to plaintiffs seeking access to sunlight.[56] The case was appealed to the Wisconsin Supreme Court. The majority recognized that – in the past – courts had consistently denied standing to such plaintiffs, but it decided to overrule that line of cases, and it decided to grant standing to such plaintiffs.[57]

I will use this case to explore more fully the relationship between legal and economic standing, and especially the considerations that should govern under KHZ a decision on whether to grant standing for a class of cases. Later, in Chapter 8, I will identify examples in which the law failed to react to a social change even though the social change rendered the law inefficient. However, in an era of rapid social change it is also possible for judges to *overreact* to social change, and to change the law even though the new social values do not justify a change in the law. The judges may *overestimate* the extent or importance of the social change. *Prah* is an example of a case in which the majority appears to have overreacted to a social change.[58] In any event, *Prah* is a useful vehicle for considering the factors that determine whether standing should be granted.

Under the law of nuisance, a person cannot *unreasonably* interfere with another person's ability to enjoy his or her property.[59] In a typical nuisance action, the defendant is putting his or her land to use in a way that is inconvenient or annoying to the plaintiff and which interferes with the plaintiff's ability to enjoy his or her land.

As a threshold matter, the plaintiff must show that he or she is not a 'hypersensitive' landowner.[60] If the defendant's conduct is only disruptive to the plaintiff because the plaintiff is unusually sensitive or vulnerable, the defendant's conduct is not a nuisance, even if the plaintiff is suffering extreme economic losses as a result.

If a court concludes that the plaintiff is not hypersensitive, the court goes on to compare the utility of the defendant's conduct with the gravity of the harm to the plaintiff.[61] Under the Restatement (Second) of Torts §827, the factors to be considered in measuring the gravity of the plaintiff's harm include: (a) the extent of the harm involved; (b) the character of the harm involved;[62] (c) the social value that the law attaches to the type of use or enjoyment invaded; (d) the suitability of the particular use or enjoyment invaded to the character of the locality; and (e) the burden on the person harmed of avoiding the harm. The factors to be considered in measuring the utility of the defendant's conduct include (a) the social value that the law attaches to the primary purpose of the conduct; (b) the suitability of the conduct to the character of the locality; and (c) the impracticability of preventing or avoiding the invasion (Restatement [Second] of Torts §828).

The Restatement (Second) of Torts' approach to nuisance law is consistent with KHZ's approach to benefit–cost analysis. To determine the plaintiff's WTA or WTP, we need to know both the seriousness of the harm caused by the defendant and the plaintiff's opportunity cost. Similarly, to determine the defendant's WTA or WTP, we need to know both the value of his conduct to him and his opportunity cost. The Restatement (Second) of Torts §827 and §828 asks us to consider both the value of the defendant's conduct to the two parties and their opportunity costs, allowing us to determine their WTPs and WTAs.

Furthermore, the Restatement (Second) of Torts' consideration of whether the plaintiff's use or the defendant's use is more consistent with the neighborhood helps us determine the opportunity costs of each, especially when the best way to avoid the injury is for one of the parties to move. It is probably more efficient to make a person change his or her lifestyle to fit the needs of the neighborhood (either by moving or by adopting some measure that reduces the harm of the invasion) than to make the whole neighborhood change to fit the needs of one party.

The Restatement (Second) of Torts also incorporates the regard for others, by considering the social value that the law attaches to the plaintiff's use and the defendant's use. If society attaches 'value' to ensuring that the plaintiff wins and the defendant loses, then the regard for others favors giving the right to the plaintiff. Similarly, if society is willing to pay or willing to accept payment to ensure that the defendant wins, the regard for others is in favor of the defendant.

If a nuisance is proven, the plaintiff is typically entitled to damages for the past interference with his property and to an injunction against future interference.[63] Injunctions are available to plaintiffs who have suffered irreparable injuries – that is, injuries for which damages would be inadequate.[64] Since the law views each parcel of land as unique, an injury to land is often deemed to be irreparable.[65] On occasion, courts will recognize that a nuisance has occurred but will limit the remedy to damages; however, this is an atypical result.[66]

Even if the plaintiff cannot convince the court that the defendant's use is a nuisance, the plaintiff can prevent the harm by convincing the defendant to give him or her a restrictive easement or a covenant.[67] On the other hand, if something is held to be a nuisance, the defendant can purchase the right from the plaintiff to continue committing the nuisance. Therefore, the consequence of a court declaring that something is not a nuisance is that the invasion will continue unless the WTP of the plaintiff is higher than the WTA of the defendant, after transactions costs. On the other hand, the consequence of a court declaring that something is a nuisance is that the invasion will not continue unless the WTP of the defendant is higher than the WTA of the plaintiff, after transactions costs. Since WTA is higher than WTP for normal goods, declaring something to be a nuisance increases the odds that the activity will be stopped, but it does not guarantee it.[68]

The Restatement's threshold requirement that the plaintiff be putting his land to a typical use, rather than a hypersensitive use, is efficient as well. In essence, this requirement means that the law of nuisance denies standing to hypersensitive plaintiffs. It is not clear whether considering the regard for others would lead us to conclude that hypersensitive plaintiffs should be denied standing. However, it is efficient to deny standing to hypersensitive plaintiffs, because hypersensitive plaintiffs – as a *class* – will frequently be the least-cost avoiders. The least-cost avoider is the one whose money value for a change (WTA or WTP, depending on who has psychological ownership) is the lowest. Therefore, refusing to give the right to the least-cost avoider is efficient, by definition, since the least-cost avoider will lose less than the rest of the affected parties will gain.

Almost by definition, hypersensitive plaintiffs will usually be outnumbered by potential defendants. By 'potential defendant,' I mean a person who is using his land in a way which *actually* disrupts at least one hypersensitive person. For example, suppose the average member of a society is not bothered by children, but that a small percentage of hypersensitive people – curmudgeons – are seriously annoyed if any of their neighbors within a one mile radius has a child in their home. There are almost certainly more people who are currently raising children than there are curmudgeons. However, not every person who is raising a child is a potential defendant; only the people who live within one mile of a curmudgeon are potential defendants. Since a mile is a considerable distance, it is extremely likely that there are more potential defendants than there are curmudgeons.

There is no basis for assuming that any *one* potential defendant's cost to avoid the injury is lower than the plaintiff's cost to avoid the injury.[69] However, the cost of requiring all of the potential defendants to avoid injuring all of the hypersensitive plaintiffs will very frequently be higher than the cost of placing the burden on all of the hypersensitive plaintiffs to avoid being injured.

However, in some cases hypersensitive plaintiffs will not outnumber potential defendants. Suppose that a curmudgeon is bothered only if one of his next-door neighbors has a child. In a typical community of twenty people, there might be nine people who are not raising children but who are not bothered by children, nine people who are raising children but who do not live near a curmudgeon, one curmudgeon, and one person who is raising children and who lives near a curmudgeon. In this hypothetical community, curmudgeons are bothered by something that 95 percent of the community is willing to tolerate, so curmudgeons are probably hypersensitive. However, there is only one potential defendant and one potential plaintiff, so there is no basis for assuming that the plaintiff's cost to relocate is higher than the potential defendant's cost to relocate.

However, even when the hypersensitive plaintiffs are not outnumbered by potential defendants, it is still efficient to deny standing to hypersensitive plaintiffs because this results in lower transactions costs, in the form of information costs. The hypersensitive plaintiffs know they are hypersensitive, but the potential defendants do not know who the hypersensitive plaintiffs are. If hypersensitive plaintiffs had standing, every time a person wanted to move – or to put their property to a new use – they would have to ask all of their neighbors if they were hypersensitive. This would result in substantial information costs. Of course, the hypersensitive plaintiffs might argue that they do not know who the potential defendants are. However, the cost of requiring all of the hypersensitive people to identify all potential defendants is almost certainly lower than the cost of requiring every homeowner to identify the potential hypersensitive plaintiffs.

To return to the example with a community of twenty people: if curmudgeons have standing, there will be ten people who will have to ask all of their neighbors if any of them are bothered by children. If curmudgeons do not have standing, then there is only one person who has to ask his neighbors if any of them plan on having children.

Interestingly enough, historically, plaintiffs seeking access to sunlight were not denied standing on the grounds that they were hypersensitive.[70] Instead, they had previously been denied standing because the law of nuisance recognized three broad social policies which were widely accepted in the nineteenth and early twentieth centuries, and which, if true, would justify the denial of standing.[71]

First, society had a strong belief that a landowner should be able to put his land to any use he wished, so long as he did not cause physical damage to a neighbor. If a plaintiff could stop the defendant from developing his property simply to ensure the plaintiff's access to sunlight, society would feel that the defendant was being treated unfairly, and this sense of unfairness would cause society to experience a loss as a result of the regard for others.

Second, sunlight was valued only for its aesthetic qualities to its owner, and it was thought that the owner could acquire equivalent illumination through artificial devices. In other words, it was believed that the plaintiff seeking sunlight had a low WTA and WTP, since sunlight was of relatively little value, and the opportunity cost was simply the cost of purchasing artificial light, which was relatively low.

Third, society had a significant interest in encouraging property development. America was in the middle of a growth period that was almost universally viewed as necessary to its future. That is, economic growth or development as defined by market goods was highly valued relative to non-market amenities. It was believed that American society experienced a significant gain whenever land in America was developed, and that judges would inflict a loss on society if they recognized a right to sunlight and allowed plaintiffs to prevent development. In other words, America had a direct interest in encouraging development, and experienced a gain when development was allowed.

Prah concluded that a series of social changes had occurred in the late twentieth century which undermined the three social goals outlined above. First, sunlight had become something more than just an aesthetic luxury, it had become an energy source. Therefore, the value of sunlight to the plaintiff is likely to be higher than it was before. Furthermore, the opportunity cost of losing sunlight is higher, since one cannot generate solar energy artificially. Artificial devices can provide illumination, but they cannot be used to generate electrical energy.

Second, the value of non-market amenities had grown relative to traditional market growth since the nineteenth century. Today, society is less willing to encourage traditional market growth at the expense of environmental and other amenities.

Third, America is rapidly depleting its supply of fossil fuels, and significant public policy was aimed at experimenting with and developing alternative energy sources. Therefore, allowing the plaintiff to develop solar energy would likely result in a *direct* benefit to American society, since it lessens the burden on fossil fuels.

Fourth, American attitudes towards property owners have changed, and few Americans still believe that a landowner should have a completely unrestricted right to develop his property. Today, Americans regard a relatively large degree of regulation of land use as reasonable, even when one has not physically injured his neighbor's property. Therefore, the regard for others is less likely to favor allowing the defendant to use his property in a way that obstructs sunlight, even if the defendant is not causing a physical harm to the plaintiff's property.

In light of those four changes, the court concluded that it is no longer reasonable to *assume* that it was in America's best interests to deny standing to plaintiffs seeking access to sunlight. Therefore, it is efficient to grant standing to people seeking access to sunlight, so that a court can determine, on a case-by-case basis, whether a particular plaintiff's need for sunlight is greater than a particular defendant's need for development. The Wisconsin Supreme Court remanded, directing the trial court to consider the factors specified in the Restatement to determine whether Maretti's construction actually constitutes a nuisance.[72]

Judge Callow argued in dissent that the court should continue to deny standing to plaintiffs seeking access to sunlight.[73] He made three arguments to support his conclusion. First, he argued that the state legislature is in a better position to determine whether there has been a change in the regard for others than the courts are.[74] Therefore, the courts should continue to deny standing to plaintiffs seeking access to sunlight until the legislature grants this right to plaintiffs. In fact, he noted that the legislature had actually drafted a statute that governed one's right to sunlight, and argued that the court was wrong to ignore that statute.[75] Under the statute, one who builds a solar collector can prevent a neighbor from blocking his access to sunlight only if the plaintiff received a solar access permit from the state before the defendant received a permit to build his house from the local subdivision and the city. In this case, Prah apparently had never received a permit from Wisconsin, and Prah did not tell Maretti that he had built a solar plant until after Maretti had received a permit from the local subdivision and the city. Therefore, under the recently adopted Wisconsin statute, Prah had no right to prevent Maretti's construction.

Callow's argument that the judiciary should let the legislature decide what is in the public interest and what the regard for others favors is a common argument, but it is not self-evidently correct. However, in this case the legislature had actually acted, and it had drafted a statute which struck a balance between the interests of solar power users and the interests of people who wished to develop their property. The legislature's 'first in time' approach to the issue of conflicts between solar power users and other landowners is a reasonable one, and the majority probably should have at least considered it.[76]

Second, Callow argued, in essence, that courts should only recognize the regard for others in an action alleging a public nuisance, not a private nuisance.[77] Callow's argument is not a persuasive one, at least under KHZ. The regard for others would probably be *more* strongly opposed to a defendant who committed a public nuisance than it is opposed to a defendant who committed a private nuisance, but there is no reason to ignore the regard for others in private nuisance actions. If the regard for others is ignored in private nuisance actions, courts would frequently reach inefficient decisions, by KHZ's definition of efficiency.

Third, Callow argued that even if solar power is of greater value today than it was in the nineteenth century, and even if the regard for others favors plaintiff's in Prah's position, it is *still* true that Prah is a *hypersensitive* plaintiff, and so it is still efficient to deny standing to Prah.[78] Callow notes that whether a plaintiff is hypersensitive is largely a question of relative numbers.[79] A hypersensitive plaintiff is a plaintiff who is bothered by something that most people would not find bothersome. It may be true that Prah is engaging in a socially useful activity by experimenting in solar energy, but the fact remains that most people would not have been bothered by Maretti's construction. Judge Callow analogized to the history of the law's treatment of horses and cars. When the car was first invented, it was frequently held to be a nuisance to horses. Many more people owned horses than owned cars, and so it made sense to require car owners to restructure their lives to reduce the impact on horses, rather than requiring horse owners to restructure their lives to suit car owners. Later, when cars became commonplace, the *horse* was held to be a nuisance. Callow suggests that solar energy is still in such an early stage of development that solar energy users like Prah are hypersensitive, while home-builders like Maretti are behaving reasonably.

Callow's third argument is highly persuasive. The majority is almost certainly correct in arguing that society's attitude toward the value of sunlight has changed,[80] but Callow is almost certainly correct in responding that society has not changed enough to justify a new legal rule.[81] Despite the social changes that the majority discusses, the fact remains that the vast majority of homeowners in Wisconsin would not be bothered by Maretti's construction, since the vast majority of homeowners in Wisconsin do not rely on solar power for heat and hot water. Therefore, solar power users like Prah are hypersensitive. While society has changed, society has not changed *enough* to make solar energy use more widespread. Just as the car eventually succeeded the horse, it may be that solar energy will eventually become so valuable that one who desires access to sunlight should not be considered hypersensitive. However, it seems unlikely that Wisconsin had reached that point in 1980, so the majority's decision was premature.

Standing and the question of whether harm occurs where it is unknown

The question of standing is extremely important for those who claim non-use values for environmental goods. There are two types of non-use value: the value placed on the very existence of a good (existence value) or the value placed on being able to pass the good on to others (bequest value). It is probably true that non-use value mainly represents the value one places on the existence of the good for others to use, whether they are future or existing users.[82] Both court decisions and economic analyses have been inconsistent about who has standing with respect to non-use value. In the case of the Nestucca oil spill, the populations of Washington and British Columbia were used for estimating damages, while in the case of the Exxon Valdez spill, the population of the entire United States was held to be the potentially affected population (Dunford *et al.* 1997). In a more recent case, *Montrose Chemical Corp.* v. *Superior Court*, the Trustees defined the potentially affected population as the English-speaking households in California (Dunford *et al.* 1997).

The potential dam removal on the Elwha River on Washington's Olympic peninsula illustrates the importance of this issue.[83] By far the largest benefit from removing the dams on the Elwha is found for the general population of the United States. Nevertheless, a study showed that the majority of that population had never heard of the possibility of dam removal anywhere in the United States improving the fish habitat (71 percent), never heard of the possibility of dam removal specifically on the Elwha (86 percent), and probably had never even heard of the Elwha (Loomis 1995). The contingent value survey nevertheless found that the best estimate of the WTP value of removing dams on the Elwha for the US population outside of Washington State was about $6.3 billion per year, for ten years (Loomis 1995). Most of this value is non-use value.

'[N]on-use values reflect the utility that people obtain from natural resources based solely on the knowledge that they have about the services of those resources' (Dunford *et al.* 1997). Dunford *et al.* (1997) argue that without specific knowledge of the injury or of the potential gain, there can be no loss. In this regard, use values and non-use values are thought to be fundamentally different. The reasoning is this: for a use good, one may miss an opportunity for what would have been available in the future, even though, if the opportunity is not there, one may never be aware that it was an opportunity missed. This cannot be true for a non-use good, because value arises solely from knowledge and not from use. Without knowledge of the good, the good has no value. Contingent valuation surveys, by their very nature, inform a sample of people about a possible event or decision which (having learned about it) they may then value. But, the reasoning continues, it is a mistake then to use their informed value to represent the value of those who are ignorant.

This argument fails, since it ignores the relation of wealth to value. People who care about salmon runs and free-flowing rivers care about environmental wealth. They care about the Elwha River as belonging to a class of goods that constitute this wealth. Those who put a non-use value on species preservation may not know about a particular species, but may be reasonably said to care about it as part of a genus or class they do care about. Even if people never hear about the Elwha, they have a sense of their environmental wealth, and have knowledge of what has happened to salmon runs and free-flowing rivers.

Consider the analogy of a rich man who owns many businesses that are run by others. We would say that he suffers a loss when one of his businesses suffers as a result of a poor decision, even if he never knows of the loss or of that decision, and even if he does not spend most of his wealth. He knows the magnitude of his wealth, even if he does not know each project that adds to or subtracts from it. He knows about changes in his wealth. As a result of a decision he knows nothing about, he suffers a psychological loss associated with the decline in wealth. So, also, does one who regards the environmental wealth of the nation as partly her own suffer a psychological loss from the deterioration of this wealth, even when she has no knowledge of the particular event that decreases it.

The benefit–cost analyst would say that insofar as a particular loss leads to a loss of environmental wealth, and insofar as environmental wealth is valued, there is a psychological, and therefore an economic, loss. The analyst would point out that non-users who do not know about the particular loss at the time of the contingent valuation survey may know about it later, and suffer a loss in environmental wealth that is linked directly to it. The loss to non-users from destruction of particular environmental amenities is real and important. The implication is that what non-use users value is not the specific environmental good, but the benefits for others that flow from this class of good.

5.7 THE EXISTING PRACTICE

The Practice in Environmental Cases

In practice, the issue of whether to use the WTP or the WTA rarely arises explicitly, except in defining what effects are benefits (use the WTP) and what are costs (use the WTA). The panel of experts on the use of contingent valuation methods to assess natural resource damages notes that 'virtually all previous [contingent valuation] studies have described scenarios in which respondents are asked to pay to prevent future occurrences of similar accidents,' without regard for the issue of whether WTP or WTA is the appropriate measure (Arrow *et al.* 1993, pp. 4601–4614). The panel states that 'the willingness to pay format should be used instead of the compensation required because the former is the conservative choice' (ibid., p. 4608). This is incorrect as a matter of principle; the choice of a welfare criterion should not be a question of being conservative, it should be a question of selecting the right measure. Perhaps we should adopt a conservative valuation of the right measure, but that is a different matter.

WTP and WTA and the Practice in the Law of Remedies

Although the government rarely *explicitly* uses WTP and WTA in making decisions, courts frequently make *implicit* use of WTP and WTA. In many lawsuits, one of the most fiercely disputed issues is the proper measure of damages.[84] While lawyers and judges rarely speak in WTA and WTP terms, they frequently suggest rules for measuring damages which approximate one or the other measure. Thus, a dispute about the proper measure of damages may be a dispute about whether WTP or WTA is the appropriate measure.

The threshold question, from a remedies perspective, is whether a party is entitled to damages at all. This is essentially a question of standing. The legal rule is that there cannot be recovery in the form of damages unless there has been an injury which the law recognizes.[85] When a party seeks damages without having suffered an injury (or having suffered an injury which the law does not recognize), judges dismiss such a claim as a mere request for a 'windfall.' This simple statement of the requirement for standing closely parallels the rule I have suggested for economic standing. My rule is that a party should have standing to have his or her gains or losses considered in a legal decision when the weight of public opinion, in the form of the regard for others, supports granting their gains or losses standing. Because America is a democratic country, the fact that a party's alleged injury is or is not recognized by law is *some* indication that America's regard for others does or does not support granting them standing, but, of course, the law does not always reflect the citizens' preferences perfectly.

Assuming that a party is entitled to damages, the next question is the proper measure of damages. In general, the rule for compensatory damages is that a party should be restored to the position he would have been in, had he not suffered the unlawful injury.[86] This rule resembles WTA, rather than WTP. In order to determine the position a person would have been in but for an unlawful injury, one must recognize the substitution effect, income effects, and loss aversion. If these effects were ignored in the calculation of damages, a party would not be restored to the position he would have been in without the unlawful injury. Thus the general rule of law is to use the WTA measure for damages when a person has suffered an unlawful deprivation.[87] This is consistent with my approach, since a party who has suffered an unlawful injury has almost certainly been deprived of something to which the party had psychological ownership, so the WTA measure is appropriate.

In practice, however, courts frequently use measures of damages which are much closer to WTP than to WTA.[87] For example, in many cases the measure of damages for a person who has been deprived of a good is the market value of the good. Clearly, the market value of a good will be much closer to WTP than WTA. A person's WTP will not be more than its market value (since he would not be willing to pay $10 for something that he could get on the market for $5), but his WTA may frequently be much higher than the market value (because of sentimental value, difficulties in finding a replacement, or personalized modifications that increase the good's value to him but decrease its value to the general public). However, courts generally do not use the market value for goods unless that is a reasonable estimate of their value to the owner, as in the case of goods that are held for resale. The market value is not used to measure damages for goods that the owner bought for his use or convenience.[88] Again, the courts' approach closely parallels the approach of KHZ. From KHZ's perspective, the market value would be the proper measure of damages only for commercial goods. Goods that are held for resale are clearly commercial goods, at least in most cases. The courts' use of the market value for commercial goods is efficient, as is the courts' refusal to use the market value for consumer goods.

However, while courts do not use the market value for non-commercial goods, they do not use a 'pure' WTA measure either.[89] In practice, courts usually refuse to recognize sentimental value.[90] In a majority of cases, the rule is that damages based on sentimental value are unavailable in tort or contract claims involving injury to property.[91] Even those jurisdictions that allow recovery of sentimental value only allow it in rare instances.[92]

In order for WTA to be measured correctly, sentimental value must be recognized. Suppose I inherited a silver bracelet with a market value of $80 from my grandmother. Suppose a friend offers to buy the bracelet for $100, but I refuse. Clearly, my WTA is more than $100. The fact that I probably said 'no' for sentimental reasons does not change the fact that my WTA is more than $100. If the bracelet were to be stolen, and a court were to give me $80 – or even $100 – in damages, it would not restore me to the position I would have been in, but for the theft of the bracelet. Put another way, courts will give damages based on WTA rather than WTP when the plaintiff can show that WTA and WTP differ for objective reasons, but will not give damages based on WTA when the WTA figure is large for subjective reasons, such as sentimental value.

One troubling case in which sentimental value was rejected is *Furlan* v. *Rayan Photo Works*. In this case, the plaintiff sent his only picture of his mother to a pharmacist, and asked him to enlarge it.[93] The pharmacist negligently damaged the photo, essentially ruining it. The court limited the plaintiff's damages to $5, since any damages aside from the $5 figure would represent 'sentimental value' or 'emotional distress,' neither of which is recoverable (at least in New York) when property is negligently damaged.[94] Intuitively, we probably feel that Furlan suffered more than a $5 loss, and that $5 does not restore him to the position he was in before Rayan Photo Works destroyed his mother's picture. Furthermore, we can safely assume that Furlan would not be 'willing to accept' $5 in return for his mother's photograph.

Nonetheless, *Furlan* may have been a KHZ efficient result. Recognizing sentimental value would subject society to considerable transactions costs because of the difficulty of accurately determining a person's sentimental attachment to a good. It would place large transactions costs on defendants (who would have to guess the sentimental value of items in order to determine the efficient level of caution when working with the items) and on the courts (who would have to evaluate claims of sentimental value). Although *Furlan* does not speak explicitly in transactions costs terms, it is clear that what the court had in mind were the administrative difficulties of measuring sentimental value:

> An injury to the feelings, independently and alone, is something too vague to enter into the domain of pecuniary damages; too elusive to be left, in assessing compensation, to the discretion of a jury. The extent and intensity of such injuries depend largely upon individual temperament and physical, mental and nervous conditions. Those conditions are shadowy, unequal, and uncertain in the extreme.[95]

Put another way, when it comes to avoiding damage to goods whose value is largely sentimental, the least-cost avoider is probably the plaintiff, not the defendant. In other words, precisely because sentimental value is known to the plaintiff, and is usually unknown to the defendant, it might be unreasonable to expect a defendant to realize that an item carries great sentimental value and to take great care in protecting the item.

However, some jurisdictions have recognized limited situations in which sentimental value is recoverable. There are two classes of such exceptions. First, sentimental value is recoverable in a contract case in which the breaching party *knew* that the other party had entered into the contract for purely sentimental or emotional reasons.[96] Second, sentimental damages are recoverable when the item is one that is generally capable of creating an emotional attachment, and where limiting the plaintiff's recovery to the market value of the item would be manifestly unjust.[97]

Windeler v. *Jewelers* is an example of a case in which the defendant knew that the plaintiff had entered into the contract for purely sentimental and emotional reasons, and in which sentimental value was recognized.[98] The plaintiff had given the defendant six of her rings, asking him to reset their stones in a new ring which she would then present to her daughter as a family heirloom. The defendant sent the rings to a third person by *insured* mail, rather than *registered* mail, a practice which the jury determined was negligent.

The court noted that, in this case, the defendant *knew* that the rings were of great sentimental value to the plaintiff. For one thing, the plaintiff told him this when they made the contract. For another, when the defendant called the plaintiff to inform her that the rings were lost, he advised her to sit down first, suggesting that he knew the loss would be a tremendous emotional blow to her. As a result of losing the rings, the plaintiff suffered severe headaches, had difficulty sleeping, and began to cry frequently. The court held that when a defendant knows that a plaintiff is entering into a contract which directly relates to the 'happiness and comfort of the plaintiff,' the plaintiff may recover both for mental distress and for the sentimental value of the lost property.

Campins v. *Capels* is an example of the second circumstance in which sentimental damages are recoverable – a case in which the lost items were ones that would have sentimental value to a typical person in the community and were of value for almost purely sentimental reasons.[99] The plaintiff's home had been burglarized, resulting in the theft of a wedding ring and three 'national racing championship rings.' The defendant had received the rings from the thieves, and had then melted them down so that he could recast them and sell the new jewelry. Interestingly enough, the plaintiff did not allege that his wedding ring had any sentimental value (he asked for the market value of the ring), but he did argue that the championship rings had great sentimental value.[100]

The court noted that the plaintiff's 'sentimental' attachment was not an example of a 'mawkishly emotional' or an 'unreasonable emotional' attachment to the championship rings.[101] Rather, the rings were valuable because they were a memento of the 'blood, sweat and tears' the plaintiff had gone through to earn them. The court notes that there is *no* 'readily available' market for the buying and selling of championship rings. In other words, virtually all of the value of the rings stems from their emotional significance. The court concluded that the injustice which would be done by giving the plaintiff nominal damages outweighed the difficulties involved in proving sentimental value with certainty. The court decided that a jury could estimate the sentimental value of goods with reasonable accuracy, particularly since sentimental value is available only for goods that are 'generally capable' of creating emotional attachments. However, the court held that a plaintiff cannot demonstrate sentimental value by arguing that he would not have sold an item at some specific price.[102] The court does not explain the reason for this rule, and the rule is inconsistent with the basic definition of WTA. However, the reason is probably that it is too easy for plaintiffs to inflate the emotional value of goods with such self-serving statements, and it would be difficult (if not impossible) for a defendant to *disprove* such a statement.

It is important to note that even in the jurisdictions which allow sentimental value, one must show that a good has virtually *no* market value, not simply that the market value is much lower than the plaintiff's WTA, if sentimental value is to be included. For example, in *Carye* v. *Boca Raton Hotel & Club*, the plaintiff's jewelry was stolen while the items were entrusted to the defendant.[103] The jewelry had been accumulated over the course of the plaintiff's 48-year marriage, and the court did not dispute that the rings had significant and reasonable sentimental value to the plaintiff. However, the court denied recovery for sentimental damages because the market value of the rings was considerable. Furthermore, unlike *Windeler*, in this case the plaintiff had not told the defendant that the items were of special emotional significance (it is not clear, in any event, whether Florida would have followed the logic of the *Windeler* case).[104]

It is interesting to note that in both of the tests for sentimental value there are two justifications for awarding the plaintiff sentimental value. First, in each case the rule ensures that the defendant is on notice that the goods have sentimental value. When a contract is formed and the plaintiff specifically informs the defendant that the good has great emotional significance, the defendant can hardly be heard to say that he could not have known that he should take special care of the item. Similarly, when a good is such that the typical person in the community would attach sentimental value to it, the defendant can reasonably be expected to know that this particular plaintiff attached sentimental value to the item as well. The fact that the defendant is on notice of the sentimental value of the item essentially decreases the transactions cost of requiring the defendant to pay for sentimental damages.

Second, in each case the regard for others would likely be strongly in favor of recognizing sentimental damages. When a plaintiff makes a contract because of his sentimental attachment to a good, and the defendant knows this, it seems fair to require the defendant to pay for the sentimental value of the good if he negligently damages or loses it. The plaintiff's high sentimental value is what led him to make the contract in the first place – a contract that would have profited the defendant had the defendant performed it adequately. Having benefited from the plaintiff's sentimental value before the breach occurred, the defendant cannot destroy the plaintiff's sentimental value and refuse to compensate the plaintiff for it. Similarly, when an item has great sentimental value and virtually no market value, and when *most* people in the community would attach sentimental value to the item, distributional justice seems to require a recovery that includes sentimental value. Otherwise, the defendant could knowingly inflict a tremendous loss on the plaintiff without having to reimburse any of the damage that he has caused.

It is not clear whether *Furlan* is reconcilable with *Windeler*, since it is not clear whether Rayan Photo Works knew that Furlan was entrusting them with a picture that had great sentimental value to him.[105] *Furlan* is completely inconsistent with *Campins*, however.[106] Most people would attach special value to their only picture of their mother, and it is also true that there is virtually no market for old photos (indeed, Furlan received *nominal* damages, not the *market value* of the picture, which suggests that the court determined that there was no market for old photos).[107] In order to determine whether *Furlan* or *Campins* is the better rule of law, an economist would have to quantify sentimental value, the transactions costs of determining sentimental value when the conditions of *Campins* are satisfied, and the regard for others, something which I do not attempt here.[108] Both *Furlan* and *Campins* are reasonable predictions of what the most efficient rule is, but neither engages in the type of analysis which would be necessary to establish its superiority beyond doubt.[109]

5.8 SUMMARY

I have said that two things are involved in valuing a good: the value of the item itself, and the value of the law that determines ownership of the good. The value of the goods to the thief should be considered if we are addressing the question of whether or not *theft* should be illegal. A benefit–cost standard may be applied to the issue of whether or not standing should be granted. Where the value to a defined group from granting it standing is greater than the loss of value to others from granting it standing, the economist can argue on benefit–cost grounds for granting standing to the defined group.

Where the issue is whether the jurisdiction should have the power to produce a self-regarding analysis, or whether the jurisdiction should exist at all, or whether the foreigner should have standing, the values to the foreigner are liable to be relevant to that discussion. Again, these matters cannot be separated from legal determination of rights granting standing.

The benefit–cost analyst should not give or take away standing where the courts have not done so.[110] To do so would both make the analysis irrelevant to the real world and show a misunderstanding of the proper context of benefit–cost analysis as an adjunct to the law. Where the courts have not decided standing, the analyst can, however, show the effects with and without standing being granted.

The whole process of requiring environmental impact statements as part of the relicensing process suggests a public stake in environmental protection. Moreover, the policy process surrounding the issue of dam removal on the Elwha has been directed, in part, by an act of Congress. Therefore, the FEIS is correct in including estimates of this non-market value (Flatt 1994).

NOTES

1. It is widely recognized that the invariance part of the Theorem requires the qualification 'income effects aside,' and less widely recognized that it also requires the further qualification of 'no loss aversion'. To these qualifications one should also add that of 'no substitution effects'.
2. The use of the WTA to represent the sense of a loss restored is the correct measure even if loss aversion does not exist.
3. For example, see Kennedy (1981) and Coleman (1980, p. 509). However, Heyne (1988, p. 53) furnishes a sufficient counter argument.
4. Long before Posner incorrectly complained about the indeterminacy, others pointed out the problem of the unallocated portion of the sort shown in Figure 5.1. For example, see Mishan (1971).
5. Note that in this case Hovenkamp's (1991) suggestion of using the WTA is wholly contrary to the KH criteria.
6. This is only true for those natural resources whose value lies purely in their commercial exploitation and is profoundly untrue for others, such as the Grand Canyon and Glacier National Park. If the owner of a natural resource values it purely for commercial exploitation, it would be a commercial good, and the owner's WTA and WTP would not differ. In Chapter 5, I show that the initial assignment of a right to a good makes no difference when a commercial good is involved, but makes a profound difference otherwise.
7. Minkler (1998).
8. Assigning it to the party with the higher WTP may not reduce transactions costs, if the party with the higher WTP has higher transactions costs than his competitor. Suppose A can buy the good from the government at a transactions cost of $5 (and sell it to B at a transactions cost of $2) while B would have a transactions cost of $10 if he tried to buy the good from the government. In this case, transactions costs would actually be lower if A bought the good and sold it to B. However, if A's WTA and WTP differed by more than $3, it would still be more efficient for B to receive the good initially.
9. The same right might be a commercial good to one party and a non-commercial good to another person. We can not determine whether or not something is a commercial good in the abstract, we can only determine whether a particular person views a good as a commercial good.
10. Note that not all business assets are commercial goods. For example, a businessman who owns a steel mill might value it both for profits and for the pleasure of employing people in his community. In the latter case, the steel mill is not a commercial good.
11. The general rule is: Where one class of claimants values the right more than other classes, efficiency requires that the right should go to the claimants who value it the most. This rule holds even where markets ensure that the right will eventually end up in the hands of those who value it the most, as the rule avoids the transactions costs of getting the right into the hands of those who value it the most.
12. Underlying this proof is a notion that preferences are to be taken as given. And it is true that in benefit–cost analysis preferences are usually taken to be given. However, efforts to change preferences to accord with the law may themselves be KH efficient. Underlying this proof is the notion that changing preferences to be in accord with the law cannot be described as efficient.
13. See Levy and Friedman (1994) for a discussion of the concept of ownership in federal environmental law.
14. Ibid. These are the rules of adverse possession, limitations on recovery of lost profits, contract modifications, gratuitous promises, opportunistic behavior, and repossession. To these I would add limitations on recovery of property from theft.
15. See *Heninger* v. *Dunn*, 101 Cal. App. 3d 858, 162 Cal. Rptr. 104, 106–07 [1980]; *Newsome* v. *Billips*, 671 S.W.2d 252, 255 [Ky. App., 1984]; *Trinity Church* v. *John Hancock Mutual Life Ins.*, 502 N.E.2d 532 [1987].
16. *State of Ohio* v. *U.S. Department of the Interior*, 880 F.2nd 432 (D.C. Cir. 1989).

17. For simplicity I have assumed that the WTP and WTA are linear in the amount of the good.
18. See the discussion of dueling in Chapter 8.
19. The calculation is as follows: \$200,000 + 0.5(\$680,000 – \$200,000) = \$440,000.
20. The calculation is as follows: \$300,000 + 0.5(\$325,000 – \$300,000) = \$312,500.
21. *New York Times*, Sunday, April, 21 (1996).
22. *New York Times International*, Wednesday, October, 22, 1997, at A4.
23. The Headwaters Grove in Northern California considered previously is another example.
24. Of course, many would argue that one's values are a product of genetics as well as culture.
25. The treatment of standing here is similar to that in Zerbe (1991, 1998b).
26. This is course different from legal standing. A thief has legal standing to appear in court. I shall argue that he does not have economic standing to have his value for the stolen goods count unless the issue is whether or not theft itself should be illegal.
27. Preferences are said to be reflective when a choice x is at least as good as itself, and transitive when an ordering such as $A > B > C$ implies $A > C$ (where $>$ means 'is preferred to'). See Boadway and Bruce (1984, pp. 34f). Other assumptions are sometimes made.
28. The presence of these different questions may explain explicitly why some studies consider the value of the goods to the thief and others do not.
29. Now an issue might be raised as to whether or not the company has standing to have the \$2 search costs counted. I would hold that where resource costs are involved – as in the case of the \$2 search costs – they should be counted in the benefit–cost calculation. The part of society that is not the company loses something from the \$2; it does not lose from the transfer of the \$15. It is, of course, possible that the deterrence value of requiring the money to be returned would exceed the return costs, even if these search costs were greater than \$15.
30. This example is based on a reworking of an example offered by Dworkin (1980, pp. 197f).
31. See Des Jarlais, Deren and Lipton (1981). According to Des Jarlais *et al.* (1981), among those who have valued goods in the hand of the thief are Becker (1968), Polinsky (1980 and 1983), Polinsky and Shavell (1979), and Faith and Tollison (1983). Among those who have argued or undertaken analyses contrary to this position are Stigler (1970), Shavell (1985), Trumbull (1990), and Zerbe (1991).
32. The eminent benefit–cost analyst Arnold Harberger tells me that he refuses as a matter of policy, and I suspect of principle, to perform a benefit–cost analysis from any but a national perspective.
33. Most states follow the rules of premises liability outlined here. See *Ocampaugh* v. *Seattle*, 588 P.2d 1351, 1358 (Wash. 1979). Some states have rejected the doctrine of licensee, invitee, and trespasser, and therefore have little need for the exceptions to those rules. See, for example *Rowland* v. *Christian*, 443 P.2d 561 (Cal. 1968).
34. See *Schock* v. *Ringling Bros.*, 105 P.2d 838, 841 (Wash. 1940). There are subtle, but legally significant, differences between the duties owed to an 'invitee' and a 'licensee,' but these differences are beyond the scope of this book. See generally *Tincani* v. *Inland Empire Zoological Society*, 875 P.2d 621 (Wash. 1994). For simplicity's sake, I refer to all visitors with permission to be on the owner's land as 'guests,' without distinguishing between invitees and licensees.
35. See *Schock*, 105 P.2d 838.
36. See *Curtis* v. *Tenino Stone Quarries*, 79 P. 955, 956 (Wash. 1905) stating 'To hold, as a general and universal rule of law, that the owners of mills and factories must so construct and maintain their premises as to be reasonably safe for trespassers … would be destructive of all industry and all property rights.'
37. See ibid. Courts do not use the term 'least-cost avoider'; rather, they say that owners are not insurers of every trespasser, or that the cost of protecting trespassers would be unreasonably burdensome. See *Schock*, 105 P.2d at 843.
38. See *Curtis*, 724 P. at 96.
39. This issue is complicated to some degree by the doctrine of 'implied' invitations. For

example, a homeowner with a welcome mat at the front door has made an implied invitation for people to come on to their property and knock on the door. Of course, it is not easy for a homeowner to anticipate an 'implied' guest. However, the scope of invitation for implied guests is fairly limited; they can only walk on to the property and knock on the door: any other use of the property is a trespass. Since implied guests may only use a small part of a person's property, the property owner needs to make only a small part of his or her property safe.

40. The 'tender years' exception is on the shakiest ground, economically speaking, and interestingly enough it is also on the shakiest legal ground. Compare *Sherman* v. *Seattle*, 356 P.2d 316 (Wash. 1960) with *Meyer* v. *G.E.*, 280 P.2d 257 (Wash. 1955).
41. See *Schock*, 105 P.2d at 842
42. See *Katko* v. *Briney*, 183 N.W.2d 657, 660 (Iowa 1971) (noting that value of human life to the individual and to society outweighs a landowner's interest in excluding wrongful intruders).
43. This assumes that we are dealing with a mere trespasser, not with a trespasser who intends to commit a more serious crime or tort while he is on the owner's property.
44. It can be established that a dangerous condition was an attractive nuisance if he or she proves that the following five elements are met: (1) the condition is 'dangerous in itself,' (2) the condition is 'attractive and alluring to children,' (3) the child's immaturity rendered him or her unable to appreciate the danger, (4) the condition was left exposed and unguarded, (5) it was 'reasonably practicable' for the owner to restrict access to the condition or to render it harmless. See *Ochampaugh* v. *Seattle*, 588 P.2d 1351, 1354 (Wash. 1979). A condition is not dangerous in itself if it was dangerous only because the child disturbed it. See *Holland* v. *Niemi*, 345 P.2d 1107–1108 (Wash. 1959).
45. See *Ocampaugh*, 588 P.2d at 1353; *Mail* v. *Smith Lumber and Shingle Co.*, 287 P.2d 877, 878 (Wash. 1955).
46. See *Helland* v. *Arland*, 126 P.2d 594 (Wash. 1942) (noting that 'some few courts, among which is ours, have repudiated the idea that a child as young as [five years] can *in any real sense* be a trespasser' [emphasis added]).
47. See *Ocampaugh*, 588 P.2d at 1357 (denying damages to child trespassers who drowned in a pond, since features which made the pond dangerous were 'generally known and understood by children old enough to be allowed to play at such places').
48. See ibid., *Mail*, 287 P.2d. at 878 (stating 'If the doctrine of attractive nuisance is extended or applied without regard for the proper balancing of legal responsibilities and liability as between parents and landowners … there is the danger that landowners would … become the insurers of the safety of children playing upon such landowners property.'); *Meyer*, 280 P.2d at 258 (stating 'The presence of danger to an unattended infant is not necessarily a test of anything but the need of parental care.') But see *Sherman*, 356 P.2d 316 (imposing liability on the landowner without considering the significance of the lack of parental supervision over the three-year-old).
49. See *Sherman*, 356 P.2d 316. A six-year-old child is not of tender years. See *Ochampaugh*, 588 P.2d 1351.
50. See *Sherman*, 356 P.2d 316.
51. Compare *Sherman*, 356 P.2d 316 with *Meyer*, 280 P.2d 257.
52. *Sherman*'s attempt to distinguish *Meyer* on the grounds that *Sherman* dealt with a child intruding on to a *portion* of land without permission is unconvincing, since an invitee who exceeds the scope of his invitation is a trespasser. Compare *Sherman*, 356 P.2d 316; with *Meyer*, 280 P.2d 257.
53. See *Prah* v. *Maretti*, 321 N.W.2d 182, 184 (Wis. 1982).
54. See ibid. at 185 (noting that Maretti had received permission to build his home from both the subdivision and the city).
55. See ibid. at 188–189. Before *Prah*, the only way to acquire a protectable interest in sunlight under the common law was to convince one's neighbor to give him an express easement for sunlight. An easement is essentially a contract between two landowners, which either grants one person the right to use another person's land in some limited way, or which prevents a person from using his own land in a particular way. In this

particular case, Prah and Maretti attempted to negotiate an agreement but were unable to reach a compromise. See ibid. at 185.

56. See ibid. at 184.
57. See ibid. at 189.
58. See ibid. at 194 (dissenting opinion).
59. See ibid. at 187.
60. See ibid. at 197 (dissenting opinion).
61. See ibid. at 187.
62. By 'character of the harm' the Restatement means that nuisances which cause physical damage to a structure on real property are in general more serious than personal discomfort or annoyance. The Restatement's justification for treating physical damage as more important than personal discomfort is that the former is much easier to prove than the latter. If the Restatement is simply making a prediction that plaintiffs will be successful more often when they produce evidence of physical damage to their property, since physical damage is easier to prove than discomfort, this distinction is sensible. If the Restatement is making a prescription that preventing or reimbursing people for personal discomfort be treated as less important than preventing or reimbursing physical damage, even when the economic injury (WTA or WTP) is the same, that distinction is not sensible. Whether an injury has been proven is a separate issue from the weight that should be given to an injury once it has been proven.
63. See ibid. at 184.
64. See *Stokes Cty. Soil Conservation Dist.* v. *Shelton*, 67 N.C. App. 728 (1984).
65. See *United Church of the Med. Ctr.* v. *Medical Ctr. Commn*, 689 F.2d 693, 701 (7th Cir. 1982).
66. See *Lopardo* v. *Fleming Cos.*, 97 F.3d 921, 930 (7th Cir. 1996).
67. See *Prah*, 321 N.W.2d at 188. Easements or covenants are special types of agreements. They are essentially contracts in which a party either agrees to allow another person to use his property, or agrees not to use his own property in a certain manner. The law of property sometimes creates an easement or covenant even when there is no express agreement (such as an easement by prescription).
68. Declaring something to be a nuisance also has a distributive effect, since the plaintiff's wealth is increased at the expense of the defendant. The plaintiff's wealth will increase because either a harmful activity will be prevented, or the plaintiff will receive a sum of money that is at least as valuable to him as preventing the activity.
69. Indeed, almost by definition, it will usually be harder for the hypersensitive plaintiff to find a new home that suits him or her, since there will be relatively few places where the hypersensitive plaintiff would be comfortable. A defendant who wants to put his land to a reasonable use would probably have relatively little difficulty finding a neighborhood which would tolerate that use.
70. See ibid. at 188–189.
71. See ibid. at 189–190.
72. See ibid. at 192.
73. See ibid. at 193–199.
74. See ibid. at 195.
75. See ibid. at 195–196.
76. In addition, the legislature's rule might have reduced the transactions costs of both those seeking access to sunlight and those seeking the right to build a home on their property. Whether or not a person had a solar access permit is publicly available information. Under the legislature's approach, it would be relatively easy for solar power users to express their need for sunlight, by requesting a permit. Similarly, it would be relatively easy for people who wish to build a home to find out whether any of their neighbors had a permit. By thwarting the legislature's approach, the court makes it more difficult for people like Maretti to find out whether any of their neighbors has a particularly intense need for sunlight.
77. See ibid. at 194–195.
78. See ibid. at 196–197.

79. See ibid. at 195.
80. See ibid. at 188–189.
81. See ibid. at 197.
82. In this regard, it represents a type of altruism that is similar to the value one may give to the distributional effects discussed earlier.
83. See generally Elwha River Restoration (1995).
84. See for example *Furlan* v. *Rayan Photo Works*, 12 N.Y.S.2d 921 (N.Y. Mun. Ct. 1939).
85. See *Porous Media Corp.* v. *Pall Corp.*, 110 F.3d 1329, 1335, 1336 (8th Cir. 1997).
86. See *Protectors Ins. Serv.* v. *United States Fd. & Guar. Co.*, 132 F.23d 612 (10th Cir. 1998).
87. See for example *O'Connor* v. *Katz*, 186 N.Y.S.2d 790 (N.Y. Mun. Ct. 1959).
88. See ibid. at 792.
89. See for example *Furlan*, 12 N.Y.S. at 923.
90. See ibid. See also *Landers* v. *Municipality of Anchorage*, 915 P.2d 614 (Alaska 1996). But see *Campins* v. *Capels*, 461 N.E.2d 712 (Ind. Ct. App. 1984); *Windeler* v. *Jewelers*, 8 Cal. App. 3d 844 (1970).
91. See *Landers*, 915 P.2d at 619.
92. See for example, *Campins*, 461 N.E.2d at 720; *Windeler*, 8 Cal. App. 3d at 852; *Carye* v. *Boca Raton Hotel & Club L.P.*, 676 So.2d 1020, 1021 (Fla. Dist. Ct. App. 1996).
93. See ibid. at 922.
94. See ibid. at 922–924.
95. See ibid. at 924.
96. See *Windeler*, 8 Cal. App. 3d at 852.
97. See *Campins*, 461 N.E.2d at 721. See also *Carye*, 676 So. 2d at 1021.
98. See *Windeler*, 8 Cal. App. 3d at 848–852.
99. See *Campins*, 461 N.E.2d at 714.
100. See ibid. at 719–721.
101. See ibid. at 721.
102. See ibid. at 722.
103. See *Carye*, 676 So. 2d at 1020, 1021.
104. Compare *Carye*, 676 So.2d 1020, with *Windeler*, 8 Cal. App. 3d 844.
105. Compare *Furlan*, 12 N.Y.S.2d 921, with *Windeler*, 8 Cal. App. 3d 844.
106. Compare *Furlan*, 12 N.Y.S.2d 921, with *Campins*, 461 N.E.2d 712.
107. See *Furlan*, 12 N.Y.S.2d 921–924.
108. Compare *Furlan*, 12 N.Y.S.2d 921, with *Campins*, 461 N.E.2d 712.
109. Compare *Furlan*, 12 N.Y.S.2d 921, with *Campins*, 461 N.E.2d 712.
110. The Comprehensive Environmental Response, Compensation and Liability Act (CERCLA) excludes certain types of releases from natural resource damage [43 CFR SEC. 11.24(b)]. Exempt are damages previously identified in an environmental impact statement as irreversible and irretrievable, damages occurring before the enactment of CERCLA, damages resulting from other federally permitted releases, and releases associated with certain pesticide products. In a similar spirit, the Oil Pollution Act of 1990 (OPA) does not apply to discharges allowed under permits issued under federal, state, or local laws [Sec. 1002 (c)(1)], or from vessels owned or charted and operated by a federal, state, local or foreign government agency that is not engaged in commerce [Sec. 1002 (c)(2)].

6. The problem of missing values in normative law and economic analysis

6.1 INTRODUCTION

I have suggested, as a matter of logic and consistency, that all goods must be included in a welfare analysis for which there is a WTP or WTA. The acceptance of axiom 5 – which deals with missing values – would improve the consistency and logic of benefit–cost analysis. It vitiates the most widespread and persistent criticism of normative economic analysis. That criticism is that, even in principle, benefit–cost analysis ignores certain values (Anderson 1993; pp. 194f; Kelman 1981; and Sagoff 1988). Here, the term 'missing values' refers to goods ignored in normative evaluation.[1] I propose to show that missing values are not missing in principle, but have been overlooked in practice. That is, they may be missing from the analyst's discussion or from the critics critique, but are not missing, in principle, as a logical part of benefit–cost analysis, and, by definition, are not missing in KHZ analysis.

Sometimes the missing-values criticism is made explicitly, as when Kelman (1981) and Williams (Smart and Williams 1973, pp. 97–98) complain about the neglect of the value of integrity, or of moral positions, by normative economic analysis. Other complaints focus on undesirable results from normative economic analysis (Parfit 1992). These usually turn out to be, at root, implicit complaints about missing values.[2] For example, some complain about the reduced weight given to future generations as a result of the discounting process in benefit–cost calculations, and conclude that the foundations of analysis must be ethically flawed or, in this particular case, that discounting is ethically flawed (Parfit 1992, 1994). This, I will show, is another case of overlooked values. These instances of overlooked or missing values arise either from an overly narrow commodified or market view of values, or from a failure to consider what I have called the regard for others.[3] Axiom 5 – which deals with missing values – obviates these sources of criticisms.

6.2 MISSING VALUES AND THE MARKET

Market Values

In some cases, the critics of benefit–cost analysis object to what they see as the limitations of market values which are embedded in normative economic analysis; in this view, economics is concerned only with market values. In focusing on market values, normative economic analysis is seen as ignoring values that are not commodified, such as spiritual values or community values. These critics see the economist's attempt to supply a shadow price for some commodity not provided by the market (such as environmental quality or an increase in safety) as an attempt to supply a market price for goods whose value is more than just their market value. The criticism is elegantly expressed by Lumley (1997, p. 72) '[I]f a single discount rate is applied to environmental resources, the implications of non-monetary aspects of those resources are often ignored for these intangible factors are the ends to which money is not a means.' Goods which are not be purchased with money may nevertheless be ranked in monetary terms.

A basic misunderstanding of the critics is a failure to realize that, in the language of benefit–cost analysis, the market is a *metaphor* for a mechanism for determining value. Market values, in the language of the metaphor, need not represent 'mere commodities' but instead represent choices. Choices, of course, exist outside a commodity-type market. The purpose of normative economic analysis is not to monetize values, but rather to provide a ranking of choices expressed in money terms. The distinction is crucial.

For instance, the value that I place on a friendship is not one that I wish determined in a commodity market. When I harm my friend by canceling a lunch appointment at the last minute in order to attend a lecture of particular interest (Sunstein 1997, pp. 73–74),[4] I do not compensate or offer to compensate my friend by offering a sum of money. Yet I might perform other acts – perhaps acts with a monetary value – which are consistent with friendship, to show its value to me. I might offer to drive him when he needs a lift; I might give him a present; I might agree to participate in an activity he enjoys. So when I talk about the value of friendship and its value in the 'market for friendship,' I am merely calling attention to the fact that friendship has a value. More important, in missing the lunch to attend the lecture, I am making a choice, and the role of benefit–cost analysis is to reflect that choice. The value of friendship, in principle, has been neither missed nor undervalued by benefit–cost analysis.

Integrity

Integrity is a particular value that benefit–cost analysis is accused of lacking. For instance, Williams (Smart and Williams, 1973, pp. 97f) considers the case of George:

> George, who has taken his Ph.D. in chemistry, finds it extremely difficult to get a job. An older chemist who knows about the situation says that he can get George a decently paid job in a certain laboratory, which pursues research into chemical and biological warfare. George says that he cannot accept this, because he is opposed to chemical and biological warfare. The older man replies that George's refusal is not going to make the job or the laboratory go away; what is more, he happens to know that if George refuses to take the job, it will certainly go to a contemporary of George's who is not inhibited by any such scruples, and who is likely, if appointed, to push along the research with greater zeal than George would. What should George do?

Williams argues that under a utilitarian analysis, George must accept the job, since it improves the position of his family, and advances the work more slowly (a desirable aim). Similarly, the objection to the use of benefit–cost analysis made by Steven Kelman (1981) is essentially that it rests on utilitarianism, and that utilitarianism requires a sort of expediency in decision making (as in the case of George).

Yet benefit–cost analysis does not rest on utilitarianism of this sort, as Posner (1981a, Chapters 3 and 4) has noted. Normative economic analysis is concerned with ranking states of the world, where values are any that can be expressed by a WTP or a WTA, so that whether or not integrity is included in a utilitarian analysis is neither here nor there, for the conduction of a benefit–cost analysis. In Williams's example, if George (or Williams himself) chooses a world in which George has integrity over one in which he does not, then integrity would have value for a benefit–cost analysis.

Community Values

Both Mark Sagoff (1988) and Elizabeth Anderson (1993) devote a good deal of effort to distinguishing between our preferences as consumers and our choices as citizens. They maintain that benefit–cost analysis treats goods such as health, safety, and environmental quality as mere commodities, and that cost–benefit analysis assumes that the public nature of some instances of these goods is merely a technical fact about them, and not itself a valued quality. The possibility that national parks or public safety might be valued as shared goods does not enter into their evaluations. Anderson sees cost–benefit analysis as assuming that the preferences people express in private consumer choices should be those used in making public choices, as if the valuations people make as consumers exhaust their concerns (Anderson 1993, pp. 193–194).

Anderson and Sagoff assume that benefit–cost analysis measures people's valuations of non-commodity goods only as 'they are privately appropriated, exclusively enjoyed goods' (Anderson 1993, p. 193). For example, Anderson (p. 199) finds that the opportunity to earn a living is 'a need and a responsibility.' She finds, therefore, that using wage premiums for risk as the basis to estimate the cash values people place on their lives is incorrect, since these premiums also reflect the risks people feel obliged to accept in order to discharge their responsibilities. That is, using wage premium data to measure the cost of risk results is a miscalculation, since what is being measured also includes the values of responsibility and duty, which are not included in the wage premium. Sagoff uses child labor laws as an instance in which choices based on narrow, market consequentialist ends, may differ from our choice as citizens. But these views of Anderson and Sagoff are based on their assumption about the 'commodity fetishism of welfare economics: the assumption that people intrinsically care only about exclusively appropriated goods, and that they care about their relationships with others only for their instrumental value in maximizing private consumption' (ibid., p. 203). However true these characterizations of the practice of benefit–cost analysis may be, they fail as criticisms of benefit–cost analysis *in principle*. As a result, these arguments fail because they mischaracterize the goal of economics as a normative tool.

Sagoff and Anderson correctly note the distinction between publicly and privately valued goods. They incorrectly assert that benefit–cost analyses ignore publicly valued goods. This is an incorrect view of what benefit–cost analysis is attempting to capture. Benefit–cost analysis deals with choices, and their associated value cognates. The values relevant for a benefit–cost analysis are precisely those associated with choices, whether these are public preferences, or choices of individuals as citizens, or choices of individuals as mere consumers. The relationship between private and public preferences can be complex. My choice as a consumer to drive to work may fail to reflect my choice as a citizen to tax automobiles and subsidize the bus service. The fact that I do not currently use the bus service may not reflect my willingness to enhance and support it. Similarly, the value I place on preventing child labor need not arise from concern about myself directly, or about my own children, but rather from concern for others, and from my concept of a good society. Such values are relevant to choice and, therefore, to the choice between two worlds that represents the foundation for a benefit–cost framework.[5]

6.3 MISSING VALUES AND THE REGARD FOR OTHERS

The Discount Rate Problem

In benefit–cost analysis, future benefits and costs are discounted, using an interest rate referred to by economists as the discount rate. This rate is traditionally used to reflect the preferences of those affected by a decision. A widespread criticism of the use of the discount rate and, by implication, of benefit–cost analysis, is that the use of a discount rate is unethical (e.g. Parfit 1992, 1994; Schultze *et al.* 1981). The use of a discount rate is held to be unethical because it discounts the benefits to be gained and the costs to be borne by future generations. It is said that utility of future generations should count equally with the utility of the present generation (Schultze *et al.* 1981; Pearce and Turner 1989). For example, Parfit (1992, p. 86) argues that 'the moral importance of future events does not decline at *n* % per year.' This sort of criticism has been noted by economists (for example Pearce and Turner 1989; Pearce, Markandya and Barbier 1989), lawyers (Plater *et al.* 1998, pp. 107–109), and philosophers (Parfit 1992, 1994). Morrison (1998) while arguing against zero discount rates, fails to correctly account for morality.

Consider the following example of the sort of problem with which these critics are concerned:

> A project is being considered that produces substantial benefits of about 20 billion, at a cost of about 10 billion but, in addition, produces a toxic time-bomb that will cause enormous environmental costs sometime in the far future.[6] (I remove questions of uncertainty from this example.) Suppose that current waste-disposal technology will contain this waste for 500 years but that the material will remain toxic for 10,000 years. Sometime in about 500 years from now the waste will escape its sarcophagus. The estimated cost of the future environmental damage in constant, year 2000 dollars will be about $8 trillion, about the size of the current US GDP. The present value of these damages discounted at a 3 percent real social rate of time preference (SRTP), assuming the waste escapes at the first opportunity 500 years from now, is about 3 million dollars, not insignificant, but far far less than the damage that will occur in 500 years and far too small to affect the results of the benefit–cost analysis. Discounting these damages then results in the project going forward. The benefits exceed the cost by 10 billion and it is said that the project is then justified by benefit–cost analysis but that the justification leads to a bad result so that benefit–cost analysis is deficient. This siting it is said would nevertheless be unfair to future generations and on this basis it is argued that the use of the discount rate is inappropriate or unfair or unethical.

A commonly proposed solution is to argue that lower, or possibly zero (or even negative), discount rates should be used, as they can avoid such time-bomb results (for example Schultze *et al.* 1981). Another suggested solution is to not use discount rates at all (Parfit 1994). This sort of argument is, I believe, a moral plea about what our sentiments should be towards future generations, but not an effective statement about what discount rate should be used. However, the reasoning used to conclude that use of discount rates is immoral is not wholly coherent. The proposed solution is ad hoc and, if generally applied, will lead to other ethical problems – for example, the adoption of projects that give fewer benefits to both present and future generations.

To arrive at a correct approach, we must consider why we find the result in the nuclear plant example unacceptable. To argue that the proposed project is unethical is to call attention to a harm that was not previously identified. This argument for unacceptability, which is the benefit–cost argument, is not based on the preferences of future generations, which we cannot know exactly, but on our own preferences, based on our empathy with future generations. There are, then, missing values, and the missing values are our own, in the form of our regard for others.

A solution (Lesser and Zerbe 1995) is inherent in the criteria for KHZ that were developed in Chapter 2 of this book. What is missing from the traditional analysis is our *regard for others*. The current generation will have a WTP or a WTA to prevent this unfair result. The missing values can be expressed in terms of the willingness to accept (or pay) and are, therefore, a required part of a KHZ analysis.

In the above example, what the use of the discount rate is telling us is that we might invest less than a penny today, and create sufficient wealth to compensate all harm inflicted 500 years from now. If we were to invest the $10 billion benefits today, the net wealth creation in 500 years would be about $\$2.62 \times 10^{16}$, or about 3200 times the current US GDP. The proposed project could, at the insignificant cost of less than a penny, generate sufficient revenue to fully compensate for future damages, and, if the net benefits are fully invested, will produce a truly stupendous payoff 500 years later for people then living (of course, the mechanisms to achieve compensation may not exist, and I will address this issue later). So, we will say that the use of the discount rate is appropriate, insofar as it furnishes present generations with useful information.

However, the members of the present generation may have an expectation that future generations should be free of problems caused by the current generation. An unfair result is a loss to those who expect fairness and care about unfairness. Thus, in a caring society, harm to future generations would be a loss to the present generation, and the WTA would be the correct measure of value. Evidence from Kunreuther and Easterling (1992, p. 255) and from Svenson and Karlsson (1989) suggests that, at least as regards nuclear waste disposal, individuals tend to not discount its future consequences.

KHZ departs from KH with respect to the issue of whether or not future generations will, in fact, be compensated. For KH, only potential compensation is considered. All that the traditional benefit–cost analysis shows is that the future generations could, in principle, be more than compensated. They may, of course, not be actually compensated.

By KHZ's standards, however, and in particular by the missing values axiom, a project in which future generations are compensated is different from one in which they are not. KHZ then requires that we consider two projects, one in which future generations are not compensated and one in which they are. The WTA of present individuals could be quite different for the two projects. For the non-compensated project, the WTA of some present individuals might well be infinite, on ethical grounds. If, however, future generations are to be fully compensated, the present generations might conclude that they have no ethical loss.

Suppose, nevertheless, that present individuals care little about fairness or unethical outcomes – their WTA is small so that, as a result, the non-compensated project passes the benefit–cost test. One can view this as an unethical result, but the result arises not from the use of the discount rate but from the sentiments of society. The task of the critic of using discount rates is to reform the sentiments of society, not to suggest that using the discount rate is improper.

Table 6.1 shows the KHZ solution to the discount rate problem. When people care about the future their choice is between a project with compensation and one without. In this case, the project with compensation has a net present value of $997 million. The project without compensation has a negative net present value. When people care about future generations, the project with compensation is superior ethically and in benefit–cost terms to the project without compensation. When people do not care about others, the project without compensation is superior, in benefit–cost terms. The moral issue, however, is not the discount rate, but rather what people care about.

There are a number of often elegant approaches to calculating future value that involve manipulation of the discount rate. These are often suggested in connection with protecting current environmental assets for future generations (Heal 1998; Chichilnisky 1997). Yet, all of these admirable suggestions are attempts to incorporate the sentiments of their authors into a discount rate approach. KHZ suggest that this is not the way to go about incorporating ethical concerns. Ethical concerns about future consequences can be treated by giving value to these ethical concerns, rather than by adjusting the discount rate.

Of course, it may be that a general compensation to future generations is insufficient to satisfy present moral sentiments. What could be required might be compensation of the specific individuals harmed. As Robert Lind (1999,

Table 6.1 The discount rate problem resolved

	Where people care about the ethics of harming future generations		**Where people do not care about the ethics of harming future generations**	
	The project **with** compensation (billions)	The project **without** compensation (billions)	The project **with** compensation (billions)	The project **without** compensation (billions)
Present value of benefits	$20	$20	$20	$20
Present value of ordinary costs	$10	$10	$10	$10
Present value of harm to future generations	$0	$0.003 billion	$0	$0.003
Present value required to compensate future generations	$0.003	$0	$0.003	$0
Present value of ethical harm to present generation	0	A large number – probably infinite	0	0.003 (standing) 0.00 (no standing)
Net present value (billions)	**$9.997**	**Negative**	**$9.997**	**$9.997 (standing) $10.000 (no standing)**

p. 175) points out, designing and implementing such intergenerational transfers is virtually impossible. It may, then, be impossible to ensure that the future individuals who are harmed will be compensated. In this case, the project may be inefficient, since people care about compensation, but such compensation is impossible (see Table 6.1). The major cost is to the present generation, and lies in their aversion to the unfairness that would be imposed on the future generation. Although the project would be inefficient, the discount rate used to evaluate it would not change. Similarly other projects might fail the KHZ efficiency test because compensation might not be possible, as for instance in the case of possible destruction of an unique environmental good.

The solution to the ethical dilemma of the discount rate problem is, then, to acknowledge ethical concerns as ethical concerns, and seek an ethical solution, while acknowledging the values that commend use of a discount rate. For to not use the discount rate is simply to ignore a fact arising from the productive aspect of nature. To use a discount rate that is below the rate at which people will trade off present for future consumption, that is, a rate of time preference, will lead to economic inefficiency, by justifying investment with insufficient returns. To use a rate that is too low attempts to cope with inequity by adjusting prices. The result is that an inequity appears to be an inefficiency.

6.4 INCOME DISTRIBUTION

No criticism of the KH criteria has been more widespread than the one that the KH criteria neglect distributional effects. Little (1957 [1950]) pointed out that all criteria – whether KH or not – rest on value judgments; they are inescapable in normative economics. The important thing is to make the judgments clear. Little proposed that in addition to the hypothetical compensation test there also be a distributional test. Thus, a movement from A to B is desirable if (1) it passes a compensation test, and (2) B is distributionally superior to position A. He did not, however, suggest what the distribution test might be. Earlier, before the advent of the KH test, Pigou (1932) had suggested a dual test, and had proposed that greater equality in income was a good thing. Under Pigou's test a new position was better than an old if, for an unchanged allocative efficiency, it showed an increase in the equality of distribution. Little's work ushered in an outpouring of literature about the use of distributional tests as a tool for judging economic policy.

In the modern era, the views of the former Solicitor General of the United States, Charles Fried (1978, pp. 93f) are representative. He sees the economic analysis of rights as using a concept of efficiency that is removed from distributional questions. He holds that economic analysis does not consider whether the distribution is fair or just. He then concludes from this that the fact that a given outcome is efficient does not give it 'any privileged claim to our approbation' (1978, p. 94). The view that efficiency is unconcerned with distributional issues, or with fairness, is widespread in both law and economics (for example Posner 1984); however, it is based on practice, and not on logic.

The desire to separate distribution from efficiency arises from a misunderstanding and is inconsistent by definition with the KHZ criteria. Thus, this potent criticism of KH does not apply to KHZ, and, to this extent, it increases the acceptability and usefulness of KHZ.

Is Efficiency Equitable?

The basic problem, as Hammond (1985, p. 427) notes, is the difficulty of determining 'what constitutes a good distribution of income.' But benefit–cost analysis has an answer to that problem. A good distribution of income is that distribution which people are willing to purchase, in benefit–cost terms. It is true that the KH criteria is applied as if every dollar be weighted the same (in utility terms) regardless of who receives it, *by the person who receives it.* Yet the KH criteria implicitly, and the KHZ criteria explicitly, do not require that each dollar received by one person *be weighted the same by other people*. The KHZ criteria require that the valuations *others* place on a change in income for others be included, since the distribution is itself one of the goods being valued. The regard of some for the social welfare of others is well established, according to Fay Cook and Edith Barrett (1992). Posner (1987a, p. 23) speaks about the problem in which 'if the initial allocation is thought to be unjust, the change, while increasing the wealth of society, may actually be carrying it further away from the just allocation.' If we care about justice, however, the change is, in fact, not KH efficient, unless the gain in other forms of wealth is sufficient to offset the loss from a less equitable income distribution.[7]

Treating Income Distribution as Another Good: Income Distribution in General

Under KHZ, income distribution is to be considered as just another good (Appendix 6A shows this formally). In speaking of income distribution, I speak in three senses. First, there is the matter of the general distribution of income, in which the identity of the people does not matter. Second, there is income distribution in which the characteristics (aside from income) of the people matter (non-characteristic autonomy). Third, there is specific compensation, in which the names or identities of individuals matter (no autonomy).

Here, I am not concerned with income distribution in general, but with the distributional effects of particular projects. First Harberger (1978), and then Zerbe (1991, pp. 102–103), suggested an approach for determining the value of income distributional effects of a project. Table 6.2 shows an application of the Harberger approach. We assume that there are 100 rich, 100 middle income, and 100 poor people in a society. All are affected directly by a proposed project. Suppose that figures are in thousands of dollars. The example shown in Table 6.2 summarizes the gains and losses from the project, in which the rich gain \$50, the middle income gain \$5, and the poor lose \$30 directly. The gains and the losses show the results of the project, without taking into account the regard of others. Without consideration of the regard for others, the project appears to be KH efficient. The table then shows the results of applying the KH or wealth-maximization criteria.

Table 6.2 Traditional KH efficiency: No consideration for others (in thousands of dollars)

	Gains	Losses	Net benefits
Rich	\$100	\$50	\$50
Middle income	\$60	\$55	\$5
Poor	\$30	\$60	–\$30
Total	\$190	\$165	\$25

But, the gains and losses of Table 6.2 do not take into account the WTP or WTA for a change in income distribution. It is, for example, not enough to claim that a policy that puts an incinerator in the poorest neighborhood is efficient since those harmed *could* hypothetically be compensated for by some other efficient alternative means, if other people care about income distribution.

Now suppose that others are willing to pay to avoid changes to income distribution in which the poor in general suffer absolute losses. Harberger (1978) and Zerbe (1991, pp. 102–103) point out that the WTP is limited by the cost of compensating the poor in general by the most efficient alternative means. That is, the amount one would pay for a good is limited by the price of a substitute. The substitute in this case is the cost of achieving a similar distributional result by the most efficient alternative means. We will call this value the distributional benefit, and it may be positive in the case of a transfer that benefits the poor, or negative in the case of a project in which the poor lose. I assume, following Harberger, that the transfer costs amount to 20 percent of the amount transferred. If the poor were fully compensated, then, by

Table 6.3 KHZ efficiency: Regard for income distribution

	Gains	Losses	Net benefits
Rich	$100	$50	$50
Middle	$60	$55	$5
Poor	$30	$60	–$30
Distributional benefit (the regard for others)			–6
Total	$190	$165	$19

the most efficient means available, the $30 in required compensation would cost 20 percent of their $30 loss, or $6. The results are shown in Table 6.3. The project with compensation yields net benefits of $19. Although the project has negative distributional consequences, and although we have included the value of a more equitable income distribution in the project analysis, the project remains efficient because of the net wealth it creates.

The Regard for Others and the Compensation of Particular People: Horizontal Equity

Table 6.4 shows the evaluation when others care about changes in income distribution. What is generally more appropriate and important for the analysis of a particular project is the question of justice for those harmed. That is – the question of particular compensation for those who lose from the project (Michelman 1967). Table 6.3 does not account for the regard for others with respect to the particular compensation of those harmed. This is a matter of horizontal equity. In some cases, others will care about the compensation of the particular people who would be harmed by the project if they are not compensated.[8] The fact that others do care is illustrated by the large and expanding literature on environmental justice.

In these sorts of cases, to redistribute income to the general class of poorer people other than those affected by the incinerator may not be a good substitute for compensating the particular people who are being harmed. Where this is the case, the WTP for compensation is not limited by the cost of the most effective means of compensating the poor. Rather, the WTP for the particular compensation must be taken into account.

Suppose that each of the rich people is willing to pay $.005 for each $1 of compensation needed in order to fully compensate the poor who are harmed in this project. Each of the middle-income persons is similarly willing to pay $.001 cent for each $1 of compensation provided to the poor. In this example,

Table 6.4 KHZ efficiency when losses to particular people are taken into account

	Gains	Losses	Compensation loss	Net benefit
Rich	$100	–$50	–$15	$35
Middle income	$60	–$55	–$3	$2
Poor	$30	–$60	$0	–$30
Total	$190	–$165	–$18	$7

if compensation is not carried out, there are losses to others. Table 6.4 incorporates these losses, assuming that compensation is not provided. The net benefit of the project is, then, not $25, as was the case when no account was given to the regard for others, but much less: $7.

But this same project appears very different if compensation is actually provided. The net benefit must, however, take into account the administrative costs of the compensation. Suppose that these are 20 percent of the amount of compensation, or $6, and that this cost is borne by the rich and by the middle-income group at the ratio of 2 to 1. The result is shown in Table 6.5. Despite the substantial administrative costs, net benefits are now higher than was the case shown in Table 6.4.

Table 6.5 KHZ where others value compensation and compensation is given

	Gains	Losses	Transfer	Cost of compensation	Net benefit
Rich	$100	–$50	–$20	–$4	$26
Middle income	$60	–$55	–$10	–$2	–$7
Poor	$30	–$60	$30	0	0
Total	$190	–$165	0	–$6	$19

Clearly, where the net benefits from compensation to others exceed the administrative costs of compensation, compensation is efficient.

6.5 WHEN SHOULD DISTRIBUTIONAL EFFECTS BE IGNORED?

The general rule is that distributional effects should be considered when the (probable) benefits from doing so exceed the (probable) costs. Otherwise, they should be ignored. This rule does not, however, necessarily lead one to ignore distributional effects, as some writers have maintained. In the case of the incinerator, net benefits increased from $7 when no compensation was given to $19 when compensation was given.

Posner (1992b, pp. 461–463) concludes that there is no reason to suppose that policies designed to move society closer to equality will increase economic welfare.[9] Posner's analysis is, however, based on the assumption that to say anything about distributional considerations requires the assumptions of differences in the marginal utility of income among income classes. He points out that he does not wish to make assumptions about the marginal utility of income among income groups, so he cannot say that a policy of redistributing from one group to another increases total utility.

We have seen, however, that it is not necessary to make assumptions about differences in the marginal utility of money in order to address questions of income distribution. The KH or KHZ criteria, of course, assume there are no differences in the marginal utility of money; yet, by incorporating the regard for others, they require a consideration of distributional and compensatory effects.[10] Posner fails to realize that the KH or wealth-maximization tests can be applied to distributional considerations, on the same basis as for any other good. The issue for economic efficiency, then, is not whether total utility increases – something which is unknowable in any event – but rather whether or not a distributional change passes a compensation test.

More practically, Mitchell A. Polinsky (1983) has pointed out that tax and welfare programs are typically the cheapest way to redistribute wealth. On this basis, he argues that KH efficiency considerations should shape ordinary legal doctrine, such as tort and contract law, and should govern benefit–cost analysis. Notwithstanding widespread approbation of this sentiment,[11] as a general guide it is incorrect. In the evaluation of a project with distributional implications, the existence of alternative and less expensive redistributive methods does not mean that distributional effects should not be considered. Rather, Polinsky's observation affects the way in which the effects are valued (Zerbe 1991, pp. 102–103). The value of the redistributive effects cannot be greater than the costs of achieving them by the most efficient alternative method. The existence of cheap alternative methods of achieving redistribution will limit the size of the potential benefits to be gained. In some cases, however, actual compensation may have special value as shown in the discussion accompanying Table 6.5. Here, there are net benefits from actual compensation. In these cases, Polinsky's observation is no guide at all.

6.6 AN APPLICATION TO TAX POLICY

It is a well-known proposition of welfare economics that a tax should be levied so as to least distort the individuals' choices. This means that the efficient tax is one in which choices cannot affect the magnitude of the tax. Thus, a lump-sum tax, in which every person pays the same amount regardless of his or her actions, is judged the efficient tax. Similarly, a tax on a good that is in relatively inelastic demand is superior to a tax on a more elastic good, since the excess burden of the tax on the more inelastic good will be greater.

One of Margaret Thatcher's most hated actions was the enactment near the end of her term of a lump-sum tax, on the recommendation of her economic advisor. Insulin is a good that is in inelastic demand, as are body parts for transplant operations. However, taxes on such goods would likely be seen as unfair, so that the suggestion that it would be efficient to levy a tax on them may be incorrect, because of the regard for others.

Thus, the KH efficient tax will sometimes be at variance with the best tax. Once it is recognized, however, that the distributional effects of the tax are to be incorporated into the considerations of efficiency, then the paradox of apparently efficient but unwise tax policy is resolved. On the basis of KHZ no one would recommend as efficient a lump-sum tax nor a tax on insulin or on transplants.

6.7 FAIRNESS AND THE REGARD FOR OTHERS

Happyville

Paul Portney (1992, pp.131–132) posed the following problem:

> You have a problem. You are Director of Environmental Protection in Happyville, a community of 1,000 adults. The drinking water supply in Happyville is contaminated by a naturally occurring substance that each and every resident believes may be responsible for the above-average cancer rate observed there. So concerned are they, that they insist you put in place a very expensive treatment system to remove the contaminant. Moreover, you know for a fact that each and every resident is truly willing to pay $1,000 each year for the removal of the contaminant.
>
> The problem is this. You have asked the top ten risk assessors in the world to test the contaminant for carcinogenicity. To a person, these risk assessors –

including several who work for the activist group, Campaign Against Environmental Cancer – find that the substance tests negative for carcinogenicity, even at much higher doses than those received by the residents of Happyville. These ten risk assessors tell you that, while one could never prove that the substance is harmless, they would each stake their professional reputations on the substance being harmless. You have repeatedly and skillfully communicated this to the Happyville citizenry, but because of a deep-seated skepticism of all government officials, they remain completely unconvinced and truly frightened – still willing, that is, to fork over $1,000 per person per year for water purification.

First, what are the annual benefits of removing the contaminant from the Happyville drinking water system? Second, suppose that: (1) the contaminant was not naturally occurring, but rather the result of industrial contamination; (2) our estimate of $1,000 per person for annual willingness to pay for purification was based on a state-of-the-art contingent valuation study; and (3) a lawsuit had been brought against the source of contamination. If the answer to your first question was $1,000,000 in annual benefits, would you be willing to support a judgment of $1,000,000 in annual damages against that source?

The analysis of this problem cannot be properly be separated from issues of distributive justice. Few would object if the people of Happyville pay, perhaps foolishly, to remove the offending substance. They will feel differently if they themselves have to pay, and they will feel differently about paying for a project they regard as foolish or wasteful than they would about paying for a project they thought made good use of resources. Thus, the benefit–cost analyst could suggest that if non-residents of Happyville are required to pay for treating the drinking water for Happyville, they are apt to suffer special losses, to the extent to which they believe their money is going for an irrational or wasteful cause. If our tax money is being spent foolishly, we suffer a larger loss, since, in addition to the taxes we pay, we have a sense of waste.

For example, Douglas Easterling (1992, p. 442), in a nice piece of work, has shown that opposition to local placement of storage facilities for high-level nuclear waste is less when residents believe that the site chosen is the safest site. A project that imposes a harm may be felt differently and may generate different WTA measures of loss when it is felt that the process of choice is fair and that the outcome is the most efficient. Similarly, Cook and Barrett (1992, p. 93) show that the effectiveness of welfare programs helps explain the level of public support for them.

> Groups defined on the basis of age, color, income, or sex show the same pattern of support (though not the same level of support) on the basis of how appropriate the program is thought to be for the problem addressed and the deservedness of recipients.

Returning to the problem of Happyville, we – as non-residents of Happyville – are unlikely to object if the residents of Happyville spend only their own money. Those who pay are likely to feel different about the project if they believe it to be efficient rather than inefficient. The problem of Happyville as given is incomplete, because the issue of who pays is not addressed. People will care about who pays, as well as how much is paid.[12]

6.8 MICHELMAN AND MISSING DEMORALIZATION COSTS

Related issues arise in Frank Michelman's (1967) treatment of whether government action should be a government taking of property and therefore subject to compensation. He considers *efficiency gains* separate from *demoralization costs* and from *settlement costs*. Michelman defines efficiency gains as

> the excess of benefits produced by a [government's) measure over losses inflicted by it, where the benefits are measured by the total number of dollars which prospective gainers would be willing to pay to secure adoption, and losses are measured by the total number of dollars which prospective losers would insist on as the price of agreeing to adoption. (1967, p. 1214)

He defines demoralization costs as

> the total of (1) the dollar value necessary to offset disutilities which accrue to losers and their sympathizers specifically from the realization that no compensation is offered, and (2) the present capitalized dollar value of lost future production (reflecting either impaired incentives or social unrest) caused by demoralization of uncompensated losers, their sympathizers, and other observers disturbed by the thought that they themselves may be subject to similar treatment on some other occasion. (1967, p. 1214)

And settlement costs are

> the dollar value of time, effort, and resources which would be required in order to reach compensation settlements adequate to avoid demoralization costs. Included are the costs of settling not only the particular compensation claims presented but also those of all persons not obviously distinguishable by the available settlement apparatus. (1967, p. 1214)

Michelman (1967) labels as B the benefits of a government action, and as C the costs of the action, where B and C are part of efficiency gains. Both types of gains are measured by the WTP and the WTA the government action, not counting demoralization and settlement costs. A utilitarian could do a project only if $(B–C) > \min(D,S)$. That is, a project is worthwhile only if the net efficiency benefits exceed the lesser of demoralization and settlement costs. For a worthwhile project, compensation should be made if settlement costs are lower than demoralization costs. But if settlement costs are higher than demoralization costs, then no compensation should be paid. That is, compensate if $D > S$; otherwise, do not compensate.

William Fischel (1996, p. 147) argues that Michelman's analysis introduces value considerations broader than those of KH. He notes that 'Michelman's standard is however, less permissive than the KH criteria, which says simply that the government should do projects if the gainers can compensate the losers but does not require that it actually make the compensation.' Fischel is arguably incorrect in his characterization of the KH standard as excluding certain goods; but, clearly, KHZ does not exclude these goods, though Fischel is certainly correct when he says that economists usually do not consider demoralization costs.

Michelman (1967) introduces projects that can be defined between two states as differences in terms of WTP or WTA. These states, then, I argue, are goods that economists consider, or logically ought to consider, as part of the application of KH criteria. They are, by definition, to be included in KHZ analysis. The point is that the context in which a prospect is offered will affect its valuation. A watch that is stolen may be regarded differently from a watch that is lost, as Fischel (1996, p. 145) notes: 'The watch is gone in both cases, but the very knowledge that it was stolen may make you feel worse.'

What both Michelman and Fischel are correctly pointing out is that a project with compensation is different from one without it. It is a different project, so it is not surprising that it involves different costs and benefits. Expected benefits are also closely related to distributional context.

If compensation is not to be given, a project is KH acceptable if $B > C + D$. If compensation is proposed, the test is now $B > (C + S)$. D and S are simply costs to be entered into the cost side of the equation. Thus, the existence of D and S suggests, where compensation is considered, that there are two different projects, one with and one without compensation.[13]

6.9 A CHRISTMAS CAROL: THE EFFICIENCY GAIN FROM CHRISTMAS GIVING

In Chapter 3 we considered an analysis of Christmas giving as an example of the misapplication of the concept of economic efficiency as it calculated economic waste (deadweight loss) without suggesting that there existed any superior alternative to Christmas giving (Waldfogel 1993, p. 1328). But the analysis of Christmas giving is deficient in another aspect. It calculates inefficiency while leaving out economic values. As I mentioned in Chapter 3, Waldfogel suggests (p. 1328) that gift-giving may, in general, create inefficiency ('a deadweight loss') because 'the gifts may be mismatched with the recipients' preferences.'

He estimates (p. 1328) that 'holiday gift-giving destroys between 10% and a third of the value of gifts.' In determining value, Waldfogel and others (Solnick and Hemenway 1996; List and Shogren 1988) asked the subjects of the survey to exclude 'the sentimental value' of the gift when estimating how much they would be willing to pay and willing to accept for the gifts. The material value is the value of a good aside from its sentimental value.

Sentimental Value as a Missing Value

However, there is no reason to separate sentimental value from material value when one calculates deadweight efficiency effects.[14] Because Waldfogel (1993) arbitrarily ignores part of the value of production or consumption, his work cannot be used to make a general statement about efficiency loss. The point of measuring deadweight losses is to be able to say something about policy – for example to suggest more efficient policy and how to reduce waste. Indeed, the really interesting finding in the surveys of Waldfogel (1993) and others is that substantial sentimental value exists.

In Waldfogel's (1993) work, the yield of the gift is the ratio of the material value placed on the gift by its recipient to its cost, as estimated by the recipient. If the yield is greater than 1, the gift giving is said to be efficient. If equal to one, it is said to be neutral. If fractional it is estimated to be inefficient and the gift is said to incur a deadweight loss.

Waldfogel finds that gift-giving results in a fractional yield. Solnick and Hemenway (1996) and List and Shogren (1988), however, provide estimates that suggest greater than one yields, so that Christmas gift-giving results instead in a gain in material value. In all cases, however, the authors attempt to separate the sentimental value of the gift from its material value, by asking questionnaire respondents to separate these two values.[15]

Although Waldfogel asks the survey recipients to exclude 'sentimental value' in calculating the value of their gifts, he does not define sentimental value for them, nor does he define it in his article. Solnick and Hemenway (1996) or List and Shogren (1988) also fail to define sentimental value. What is sentimental value? I will say that sentimental value arises primarily from the thoughtfulness of the gift. I elicited comments about its content and context in discussions with colleagues.[16] Their remarks are shown in quotes below. In general, sentimental value appears to be created because the gift makes one feel valued.[17] 'A gift that was thoughtful and uniquely personal would be most likely to have sentimental value.' 'One might find a gift thoughtful because of the memory it evokes. One might care for a gift because one recognizes the thought that went into the gift even if the gift had little material value to the recipient.' 'I would care a good deal about a gift of a lump of dirt from Lake Ann, where my husband proposed to me.' One might care for a gift beyond (though perhaps related to) its material cost because it confers a sense of status on the recipient. 'I have a sentimental value for any (non-cash) gift that one gives me as it shows someone cares about me. One might care for a gift just because it was unexpected.' Sometimes a gift might have sentimental value in itself. 'I received a family heirloom whose value to me is very far above its value in the market place.'

Similarly, one might return a gift without losing its sentimental value. 'The fact that I return and exchange a gift does not mean it has no sentimental value. I was given a sweater the wrong size and exchanged it for an identical one of the same size, but the gift retained its sentimental value. Even if I exchange a gift for a completely different sort of gift, that does not mean receiving the gift has no sentimental value. I look at this exchange as the same sort as exchanging the sweater for one of the right size. Yet, if I were given cash, this would have no sentimental value and the sentimental value from the sweater would not have been realized.' Yet even cash may have sentimental value, if it reflects a particular thoughtfulness on the part of the giver. 'If cash was what I most needed, a gift of cash that recognized my need would have sentimental value if I felt it was a thoughtful recognition of my need. Yet, aside from this case, cash would almost never create sentimental value for me.'

In addition to sentimental value created for the recipient, sentimental value may be created for the giver. After all, the giver is the decision maker in the transaction. 'I gave my husband a framed picture from a happy time together and this gift meant a great deal to both of us.'

In addition, gift-giving often has a value that reflects a moral or social value (Cheal 1988; Landa 1994; Titmuss 1971). The Northwest Coast Native American Potlatch comes to mind. Aristotle defines friendship as a relationship arising out of duty, gratitude, love, care, or just common interest, and gift-giving relates to all of these values. Giving may reaffirm and strengthen a relationship and enhance social stability. For instance, in a hierarchical society, gifts may be finely graded to reflect the recipients' positions in the hierarchy. And, insofar as gifts help to forge a culture or a community, they may lower costs for the larger society, so that their value goes beyond the individuals in the exchange (Landa 1994).

The welfare comparisons of gifts or grants of goods rather than of money generally conclude that the gift of a good is inefficient because a gift of money always creates a wider range of choice (third party effects aside). Thus, the argument goes, a gift of money will result in the recipient's attaining a welfare position as high as and possibly higher than would the gift of the good. The welfare position will be higher for the money grant in the case where one desires less of the good than one was given. If non-cash gifts are more likely to have sentimental value than cash gifts, then this traditional welfare conclusion no longer holds.

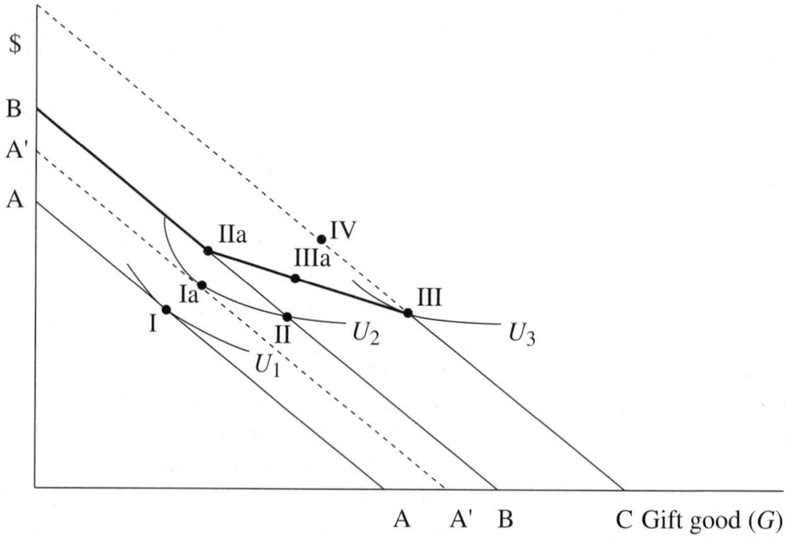

Figure 6.1

In Figure 6.1 the amount of the gift good (*G*) being given to the recipient is shown on the horizontal axis, and the recipient's money is shown on the vertical axis. *G* could represent the number or amount of any one type of gift, whether it is roses or luxury sedans, so long as it is consistently used to measure one type of gift. In order to focus on sentimental value, I assume for purposes of this analysis that Waldfogel (1993) is correct and that the material yield is fractional. Point I on budget line AA shows the equilibrium amount of the good and income prior to receiving the gift good. Suppose the recipient now receives an additional amount, AB, of the gift good. The consumer moves to U_2 at II. The budget line BB runs through the new allocation of the good at II, but since the consumer is on U_2 below BB, there is a fractional yield. The loss as compared with receiving cash is then BA. But if an amount of money equal to the cost of the gift were given to the consumer, he or she would be able to purchase less of the gift good by moving northwest along the budget line to achieve a higher equilibrium welfare position at say IIa. Similarly, if the consumer could sell the gift good, he or she could move to this same higher equilibrium IIa, except for the loss created by transactions costs.

Suppose, however, that the gift has sentimental value. This is a value that is not redeemable in cash; it cannot be realized by selling the gift. It can, however, be measured in terms of a quality-enhancing attribute for the recipient of the good. For instance, the sentimental value of the gift good places the person at, say, III. At III the person has the same money income and the same material amount of the good as at II, but has a larger total amount of gift good than at I or II because sentimental value is included (the slope of the budget line CC that goes through III reflects the market price of the good).

I call the yield based on material value plus sentimental value the total yield. If the material good cannot be sold, then III is the equilibrium. At this point the total yield may be either greater than 1 or fractional, depending on the marginal rate of substitution (MRS) for the good. If the recipient could sell the good without destroying its sentimental value, he or she could achieve a higher level of welfare by moving northwest along the budget line CC to some point such as IV. At IV the total yield is greater than 1, because IV must lie above IIa (by CB), since the material value is the same at IV and IIa but point IV contains sentimental value in addition to material value.

Selling the good may, however, destroy its sentimental value. Consider three possibilities. If selling any amount of the material good destroys all of its sentimental value, then positions III or IIa are the possible equilibria depending on the marginal rate of substitution (MRS) for the good. With a higher MRS for the gift good, the equilibrium will be at III and the yield will be greater than 1. With a sufficiently low MRS, U_3 can lie below IIa so that IIa is the equilibrium. If none of the sentimental value is destroyed until the last unit of the good is sold, then the seller will move from III toward IV, but just before reaching IV the budget line would drop to BB. The equilibrium would lie between III and IV, and the total yield would be greater than 1. In an extreme case with a sufficiently low MRS for the good, all of the gift could be sold and equilibrium could be at IIa with a neutral yield. Finally, we might posit a linear relationship between the loss of sentimental value and the amount of the material good sold. In this case, the relevant budget line is the heavier line, BIIa III IIIa C. Equilibrium can occur anywhere along this from III to IIa depending on the MRS, with a greater than 1 total yield, unless the equilibrium is at IIa, in which case the yield is neutral.

The conclusions, then, are: (1) if the material good cannot be sold, the total yield may be greater than 1 or fractional depending on the MRS for the good; (2) if the good cannot be sold, the existence of sentimental value will reduce the chance of a fractional total yield; (3) if the material good can be sold, the yield will be greater than 1 or neutral, transaction costs aside; (4) if the material good can be sold and there is no loss of sentimental value, there is a greater than 1 total yield; and (5) if the good can be sold but there is some loss of sentimental value, the yield will be greater than 1 or neutral.

A survey

To test the existence and importance of sentimental value in holiday gift-giving, a contingent-value questionnaire, consisting of twelve questions, was

Table 6.6 The importance of sentimental value

Question	Mean response/ proportion yes	95% confidence interval
Sentimental value is determined by the thoughtfulness of the gift. (7 = Strongly agree; 1 = Strongly disagree)	4.500	4.155 – 4.845 *N* = 126
Sentimental value is determined by who gives the gift. (7 = Strongly agree; 1 = Strongly disagree)	4.794	4.454 – 5.133 *N* = 126
Sentimental value is determined by memories the gift evokes. (7 = Strongly agree; 1 = Strongly disagree)	4.810	4.495 – 5.125 *N* = 126
Did any of the gifts you received have sentimental value? (Yes or No)	91.35%	87.53% – 95.17% *N* = 208
What percentage of the gifts had sentimental value? (Percentage)	23.33%	19.00% – 27.66% *N* = 171
Would a gift of cash have had sentimental value? (Yes or No)	23.14%	14.23% – 32.05% *N* = 121
Would a gift of cash you received as a gift be as likely as a non-cash gift to have sentimental value? (Yes or No)	2.63%	0.00% – 11.81% *N* = 114
Would a gift certificate be as likely as non-cash, non-gift certificate to have sentimentalvalue? (Yes or No)	36.11%	27.05% – 45.17% *N* = 118
Sometimes a gift giver asks us what we want. Sometimes the giver surprises us with the choice of gift. Do you value the surprise factor in receiving a gift, holding constant the overall quality of the gift in your eyes? (Yes or No)	99.12%	89.94% – 100% *N* = 114

Table 6.6 continued

Question	Mean response/ proportion yes	95% confidence interval
If a gift had sentimental value, would the sentimental value increase your reluctance to part with the gift? (Yes or No)	100.00%	91.05% – 100% $N = 120$
By how much would sentimental value raise your selling price as a percentage of the value of the estimated cost of the gift? (Percentage)	40.84%	31.51% – 50.17% $N = 102$
Did any of the gifts you gave have sentimental value to you the giver? (Yes or No)	70.14%	63.97% – 76.32% $N = 211$
Did the existence of sentimental value increase the pleasure you had in giving gifts? (Yes or No)	99.37%	91.60% – 100% $N = 159$
Did the existence of sentimental value increase the amount you would have paid for the gifts? (Yes or No)	86.79%	79.02% – 94.56% $N = 159$
By what percentage of the estimated costs did the existence of sentimental value increase the amount you would have paid? (Percentage)	59.07%	51.53% – 66.61% $N = 124$

given to graduate students from two different departments at the University of Washington. The results are shown in Table 6.6.

The survey supports the claims made that gifts can have sentimental value to the recipient,[18] the new claim that they can have sentimental value to the giver also, that this value can raise the price the giver is willing to pay or the price at which the recipient is willing to sell and, importantly for my purposes, that gifts of cash do not generally carry sentimental value and that gift certificates are less likely than non-cash gifts to carry sentimental value.

Waldfogel's results suggest that gift-giving may destroy about 13 percent of the material value of the gift if the WTA measure is used.[19] His estimate of material yield of 87 percent means that a gift that costs $100 is worth only $87 to the recipient, not including sentimental value.[20] The survey suggests about 23 percent of gifts received had sentimental value. If we apply this percentage also to gifts given, and assume that on the average gifts with sentimental value cost the same as the average gift, then the total value of gift giving is 109 percent of material value, accepting Waldfogel's 87 percent figure for material yield for gifts received. If material yield is 100 percent, total value would be 123 percent of material value. On the basis of these results, as well as the results of Solnick and Hemenway (1996), no case can be made that there is a deadweight loss from Christmas giving.[21] In fact, there appears to be substantial gain.

According to an estimate used by Waldfogel (1993, p. 1226), holiday gift-giving in 1992 totaled about $38 billion. Assuming Waldfogels' fractional yield, nevertheless, the total value of the exchanges generated by this $38 billion would have been about $47 billion by my estimates of which about $14 billion was sentimental value. Economic efficiency suggests that Christmas achieves a 'God bless us [almost] every one' rather than a 'bah, humbug!' Economists doing normative economic analysis should take values as they are, not as they wish them to be (Zerbe 1998b).

Slavery

KH has been criticized because it does not always tell us the right thing to do (Dworkin 1980; Kelman 1981). One example used is that of slavery, and Dworkin faults KH on the grounds that it is not always able to condemn slavery as inefficient. Posner (1980) has offered the major defense. He maintains that wealth maximization probably condemns slavery as inefficient, since a person could, if he chose, be more productive in the sense of producing a greater physical output as a free person than as a slave.[22] This argument is technically incorrect, but, more important, it is a misguided defense as well.

It is technically incorrect because it ignores those sentiments that must be taken into account in determining efficiency, even if we confine ourselves to the sentiments of the slave and of the owner, and ignore the regard for others. Consider, first, only the transactions between the slave and the owner. Imagine that the status quo position is one of slavery. The efficiency question is, then, whether the WTP of the slave is greater than the WTA of the owner. Even if the slave could be more productive free, and capital markets were perfect, so that the slave can borrow against future earnings, we cannot say whether or not the WTP of the slave would be greater than the WTA of the owner. The owner may have a taste for owning a slave and may be willing to suffer the financial loss inherent in retaining the slave because the psychic gain is greater than the financial loss. Posner's mistake arises partly from his focus on efficiency in terms of mainly material wealth, but primarily from ignoring the regard for others.

Posner's defense ignores the regard for others.[23] The fact is that one cannot maintain that slavery – at least by the 1850s in the United States – was efficient on the basis of available evidence, Professors Fogel and Engerman notwithstanding. Professors Fogel and Engerman (1974) maintain that slavery was efficient. What they show, instead, is that it was economically viable. They answer in the negative the question 'if slavery had been eliminated, would the GNP have been greater?' I see no reason to doubt their answer that it would not have been.

But to determine whether or not slavery was efficient is a different question from the one Fogel and Engerman, as well as Posner, addressed. A different question would have had to be asked and answered: 'would the WTP of those opposed to slavery have been greater than the WTA of slaveholders?'[24] To this question, no answer has been provided. That slavery might not have been efficient is suggested when we consider the sentiments of others, and the social antipathy to it that was already growing.[25] One cannot imagine that the practice would have survived the turn of the century, even without the Civil War.

However, KHZ cannot always condemn slavery. Even KHZ cannot condemn it in time periods in which the legality of slavery accurately reflected the prevailing sentiments. However, this is not a reason to condemn either KH or KHZ. It is simply a limitation of the measures KHZ and KH use, and should be noted. Neither KH nor KHZ purports, nor should purport, to tell us the right thing to do, in a morally transcendent sense. The moral basis of the KH and KHZ criteria cannot rise above the sentiments of the times. This is its defect, but it is also its strength.

APPENDIX 6A

Consider the derivation of a social welfare function that meets the KH requirement. A social welfare function involves a decision rule. Consider social welfare as a function of the utilities of all of the individuals in society so that welfare is

$$W = (U_1, U_2, \ldots, U_N) \tag{6.1}$$

A change in welfare is found by totally differentiating equation (6.1) to give:

$$dW = \sum_{i}^{N} \frac{\partial W}{\partial U} dUi \tag{6.2}$$

Thus, a change in welfare is given by the change in the *i*th person's utility dU_i multiplied by the social weight given to the *i*th person's utility. The utility of the *i*th person is a function of goods and services consumed. That is

$$Ui = (X_1, X_2, \ldots, X_m) \tag{6.3}$$

and thus a change in the utility of the *i*th person is:

$$dU_i = \sum \frac{dU_i}{dX_{ij}} dX_{ij} \tag{6.4}$$

A well-known result of consumer welfare theory is that the additional utility given to the *i*th person by a new unit of good X_j is just the price (explicit or implicit) times *i*'s marginal utility of income or

$$\frac{dU_i}{dX_{ij}} = \frac{dU_i}{dY_i} P_j \tag{6.5}$$

where Y represents income and P_j represents the price of good X_j. The term $\partial U_i / \partial Y_i$ is *i*'s marginal utility of income – that is, the utility of an additional dollar. Substituting equations (6.4) and (6.5) in equation (6.2) gives

$$dW = \sum_i \sum_j \frac{\partial W}{\partial U_i} \frac{\partial U}{\partial Y_i} P_j dX_{ij} \tag{6.6}$$

Therefore, a change in welfare is the sum of all of the income changes for an individual, $\Sigma_j^M P_j dX_{ij}$, multiplied by that individual's marginal utility of income, $\partial U / \partial Y_i$, times the marginal social weight given to that individual, $\partial W / \partial U_i$, summed over all individuals. Equation (6.6) can be rearranged to give

$$dW = \sum_i \sum_j P_j dX_{ij} + \sum_i \sum_j \frac{\partial W}{\partial U_i} \frac{\partial U}{\partial Y_i} P_j dX_{ij} \tag{6.7}$$

This equation has divided a change in welfare into two parts: an efficiency effect, which is the first expression on the right-hand side of the equation, and a distributional effect, which is the second expression on the right-hand side. The efficiency effect is the sum of the changes in income unweighted by the person's marginal utility of income or by the social weight given to the *i*th person's utility. The KH measure of welfare assumes that everyone's utility is counted the same, that it has a weight of 1, and that the marginal value of a dollar is also the same for everyone so that it also has a weight of 1. These assumptions make the last expression on the right-hand side equal to 0, so that we are left with simply

$$dW = \sum_i \sum_j P_j dX_{ij} \tag{6.8}$$

On this basis it is said that the KH measure does not consider distributional effects. The distributional part of the equation that has disappeared depends on the marginal utility of income and on some rule for giving weight to each person's utility. What is not commonly realized is that the efficiency part of the equation, that is, equation (6.8), itself embodies a distributional component. The various X_j goods that are contained in equation (6.8) are as broadly conceived as possible; any good that gives rise to utility is contained as one of the X_j goods. Such a good is income distribution, which can be regarded as just another good, and should therefore be treated similarly. A change in income distribution has a value and thus an implicit price P_j and will give rise to a change in income and in utility for those who place a value on income distribution.[26] The change in income is counted the same regardless of who obtains it; the effect on each person is measured by his or her WTP or WTA, and the change in utility is counted equally for all, so that the valuation process for the change in income distribution meets the requirements of the KH test.

This result can be modeled explicitly. Measure the weight that person i gives to an increase in income for person k as W_{ki}. The willingness of i to pay for an increase in person k's income will then be W_{ki} (Y) where Y is income. Person k may also care about person i measured by W_{ik}. An increase in k's income will then increase i's satisfaction which in turn will increase k's satisfaction, and so on. The effect of these interactions can be taken into account by the 'interdependence multiplier,' which is $M_{ki} = 1 / (1 - W_{ki}W_{ik})$. Now instead of including a distribution good as one of the dX_{kj}'s, treat it separately so that equation (6.8) becomes[27]

$$dW = \sum_j \sum_k \sum_i M_{ki} W_{ki} P_j dX_{kj} \qquad (6.9)^{28}$$

For convenience, call the sum of the $M_{ki}W_{ki}$ the *marginal social value* of i's income, and designate it as Π_{ki}. Equation (6.9) can then be written as

$$dW = \sum_j \sum_k \sum_i P_j dX_{kj} - \sum_j \sum_k \sum_i (1 - \Pi_{ki}) P_j dX_{kj} \tag{6.10}$$

Equation (6.10) may reasonably be regarded as the fundamental equation of benefit–cost analysis.[29] The first term on the right-hand side is the change in efficiency when distributional effects are not considered. The second term represents the value of distributional effects as measured by the WTP or WTA.

NOTES

I would like to thank Leigh Anderson, Alison Cullen, Patrick Dobel, Richard Parks and Diane Zerbe for useful suggestions on the section on sentimental value.

1. Missing values have a particular meaning in statistics that is different from the meaning here.
2. For example, complaints about efficiency as an incorrect value (Dworkin 1980).
3. To mention a few example: Kelman (1981), Williams (1983), Waldfogel (1993).
4. Sunstein (1997, p. 81) notes that 'we may believe that goods are comparable without believing that they are commensurable.' I would say further that the use of monetary figures to rank preferences can be done even where the choices are not made with respect to a monetized frame of reference. We do not think of friendships in terms of money, but we make trade-offs with respect to them. The problem of the effect that using the discount rate has on future generations and the problem of estimating losses are endemic to any decision process that uses information.
5. Critics say that these values are difficult to quantify (although a benefit–cost framework is not limited to quantification) or to capture. This is, however, an empirical issue and the one for which the critics I discuss offer no evidence.
6. Cases in which this sort of issue has risen include *Baltimore Gas & Electric* v. *Natural, Resources Defense Council*, Inc. 462 U.S. 87, 1983, and *Pacific Gas and Electric Co et al.* v. *State Energy Resources Conservation and Development Commission et al.* 461 U.S. 190, 1991.
7. Posner (1987a, pp. 23–24) finds it a 'serious problem' that KH does not consider the distribution of wealth and that its measures of value are nevertheless dependent on the distribution of wealth.
8. There is an additional problem. The incinerator may reduce the income of those in the neighborhood such that it is a fortiori KH efficient to later locate yet another disamenity there. This process can result in a cycle of continuing additional burdens for those adversely affected.
9. Posner's assertion is incorrect even without consideration of the regard for others. There is evidence that greater equality can increase political, and therefore economic, stability, resulting in a greater national income. See references in Ellickson (1991 p. 179, n. 42).
10. Of course, a case can be made that KH is a good guide to maximizing total utility, but in my view this is a case that economists should resist making. The concept of utility as something measurable is one that is unreal, unscientific, and of no value. For the analyst at least, what is important with respect to KH or any other normative rules is whether or not there is acceptance of the criteria. The first principles of any normative criteria rest on acceptance.
11. For example, Ellickson (1991, p. 177) accepts this argument.
12. This is consistent with the asymmetric value function of Kahneman and Tversky (1979). Thaler (1991, pp. 11f) points out that a sense of waste is recorded as a loss.
13. We might, in fact, argue that there are four projects, since there are, in addition, the project that is KH efficient and the one that is not KH efficient.
14. Solnick and Hemenway (1996, p. 1301) recognize this, as they note that social aspects of gift-giving are often responsible for the value created in the real world.
15. It is unclear that this was done successfully. Solnick and Hemenway (1996) show that the material value of the gift as a percentage of its costs (the 'yield') as estimated by survey respondents varied directly with its sentimental value.

16. These colleagues included Alison Cullen, Robert Plotnick, Leigh Anderson, Marieka Klawitter, John Madison, and Patrick Dobel.
17. My wife, a psychoanalyst, suggests that a gift may create negative sentimental value. A gift that is thoughtless may be worse than a neutral gift. Steve Vinyard pointed out to me the instance in which Homer Simpson gave his wife a bowling ball custom made to fit his fingers and with 'Homer' stamped on it.
18. Waldfogel (1993), Solnick and Hemenway (1996) and List and Shogren (1988).
19. I focus on the WTA rather than the WTP estimates of Waldfogel, as the former seem conceptually correct.
20. The results of List and Shogren (1988), however, suggest that the sentimental value as a percentage of cost is 127 percent and that the total yield (total value divided by cost) is about 254 percent.
21. This is true even if we take the extreme estimate that the material loss is one-third of the cost.
22. For example, see Posner (1980, pp. 501–502). Posner notes (1980, p. 1), 'For example, if we started with a society where one person owned all the others, soon most of the others would have bought their freedom from that person because their output would be greater as free individuals than as slaves, enabling them to pay more for the right to their labor than that right was worth to the slave owner.'
23. Similar criticisms can be made about Posner's discussion of rape. The regard for others is, however, recognized by Calabresi and A. Douglas Melamed (1972, pp. 1089, 1112). They note, '[I]f Taney is allowed to sell himself into slavery, or to take undue risks of becoming penniless, or to sell a kidney, Marshall may be harmed, simply because he is a sensitive man who is made unhappy by seeing slaves, paupers or persons who die because they sold a kidney' (1972, p. 1112).
24. If the possession of slaves is regarded as a matter of rights in dispute, the WTA of both parties will also play a role, as I showed earlier
25. *Uncle Tom's Cabin* was the greatest fiction success of the nineteenth century. Alfred Kazin, 'Introduction,' *Uncle Tom's Cabin*, Bantam Books, 1981 at vi. It was not for nothing that President Lincoln greeted Mrs. Stowe as 'the little woman who wrote the book that made this great war' (Kazin, p. ix). Kazin also notes that 'Mrs. Stowe had brought to her indictment of slavery … a moral passion that in the book is the most powerful antagonist of slavery and one that so worked on people's feelings from 1852 to the end of the Civil War that no other single book can be said to have contributed so much to the end of slavery' (Kazin, p. viii).
26. Strictly speaking, the price may differ for all of the i persons, and thus the P term should have an i designator as well.
27. The interdependence multiplier can be derived by laying out the infinite series of interactions which are a multiplicative series yielding an M_{ki} (see Zerbe and Dively 1994).
28. For example, if Derek receives an income increase of $50 and Amartya an increase of $100, the total money measure of the welfare increase using KH would be $150. If Derek and Amartya care about each other so that Derek weights an increase in Amartya's income by 0.1 and Amartya weights Derek's income by 0.2, the total money measure of the increase in KH welfare is $173.40. If each person is governed by the golden rule and cares about the other as much as (or more than) himself so that W_{ik} and W_{ki} are both 1 (or greater), the increase in welfare would be infinite.
29. However, in order for equation (6.10) to be complete, time needs to be introduced. To do this is straightforward.

7. The failure of market failure

7.1 INTRODUCTION

The failure to include transactions costs when considering whether a rule or practice is efficient is one of the most pernicious problems in economics. It has led to endless difficulties. This chapter delineates the role of transactions costs in considering efficiency. It shows that a proper consideration of transactions costs reveals the market failure approach – and the prescriptions for government intervention based upon it – to be incoherent.

Axiom 7(a) states: 'Transactions costs are to be included in evaluating an economic change or in determining economic efficiency.' This simple axiom has powerful implications for the concept of market failure and the question of the proper role of government in the marketplace. This question is an old and fundamental one. Public officials throughout the world grapple with this issue, deciding which public services to provide or how to regulate the activities of individuals and firms, a task made more urgent by recent efforts to privatize public responsibilities and 'reinvent' government. In the search for objective standards by which such decisions can be made, public officials increasingly have turned to the concept of market failure. Use of the market failure concept is widespread, both in teaching curricula and in practicing government circles.

This chapter demonstrates once again the limitations of the market failure concept. Its shortcomings have been known for some time, but with little consequence, since its use continues to be widespread. In this chapter I summarize the conceptual problems of the market failure idea. I further show how market failure analysis leads to conclusions about the efficiency of government intervention that are not supported by empirical studies. An alternative economic approach, which emphasizes the concept of transactions costs, buttresses this criticism and provides a better grounded conceptual framework for understanding issues of government intervention. In general, this approach provides a better method for understanding the nature of collective action, although it is not a diagnostic tool in the same sense that the market failure concept purports to be.

7.2 A SHORT HISTORY OF THE MARKET FAILURE CONCEPT

The concept of market failure initially appeared as a means of explaining in economic terms why the need for government expenditures arises. It constituted, according to its presenters, 'a normative judgment about the role of government and the ability of markets to establish mutually beneficial exchanges' (Dahlman 1979, p. 143).

Presenting the traditional approach, Arthur C. Pigou (1932, p. 173) argued that the divergence between the values of marginal private and marginal social net product would not 'make the national dividend a maximum; and, consequently, certain specific acts of interference with normal economic processes may be expected...to increase the dividend.' In his classic article 'The Pure Theory of Public Expenditure,' Paul Samuelson (1954, p. 388) observed that no decentralized pricing mechanism could be used to determine the optimal level of goods characterized by collective consumption. In such cases, as the authors of one modern textbook agree, 'the market has no choice but to fail' (Skaggs and Carlson 1996, p. 543). In one of the leading textbooks on the new science of policy analysis, David Weimer and Aidan Vining reach a conclusion that appears frequently in the literature:

> When is it legitimate for government to intervene in private affairs? In the United States, the normative answer to this question has usually been based on the concept of *market failure* – a circumstance where the pursuit of private interest does not lead to an efficient use of society's resources or a fair distribution of society's goods. (Weimer and Vining 1992, p. 30)

Textbooks on microeconomics and public finance commonly present the concept of market failure as a general justification for government intervention (Browning and Browning 1992, p. 657; Boardman *et al.* 1996, p. 99).

As it matured, the market failure concept took on an additional characteristic – that of a diagnostic tool by which policymakers learned how to objectively determine the exact scope and type of intervention needed (Weimer and Vining 1992; Boadway and Wildasin 1984; Hyman 1990; Procaccia 1996). Expansion of this normative concept into a diagnostic tool appeared in conjunction with the growth of policy analysis as a field of study and university training. One scholar argues:

> The welfare theorem lets [us] classify inefficiencies as due to monopoly externalities, and so on. This helps us to understand and perhaps to solve such inefficiencies just as a doctor's diagnosis ... is part of treatment. (Farrell 1987, p. 1160)

To employ the diagnostic approach, analysts attempt to identify the precise type of problem that gives rise to the market failure, as well the different types of bureaucratic malfunctions (non-market failures) likely to occur when public officials attempt a cure. Use of this 'double market failure test' (Weimer and Vining 1992, p. 179) is presented by advocates of the approach as an essential part of the diagnostic process. Like doctors attempting a cure, policy analysts must render a diagnosis of the underlying disease and consider the dangers of treatment, including side effects. Accordingly, policy analysts argue that the existence of a market failure 'provides a necessary, not a sufficient justification for public policy interventions' (Wolf 1979, p. 138; Weimer and Vining 1992, p. 13). Sufficiency is established when the gains from government intervention outweigh the dangers of government intervention.

In keeping with the diagnostic model, different treatments are favored for different afflictions. In their textbook *Public Sector Economics*, Boadway and Wildasin (1984, p. 61) suggest that 'while typically the remedy for market failure due to public goods is for the public sector to provide the good, the remedy for externalities is often to provide incentives to the private sector to produce the correct amount.' In the legal literature, Frankel (1995, p. 295) echoes this with the suggestion that in situations involving public goods the 'government may be in a better position to operate a firm than the private sector.' Like medical students contemplating cures, policy analysts are taught to apply the least intrusive intervention. If a market failure can be resolved by the creation of an incentive that will allow the market to correct itself, such as a tax expenditure, this is to be favored over more aggressive treatments, such as the creation of a government monopoly. Full-scale government intervention should be undertaken only when it can be shown 'that a less-intrusive generic policy cannot be utilized or that an effective contract for private production cannot be designed to deal with the market failure' (Weimer and Vining 1992, p. 179).

What began as a simple attempt to provide a normative explanation for the existence of government expenditures has developed into a quasi-scientific full-scale diagnostic test with the application of cures. Some policy analysis textbooks even present tables that allow students to identify appropriate interventions for different types of market and government failures (ibid., p. 193; Hyman 1990, pp. 158–159). This appears to be a powerful and attractive model. It looks scientific. It seems to provide an objective test for governmental intervention. It appears to be something that can be usefully taught in schools.

Inevitably, such concepts and teachings find their way into public policy. Recently the US government issued Executive Order 12866 (1993), which requires federal officials to conduct an economic analysis as a means of determining the need for proposed regulations. Guidelines for carrying out this order require officials to make a finding of 'whether the problem constitutes a significant market failure' as a prerequisite for recommending government intervention. The guidelines further provide instructions for identifying types of failures, comparing potential interventions, and guarding against 'unintentional harmful effects on the efficiency of market outcomes' (Executive Office of the President n.d., 3, 5). The resulting Regulatory Impact Analyses make reference to a variety of market failure concepts. A controversial 1994 standard that set stricter wind resistance standards for trailer homes, for example, claimed that asymmetric information and externalities necessitated government intervention into the market for manufactured housing (De Alessi 1996).

An extensive flowering of the market failure concept has occurred in the field of law. The number of law review articles and court decisions using the concept runs into the thousands, with 239 references turned up by a search of law reviews for the twelve months between June 1995 and June 1996 alone. These references occur not only in monopoly, antitrust (Kovacic 1995, pp. 1202, 1214, 1217), and environmental issues (Baron and Dunoff 1996, pp. 437, 441–443) but appear to span virtually the entire corpus of law. References are found, for example, in family law articles (Estin 1995, n. 248, n. 356, n. 357), in connection with setting product standards (Abbott 1996, p. 163), in references to the plight of refugees (Beck 1995, p. 177), in connection with health care (Kang 1995, pp. 513, 526; Jost 1995, pp. 827, 851, n. 203; Jordon 1995, p. 917, n. 18), and with regard to problems of creating markets in less-developed countries (Utset 1995, n. 7), as well as in securities law (Kitch 1995, p. 776; Letsou 1996, p. 150), the creation of financial derivatives (Singher 1995, p. 1468), moral legal theory (Baron and Dunoff 1996), contracts (Procaccia 1996, pp. 630, 635–636, n. 3; Blackman 1995, p. 1368), occupational injuries (Linder 1995, p. 94), controls on credit card interest rates (Rougeau 1996, p. 15), intellectual property (Ginsburg 1995, p. 1491, n. 102; Owen 1996, n. 149), discrimination in insurance markets (Gaulding 1995, pp. 1653, 1687), the information superhighway (Post 1995, p. 792), and zoning (Larson 1995, pp. 180–181).[1] Similarly, court decisions that refer to market failure and to externalities are made with great frequency.

Long before social scientists applied diagnostic skills to public affairs, doctors of medicine postulated that diseases of the body were caused by imbalances in bodily 'humors' (Thomas 1992, pp. 8–9). By the eighteenth century, this fit of deductive reasoning had been elevated to the level of a diagnostic procedure. The approach led to a variety of ineffective and often dangerous remedies, such as bleeding or purging. It eventually was replaced by more scientifically valid approaches, such as germ theory and the discovery of antibiotics. The theory of market failures, this chapter will show, is little better grounded than the outdated belief in bodily humors.

7.3 WHY MARKET FAILURE FAILS

A fundamental problem with the concept of market failure, as economists occasionally recognize, is that it describes a situation that exists everywhere (Nelson, 1987; Dahlman 1979). While the ubiquity of market failures seems well accepted, the consequences of this observation are not. Some people believe that this dooms the concept as an analytical tool; others disagree.

Market failures are thought to occur when the market fails to produce public goods, or gives rise to natural monopolies, or disenfranchises parties through information asymmetries, or creates undesirable income distributions. All of these problems are types of externalities, since each consists of non-monetary effects not taken into account in the decision-making process (the classic definition of externalities). Hence, when we charge that the market failure concept has certain shortcomings, we mean to apply this statement to all forms of externalities including non-market failures by governmental institutions.

The core of the argument against market failure analysis is derived from the study of transactions. Externalities arise when parties fail to engage in transactions because the cost of doing so is too high. The effect of transactions costs on market behavior was first analyzed in the 1930s, beginning with an examination of brokerage charges and other costs of exchange (Hicks 1939; Allen 1996). This quickly expanded into an analysis of the relationship between property rights and the cost of transactions. The property rights approach began with an article by Coase (1937, 1960), that is now well known in the discipline of economics. Coase argued that individuals form firms because their use of the price system is not costless. In other words, entrepreneurs create firms in an effort to reduce the transaction costs associated with using the price system. This approach was further developed mainly after Coase's 1960 article on 'The Problem of Social Cost' through the work of Alchain (1965), Demsetz (1967), Barzel (1985), Ostrom (1990), Allen (1991), and others.

The property rights approach is important because it defines the condition under which externalities entirely disappear. Transactions costs in this respect are defined as *the resources necessary to transfer, establish and maintain property rights* (Allen 1991, p. 4). As property rights become more extensive and complete, transactions costs approach zero.[2] In a similar fashion, as transactions costs decline, property rights become more complete as it is cheaper to defend them or to transfer property.

Only when property rights are perfectly clear and costless to use and enforce do transactions costs vanish. In a zero transactions cost world, with well-specified rights, there would be markets for everything and all rights would be clear (Arrow 1969), producing efficient outcomes for any collective problem that parties chose to resolve. This condition is expressed by the so-called 'weak form' of the Coase Theorem.[3]

> In a world in which property rights are fully specified and in which transaction costs are zero, the allocation of resources will be efficient. (Zerbe 1976, 1980; Medema and Zerbe 2000a and 2000b)

No such world, of course, can ever exist. This realization is critical to an understanding of why the market failure model fails. Conceptually it fails for the following reasons.

1. Externalities are defined by transactions costs. In essence, externalities come into being because the transactions costs of resolving them are too high. In this sense, every story about externalities is also a story about transactions costs.

Transactions costs define externalities in the following manner: *the net value of the externality constitutes the lower boundary for associated transactions costs.* Stated another way, transactions costs will never be lower than the net monetary impact of the externality. By 'net monetary impact' we mean the net benefits to be derived by eliminating the problem. An example may help clarify this point. Suppose one party suffers from the effects of pollution produced by a neighboring source. The pollution damage is $125,000, and the cost of installing devices to eliminate the pollution is $100,000. The damage done by the pollution is greater than the economically optimal amount, according to the definition of an externality. Pollution, in short, is being overproduced. In such a case, $25,000 represents the gain that could be made by eliminating the pollution in a situation where transactions costs equal zero. The costs of transactions (negotiations, lawsuits, contracts) will not be zero, of course. If they are less than $25,000, efforts to eliminate the externality will ensue. If the costs are greater than $25,000, then the incentive to resolve the problem will disappear.[4]

Where externalities remain, it may be inferred that the transactions costs are equal to or greater than the net value of the externality. In this sense, the net value of the externality sets the lower boundary on the transactions costs required to remove or reduce the effect. If transactions costs were less than the net value of the externality, it would pay to incur them.

2. Transactions costs are ubiquitous. Market failures may be defined as departures from the optimum with respect to an operating price system that is costless. The existence of unpriced but non-zero transactions costs mean that some trades are not created – trades that would be undertaken if the cost of the unpriced transactions were zero (or less than the net monetary impact to be gained). Failure to undertake these trades creates a market failure.

Market failures disappear only when the costs of operating the price system are zero. In the real world, however, property rights are never fully specified, so some costs of resolving them must always be incurred. Unpriced transactions costs, in essence, are everywhere (Allen 1991). Since unpriced transactions costs are ubiquitous, this gives rise to a situation in which externalities, and thus market failures, can be found wherever transactions occur.

How, then, does an analyst distinguish between externalities that require government attention and those that do not? The market failure approach owes much of its success to the fact that sophisticated users have focused on providing goods with large net benefits where government has an advantage with respect to transactions costs. For example, market failure analysts have focused on goods with high exclusion costs – such as pollution, open access goods, and the like. These are goods for which the government can better exploit its advantage in coercion to affect substantial per unit reductions in transaction costs and in which the potential markets – clean air and water, police and fire services, and the like – are large. Choice of these markets is, however, essentially ad hoc (aside from their transactions costs features).

Beyond these cases, the market failure concept can also be applied to cases that most analysts would consider trivial and not worthy of government attention, and which the analysts tend to ignore. When a neighbor fails to plant more flowers even though this would increase property values in the neighborhood by more than the cost of planting, an externality and a market failure exists. The highway driver who, by driving too slowly, fails to consider the time costs he or she imposes on other drivers creates an externality (since the government owns the highway we should probably say that a non-market failure exists). Wherever moral hazard or adverse selection may be found, externalities arise. Companies providing fire insurance worry that policyholders will ignore efficient fire prevention measures; the availability of flood insurance may induce people to build in flood-plains; government insurance for savings and loan companies may induce investments that are too risky; and, as Fischel (1996) notes, colleges granting tenure to professors may find they work too little thereafter.

Externalities exist any time there is inefficiency in the law affecting markets. A law that encourages inefficient breach of contract produces an externality, as does a tort law that sets the penalty for reckless driving so low that too much reckless driving occurs. Suppose that buying a car involves title transfer fees imposed by the state. If these fees are set too high, some trades will not be made, and the car manufacturer may then produce too few cars, just as with a monopolist.

As these cases suggest, an analyst in search of externalities and market failures can find them anywhere, providing a universal justification for any sort of government intervention that he or she might want to promote. Supporters of the market failure concept avoid this problem by focusing on failures that are 'big.' In its worst form, this amounts to little more than the substitution of the ideological biases of the analyst. In its more productive forms, it leads to a comparing the benefits of government intervention with the risk that principal–agent problems in the public sector will make the problem worse.

3. Definitional problems. As this discussion suggests, a close examination of the market failure concept gives rise to all sorts of definitional problems. This should not be surprising, as the authors of one leading theoretical text note, since 'a fully satisfying definition of an externality has proved somewhat elusive' (Mas-Colell, Whinston and Green 1995, p. 351). If the price system itself is treated as a factor of production, one could as easily say that the costs of using this price system are too high to warrant its use. In its essential form, then, the externality concept amounts to little more than the observation that the price of an input (the market system) reduces the quantity demanded.

4. The search for necessary and sufficient conditions is misleading. As noted above, analysts schooled in the market failure concept are taught that the existence of an externality is a necessary, but not a sufficient, condition for government intervention. Given the definitional problems inherent in the concept, it should not be surprising to learn that this statement is misleading.

Consider a standard example in which the byproduct of one profit-maximizing firm becomes part of the production costs of a second profit-maximizing firm – a classic externality. Let us assume that the combined producer and consumer surplus when firm one produces at the socially optimal level is greater than when it produces the externality. In this situation, 'the competitive equilibrium in the presence of externalities is Pareto suboptimal' (Just, Hueth and Schmitz 1982, pp. 271–272).[5] The optimal position is the one that would be reached if a single firm that represented the merger of firms one and two were to maximize its profits. This position can be reached by an externality tax, by merger of the firms, or by government restriction on the output of firm one. Analysts will recognize a market failure and governments may be encouraged to intervene.

But is government intervention optimal? Suppose that the transaction costs of a merger or the administrative costs of the tax or other devices used to internalize the externality are greater than the increase in consumer and producer surpluses to be obtained. The solution in which the externality continues to exist then becomes the optimum. Sufficiency is not attained, although not necessarily as a consequence of searching for principal–agent problems in the public sector.

Suppose, however, that the government may intervene with zero cost to the government and no principal–agent problems. To keep the example simple, assume that pollution produced by firm one is the problem and that it may be eliminated by installing a device costing $100,000. The pollution itself causes damage of $125,000. Typically, the analyst in search of non-market failures would see this as a case in which government intervention is justified. Yet this may not be the case. Suppose that the government intervention imposes record-keeping costs on the firm and that these amount to $26,000. Clearly, the intervention is not efficient.

It may be objected that the double market failure test would take all such costs into account. If this is the case, then the double market test amounts to a requirement to perform a full benefit–cost test after identifying a market failure. This supports our point exactly. Analysts are more likely to discover efficient interventions when they begin with transactions costs and net benefits (De Alessi 1996). This avoids the search for externalities, which as demonstrated above, can be found anywhere the analyst chooses to look and inevitably lead the analyst astray.

Moreover, to begin with market failure is to assume that it is a necessary condition for efficient intervention. Yet it is not. Let us return to the example of the firm which is generating pollution and which injures a second firm. Suppose that merger costs have fallen as a result of a more streamlined review process developed by the Federal Trade Commission. If the firms merge, we would expect the new firm to stop generating pollution, and thereby cure the externality, since generating pollution would impose costs on *itself* which outweigh its *own* gains.

Now, suppose instead that the firms do not merge, but the government devises a means of collecting the corporate income tax more efficiently which saves the firms an amount of money equal to the amount they would have saved by merging. The cheaper tax collection method is a government action unrelated to the identified externality. The cheaper method of examining mergers might be said to be a way of reducing the externality between the two firms, but it is more accurate simply to say that it is a cost-saving innovation. The two innovations are not mutually exclusive choices. *Both* should be undertaken, even though only one internalizes an externality. Hence the existence of a market failure cannot always be taken as a necessary condition for government intervention.

In general, any time government can reduce private transactions costs or its own costs of provision, it should do so regardless of whether or not an externality exists. It need not wait for the appearance of an externality to justify intervention.[6]

Many policy analysts who are aware of conceptual shortcomings such as these nonetheless do not dismiss the market failure concept. Responding to a series of charges by Nelson on the inadequacies of market failure (1987), Faulhaber (1987), for example, states:

> While I agree with both points, I do not agree that they undermine the usefulness of the concept of market failure as an analytical device. Nelson's theme that 'market failure is ubiquitous' is analogous to a physicist, who, when confronted with Newton's three laws of mechanics, throws up his hands and says, 'Yes, but friction is ubiquitous!' Generations of mechanical engineers and designers have made a good living from dealing with friction in all its incarnations, from machine tools to automobiles. The point is not that market failures exist, but how serious are those market failures. (p. 558)

Faulhaber's point is that all theoretical models make simplifying assumptions, and the fact that a simplifying assumption is not always factually correct is a poor reason to reject the theoretical model. That is true, but his analogy to Newton is misplaced.[7] Newton's laws of motion are theoretically correct, provided that friction is zero (if we ignore Einstein's theory of relativity). Since Newton's laws of motion were theoretically correct, they served as a useful foundation for physics. If a physicist wanted to relax Newton's simplifying assumption and was willing to go to the trouble of calculating the effect of friction, he or she could still use Newton's laws as a useful starting point.

In contrast, the market failure model would be theoretically flawed *even if* it accounted for transactions costs. Therefore, it cannot be 'saved' simply by adding an additional term. This is because the market failure model makes *two* mistakes. First, it assumes that the existence of an externality is a sufficient condition for government intervention. This is a mistake, since transactions costs might make it inefficient to intervene even if there is an externality. This problem could be cured by incorporating transactions costs. However, the market failure model also makes a second mistake: it assumes that an externality is a *necessary* condition for government intervention. This is a mistake, since the government may have an opportunity to reduce transactions costs – and thus improve the efficiency of the society – even if there *is not* an externality. For example, a more efficient method of collecting corporate taxes might save the corporations money without decreasing the government's revenue. This would increase the net wealth of the society, even though the government would not be 'curing' anything that could reasonably be described as an externality. Because the market failure model cannot be saved by incorporating transactions costs, it does not serve as a useful foundation for economic analysis.

A second difference between Newton's laws of motion and the market failure model is that Newton's simplifying assumption was a *sensible* one, in many circumstances. Even though friction is ubiquitous, in many cases its effect is so slight that it can be ignored and a physicist will still make a reasonably accurate prediction. In contrast, not only are transactions costs not zero, they are frequently not even close to zero. In particular, if an externality exists in an otherwise smoothly functioning market, it is likely that the transactions costs of fixing that externality are high, or the externality would have already been fixed. In other words, the market failure model assumes that transactions costs are zero in precisely those circumstances in which transactions costs are likely to be prohibitively high.

7.4 EMPIRICAL EVIDENCE AND CLASSIC EXTERNALITIES

The market failure diagnostic is a normative tool used to identify situations in which government intervention will prove efficient. The empirical test of such a tool is this: Does it justify intervention in cases where it is actually warranted? I argue that it does not. In a number of cases, the market failure concept leads to conclusions that appear incorrect when compared with actual practice. The gap between what the market failure concept tells us should occur and what we actually observe grows larger as empirical studies accumulate.

Consider the following four cases: the lighthouse, land tenancy, crops and bees, and common property. In each case, market failure analysis predicts the wrong outcome. In each case, an understanding of transactions costs helps to determine the efficient level of government intervention. Although no single concept captures the rich variety of institutional arrangements developed in practice to solve collective problems, the transactions costs approach does help to explain why some of those practices arise.

> *The Lighthouse* (Samuelson 1964, p. 45)
> Here is a later example of government service: lighthouses. These save lives and cargoes; but lighthouse keepers cannot reach out to collect fees from skippers. So, says the advanced treatise, 'we have a divergence between private advantage and money cost … and true social advantage and cost.' Philosophers and statesmen have always recognized the necessary role of government in such cases of 'external-economy divergence between private and social advantage.'

Market failure models typically consist of theoretical discussions such as these, rather than a descriptive analysis of what in fact exists. As a result, they tend to be vague and inaccurate, permitting ideological biases to be presented as scientific fact. Samuelson (1964, p. 159) notes with respect to public goods in general, and the lighthouse in particular, that 'this is certainly the kind of activity that governments would naturally undertake.'

This normative judgment is not on firm ground. Coase (1974) has examined how lighthouses were historically provided in England and Wales. Contrary to what market failure analysis would lead us to believe, most seventeenth-century lighthouses were not built or run by governmental bodies, but by private parties for private gain. Private individuals would gain a patent from the crown upon presenting petitions from ship owners and shippers (the granting of the patent, of course, was a form of government intervention – in this case a market-enhancing intervention that relied upon the government's coercive powers to create a property right). The patent allowed the private individual to build a lighthouse and levy tolls on ships. The toll was collected by agents or custom officials at port and varied with the tonnage of the vessel for each lighthouse passed (ibid., p. 364). The ship tonnage could be taken as a reasonable approximation of the level of demand for the lighthouse so that prices approximated an efficient Lindahl (discriminatory) pricing scheme.

Privately run lighthouses arose even though a governmentally chartered organization, Trinity House, had been established in 1566 and had started to build lighthouses early in the following century. Trinity House was reluctant to invest its own funds in lighthouses, yet opposed the efforts of private individuals to construct them. By 1820, twenty-four lighthouses were operated by Trinity House and twenty-two by private individuals, although many of the former had been originally built by private individuals (ibid., p. 366). The market failure approach would have us believe in the efficiency of government provision of lighthouses; actual experience provides a more complex conclusion.

The lighthouse case illustrates a key problem with the concept of public goods. As Mark Zupan (1996) has argued, the public provision of 'public goods' may have less to do with the characteristics of the goods than with the behavior of the interests providing them. Zupan argues that the providers of public goods – defense contractors, teachers, asphalt producers, and the like – join with policymakers to lobby for their overprovision because of private gain. Ironically, free-rider problems arise from the overprovision of public goods as more producers rush in to take advantage of commitments already made.

The lighthouse has been treated as a classic example of a 'public good.' Public goods are, in fact, an incoherent classification for public policy purposes, as Randall (1983) has noted. Public goods are defined with respect to two different sorts of transactions costs: exclusion costs that are high (associated with free riding) and the costs of determining individual levels of demand, required for Lindahl pricing or taxation. Randall notes:

> Nonexclusiveness and nonrivalry may be found together or separately, and the economic analysis of the two phenomena are quite different. Accordingly, a focus

> on questions of exclusiveness and rivalry permits precise analysis, while the term, 'public good' only introduces confusion. (p. 147)

Neither of these types of transactions costs, separately or together, may justify a government intervention. Although each category of transactions costs identified with public goods is relevant, creating a class of goods that combines the two will lead to errors. As the lighthouse example suggests, a variety of institutional arrangements exist, including market-enhancing government action, for handling goods characterized by high exclusion costs and non-rivalry.

Land Tenancy

Land tenancy provides another example of the way in which market failure analysis leads policymakers astray. Sharecropping or leaseholds, in which one party farms property owned by another, are examples of land tenancy and the basis for many government land reform efforts worldwide. The standard view in the economics and tenancy literature is that tenancy leads to an inefficient allocation of resources (Cheung 1969). Following the classic market failure perspective, Pigou (1932) notes:

> There can be no doubt that over a wide field some part of the investment designed to improve durable instruments of production is often made by persons other than their owners. Whenever this happens, some divergence between the private and the social net product of this investment is liable to occur. (p. 174)

This externality is said to arise from the fact that neither the tenant nor the owner fully or correctly considers the effects of their actions on the other. Inefficiencies are said to arise particularly from the disincentive for either party to make investments in the land that will maximize its productivity.[8] The disincentive is said to account for the major externality.[9] This inefficiency was thought to be particularly large with respect to sharecropping. If this were true, one would expect to observe lower crop yields under share tenancy than under alternative cultivation arrangements. Historical studies, however, do not confirm this. An examination of share tenancy in China and Taiwan prior to the land reforms of 1949, for example, shows that a well-developed system of private property rights in land existed and that the market by and large comported with the dictates of competition. For this system Cheung (1969, pp. 56–61; 1980, p. 42) did *not* observe lower ratios of labor and other inputs, a lesser degree of improvements, or lower yields on tenant farms than on owner-cultivated farms or farms employing wage labor. In addition, there is no evidence that the market values of lands under tenant cultivation were lower than the values of land under owner cultivation.

Perhaps the most frequent argument has been that, under share tenancy, farm improvements would be contracted inadequately or not at all. Yet, Cheung (1980, p. 43) finds that these 'are precisely the activities stated in every written contract that I could find.' Charges that share tenancy is less efficient than other cultivation arrangements cannot easily be sustained.

By contrast, government intervention in land tenancy can produce inefficiencies of its own. The particular mix of tenure systems on Indian reservations is inefficient not because of market failure in the traditional sense but because the trustee arrangements mandated by the federal government are so poor. Estimates by Allen and Lueck (1992, p. 448) show that the per acre value of agricultural land is 85–90 percent lower on tribal lands than on fee simple property.[10]

The transactions costs concept helps to explain the operation of different sorts of land tenure contracts. It has been used to explain the circumstances under which cash tenancy versus crop-sharing tenancy are more likely to arise. Allen and Lueck (1992) argue that the trade-off between the two types of contracts is a question of input distortion costs versus output division costs. Input distortion costs arise with cash rent because renters tend to overuse inputs supplied by landowners (for example, too much fertilizer), a consequence of the fact that the renter pays a fixed rent and gets all the proceeds from the crop (obviously a bigger problem with short-term leases than with long-term leases). So when input distortion costs are high – for example in a situation where the soil is fragile – crop sharing is favored. Crop-sharing contracts lead to high measurement and division costs, but fewer input distortion costs.

Bees and Crops

The US beekeeping subsidy has been presented in the popular literature as one of the best examples of a federal intervention that would not die. In his classic discussion of the positive reciprocal externalities that exist between beekeepers and the owners of apple orchards, Meade (1952) argues that a system of taxes and subsidies can, and must, be imposed in order to achieve efficiency. Apple farmers provide valuable services to beekeepers, since bees feed on the blossoms of fruit trees, while at the same time the bees provide valuable pollination services to apple growers.

Cheung (1973, p. 19) examined the relationship of bees to pollination as it actually exists. He found that no externality exists and instead that contractual arrangements between farmers and beekeepers have long been routine in the US. The existence of a market for nectar and pollination services can readily be observed in Washington State, the location of Cheung's study, in some cases simply by consulting the yellow pages of the telephone directory.

How is it possible that the market avoids the externality that Meade predicted? To begin with, transactions costs are very low here. Since the value of resources devoted to pollination and nectar extraction is insignificant and farmers could easily and cheaply keep bees themselves (and sometimes do), the gains from contracting with beekeepers are extremely small. This, in turn, suggests that contracting costs are minimal (Cheung 1980, pp. 46–48). There is also a well-developed system of contractual relations between beekeepers and farmers – so well developed, in fact, that although written contracts (sometimes so simple as to be recorded on postcards) are used to secure an initial arrangement among the parties, oral agreements are standard for subsequent relations. Furthermore, these oral contracts are rarely breached, owing to the presence of 'extra-legal constraints' in the form of sanctions against those who do not honor their pledges (Cheung 1973, p. 29). Thus, the presence of strong culture norms serves to lower private transactions costs. In spite of the informality of these contracts, they tend to be quite comprehensive, specifying 'the number and strength of the [bee] colonies, the rental fee per hive, the terms of delivery and removal of hives, the protection of bees from pesticide sprays, and the strategic placing of hives.' And, where hives are placed merely for honey-generating purposes (that is, no pollination is desired), prices (often paid in honey) are not necessarily fixed, but are allowed to vary with the honey yield (ibid.).[11] All of these various pieces of evidence lead Cheung to conclude, contrary to Meade's story, that 'the allocation of hives and nectar flows approximates that of a smoothly functioning market' wherein resources are efficiently allocated (Cheung 1980, p. 50). These cases offer important evidence that markets can successfully (if not fully efficiently) deal with potential externality problems under appropriate conditions.

The market failure model, ungrounded as it is in fact, ignores subtleties such as these. The existence of cultural norms defining acceptable behavior and the size of monitoring and enforcement costs affect voluntary arrangements. As Ostrom (1990, pp. 190f and 191) notes in her study of common property arrangements, models that make unrealistic assumptions about norms of acceptable behavior, monitoring and enforcement costs, and the availability of information do little to help analysts derive predictions that are precise or even approximately correct.

Common Property

One of the most famous market failure stories is that of the tragedy of the commons (Gordon 1954; Scott 1955; Hardin 1968). According to this story, community resources held in common, such as grazing land, inevitably suffer exploitation and degradation. Suggested remedies include transfer of the resources to a single government agency or privatization (Hardin 1978). Yet, as Feeny, Hanna and McEvoy (1996, p. 198) note, the assumptions of this approach 'appear to lack both descriptive accuracy and predictive power.' Empirical inspection of common property phenomena from the property rights–transactions costs perspective has uncovered a rich array of arrangements previously unexamined and a good deal of evidence contrary to the prediction of overexploitation. Overexploitation has occurred, but its incidence is not exclusive to situations of common property; it has been found under both state and private property regimes. At the same time, successful management has occurred under a variety of regimes, including communal ones (Feeny, Hanna and McEvoy 1996, p. 187; Ostrom, 1990).

Anderson and Swimmer (1997), in a study of Native American land use, provide empirical support for the assertion that the choice of private, shared, or open-access land can be explained by changes in the relative costs imposed by different constraints, a matter of transactions costs. In her extensive study of common property arrangements, Ostrom (1990) has revealed a variety of institutional arrangements for resolving disputes in areas such as meadows and forests, irrigation, groundwater, and fisheries. Ostrom and also North (1981) show that institutional arrangements are quite sensitive to transactions costs, including those imposed by litigation and by the ease of creating government institutions.

In the area of fisheries, officials in New Zealand and Canada have found that the costs of creating property rights to fish stocks often are less than the costs of imposing government restrictions on fishing. In the United States, where the government has attempted to prevent overfishing through a variety of regulations, boat owners have evaded these regulations by inefficiently changing fishing practices and technology (Lesser, Dodds and Zerbe 1997, pp. 132–137).

7.5 GOVERNMENT FAILURE: THE SALT DILEMMA

The transactions costs approach to deciding whether government intervention is justified within private markets applies equally well to deciding whether the government should intervene in the affairs of lower-level government agencies. Government agencies can be subject to externalities, just as the private sector can. The government is composed of a number of agencies, each of which has a separate budget. In considering the benefits and costs of a new project, an agency may be tempted to ignore the costs that its projects impose on other agencies or on individuals. Similarly, it might ignore benefits which are unrelated to its bailiwick. Suppose that government agency A undertakes a project that saves itself $1 million a year, but that imposes costs of $2 million a year on a *different* government agency, B. If agency A nonetheless decides to undertake the project, an externality will result.

Assuming transactions costs were zero, we would expect agency B to offer a sum of money or some other inducement to agency A to persuade it to abandon the project. If agencies frequently undertake projects that impose costs on other agencies that outweigh their own savings, this suggests that the transactions costs of interagency coordination are extremely high. Should we assume, then, that an overarching governmental body with authority over both agencies should intervene, and force A to abandon its project? Under the market failure model, the answer would surely be 'yes.' Yet, clearly, there are transactions costs that stand in the way and that explain why the 'inefficient' practice occurred.

An illustration of this dilemma is found in the Federal Highway Administration's continuing use of salt to de-ice roads. The FHA's use of salt is based on two conclusions: first, that the value of having de-iced roads is greater than the cost of purchasing and applying salt to roads,[12] and, second, that salt is less expensive than any other de-icing alternative, such as calcium magnesium acetate (CMA), which might cost as much as five times more than salt.[13]

However, Dr. Wurster of the EPA has estimated that salting roads inflicts a cost on the public of $2.91 billion a year. This is because salting roads harms the environment and corrodes automobiles and highway structures. Experts estimate that using CMA instead of salt would reduce the damage to the environment and although CMA would cost $1 billion more than salt, it would inflict $1.9 billion per year less damage on the environment and on automobiles than salt does. Therefore, forcing the FHA to use CMA instead of salt would save the public $900 million, if we ignore transactions costs.

Clearly, Dr. Wurster's report suggests that the use of salt instead of CMA is the product of an externality.[14] If transactions costs were zero, we would expect all of the people who are harmed by salt to offer a sum of money to the FHA to convince it to use CMA instead of salt. However, given the size of the class of people who are injured by salt (which includes everybody who cares about environmental goods and everybody who owns a car), it would be virtually impossible for them to coordinate their activities and negotiate a deal with the FHA: the transactions costs of doing so would not only *not* be zero, they would almost certainly be prohibitive.

Inasmuch as the total social cost of using salt is $900 million greater than the total social cost of using CMA, government intervention would be efficient if the transactions costs of intervening would be lower than $900 million dollars. The government could intervene by creating a rule that required the FHA to use CMA. The Supreme Court could interpret the existing laws in a way that required the FHA to use CMA, or Congress could pass a new law that required the FHA to use CMA. Under KHZ, we do not count the cost of changing the rule itself (i.e., the cost of lobbying Congress or of convincing the Supreme Court to rule in one's favor).[15] However, we do count the administrative cost of enforcing the new rule. If Congress (or the Supreme Court) ruled that the FHA must use CMA, there would be some enforcement costs, but presumably the cost of enforcing the rule would be less than $900 million dollars. We can say, then, that the present practice is probably inefficient in the sense that government intervention to cure government's own externality appears to be efficient. If this sort of example with similar numbers were to apply to private firms, presumably there would already have been a resolution. Perhaps the incentives for government officials to correct the problem are less than would be the case for profit-making entities.

7.6 ASSESSING GOVERNMENT INTERVENTION

At this point we return to the original question raised by this chapter: How is it possible to determine the proper role of government in the marketplace? We have argued thus far that the market failure idea, with its conceptual and empirical shortcomings, does not provide a reliable guide to this process. The correct normative theory rests on transactions costs, and implementing this theory is largely a matter of significant empirical inquiry.

First, the issue of government intervention is largely an empirical and not a theoretical one. As Nelson (1987, p. 556) says, 'there is no satisfactory normative theory regarding the appropriate roles of government in a mixed economy.' No theory captures the variety of institutional arrangements that have been developed to resolve collective problems. The market failure concept is not inherently empirical and as such cannot provide answers to empirical questions.

The most important empirical question is this: What are the net benefits (if any) of any particular institutional arrangement? The only general statement that can be made about government intervention on KH efficiency grounds is that government should intervene where the costs of intervention are less than the benefits. No simple diagnostic scheme can indicate whether the costs of intervention will be less than the benefits for any general class of cases. Empirical analysis invites the analyst to consider the particular costs that govern each case.

Obviously, the completion of empirical studies is more difficult and time consuming than the general search for externalities. Being ubiquitous, externalities are easy to find. Empirical studies, especially those that employ benefit–cost analysis, are hard to complete. Analysts may use the wrong formula to calculate the proportion of cost increases that fall on consumers; they may confuse expenditures with costs; they may misestimate costs or omit unintended consequences (De Alessi 1996). Policy analysts have long recognized the difficulty of completing accurate empirical studies as a guide to intervention decisions, which helps to explain why the simple diagnostic scheme offered by the market failure concept – even though ill conceived – has proved so popular.

For thinking about intervention decisions, the transactions costs concept provides analysts with insights not otherwise apparent into the relationship between government and the marketplace. It provides insights into the accumulation of institutional arrangements that exist in practice, and it avoids the endless quest for 'failures' in either the private or the public sector that provide a basis for government intervention. The transactions costs concept is correct in principle, we believe, although not all of its facets have been worked out.

The transactions costs concept invites the analyst to answer a key question: What are the transactions costs that affect the search for collective solutions, and in each case how are those costs affected by government laws and actions?

The transactions costs approach tends to restore law to a more central role in the study of government (Lowi 1992). The strengthening of private property rights often lowers transactions costs and thereby permits private parties to achieve collective solutions in situations where the costs of litigation and bargaining would otherwise be prohibitive. In such cases, government intervention through the strengthening of private property rights may improve the market. Such markets are inefficient not because of any inherent 'failures,' but because the government has neglected to provide the appropriate institutional framework.

The transactions costs approach has been used to explain much of the structure of law (Cooter and Ulen 1997; Posner 1992b). For example, the approach has been used to explain why injunctive relief is superior where bargaining is possible, but compensatory damages are more appropriate where bargaining costs are high (Calabresi and Melamed 1972). It also explains a good deal of contract behavior and contract law (Salanie 1997) and has been used well to explain government utility regulation (Goldberg 1979).

Transactions costs analysis calls attention to the characteristics of government that give it an advantage relative to other institutions in its ability to lower transactions costs. There is one such advantage: the power of coercion. A classic definition of government is that of an institution which monopolizes the use of force or coercive powers over a given territory (Weber 1958, p. 78). The government may change laws and use force to compel compliance with them; it may force payment for a good through taxation; and it may use police powers to forbid or compel actions. The most general statement that can usefully be made about government intervention is that it should perform those functions for which its powers of coercion give it an absolute advantage.

A coercive rule has the potential to benefit the public, by reducing the transactions costs of individuals within the market. The rule reduces transactions costs by reducing the individual's need to spend money on self-protection. For example, if the government did not have coercive laws against theft, most people would probably spend a lot more money protecting themselves from thieves – by hiring security guards or buying deadbolts and alarm systems – than they would spend in a country with laws against theft. Another 'cost' of 'self-protection' is theft that occurs despite the investment in self-protection. Of course, even with coercive laws against theft, most people spend some money on self-protection. However, we can safely assume that expenditures on self-protection would be much higher if there were no laws against theft.

However, a coercive rule is not necessarily efficient just because it reduces the resources people spend on self-protection. To be efficient, the reduction in the cost of self-protection must be *greater* than the transactions costs to enforce the coercive rule. There are a number of transactions costs involved in enforcing a rule: the cost of investigating violations of the rule; the cost of bringing suits alleging violations of the rule; the administrative costs of the agency that enforces the rule; the cost of the losses that occur as a result of undeterred violations of the law; and the public's cost of monitoring the government agency that enforces the rule.[16]

Suppose that a society has no laws against theft, and that the average person spends $50 on theft prevention per year and loses $100 per year to thieves. Suppose that a rule is proposed which will cost taxpayers an average of $70 a year in taxes, but which will reduce losses resulting from theft to $40 a person per year (suppose also that the taxes pay for all of the costs of enforcing the rule, including the cost of monitoring the anti-theft agency). The rule is efficient, since the cost of self-protection is $150, while the cost of government intervention is $110 a year.

There may also be a distributive justification for government intervention. This is because the cost of government intervention is normally defrayed by a progressive tax system, which reduces the burden on the poor, while the cost of self-protection is frequently (but not necessarily) imposed at a flat cost, placing a disproportionate burden on the poor. In an extreme case, a poor person may not have *any* money to spend on self-protection, but society may have a strong feeling that that person should receive at least some protection from theft. On the other hand, the cost of hiring police officers, judges, and prison wardens to prevent theft is paid for by taxes, which do not fall disproportionately on the poor. Of course, it is possible for self-protective measures to be structured so that the burden on the poor is reduced. For example, a private group could be formed to prevent theft, and it might charge membership dues on a sliding scale based on income. However, it is unlikely that the price of self-protective measures would be structured in this way. Similarly, it is *possible* for the cost of government intervention to be paid by a flat fee rather than by a progressive tax, but the cost of government intervention is *usually* progressive. Therefore, government intervention does not necessarily further distributive justice as a matter of theory or logic, but, in practice, government intervention frequently *does* further distributive justice.

Of course, if you asked most people why it is desirable to have the government prevent theft from occurring, they would not say that the rule is a good one because the reduction in the cost of self-protection is greater than the cost of government intervention. Rather, they would say that the rule is good because it prevents theft from occurring, and theft is a 'bad act' which should not occur. However, the fact that theft is a 'bad act' does not make it efficient for the government to suppress it. Socially undesirable behavior can be deterred by a variety of things, including self-protection, government intervention, and cultural norms. It is only efficient to rely on the government to suppress 'bad acts' when the government can deter them at the lowest cost, or when the *fairest* way to distribute the cost of deterring the behavior is by relying on government intervention and taxation.

What are the important market failures to which its advocates refer? They are simply instances in which there is a strong possibility that government action can lower transactions costs sufficiently to produce significant welfare gains.

Chief among the market-enhancing measures that government undertakes is the creation of institutions that strengthen private property rights. As North and Thomas (1973, p. 8) note, 'governments take over the protection and enforcement of property rights because they can do it at lower cost than private volunteer groups.' Property law, dealing with fraud, extortion, contract, and torts, is perhaps the best example of a situation in which the existence of coercive laws reduces the cost of distributing goods within the relevant markets. Changes in the law of contract or fraud are among the most important measures that government provides. These do not fit well into the market failure concept, but are easily analyzed through the transactions costs approach (Zerbe and Urban 1988).

Similarly, disagreements about measurements, a type of transactions cost, may invite regulation by the state (Eggertsson 1990, p. 27). Measurement costs are those that arise in determining the quality of a good that has many characteristics. Government efforts to supply uniform weights and measures have sharply lowered measurement costs, as have private organizations such as the Chicago Board of Trade and the New York Stock Exchange, institutions to which government has in part transferred its coercive powers. Various trade associations also provide uniform standards. Zerbe and Urban (1988) argued some time ago that licensing of day care by state government may be justified as a way of lowering costs of quality determination. Licensing of professions, such as medicine represents, at least in part, an attempt to lower measurement costs (Leffler 1978). We would not, however, call these stories of market failure. We would say simply that in many situations the government possesses advantages in obtaining consent for the use of uniform standards.

Culture can act as a substitute for government action (Ellickson 1991; Ostrom 1990). A culture in which honesty is widely practiced, for example, will reduce transactions costs devoted to preventing fraud. Similarly, private innovations of a technical nature that reduce transaction costs may allow the production of some goods that formerly were not feasible.

Better empirical analysis, more attention to net benefits, and a deeper understanding of transactions costs would all help to improve the process of policy analysis. Continued reliance upon the market failure concept will not.

The market failure model ultimately fails, like other deductive models, because it is not sufficiently derived from an empirical base (Zerbe and Medema 1997). It is not sufficiently inductive, and instead relies upon methods of understanding that derive specific propositions from general principles without much attention to observed facts. As Coase (1964, p. 195) has pointed out, there is little that can be learned from the study of theoretical optimal systems.[17] Analysts who become enamored of 'blackboard economics,' where equations are substituted for underpinnings, produce concepts that bear little correspondence to the actual social system. The world portrayed is one that exists only on the blackboard: 'the analysis is carried out with great ingenuity, but it floats in the air' (Coase 1988, p. 10). The analysis called out with KHZ, however, does not float.

NOTES

This chapter is derived from two papers (Zerbe and McCurdy 1999, 2000). In those papers we thanked Douglas Allen, Leigh Anderson, Jonathan Bendor, Greg Ellis, Elinor Ostrom, Robert Plotnick, Steve Smith, and William Zumeta for useful comments, and I would like to reiterate my thanks here. Steve Vinyard and I have added a section here dealing with non-market failure and consider the use of salt on icy roads. We have also added a section using protection against theft as an example of a situation in which government intervention may be efficient.

1. There is relatively little mention in this literature of transaction costs.
2. Such property rights may be private or public. When the government provides goods directly or supports the provision of goods and services through taxation policies, it creates a government property right with associated transactions costs.
3. The first formal statement of the Coase Theorem did not appear until 1966, when George Stigler (1966, p. 113) wrote that 'the Coase theorem ... asserts that under perfect competition private and social costs will be equal.' Since this original formulation, the Theorem has been stated in numerous ways, including: '[I]f one assumes rationality, no transaction

costs, and no legal impediments to bargaining, *all* misallocations of resources would be fully cured in the market by bargains' (Calabresi 1968, p. 68, emphasis in original) and '[I]f transaction costs are zero the structure of the law does not matter because efficiency will result in any case' (Polinsky 1974, p. 1665). Paradoxically, the Coase Theorem has spawned a huge literature dealing with the artificial world of zero transactions costs, but Coase meant to emphasize real-world analysis (see Medema and Zerbe 2000a and 2000b).

4. Of course, problems of non-convex production sets exist. Sufficiently large non-convexities in the production sets of victimized firms involve situations in which a victim is not better off with a marginal reduction in the size of the externality. The victim will not be willing to pay the polluter $100,000 for a change that will make him or her $25,000 better off if the first step along this path involves spending a dollar to get a zero improvement in welfare. The victim, unwilling to take this first step, will not know that better things lie over the horizon. Information about the overall value of reducing pollution will not be furnished. To consider the example in terms of transactions costs indicates that the problem here is one of information which is a type of transactions cost: the victim will take this first, welfare-reducing step if certain that, in the end, he or she would be better off. If both victim and polluter knew of the existence of a superior position, they could also merge to achieve it. The non-convexities argument introduces imperfect information into the model. Whether government can more efficiently supply this information or whether it can be generated through negotiations is a matter of particular circumstances and legal structure and can be determined only by a more detailed examination of the particular situation (Ostrom 1990; Medema and Zerbe 2000a and 2000b).
5. This issue is treated formally in the appendix to the 1999 article by Zerbe and McCurdy.
6. This is not a hard-and-fast rule. Where government intervenes to restrain an undesirable market, such as the market for cocaine, it may be efficient to increase transaction costs.
7. We wish to thank physicist David Boulware for useful discussion on this point.
8. See Cheung (1969, pp. 3–4, 7–8, and the references cited therein). Additional problems are said to be (1) the short duration of the leases and (2) discouragement of effort on the part of the tenant, since a portion of each unit of output must be paid to the landowner as rent.
9. The strong version of the Coase Theorem includes an invariance claim and predicts that, if transactions costs are zero (low) and there are well-defined private property rights in land, the allocation of resources will be 'the same whether the landowner cultivates the land himself, hires farm hands to do the tilling, leases his holdings on a fixed rent basis, or shares the actual yield with his tenant. In other words, 'different [observed] contractual arrangements do not imply different efficiencies of resource use' (Cheung 1969, p. 4).
10. Of course, there may be benefits not captured in the land conferred by the trustee arrangements, though it is difficult to imagine they are so great as to justify this enormous cost.
11. Cheung notes the existence of two factors that could potentially complicate these arrangements (relative to standard lease contracts), both of which relate to other levels of external effects. First, there are potential spillovers from one farmer contracting for pollination services, which could potentially lead neighbors to take strategic advantage by employing fewer hives themselves. Second, the use of pesticide sprays by one farmer may result in damage to the bees kept on nearby farms. But both of these issues are dealt with through either custom or explicit contracting (such as the payment of risk premiums for potential exposure to pesticides), depending on the circumstances. The reliance on custom here is an interesting parallel to Ellickson (1991), discussed above.
12. Although the value of having de-iced roads is hard to calculate, Plater *et al.* (1998) assume that it exceeds the cost of purchasing and applying salt, which is $200 million per year.
13. Plater *et al.*'s suggestion that CMA would cost five times more than salt is somewhat confusing. CMA costs $300 to $600 a ton, while salt costs $20 to $70 a ton. The average cost of CMA would appear to be $450/ton, compared with an average cost of $45/ton for salt. Therefore, CMA appears to be ten times more expensive than salt, not five times more expensive. However, Plater's estimated $200 million expenditure on salt includes the cost of purchasing and *applying* salt, not just the cost of purchasing it. CMA is

probably not any more expensive to *apply* than salt is, so the cost of purchasing and applying CMA might be roughly five times that of salt, not ten times.

14. Among other things, Dr. Wurster's report suggests that it might be wise to re-examine the assumption that it is efficient to de-ice roads at all. The FHA assumes that the cost of de-icing roads is only $200 million, when the actual costs borne by the public are $2.91 billion. The cost of de-icing roads would only be $1.9 billion if CMA was used, but the benefits of having de-iced roads might be less than $1.9 billion; in that case, the use of neither CMA nor salt would be efficient.
15. Given the powerful vested interests which benefit from the FHA's use of salt, the cost of changing the rule would probably be very great.
16. One reason why the government has a monopoly on coercive power may be that the cost of monitoring the government's use of force is lower than the cost of monitoring a private body which is allowed to use force. For example, suppose a private company wants a law that will give it the authority to imprison people who it believes committed crimes on its property. If we ignore the cost of monitoring the company to ensure that it does not violate the suspected criminals' civil rights, the rule might appear to be efficient. The company might be able to acquire security guards and private 'judges,' and rent or purchase facilities in which to imprison inmates, at a lower cost than the government spends on policemen, real judges, and state prisons. However, most Americans would be extremely reluctant to allow a private company to have this sort of police power, and would fear that the company would abuse the rule – by imprisoning people based on insufficient evidence, or even by imprisoning people who were not suspected of having committed a crime at all but whom the company disliked for other reasons entirely. The public cost of monitoring the company, to ensure that it did not violate people's civil rights, might be much higher than the cost of monitoring a governmental police force, judiciary, and prison. Therefore, it would be inefficient to allow a private company to enforce the criminal law.
17. In a similar vein, Coase argues that 'generalizations are not likely to be helpful unless they are derived from studies of how such activities are actually carried out within different institutional frameworks. Such studies would enable us to discover which factors are important and which are not in determining the outcome and would lead to generalizations which have a solid base. They are also likely to serve another purpose, by showing us the richness of the social alternatives between which we can choose' (Coase 1974, p. 375).

8. Of distributive justice and economic efficiency: An integrated theory of the common law

8.1 GENERAL INTRODUCTION

This chapter primarily applies two parts of axiom 5, the subsection defining a good which requires that all values be included which can conceptually be measured by a WTP or a WTA (5a) and the concept of the regard for others (5c). Here I consider issues of common law efficiency. Recall that the regard for others refers to the value people place on projects that do not directly affect them but whose effects they care about, either because they care about those affected or because they care about the principles used in determining the project outcome. They may care about the principle or rule because it may affect them or others in the future.

One of the more prominent theories of the common law is the theory that the common law is KH efficient.[1] That theory holds that the common law is best described as a system designed to promote the traditional notion of KH efficiency (Posner 1992b, p. 23).[2] Although the traditional theory offers a persuasive explanation of how many common law rules have arisen (Bruce 1984), it has also 'aroused considerable antagonism' from critics who feel that the law should not be viewed as a product of economic forces (Posner 1992b, pp. 25–26). Yet its underlying validity remains.[3]

That validity is vulnerable, however, since the theory may be invalidated through the introduction of an alternative theory that better explains common law reality (Kuhn 1970; Posner 1992b, pp. 17–18; Beutel 1957).[4] Two facts make the possibility of such invalidation particularly likely. First, the concept of KH efficiency, upon which the traditional theory is built, can be improved (Zerbe 1998b). The traditional analysis erroneously mandates that the economic efficiency of an allocative change be measured independently of the effect of that change on the distribution of wealth and the fact of compensation (Zerbe 1998b, pp. 426f).[5] This, in turn, results in either the neglect or abrogation of distributive justice concerns.[6] The second fact is that judges seek not only an efficient but a just result – one in which justice is both corrective and distributive.[7] Taken together, these facts suggest that an efficiency theory which properly considers not only traditional efficiency but also distributive justice will provide a better description of the common law than does the traditional theory. Indeed, the aim of this book is to show that an integrated theory of efficiency – namely KHZ, better explains common law efficiency than the traditional theory.

I will show that KHZ offers a better explanation of the common law by considering three common law rules which have puzzled KH theorists, but which can be resolved by KHZ. First, I consider an example from criminal law: the rule that so-called 'efficient rapes' are nonetheless illegal. Second, I consider an example from contract law: the rule that waivers of liability for negligence are normally unenforceable. Third, I consider an example from tort law: the collapse of the rule against contribution. In each example, I show that under KH the current common law rule appears to be inefficient, but that under KHZ the common law rule is efficient. In particular, I show that these three common law rules are clearly efficient once the regard for others is incorporated into our analysis.

8.2 CRIMINAL LAW: THE CASE OF RAPE

Introduction

The most infamous result of traditional economic analysis[8] is that some rapes are arguably efficient, and thus inexplicably illegal.[9] Because the possibility of efficient, and therefore legal rape is contrary to existing laws,[10] such laws are glaring (and potentially invalidating) anomalies of the traditional efficiency theory.[11] No comparable anomaly arises under KHZ, however, and it will, therefore, be demonstrated that rape law is better explained by KHZ than by traditional KH efficiency. This demonstration will proceed in four steps. First, the law of rape will be briefly recapitulated. Second, the susceptibility of rape to market analysis will be considered. Third, the traditional KH efficiency theory of rape law will be reviewed and discussed. Finally, the integrated theory of rape law will be contrasted, and an appropriate conclusion drawn.

Rape Jurisprudence

Although the prohibition against rape is now defined statutorily, it is of common law origin.[12] In early English law, as in ancient codes 'the legal treatment of rape depended on the victim's relationship with a man' (Dripps 1992, pp. 1780–1781). Thus, the 'rape of a virgin was punishable by castration and blinding' (Dripps 1992, p. 1782, citing Bracton 1968, pp. 414–415), while that of a non-virgin was a matter relegated to 'the local feudal courts or private vengeance.' Ultimately, however, the common law came to protect all women against rape (Dripps 1992, p. 1782),[13] a crime it defined as 'the carnal knowledge of a woman forcibly and against her will' (Blackstone 1900, p. 210).[14] One of the most notorious elements of the common law treatment of rape was the marital exemption, by which 'a husband who forced his wife to engage in sexual intercourse with him was not guilty of rape' (Dressler 1987, p. 516, citing Matthew Hale 1736, p. 628).[15]

This exemption is indicative of the the common law's more problematic justification for the rape prohibition itself: the conception that certain women are the property of certain men. Specifically, daughters were held to be the property of fathers, and wives that of husbands. Thus, at common law, rape was a 'property offense,' by which the rapist stole 'the property rights of the father or husband,' who were, consequently, considered the true victims of the rape (Dressler 1987, p. 520).[16]

The repugnance of this conception to contemporary sensibilities[17] erupted as the rape reform movement of the 1970s, and by the mid 1980s 'nearly all states had enacted some form of rape reform legislation'. Many of these states replaced the common law crime of rape with 'a series of gender-neutral graded offenses' (Spohn and Horney 1992, pp. 20–22).[18] Despite such statutory renovation, however, the fact remains that the law has historically punished and continues to punish, at least those acts defined at common law as rape (Dripps 1992, p. 1783).[19] An efficiency theory should be able to explain the current state of rape law.

The Susceptibility of Rape to Market Analysis

Because any economic analysis of rape assumes the existence of a market for sexual services,[20] the susceptibility of rape to such analysis has been the subject of considerable debate.[21] However, it is important to note that there does not need to be a literal 'sex market' for economic analysis of rape to be possible; all that economics requires is that the metaphor of a market helps one describe and interpret the behavior of the actors (Chapter 2).[22] Furthermore, the market does not have to be defined as one for sexual services. For example, one can posit a market for sexual intimacy or romantic happiness. Moreover, speaking of sexuality in market terms does not imply that actors choose sexual partners in a calculated exchange of money for pleasure, or power for beauty (Chapter 2).

However, many writers who have conducted an economic analysis of rape are speaking of 'sex markets' in fairly literal senses (Posner 1992a). Most proponents of an economic analysis of rape have endorsed the 'commodity theory' of sexual relations.[23] This theory holds that 'sexual cooperation is a service much like any other.'[24] Specifically, it assumes that each individual has a 'property right … to his or her own body and [thus, to] his or her own sexual service' (Dripps 1992, p. 1786).[25] As a result, such services can be 'traded in social or intimate markets in exchange for some reciprocal bundle of goods…toward the personal and societal end of maximizing wealth' (West 1993, p. 2430).

According to Posner, the commodity theory's leading proponent,[26] and contrary to the feminist prospective,[27] rape is 'simply a substitute for consensual sex, which is engaged in by normal … heterosexuals for whom the cost of consensual sex is simply too high' (West 1993, p. 2421, citing Posner 1992a, pp. 106–107, 182–183, 384–385).[28] This proposition suggests that 'a rational model of "normal" human behavior can be used to analyze the behavior of rapists' (Posner 1992a, p. 386),[29] and 'implies a putative economic explanation for the illegality of rape' (West 1993, p. 2430). According to that explanation, in the absence of market failure, the market assures efficient transactions (Cooter and Ulen 1997, pp. 37–42) but efforts to bypass the market can result in inefficient transactions.[30] As a result, attempts to 'bypass' the market must be 'discouraged by a legal sanction bent on promoting efficiency' (Posner 1985b, p. 1195). Because rape 'bypasses' the market in 'sexual relations' it should therefore be forbidden (Posner 1992b, p. 218).[31] According to this conception, 'the average forcible rapist is in effect a sex thief' (Posner 1992a, p. 182), and thus, 'rape is the theft of one's sexuality' (West 1993, p. 2430).

Opponents of economic analysis of rape argue that such 'market rhetoric' is improper because sexual services are incommensurable with market commodities (Radin 1987, pp. 1921–1925). In other words, sexual services on the one hand, and all other goods on the other, are not 'comparable in terms of their value' (Duxbury 1995, pp. 657, 660).[32] Therefore, no one measure can be used to value sexual services and all other goods, and insofar as economic analysis seeks to 'evaluate' both types of 'goods along a single metric,' it is inapplicable to the problem of rape (ibid., p. 674).

Indeed, for those who accept the incommensurability of sexual services, the phantom of efficient rape vanishes.[33] As will be explained further, efficient rape is conceivable only when it is deemed feasible to compare the value of sexual services taken by the rapist with the loss incurred by the rape victim from having such services taken without his or her consent (Posner 1992b, p. 218).[34] If sexual services are deemed incommensurable, however, it would be impossible to make such comparisons.[35] Thus, proponents of incommensurability 'would not presume collectively and objectively to value the cost of a rape to the victim against the benefit to the rapist, even if economic efficiency' were the sole motive (Calabresi and Melamed 1972, p. 1125).[36]

Nevertheless, the real question is not what consequences follow from a conclusion of incommensurability, but whether that conclusion is, itself, proper (Duxbury 1995, p. 678).[37] There are at least three general theories of the propriety of the incommensurability of sexual services.

First, Radin argues that thinking 'of rape in market rhetoric implicitly conceives of as fungible something we know to be ... too personal even to be personal property' (1987, pp. 1921–1925).[38] Thus it is argued that sexual services are so intimately interwoven with the person as to be inseparable therefrom, and thus incommensurable.[39] The problem with this theory is that it amounts to a tautology by which anything called 'personal' is automatically deemed 'incommensurable.'[40] The real question is why 'personal property' should be assumed to be 'incommensurable.'[41] Until this question can be satisfactorily addressed, the theory itself must be considered inadequate.[42]

A second theory of incommensurability holds that, given the existing distribution of wealth, commodification of sexual services is morally problematic (West 1993, pp. 2431–2432; Chamallas 1988). For example, West (1993, pp. 2431–2432) argues that given the current 'political and societal hierarchical structures,' a 'woman' may be induced 'to consent to sex, that while not rape, might very well be unwanted, unenjoyed, invasive, painful, demeaning, and dehumanizing.'[43] If such sex arises through a market transaction, it is, according to the commodity theory, nevertheless legal (West 1993, p. 2431). Thus, it is argued, 'the commodity theory of sex legitimate[s] apparently consensual transactions, even in circumstances of grossly unequal distributions of sexual power' thereby perpetuating 'our collective blindness to the pervasive systems of sexual coercion that render all of our heterosexual practices, and not just rape, morally suspect' (West 1993, p. 2431).[44]

There are at least two problems with this theory. First and foremost, its conclusion is irrelevant (Landes and Posner 1987, p. 9).[45] The law itself makes many immoral sexual acts legal and thus arguably legitimate.[46] The fact that a theory posited to explain that law reaches the same conclusion is not an indictment of that theory but an endorsement.[47] Second, because there is no necessary correlation between law and morality, a theory which pronounces a given activity legal does not necessarily pronounce it moral or otherwise legitimate.[48] Moreover, characterizing an activity as 'efficient' is not a moral justification, either (Chapter 2). It is possible, and even likely, for an immoral law to be efficient if the society's regard for others is sufficiently misinformed or unenlightened (Chapter 5). Put bluntly, a sexist law will usually be efficient in a sexist society. The solution is not to pretend that a sexist law is inefficient, but to attack – and thereby to change – the social norms (Chapter 2).

A third theory of incommensurability holds that market valuations of sexual services degrade human sexuality itself.[49] This is based on a misunderstanding of what it means to study sexuality from market perspective – a misunderstanding shared by both Posner (1992b) and his critics.[50] Contrary to Radin's (1987, pp. 1921–1925) suggestion, speaking of sexuality in economic terms is not mere 'rhetoric' to justify the exploitation of women by men. Rather, an economic analysis of rape allows one to clarify (and quantify) what is gained and lost by the rapist, the victim, and society as a whole.[51] An economic analysis of sexuality is only degrading if it ignores or undermines the importance of emotional, political, spiritual, or romantic concerns. It is tempting (and customary) to speak of these things as non-economic concerns. However, properly understood, an economic analysis of sex will incorporate all values that affect a person's behavior in a sex market. Using economics to discuss people's sexual behavior does not imply that they accept or reject potential partners in an emotionally detached or reductionist way. Since most people's 'willingness to accept' a sexual partner depends on more than the other person's beauty, money and power, an economic analysis of sex must incorporate a broader range of values. Furthermore, a properly conducted economic analysis of sex will incorporate the community's regard for others (Chapter 5). Therefore, an economic analysis of sex can be degrading only to the extent that the community's norms are degrading, since an economic analysis of sex must consider every factor that the community views as important.[52]

The Traditional Kaldor–Hicks Efficiency Theory of Rape Law

The traditional KH efficiency theory of rape law starts from the proposition that 'the substantive doctrines of the criminal law ... promote efficiency' (Posner 1985b, pp. 1194–1195). Given low transactions costs, 'the market is, virtually by definition, the most efficient method of allocating resources.'[53] Therefore, the traditional theory holds that 'the major function of the criminal law ... is to prevent people from bypassing the "market," ... in situations where transactions costs are low.' In consequence, the criminal law forbids, among other things, inefficient transactions that occur outside of the relevant market, or 'pure coercive transfers of wealth' (Posner 1992b, pp. 217–220).[54] Because rape bypasses 'the market in sexual relations,' it is often a pure coercive transfer, and should, therefore, be criminally forbidden (Posner 1992).[55] Because rape has been a crime in most cultures throughout their histories, the traditional KH efficiency theory of rape law initially seems consistent with that law and thus, at least in this sense, valid.[56]

The traditional theory encounters difficulty, however, in explaining the prohibition against so-called 'efficient rape,' that is, rape which is not a pure coercive transfer of wealth, but an impure coercive transfer with a positive social welfare effect.[57] It is important to note that although Posner coined the phrase 'efficient rape,' he is skeptical that efficient rapes exist, even in the narrow sense of the word (1985b, p. 1199). Posner, among others, attempts to justify the law's prohibition of such rapes on three major grounds.[58] First, Posner (1985b, p. 1199) seems to argue that the opportunity cost of the activity commonly called efficient rape is high enough to make such rape inefficient. Second, Posner (1992a, pp. 386–387) states that allowing so-called efficient rape 'would not really be utility maximizing, if only because of the fear it would engender in the community as a whole and the expense of the self-protective measures that this fear would incite.'[59] Third, Landes and Posner (1987, p. 158) argue that the measurement problems in comparing the hypothetical offer price of the rapist with the hypothetical demand price of the victim 'are overwhelmingly difficult and hardly worth undertaking to identify the rare rape that may in some sense be thought to increase social wealth.'

Posner's first argument has two problems. First, since utility is not measurable – as Posner (1985b, p. 1197) himself recognizes – it is impossible to compare the 'opportunity cost' of rape with the utility to the rapist or its disutility to the victim. Because Posner provides no means of measuring the gains or losses associated with rape, it is impossible to determine whether the opportunity cost of rape is 'too high.' More to the point, Posner's (1985b, p. 1199) opportunity cost argument depends on the existence of a sufficient market substitute for rape. Posner (1992b, p. 142) argues that there are a variety of markets which furnish low cost substitites for rape, such as prostitution and dating markets. To those who argue that there is no market substitute for rape, since an essential element of pleasure for a rapist is violent subjugation, Posner (1985b, pp. 1198–1199) makes two replies. First, Posner argues that many potential rapists, who are actually deterred by the rape laws, do not derive the bulk of their pleasure from violence, and therefore can find a market substitute for rape (indeed, if the rape law deterred them and they are not currently celibate, they did find a market substitute). Second, Posner argues that even rapists who prefer non-consensual sex to consensual sex probably receive some pleasure from consensual sex. Therefore, dating and prostitution are market substitutes for rape even if they are not perfect substitutes. Posner's first defense of his statement that there are market substitutes for rape is highly speculative, since it is impossible to know the psychological traits of people who would commit rape if it was not illegal. In any event, there is a wealth of psychological evidence that an essential element of the pleasure of rape to people who actually commit rape is the forcible subjugation of the victim (Schwartz 1979, p. 806). Posner's second argument for the existence of market substitutes strains the concept of market substitutes past its breaking point. At some point a market substitute is so poor that forcing somebody to rely on it deprives him or her of almost as much wealth as depriving them of the good altogether. Although there may be poor substitutes for it, rape as unwanted sexual violence has no *good* market substitute (Schwartz 1979, p. 806), as Posner (1992b, p. 218) himself acknowledged in an earlier work.

Posner's (1992a, pp. 386–387) second argument, that even efficient rape is 'not really utility maximizing,' is unconvincing, because Posner does not provide any criteria to help us test or evaluate the claim. Just as the utility of a rapist and the disutility of the victim cannot be compared, the disutility of rape for the community as a whole cannot be measured. While it is true that 'the crime of rape can be supported by the idea that its deterrent effect spares [potential victims] the discomfort of worrying about being subjected to rape at some later time,' the law also 'deprives potential rapists of the pleasures of anticipation' (Schwartz 1979, p. 807, n. 33).[60] Frankly, 'there is insufficient economic reason for assuming that the reduced apprehension is greater than the deprived anticipation.' The source of the problem is that Posner (1992a, p. 386) does not view this argument as 'economic' at all, but as a 'utilitarian' argument. In fact, the effect of rape on the community as a whole can be studied economically under KHZ, through the concept of the regard for others (Chapter 2). Once the effect on the community is recognized as an 'economic' concern, it can be tested and evaluated in a meaningful way.

Posner's third argument, that efficient rapes should be illegal because the transactions costs for identifying efficient rapes would be too high, cannot be dismissed lightly (Landes and Posner 1987, p. 158). It is likely true that the cost of adjudicating claims of efficient rape would be high, precisely because it is problematic to compare the rapist's utility with the victim's disutility. However, a court might develop a low cost 'rule of thumb' to identify rapes that are likely to be efficient. For example, the ancient common law rule allowing husbands to rape their wives (Dressler 1987, p. 516) may have been such a low cost rule of thumb for determining efficiency. More importantly, it is unsatisfying to say that the primary reason for outlawing efficient rapes is that they are costly to identify. Like Posner's other explanations for rape law, it leaves open the possibility of the act of rape itself being efficient. Intuitively, it simply does not feel right to say that the reason the law condemns efficient rapes is because efficient rapes are too hard to identify. By using KHZ efficiency analysis, we can explain this intuitive sense of inadequacy in economic terms. Under KHZ, rape is never efficient, at least in modern American society, so the problem of efficient rape disappears.

KHZ Theory of Rape Law

A KHZ analysis of rape shows that the act of rape itself will be almost invariably inefficient given current social attitudes, even in the rare (and arguably non-existent) case where the rapist's pleasure exceeds the victim's pain, and not just because of transactions costs. Posner (1992b, p. 1197) compares the 'utility' of rape to the rapist with the 'disutility' of rape to the victim, which is problematic, because 'utility' is not empirically testable. KHZ's analysis of rape differs from Posner's (1992a) in two regards. First, KHZ compares the rapist's pleasure and the victim's pain by comparing the WTP of the rapist (WTP_r) with the WTA of the victim (WTA_v). No one has attempted to study WTP_r and WTA_v, but unlike 'utility' these two criteria could be measured.[61] Second, and more important, KHZ considers the economic effect of rape on society as a whole (through the regard for others: R) as well as its effect on the immediate actors. For the act of rape to be efficient, WTP_r must be higher than the sum of WTA_v and R. In other words

$$WTP_r > WTA_v + R \rightarrow \text{Rape is efficient}$$

Therefore, even in the rare (and arguably non-existent) case in which WTP_r was higher than WTA_v, rape would be inefficient if R was greater than the difference between WTP_r and WTA_v. There is a wealth of anecdotal evidence concerning R, so R may be reasonably estimated. [62] Rape is emphatically wrong by all popularly held moral standards in America.[63] Indeed, American society's disgust with rape is so intense that some segments would like to see some convicted rapists put to death.[64] Posner (1992a, 386–387) himself does not question the validity of the social conviction that rape is morally reprehensible, he simply regards this as economically irrelevant.[65] Given how widely and roundly rape is condemned, R may safely be presumed to be a very large number, probably approaching infinity.[66] Therefore, for rape to be efficient, WTP_r must be higher than WTA_v by an almost infinite amount. In other words, for rape to be efficient, the victim would have to feel only the slightest discomfort, while the rapist would have to feel an epiphany of perfect delight. As a practical matter, given current norms, rape is KHZ inefficient even when WTP_r is higher than WTA_v, so the failure to make an exception for these 'efficient' rapes is also efficient, even without considering transaction costs.

Conversely, some rapes could be efficient in a society which tolerates rape, since the results under KHZ depend on the sentiments of a community. For example, consider the ancient common law rule's exemption for husbands (Dressler 1987, p. 516). Under the norms prevailing during the Middle Ages, a woman's sexuality was regarded as the property of her husband or father (ibid., p. 520).[67] A woman who shared the norms of her age might not feel a psychological entitlement to her sexual autonomy, and thus would experience rape in WTP, not WTA terms. On the other hand, the husband might feel 'entitled' to rape his wife, and might experience rape as a change in wealth in

WTA, not WTP terms. Most communities during the Middle Ages seemingly had little or no regard for women's sexual autonomy, and society did not experience a loss when a woman's autonomy was violated by her husband, so R would be nearly zero (ibid.). In such a sexist society, rape might be efficient whenever $WTA_r > WTP_v$. Since WTA is frequently higher than WTP, rape might be efficient on a fairly frequent basis. Therefore, the ancient common law exemption may have been efficient (ibid.). Of course, the ancient common law rule may have simply reflected men's power at that time, as well as their indifference towards or ignorance of the interests of women.

The fact that the rape law of the Middle Ages may have been KHZ efficient demonstrates that KHZ does not always show us what we should do (Chapter 2). It simply allows us to evaluate the efficiency of a rule, given current social attitudes. KHZ can lead to horrifying results when a community has horrifyingly ignorant attitudes.

Furthermore, it is not unreasonable to argue that regardless of law and custom, women have always felt ownership of their bodies and of their sexual autonomies. If so, they would experience the loss associated with rape in a WTA sense regardless of what their legal rights were. This would lead to the conclusion that the ancient custom was inefficient, since its prediction that a husband's gain was lower than his wife's loss would frequently be incorrect.

The eventual abandonment of the exemption for husbands can be explained by a change in the regard for others. When social attitudes about a woman's right to her sexual autonomy changed, communities *did* experience a loss when a woman was raped by her husband. When the regard for others changed, the exemption was no longer efficient (or it was even more glaringly inefficient), and so the exemption was largely abandoned (Spohn and Horney 1992, p. 20), just as KHZ would predict.[68]

Thus, 'efficient rapes' have not been invariably illegal. When there were communities where efficient rape was possible (or when male lawmakers thought efficient rape was possible), an exemption from rape liability was recognized. The common law exemption also imposed low transactions costs, since it would be simple to determine if a rapist was a woman's husband. This shows that, contrary to Landes and Posner's (1987) suggestion, high transactions costs will not necessarily prevent a society from making an exemption for so-called 'efficient rapes,' since a society may use easily administered 'rules of thumb' as proxies for efficiency.

Posner (1992b, pp. 218–219) discusses the ancient common law's exemption for husbands, but he apparently does not view it as an 'efficient rape.' Rather, Posner suggests that marital rape was not really rape at all in traditional communities: marital rape was at most a 'dilute[d]' form of rape. In essence, marriage was a market in which men offered their services as protectors and providers, and women offered their services as sexual partners.

Although women did not consent to be raped, they consented to a social order in which fairly frequent marital rapes were inevitable, and where marital rape was unpunished.[69] Though Posner acknowledges that there is a difference between having the right to 'demand something' and having 'the right to take it by force,' he urges that the sense of impropriety is 'dilute[d]' in such cases.[70]

For Posner, wealth maximization apparently refers both to KH efficiency and to increasing productivity; indeed, at some points in his writing he incorrectly views KH efficiency and productivity as synonymous.[71] Therefore, Posner (1992b, pp. 218–219) believes that rape law, and, indeed, all law, is most efficient when it maximizes productivity. In traditional communities, the most prized goods that women produced were sexual and procreative services. A law which prevented men from raping their wives would reduce the productivity of women in that community. The law of rape changed when women's productivity changed. When increased numbers of women began working, their productivity increased and expanded beyond providing sexual and procreative services. When women's productivity increased they became wealthier as a class, and were therefore less willing to sacrifice sexual autonomy in return for protection. KHZ would similarly expect women's WTP for marital rape to increase as women became wealthier, since WTP, to a greater extent than WTA, is dependent on the woman's wealth.

The problem with Posner's discussion of the marital exemption is that it is incomplete, because it ignores the roles of psychological reference points and the regard for others. Productivity is not synonymous with KH efficiency (let alone KHZ), since it does not recognize the psychological difference between gains and losses. The fact that women became more 'productive' (at least in a materialistic sense) when they entered the work force in larger numbers may explain why more women were 'willing to pay' for less abusive husbands, but it does not explain why the legal rules were changed. In fact, even if the rules for rape had not been changed, we would expect a higher percentage of working women to avoid marital rape by 'buying' non-abusive husbands. Posner may mean not only that women were individually willing to pay for non-abusive husbands, but that they were collectively willing to pay for a change in the social order, but it is not clear that he is saying this. Assuming Posner is saying this, his argument is incomplete: the same norm that legitimated marital rape would have excluded women from the work force. For women's productivity to change, the norms regarding women's roles as producers would have to change as well.

In contrast, KHZ sees the change in rape law as reflecting a change in norms, as well as a change in women's bargaining position. KHZ does not quarrel with Posner's suggestion that women's willingness to tolerate abuse – individually and collectively – changed when they became less dependent on men for financial support. KHZ simply points out that the change in norms was an important factor in changing the law. Indeed, there was most likely a complex relationship between women's increased presence in labor and political markets and the collapse of the norms that excluded women from the work force and which tolerated marital rape. When the norms changed, rape was no longer seen as something that a woman had to 'bargain' to avoid. Marital rape was seen as a 'bad bargain' for the entire community, because the entire community suffered a loss when a woman was raped by her husband. Therefore, the community made marital rape illegal without inquiring into the husband's pleasure or the wife's pain, because no amount of pleasure on the husband's part would overcome the community's sense of loss. When the community's norms were different, marital rape may not have been a bad bargain for the entire community, and it may have been KHZ efficient to leave marital rape up to the market – in other words, to place the burden on women to avoid marital rape by 'purchasing' non-abusive husbands.

Thus, KHZ efficiency theory is better able to explain rape law than its traditional counterpart. In modern American society, all rapes are inefficient under KHZ, while some may be efficient under KH. Furthermore, KHZ offers a better explanation than Posner does as to why the law used to allow exemptions from rape liability, but does not do so (to the same extent) today. The result is that, ceteris paribus, the criminal law is better explained by KHZ than by traditional KH efficiency (Schwartz 1979, pp. 812–813).

8.3 CONTRACT LAW: THE CASE OF EXCULPATORY CLAUSES

Introduction

An exculpatory clause is a contract clause that purportedly releases one of the parties to the contract 'from liability for his or her wrongful acts' (*Black's Law Dictionary* 1990).[72] Exculpatory clauses, which putatively relieve a party from liability for that party's own negligence, form another body of jurisprudence better explained by KHZ than by traditional KH efficiency. This will be shown in three stages. First, the relevant law will be reviewed. Second, the traditional KH efficiency theory of that law will be explored. Finally, the integrated KHZ theory of exculpatory clause jurisprudence will be compared.

Exculpatory Clause Jurisprudence

'In general contract law favors enforcement of agreements without judicial review of either the overall fairness or individual terms of the exchange'

(Schell 1993, p. 433).[73] Nevertheless, there are times when 'a court will decide that the public interest in freedom of contract is outweighed by some other public policy, and will refuse to enforce the agreement or some part of it on that ground' (Farnsworth 1982, pp. 52–53).[74] One of the most important public policies under which contracts have been held unenforceable is that against the commission or inducement of torts (Restatement of the Law, Second, of Contracts §§192 and 194; Farnsworth 1990, pp. 352–353, 1982, p. 332). It is under this policy that courts have held certain exculpatory clauses unenforceable.[75] Though it is true that the enforceability of exculpatory clauses varies with the nature of the tort liability such clauses purport to excuse, only clauses purporting to excuse a party from liability for personal injuries resulting from their own negligence will be considered here.[76] Such clauses are generally held unenforceable at least if (1) the parties did not have equal bargaining power or (2) the public interest is involved (Eisenberg 1993, p. 110; Talbott 1988, p. 30, citing *Schlobohm* v. *Spa Petite*, 326 N.W.2d 920, 925–926 (Minn. 1982)).[77] The public interest has been held to be involved in services provided by '[c]ommon carriers, hospitals and doctors, public utilities, innkeepers, public warehousemen, employees, and [in] services involving extra-hazardous activities' (Talbott 1988, p. 30).[78] In other recreational situations, such as auto racing, gymnasiums and health clubs, spas and gyms, sky diving, and horse and saddle rental, exculpatory clauses excusing the party from liability for personal injury caused by that party's negligence have been upheld (ibid.).[79]

The Traditional Kaldor–Hicks Efficiency Theory of Exculpatory Clause Jurisprudence

There is a paucity of literature regarding the traditional KH efficiency of clauses seeking to excuse liability for personal injuries caused by negligence.[80] However, it seems clear that, in the absence of third-party effects or other market failures, the enforcement of a contract 'makes [the parties to that contract] better off, as measured by their own desires, without making anyone worse off' and is, therefore, traditionally KH efficient.[81] Consequently, the non-enforcement of certain exculpatory clauses can only be explained under the traditional theory as a response to market failure; and, indeed, the rule has been rationalized as necessary to protect consumers against overreaching monopolists.[82] According to this rationalization, a promisor individual is unable to effectively bargain with a promisee institution, and, as a result, must either agree to exculpate the promisee for its negligence in the performance of the underlying service or go without that service altogether (Posner 1992b, p. 114).[83] Therefore, it is argued, society is forced to endure a supercompetitive price for the underlying service, a price equal to the explicit monetary price for that service plus the value of the exculpatory clause, and this, by definition, is traditionally KH inefficient.[84] As a result, non-enforcement of exculpatory clauses might seem efficient where such clauses appear in contracts for the sale of goods and services in monopolized industries. Indeed, this result would be consistent with the current legal standard, which makes inequality of bargaining power a consideration in enforcability.[85] Thus, the traditional efficiency theory seems to explain why exculpatory clauses excusing a party from liability for personal injuries resulting from its own negligence are held unenforceable in at least some cases.[86]

The problem with this conclusion is that the assumption upon which it relies is too often false. Although many exculpatory clauses are agreed upon between an individual promisor and an institutional promisee, it does not follow that the institutional promisee is always a monopolist, or even that it exercises significant market power with respect to the terms of the sales contract. Indeed, if there is any competition among institutional promisees in their respective product markets – as there undoubtedly is between most common carriers, hospitals, doctors, innkeepers, public warehousemen, and perhaps even public utilities – such institutional promisees will have an incentive to engage in non-price competition.[87] Thus, if one promisee offers unattractive contract terms, a competing promisee, wanting sales for himself, 'will offer more attractive terms,' and this process 'will continue until the terms are optimal,' that is, until the competitive price[88] is reached (Posner 1992b, p. 114).[89] Thus, because there is competition among the institutional promisees in their respective product markets, such products will, other things being equal, be sold at competitive prices, and the use of exculpatory clauses will merely be a component of such prices. Therefore, exculpatory clauses are, at least theoretically, the result of competition rather than monopoly, and because they are a part of a contract that 'makes' its parties 'better off, as measured by their own desires, without making anyone worse off' they are traditionally KH efficient (Cooter and Ulen 1997, p. 167).[90] Thus, the non-enforcement of exculpatory clauses cannot be explained economically as a response to market failure. Indeed, such non-enforcement is entirely inexplicable under the traditional KH efficiency theory.[91]

An Integrated Theory of Exculpatory Clause Jurisprudence

Such non-enforcement may, however, be explained under an integrated approach. Recall that, broadly speaking, the integrated efficiency standard, unlike its traditional counterpart, incorporates the change in the distribution of income caused by an allocative change in the calculation of the efficiency of that change. Because KHZ uses the regard for others to measure the value of an increase in distributive justice, the relevant change in the distribution of income has a value equal to the difference between the aggregate WTP for that change and the aggregate it WTA (Zerbe and Dively 1994, p. 80). Therefore, an allocative change is, at least, KHZ efficient, if the difference between the immediate gainers' gain, *G*, and the immediate losers' loss, *L*, plus the value of the change in income distribution, *R*, is positive.[92] That is

$$(G - L) + R > 0 \rightarrow \text{KHZ efficiency,}$$

where $R = WTP - WTA$, or substituting,

$$(G - L) + (WTP > WTA) > 0 \rightarrow \text{KHZ efficiency.}$$

To determine whether a rule against the enforcement of the relevant exculpatory clauses is KHZ efficient, 'we must decide on the starting point, on the status quo position, in order to determine for whom the WTA applies and to whom the WTP applies' (Zerbe 1998b, pp. 432f). Because a rule against the enforcement of the relevant exculpatory clauses was determined to be traditionally KH inefficient, the KHZ analysis presented here will start with a presumption of enforceability, and will consider the KHZ efficiency of a change to unenforceability, that is, to the current rule.

From the above discussion of the traditional theory, it is clear that, when the relevant product market is competitive, the quantity $(G - L)$ must be positive. Hence, assuming competition, a prohibition against the relevant exculpatory clauses will be KHZ inefficient only if *R*, the value of the change in income distribution, is a negative number of greater magnitude than the quantity $(G - L)$. There is, however, good reason to believe that *R* is actually positive. That is, there is good reason to believe that there is large WTP for the change in income distribution that results from a change from the enforcement to the non-enforcement of the relevant exculpatory clauses.

If such clauses were enforced, they would create what Talbott (1988, p. 40) describes as a 'benefit spreading effect,' that is, 'they would have the effect of replacing a relatively small number of relatively large benefits (payments of compensation to the injured) with a relatively large number of relatively smaller benefits (to all who execute the waiver).'[93] Because 'there is a strong sense that something is wrong' with an 'outcome in which the uninjured benefit, while the injured are left substantially uncompensated,' the vast majority of society is probably willing to pay at least a small amount to ensure that the injured receive just compensation (Talbott 1988, p. 35).[94] This the majority can do by prohibiting the enforcement of exculpatory clauses. For, as Talbott (1988, p. 32) stated, such a prohibition spreads costs by replacing 'relatively large costs to a relatively small number of people (those who are actually injured) with relatively small costs to a relatively large number of people (in this case, all [promisors]).' Hence, *R* is probably positive, and the prohibition against exculpatory clauses is KHZ efficient.

Because the non-enforcement of exculpatory clauses which purport to relieve a party of liability for that party's own negligence is KHZ efficient but traditionally KH inefficient, the jurisprudence of such exculpatory clauses is better explained by an integrated approach to efficiency than by traditional Kaldor–Hicks efficiency. The ultimate result is that, other things being equal, contract law is better explained by integrated than by traditional efficiency.

8.4 TORT LAW: THE CASE OF THE MOVEMENT TOWARD CONTRIBUTION AMONG NEGLIGENT JOINT TORTFEASORS

Introduction

The modern movement to 'substitute ... contribution for no contribution' among negligent 'joint tortfeasors' is among the 'most important counter-examples' to the traditional KH 'efficiency theory of the common law,' for although that theory posits that no-contribution is more efficient than contribution, the movement toward contribution has continued unabated (Posner 1992b, p. 255).[95] Thus the contribution rule movement is a troubling paradox for the traditional efficiency theory, and makes the traditional theory vulnerable to invalidation by a theory with better explanatory power.[96] However, under KHZ the paradox disappears. Indeed, the movement toward contribution seems KHZ efficient. It will therefore be argued that the movement from no-contribution to contribution, and, hence, contribution jurisprudence itself, is better explained by integrated than by traditional efficiency. That argument will proceed in three steps. First, contribution jurisprudence will be summarized. Second, the traditional KH efficiency theory of that jurisprudence will be reviewed. Last, KHZ's view of contribution will be presented.

Contribution Jurisprudence

The law of contribution exists because injuries are often caused by the negligence of more than one actor (Kornhauser and Revesz 1989).[97] In such circumstances, the common law sometimes rendered the actors jointly and severally liable, and, accordingly, dubbed them 'joint tortfeasors.'[98] When negligent actors are held jointly and severally liable for an injury, the injured plaintiff may proceed jointly against all the injurers (Stanley 1994), and, if successful in obtaining a judgment, may satisfy it in whatever proportions he or she chooses. Alternatively, the plaintiff may recover all damages from only some or only one of the injurers (Landes and Posner 1980).[99] If the plaintiff chooses the latter approach, the question of whether to allow contribution arises (Cooter and Ulen 1997, p. 301). This subsection will summarize contribution jurisprudence in three steps. First, what has been termed the general common law rule against contribution will be discussed (Leflar 1932). Second, the movement toward contribution among negligent joint tortfeasors noted by Posner (1992b, p. 255) will be described. Finally, the effect of contribution on pretrial settlement will be considered.[100]

Contribution must be distinguished from indemnity.[101] Keeton *et al.* (1984, p. 341) define contribution as 'an order distributing loss among tortfeasors by requiring' each non-paying tortfeasor 'to pay a proportionate share to one who has discharged their "joint" liability.'[102] Although it is often flatly said that the common law allowed no right to contribution among negligent joint tortfeasors, it seems that, at least prior to 1799, and probably as late as 1894,[103] the common law did allow contribution (Rose 1980). Unfortunately, that rule was founded in perspicacity (Keeton *et al.* 1984, p. 337),[104] and was ultimately lost to confusion (Cavanaugh 1987; Landes and Posner 1987, p. 204).[105] The source of that confusion, and the origin of what is commonly termed the 'general rule' at common law (Higgenbotham and Wiggins 1990, pp. 700–701), was the English case of *Merryweather* v. *Nixan* (Reath 1898).[106] *Merryweather* itself involved an intentional tort,[107] and held only that contribution is not permitted in cases of intentional misconduct (Cavanaugh 1987, p. 1285).[108] It thus stated an exception to what was actually the general rule that contribution was allowed among negligent joint tortfeasors.[109] For a time, later English cases continued to recognize the distinction between intentional and negligent torts by permitting 'contribution among tortfeasors' provided that the underlying act 'was unintentional and not malicious' (Schwartz *et al.* 1979, p. 782).[110] Similarly, the early American cases applied a rule against contribution to cases involving intentional torts, but allowed contribution in those involving neglience (Keeton *et al.* 1984, p. 337).[111] Nevertheless, whether through an erroneous construction of *Merrywether* or through a misguided expansion of its holding (Cavanaugh 1987, p. 1285), the distinction between negligent and intentional torts was gradually lost, and a rule barring contribution in all tort cases was erected in its place (Higgenbotham and Wiggins 1990, p. 701; Schwartz *et al.* 1979, p. 782; Stanley 1994, pp. 3–4).[112] The majority of American courts proceeded to apply this rule, refusing to allow contribution even among negligent joint tortfeasors (Keeton *et al.* 1984, p. 337; Easterbrook, Landes and Posner 1980).[113] Indeed, the rule became so firmly entrenched that, until the 1970s, for a period of more than a century, only nine American jurisdictions allowed contribution among negligent tortfeasors (Keeton *et al.* 1984, pp. 337; Schwartz *et al.* 1979, p. 782).[114]

Despite its prevalence, however, the rule against contribution was vigorously attacked for its apparent inequity.[115] As Fleming (1983) observed, given the link forged by notions of natural justice between tort liability and fault, 'it was difficult to resist the demand for permitting contribution between tortfeasors' as a means of ensuring 'a "fair" distribution of the loss in accordance with' each tortfeasor's 'responsibility.'[116] In consequence, many courts, although constrained by stare decisis, strained to avoid inequity while retaining the underlying rule.[117] Gradually, however, the rule began to be discarded (Schwartz *et al.* 1979, p. 784). First courts (Kornhauser and Revesz 1989, p. 841, n. 48)[118] and then legislatures began to permit contribution between negligent tortfeasors.[119] Indeed, England itself allowed for contribution in 1935[120] and in 'recent years the trend, both of the legislation and of decisions in absence of it, has been toward recognition of the right of contribution' (Restatement (Second) of the Law of Torts §886A, comment a).[121] This trend is called 'the movement toward contribution' by Landes and Posner (1987, p. 219).

In an effort to approach the trend to abandon the common law rule against contribution consistently (Higgenbotham and Wiggins 1990, p. 702; Schwartz *et al.* 1979, p. 784), several model statements of the law have been drafted (Kornhauser and Revesz 1989, p. 841, n. 48). Among these are the Uniform Contribution Among Tortfeasors Act,[122] the Uniform Comparative Fault Act,[123] the Restatement (Second) of Torts,[124] and the Restatement of Restitution.[125] Although variations of each appear among state statutes, the 'approaches that the states have taken to [contribution] are remarkably fragmented' (Eggen 1995, pp. 1701–1702).[126] In general, however, the existing 'judicial and statutory rules are similar in that they all provide for contribution if three elements are present': (1) a common liability on the part of the parties to the action, (2) a legally mandated discharge of that liability, and (3) the placement of an unequal portion of that liability upon the party seeking contribution (Schwartz *et al.* 1979, p. 786).[127]

One of the most difficult issues in contribution jurisprudence is that of the effect of contribution on the pretrial settlement of litigation (Keeton *et al.* 1984, p. 340).[128] While a settling defendant is, by virtue of covenant with the original plaintiff, usually protected from efforts by that plaintiff to collect any part of a related subsequent judgment (Easterbrook, Landes and Posner 1980, p. 333), that defendant may remain subject to a claim for contribution by joint tortfeasors bound by the judgment (Fleming 1983, p. 235).[129]

The dilemma is that allowing contribution may discourage settlement,[130] but by prohibiting it may impair equity.[131] Thus, any gain in KH efficiency that would flow from preventing contribution would be met by an equivalent sacrifice of distributive justice.[132] The common law seems to have given more weight to equity, for the majority rule was that a settling defendant is not released from contribution (Keeton *et al.* 1984, p. 340), and, indeed, this remains the rule in England today (Fleming 1983, p. 235, citing *Dutton* v. *Bognor Regis*, Q.B. (1972, pp. 373, 399)). However, the statutes are divided, 'without any semblance of consensus' (Restatement (Second) of Torts, comment m). The 1935 Uniform Contribution Among Tortfeasors Act allowed contribution, but the 1955 revision took the opposite approach (Fleming 1983, p. 235).[133] The Restatement (Second) of Torts simply refuses to take any position.[134]

Yet, in part because of the troubling conundrum of settlement effects, the law of contribution remains dynamic and controversial.[135] Under traditional efficiency theory, it remains something of a mystery.

The Traditional KH Efficiency Theory of Contribution Jurisprudence

That mystery stems from a paradox, for while there is an undeniable trend toward contribution in Anglo-American law, the traditional efficiency theory would have predicted the opposite result (Landes and Posner 1987, pp. 27–28; Posner 1992b, p. 255).[136] Indeed, according to that theory, contribution among negligent tortfeasors[137] is patently inefficient.[138] It is thought to be inefficient even though both contribution and no-contribution can, under certain conditions, 'provide incentives for efficient accident avoidance' (Landes and Posner 1987, p. 201),[139] because contribution is both 'more costly to administer' (Posner 1992b, p. 189) and, at least when tailored to maximize its equitable effect, a significant disincentive to pretrial settlement (Landes and Posner 1987, p. 202; Stanley 1994, p. 6). Thus, a movement from no-contribution to contribution would increase administrative cost but would have no effect on the level of accident deterrence, and would, accordingly, be traditionally KH inefficient.[140] This subsection will explain that result in two steps. First, the deterrent effects of no-contribution and contribution will be considered. Second, the administrative costs of each will be compared.

In considering the deterrent effect of the rules of no-contribution and contribution, several important assumptions are traditionally made.[141] With respect to the actors themselves, it is generally assumed that (1) all actors have perfect information,[142] (2) the defendants are solvent,[143] (3) the actors are risk neutral,[144] and (4) the actors are rational.[145] With respect to legal background principles, it is similarly assumed that (1) a negligence regime prevails,[146] (2) 'negligence and due care are correctly defined from an economic standpoint' (Landes and Posner 1987, p. 197),[147] (3) liability is joint and several,[148] (4) a rule of contributory negligence is employed (ibid., p. 194),[149] (5) where liable, an actor is responsible for the full loss caused by its actions (Di Cola 1992, p. 1556),[150] (6) liable actors pay for damages that are attributable to non-negligent actors (ibid., pp. 1556–1557; Kornhauser and Revesz 1989, pp. 841–843),[151] and (7) there is no legal error in deciding cases.[152]

A further assumption pertains to the type of activity that gives rise to the underlying tort. All activity that may result in a tort may be classified as either a 'joint care' (Landes and Posner 1987, pp. 60, 190–191) / 'bilateral precaution' (Cooter and Ulen 1997, p. 275) case or an 'alternative care' (Landes and Posner 1987, pp. 60–61, 191, 198) / 'unilateral precaution' case (Cooter and Ulen 1997, pp. 275, 302).[153] In the former, efficiency requires both the victim and the potential injurers to take precaution against an accident.[154] In the latter, alternative care / unilateral precaution case, 'optimal accident avoidance requires that only one potential injurer take care.'[155] Since the question of employing contribution or no-contribution only arises in the joint care / bilateral precaution case,[156] the efficiency of these rules will be considered under an assumption of bilateral precaution.[157]

Given these assumptions, both qualitative and quantitative analyses become possible (Balkin 1987). In the joint care / bilateral precaution case, under a negligence regime,[158] 'the no-contribution rule, by imposing residual liability on each' negligent injurer, 'creates the optimal incentive for each' person 'to take precaution' (Cooter and Ulen 1997, p. 302).[159] To see why, qualitatively consider the case of two potential injurers.[160] If one satisfies the legal standard of care, while the other does not,[161] the latter will be responsible for the entire expected social cost of any resulting accident (Cooter and Ulen 1997, pp. 302–303).[162] Because the cost of compliance with the legal standard is, by definition, less than the expected social cost (Landes and Posner 1987, p. 196; Kornhauser and Revesz 1989, pp. 847–848),[163] however, at least one of the potential injurers will always have an incentive to comply, and if one has an incentive to comply, it follows that the other must as well (Landes and Posner 1987, p. 196). Thus, 'when the negligence standard is combined with the no-contribution rule in a case involving joint care, all parties have incentives to select levels of care that minimize the total cost of an accident.'[164]

This proposition may also be proven more formally through consideration of the expected social cost function. The expected social cost of an accident has been defined as the sum of the cost of precaution plus the cost of expected harm from an accident (Cooter and Ulen 1997, p. 271), and, hence, the expected social cost function is expressed as follows

$$C_s(x, y, z) = p(x, y, z)D + A(x) + B(y) + C(z)$$

where C_s = expected social cost of an accident as a function of the parties' levels of care; x = potential injurer A's level of care; y = potential injurer B's level of care; z = victim C's level of care; $p(x, y, z)$ = probability of an accident as a function of the parties' levels of care; D = victim C's damages from an accident; $A(x)$ = A's cost of care; $B(y)$ = B's cost of care; $C(z)$ = C's cost of care; x^* = level of care of A that minimizes C_s; y^* = level of care of B that minimizes C_s; and z^* = level of care of C that minimizes C_s (Landes and Posner 1987, pp. 193–194).

Because the two[165] potential injurers are assumed to be rational, each will choose and employ a level of precaution which minimizes its total expected loss,[166] that is, the sum of its expected losses from liability plus the cost of precaution (ibid., p. 195; Cooter and Ulen 1997, p. 273). In a joint tort, under a rule of no-contribution, the victim plaintiff determines, by choice of suit, the allocation of damages, D, between A and B, ex post (Easterbrook, Landes and Posner 1980, p. 347), and hence, that allocation is ex ante uncertain (Landes and Posner 1987, pp. 194–195). Therefore, A's total expected loss may be expressed as

$$s^A p(x, y, z^*)D + A(x)$$

and B's total expected loss expressed as

$$s^B p(x, y, z^*)D + B(y),$$

where s^A = the product of the probability that C sues both A and B and the expected fraction of the subsequent damages imposed on A given that both are sued; s^B = the product of the probability that C sues both A and B and the expected fraction of the subsequent damages imposed on B, given that both are sued (ibid., p.194; Easterbrook, Landes and Posner 1980, pp. 345–346);[167] $z < z^*$; $x < x^*$; and $y < y^*$ (Landes and Posner 1987, p. 195). Given that all actors are assumed to have perfect information, $s^A + s^B = 1$.[168]

Assuming that s^A and s^B are positive, each potential injurer's total expected loss will vary with the level of precaution chosen by the other injurer.[169] Thus, with respect to potential injurer A, if B is expected to and does employ precaution y^*, A's total expected loss will be either $A(x^*)$ if A is non-negligent, or $p(x, y^*, z^*)D + A(x)$ if A is negligent. By definition, however, x^* is the level of care of A that minimizes C_s (ibid.). Thus, $p(x, y^*, z^*)D + A(x) > p(x^*, y^*, z^*)D + A(x^*) > A(x^*)$, given that A will choose that level of precaution which minimizes its total expected loss (Easterbrook, Landes and Posner 1980, p. 345; Kornhauser and Revesz 1989, p. 836). If B is non-negligent, A will choose to be non-negligent and employ precaution x^* (Landes and Posner 1987, p. 195).[170] If, however, B is expected to employ precaution y,[171] A's total expected loss will be either $A(x^*)$, if A is non-negligent, or $s^A p(x, y, z^*)D + A(x)$, if A is negligent (ibid., p. 195). Thus, given that A will choose that level of precaution which minimizes its total expected loss, A will only choose the negligent level of precaution x if (ibid., p. 196)

$$s^{A}p(x, y, z^{*})D + A(x) < A(x^{*})$$

B, however, will select the negligent level of precaution y only if (ibid.)

$$s^{B}p(x, y, z^{*})D + B(y) < B(y^{*})$$

If (1) $s^{A}p(x, y, z^{*})D + A(x) < A(x^{*})$ and (2) $s^{B}p(x, y, z^{*})D + B(y) < B(y^{*})$, then (ibid.)

$$(s^{A} + s^{B})p(x, y, z^{*})D + A(x) + B(y) < A(x^{*}) + B(y^{*})$$

Nevertheless, because x^{*} and y^{*} are, by definition, the levels of precaution which minimize C_s (ibid.)

$$(s^{A} + s^{B})p(x, y, z^{*})D + A(x) + B(y) > p(x^{*}, y^{*}, z^{*})D \\ + A(x^{*}) + B(y^{*}) > A(x^{*}) + B(y^{*})$$

Therefore, inequalities (1) and (2) cannot simultaneously hold, and, as a result, even if $s^{A}p(x, y, z^{*})D + A(x) < A(x^{*})$,[172] $s^{B}p(x, y, z^{*})D + B(y) > B(y^{*})$, and, it follows (1) that B will be expected to select the non-negligent level of precaution y^{*}[173] and (2) that, as a result, A will also choose the non-negligent level of precaution x^{*} (ibid.). Conversely, if $s^{A}p(x, y, z^{*})D + A(x) > A(x^{*})$, given that A will choose that level of precaution which minimizes its total expected loss, A will still choose the non-negligent level of precaution x^{*}. The same analysis is applicable to potential injurer B.

Therefore, given the assumptions discussed above, under a rule of no-contribution, both potential injurers will always have an incentive to adopt the non-negligent level of precaution and, hence, a rule of no-contribution will provide incentives for efficient accident avoidance (Posner 1992b, p. 188).[174]

A rule of contribution, however, will provide the same incentives.[175] Indeed, it follows from the above analysis of the no-contribution rule that 'any allocation rule ... under which the sum of the tortfeasors' expected shares [s^{A} + s^{B}] in joint care cases sum to one' will 'provide incentives for efficient accident avoidance' (Landes and Posner 1987, p. 201).[176] To understand this, consider pro rata contribution, the rule of contribution in some jurisdictions, which requires each joint tortfeasor 'to pay a pro rata share, arrived at by dividing the [total] damages by the number of tortfeasors' (Keeton *et al.* 1984, pp. 340–341).[177] Under such a rule, potential injurer A's total expected loss may be expressed as

$$(1/n)p(x, y, z^*)D + A(x)$$

and potential injurer B's total expected loss expressed as

$$(1/n)p(x, y, z^*)D + B(y)$$

where n = the number of potential injurers (Landes and Posner 1987, p. 201). Recall (1) that because the potential injurers are assumed to be rational, each will choose and employ a level of precaution which minimizes its total expected loss and (2) that each potential injurer's total expected loss will vary with the level of precaution chosen by the other injurer. With respect to potential injurer A, if B is expected to and does employ non-negligent precaution y^*, it follows from the above analysis that A will also employ non-negligent precaution x^* (Landes and Posner 1987, p. 197). If B is expected to select precaution y, A's total expected loss will be either $A(x^*)$, if A is non-negligent, or $(1/n)p(x, y, z^*)D + A(x)$, if A is negligent. Given that both potential injurers are assumed to employ a level of precaution which minimizes their respective total expected losses, A will select precaution x only if $(1/n)p(x, y, z^*)D + A(x) < A(x^*)$ and B will select precaution y only if $(1/n)p(x, y, z^*)D + B(y) < B(y^*)$. Nevertheless, it follows from the above analysis that even if $(1/n)p(x, y, z^*)D + A(x) < A(x^*)$, $(1/n)p(x, y, z^*)D + B(y) > B(y^*)$, and, therefore, that (1) B will be expected to select the non-negligent level of precaution y^*[178] and, as a result, (2) A will also choose the non-negligent level of precaution x^* (Landes and Posner 1987, p. 197; Easterbrook, Landes and Posner 1980, p. 349). Conversely, if $(1/n)p(x, y, z^*)D + A(x) > A(x^*)$, given that A will choose that level of precaution which minimizes its total expected loss, A will still choose the non-negligent level of precaution x^* (Landes and Posner 1987, p. 197; Easterbrook, Landes and Posner 1980, p. 349). A similar analysis is applicable to potential injurer B.

Therefore, given the aforementioned assumptions, a rule of contribution will also induce both potential injurers to adopt the non-negligent level of precaution, and, hence, the deterrent effects of no-contribution and contribution are identical.[179]

However, their respective administrative costs are not identical (Landes and Posner 1987, pp. 201–202; Easterbrook, Landes and Posner 1980, pp. 349–350). The administrative costs of either allocation rule are determined by both (1) the rate of pretrial settlement of cases and (2) the costs of those trials which actually occur (Easterbrook, Landes and Posner 1980, p. 354). Each determinant will be considered, first with respect to no-contribution and then with respect to contribution.

A no-contribution rule is said to produce incentives to settle (Di Cola 1992, p. 1555; Stanley 1994, pp. 6, 59–69). To prove this result, several assumptions are usually made: first, that there are multiple potential defendants; second, that all actors are rational; and, third, that all are risk neutral (Easterbrook, Landes and Posner 1980, p. 356). Given these assumptions, it may be shown that the victim plaintiff will always have an incentive to settle with at least $n - 1$ defendants, where n equals the total number of prospective defendants, and, conversely, that $n - 1$ defendants will always have an incentive to settle with the plaintiff (ibid., p. 357). Qualitatively, given that the plaintiff is assumed to be risk neutral, it will prefer to settle with at least one defendant because any positive settlement represents a certain amount which is, by definition, of greater value than an expected equivalent amount (Easterbrook, Landes and Posner 1980, p. 356). For the same reason, the plaintiff will continue to settle with additional defendants at least until it has settled with all but one. More formally, in the absence of any settlement, the value of plaintiff C's expected claim, $V_{EC}{}^{C}$, is

$$V_{EC}{}^{C} = p^{C}D,$$

where (1) $p^{C} < 1$ and (2) p is constant (ibid., p. 357, n. 59). Settlement with the first defendant, defendant 1, for $S_1 > 0$ results in

$$V_{EC1}{}^{C} = S_1 + p^{C}(D - S_1),$$

and, given that $p^{C} < 1$, $V_{EC1}{}^{C} = S_1 + p^{C}(D - S_1) > V_{EC}{}^{C}$. As a result, because C is assumed to be rational, C will settle with defendant 1, and after settlement with $j - 1$ defendants, where $1 < j < n$, C will have an incentive to settle with j because

$$V_{ECj}{}^{C} - V_{ECj-1}{}^{C} = S_j(1 - p^{C}) > 0,$$

where $S_j > 0$ and $p^{C} < 1$. Because C has an incentive to settle with defendants 1 through j, where j includes all defendants up to $n - 1$, C has an incentive to settle with at least $n - 1$ defendants. Therefore, given the aforementioned assumptions, under a rule of no-contribution, the victim plaintiff will always have an incentive to settle with at least $n - 1$ defendants, where n equals the total number of prospective defendants.

Similarly, given the above assumptions, under a rule of no-contribution, at least $n - 1$ defendants have an incentive to settle with C.[180] To understand this, assume that defendant A's expected liability upon trial is

$$V_{EL}{}^{A} = 1/(n - n_s)[p^{A}(D - n_sS],$$

where n_s equals the number of defendants who have already settled.[181] S equals the average settlement per defendant. P^{A} equals defendant A's estimate of the probability that C will win at trial (ibid., p. 357, note 60). Because defendant A is, by assumption, rational, an offer to settle for less than $V_{EL}{}^{A}$, defendant A's expected liability upon trial, would induce A to settle with C (ibid., p. 357, n. 60). The above analysis of plaintiff C's incentives indicates that C will accept any positive settlement from $n - 1$ defendants, and since $V_{EL}{}^{A}$ is positive, there must be a set of settlements at which defendants $n - 1$ will be induced to settle with C. Therefore, under a rule of no-contribution, the plaintiff and $n - 1$ defendants will have incentives to settle rather than proceed to trial.[182] Indeed, under a rule of no-contribution, defendants compete to settle because the expected liability of the non-settling defendants increases as each defendant settles.[183]

The settlement effects of contribution are significantly less sanguine.[184] Although many varieties of contribution could be devised,[185] 'two broad classes ... appear to capture the essential features of contribution' and thus, provide the subject of this analysis (ibid., pp. 360–361).[186] First, a 'traditional' contribution rule allows joint tortfeasors who lose at trial to obtain a contribution from settling defendants (ibid., pp. 360–361).[187] Second, what is known as a 'settlement bar' rule 'forbids non-settling defendants to obtain any contribution from settling ones' (Landes and Posner 1987, p. 203).[188]

The first rule may be modeled both for the case where contribution is certain and for that in which it is uncertain (Easterbrook, Landes and Posner 1980, pp. 361–363). Where contribution is certain, defendants have no incentive to settle (ibid., p. 362; Landes and Posner 1987, p. 202). If the defendant settles, then its total loss is $1/n$.[189] If, however, the defendant goes to trial, its total loss will vary with the outcome: if the defendant is successful, its total loss is zero; if, however, the defendant loses, given that 'pro rata contribution is assured,' its total loss will be only $1/n$ (Easterbrook, Landes and Posner 1980, p. 362). Therefore, under a traditional rule of contribution where pro rata contribution is certain, the defendant 'has nothing to lose and everthing to gain from refusing to settle and going to trial'.

Where pro rata contribution is uncertain, however, the result is more similar to, but nevertheless more administratively costly than, that under the no-contribution rule. Specifically, if contribution is uncertain, then, just as was the case under no-contribution, $n - 1$ settlements will be induced (Easterbrook, Landes and Posner 1980, p. 362). Conversely, defendant n will be less likely to settle under a rule of uncertain traditional contribution than under a rule of no contribution (Easterbrook, Landes and Posner 1980, p. 362, n. 69). Therefore, a traditional rule of contribution is overall less likely to induce settlement than a rule of no contribution and is, consequently, more administratively costly.[190]

A settlement bar rule need not be (Di Cola 1992, p. 1556). Indeed, 'as a first approximation, this rule is equivalent in its effect on settlement to a rule of no contribution' (Easterbrook, Landes and Posner 1980, p. 363).[191] Nevertheless, some commentators note that a settlement bar rule could quite possibly abrogate the fairness objectives underlying a rule of contribution (Landes and Posner 1987, p. 203).[192] Therefore, courts which choose to apply such a rule must 'hold a fairness hearing before approving the settlement' which would make the settlement bar rule more administratively costly than the no-contribution rule (ibid.). Because both the traditional and settlement bar versions of the contribution rule either (1) induce a lower rate of pretrial settlement than a no-contribution rule or (2) require greater administrative expense to produce the same rate, the no-contribution rule is generally considered to be, other things being equal, less administratively costly.[193]

A no-contribution rule leads to lower administrative costs than a contribution rule would, because if contribution is allowed, this 'requires the courts to decide another issue and supervise another set of transfer payments' (Posner 1992b, p. 189). Specifically, a rule of contribution would increase trial costs by either bringing additional defendants into the original suit, or by requiring subsequent litigation by which the original defendants may force non-party joint tortfeasors to contribute (Easterbrook, Landes and Posner 1980, pp. 349–350; Landes and Posner 1987, pp. 201–202).[194] Although it may be argued that a mechanical contribution rule, such as the pro rata rule discussed above, would result in only an insignificant increase in trial costs, such a rule (1) may not actually reduce trial expense and (2) even if properly corrected to do so, would probably raise fairness objections (Landes and Posner 1987, p. 202). Therefore, it seems that the trial costs are greater under a rule of contribution than under a rule of no-contribution, and, thus, given the foregoing settlement analysis, the latter may conclusively be said to be less administratively costly than the former (ibid., p. 201).[195]

To summarize, although the rules of contribution and no-contribution both produce incentives for efficient accident avoidance, contribution is more costly to administer.[196] Thus, according to the traditional KH efficiency theory, 'contribution seems to be a less efficient rule than no contribution,' which raises the question of 'why so many states have abandoned the common law approach' of no-contribution (ibid., p. 219). It is a question which remains unanswered under the traditional theory; indeed, under that theory it is a paradox without a solution.[197]

An Integrated Theory of Contribution Jurisprudence

That paradox finds a solution in KHZ's integrated theory of the common law. Recall that, broadly speaking, the integrated efficiency standard, unlike its traditional counterpart, incorporates the change in the distribution of income caused by an allocative change into the calculation of the efficiency of that change.[198] The relevant change in the distribution of income has a value equal to the difference between the aggregate WTP for that change and the aggregate WTA (Zerbe and Dively 1994, p. 81). Therefore, an allocative change is KHZ efficient if the difference between the immediate gainers' gain, G, and the immediate losers' loss, L, plus the value of the change in income distribution, R, is positive.[199] That is

$$(G - L) + R > 0 \rightarrow \text{KHZ efficiency}$$

where $R = WTP - WTA$, or substituting,

$$(G - L) + (WTP > WTA) > 0 \rightarrow \text{KHZ efficiency}$$ [200]

To determine whether a rule of contribution is KHZ efficient, we must decide on the starting point – on the status quo position – in order to determine for whom the WTA applies and to whom the WTP applies (Zerbe 1998b, pp. 432f). Because the focus of concern is the movement toward a rule of contribution from a rule of no-contribution among negligent joint tortfeasors,[201] that starting point may most appropriately be defined as one in which the rule of allocation is no-contribution. In a movement from a rule of no-contribution to one of contribution, the immediate gainers are those defendants who, unsuccessful at trial, can now obtain contribution from other joint tortfeasors who were not parties to the original suit. Among the immediate losers are those previously non-party joint tortfeasors from whom the unsuccessful defendants may now obtain contribution. Nevertheless, because the unsuccessful defendants gain the same amount as the non-party joint tortfeasors lose, this is merely a transfer of wealth, and, thus, is of no consequence to the $G - L$ calculation (Easterbrook, Landes and Posner 1980, pp. 349–350).[202] What is of consequence to that calculation is the loss in judicial economy caused by the increase in administrative cost in moving from a rule of no-contribution to one of contribution which may be modeled as $L > 0$ (Keeton *et al.* 1984, p. 338).[203] Because this loss is not offset by a compensating gain in accident deterrence, G equals 0. Therefore, $G - L < 0$.

It follows that, for the movement from no-contribution to contribution to be KHZ efficient, R must be a positive number of greater magnitude than $G - L$. Here, R may be defined specifically as the value of the change in the distribution of wealth brought about by the movement from no-contribution to contribution. That change is a transfer between two parties, both equally responsible for a loss, of one party's fair share of that loss to another party who has already discharged the entire loss (ibid., pp. 337–338). The value of that change is, as described above, equal to the aggregate WTP for the change minus the aggregate WTA it. Although, as in the case of rape, there are no empirical studies of either WTP or WTA for the change in the distribution of wealth induced by a change from no-contribution to contribution, there is a vast amount of anecdotal support for the proposition that, in this case, WTP far exceeds WTA.[204]

The aggregate WTP for the movement from no-contribution to contribution among negligent joint tortfeasors is almost undoubtedly a very large positive number, perhaps even one approaching infinity. The support for this proposition is ubiquitous.[205] For example, Keeton *et al.* (1984, p. 338) note that the primary impetus for the change from no-contribution to contribution was 'half a century of vigorous attack upon the original rule.' Prosser (Keeton *et al.* 1984, pp. 337–338) said this of the no-contribution rule:

> There is an obvious lack of sense and justice in a rule which permits the entire burden of a loss, for which two defendants were equally liable to be shouldered on to one alone, according to the accident of a successful levy of execution, the existence of liability insurance, the plaintiff's whim or spite, or the plaintiff's collusion with the other wrongdoer, while the latter goes scot free.

These remarks indicate that the movement from no-contribution to contribution among negligent joint tortfeasors was caused by a popular dissatisfaction with the inequity entailed by a rule of no-contribution.[206] This, in turn, is indicative of a large aggregate WTP for that movement, even if the WTP of each individual is relatively slight, for, as I (1998a, p. 354; 1998b, pp. 437f) noted, the concern or regard for others, which underlies the WTP, is a concern for what people regard as fair outcomes for others.[207] Thus, the aggregate WTP is probably a very large positive number.

The aggregate WTA of the movement from no-contribution to contribution is, however, probably a very small positive number. The rule of no-contribution among negligent joint tortfeasors seems virtually bereft of supporters.[208] Assuming that what supporters there are are not substantially more wealthy and more adamant than those who oppose a rule of no-contribution, the aggregate WTA is probably very small compared to the aggregate WTP.

As a result, $(WTP - WTA)$ is probably a very large positive number and thus probably a number in excess of $G - L$. Thus, the movement from no-contribution to contribution, although inefficient under the traditional theory, is KHZ efficient, and therefore KHZ's integrated efficiency theory is better able to explain contribution jurisprudence than is its traditional counterpart. The ultimate result is that, other things being equal, tort law is better explained by integrated than traditional efficiency.

8.5 CONCLUSION

I sought to test the distributive justice critique's suggestion that the common law is better explained by the integrated efficiency theory than by its traditional counterpart. That test proceeded in two steps. First, 'descriptive capacity' – the most appropriate standard by which to evaluate this theory – was explicitly considered. Second, the descriptive capacity of both theories was compared through a three-part survey of common law doctrine.

That survey began with the criminal law of rape, and found that, although under the traditional theory some rapes should be legal, under the integrated efficiency theory, all rapes should be illegal. Therefore, rape law was shown to be better described by the integrated theory than by its traditional counterpart.

Next, exculpatory clause jurisprudence was considered. Although such jurisprudence generally holds that exculpatory clauses purporting to exclude liability for negligence are unenforceable, only the integrated theory reached this result. Therefore, the integrated theory was shown to provide a better description of exculpatory clause jurisprudence than the traditional theory.

Last, the tort law movement toward contribution among negligent joint tortfeasors was considered. This movement is inexplicable under the traditional theory, but predictable under the integrated theory. Therefore, it was shown that contribution jurisprudence is also better explained by the integrated theory than by the traditional efficiency theory.

Given that the law of rape, exculpatory clauses, and contribution are better described by the integrated theory than by its traditional counterpart, the former, other things being equal, provides a better description of the common law than does the latter. Nevertheless, because there is a distinct lack of empirical evidence in this regard, the traditional KH efficiency theory should be replaced by the integrated theory only if a sufficient quantum of future research confirms or expands this result.

NOTES

Brian Wasankari wrote the orginal version of this chapter as his analytic paper for law school under the supervision of Richard Zerbe. It was modified later by Steve Vinyard and Richard Zerbe. The modified version appears in *Research in Law and Economics*, volume XIX, 2000. It was written before I had fully developed the approach to economics presented in this book, and I have additionally modified the published version to better, though not perfectly, fit here.

1. The theory will also, at times, be called simply 'the traditional theory.' For a general exposition of that theory see, for example, Posner (1992b). It is apparently not the only theory. Parsons (1983) criticizes Posner's traditional efficiency theory and attempts to offer some solutions. Moreover, there are well-respected non-economic theories, such as those of Dworkin (1986) and Rawls (1971).

2. We critique the traditional notion in part (II).
3. Posner (1992b, p. 26) notes that 'the [traditional Kaldor–Hicks] economic [efficiency] theory of law is the most promising theory of law extant.'
4. Byrns and Stone (1992, pp. 15–16) note that any theory can be supplanted by one with superior explanatory power.
5. Flatt (1994, p. 95) notes that 'if society is willing to spend money that has no perceivable effect beyond an alteration of the allocation of a risk, the allocation of that risk must be a value.'
6. Posner (1987a p. 23; 1992b, p. 264) neglects these concerns.
7. See our discussion in part (II)(B)(2)(c).
8. That is, of the traditional KH efficiency theory of the common law.
9. The first efforts to apply economic analysis to rape law were made by Posner (1992b, pp. 67, 357–358), who originally found rape inefficient, and, thus, rape laws efficient and Calabresi (Calabresi and Melamed 1972, pp. 1089, 1125–1126), who presented an analysis which stopped short of the question of efficiency. In an effort 'to search for the limitations on the reach of economic concepts,' Schwartz was apparently the first to argue that rape could be efficient (1979, pp. 799, 813). A 'deservedly esoteric literature' has sprung forth (Posner 1992a, p. 182).
10. Posner (1992b, p. 263) notes that 'common law courts ... would have no patience for "efficient rape."' Indeed, not only is every rape, 'efficient' or otherwise, both a crime and a tort in all Anglo-American jurisdictions, but the only court to so much as implicitly mention an economic analysis of rape law did so derisively. See United States v. *Bishop*, 66 F.3d 569 (1995).
11. Of course, the traditional theory's inability to explain rape law is only grounds for invalidating it to the extent that KHZ provides a superior explanation. At the close of his discussion of rape, Schwartz (1979, p. 812) noted that in 'mathematics, an equation can be proved invalid by showing that there is one value of "*x*" for which the equation does not hold' and that insofar 'as economic principles are dogmatically advanced as theorems,' the example of efficient rape could 'have that power.' Since the theory of 'efficient rape' is founded on a misconception of KH efficiency (see part (II)(C)(1)), it may ultimately fall silent under an integrated analysis – a result, interestingly enough, supported by Schwartz's (1979, p. 813) own argument.
12. Dressler (1987, p. 515) states that 'the common-law offense of rape has largely been carried over to modern times by statute.'
13. It is, however, more accurate to say that the common law protected a male's property interest in a female, or at least in her sexuality (see, for example, Brownmiller 1975, pp. 16–30 and Wald 1997).
14. 'Carnal knowledge,' in turn, meant 'sexual intercourse,' which implied 'genital copulation' (Dressler 1987, p. 516, n. 1), and more specifically and exclusively, 'penile–vaginal penetration' (Spohn and Horney 1992, p. 22). As Dressler (1987, p. 516, n. 1) observes, 'Oral and anal intercourse do not constitute rape although they frequently were and are punishable independently' and 'sexual emission is neither sufficient nor necessary' for criminal liability. Note, however, that this definition appears to be derived from the Statutes of Westminster in the reign of Edward I, adopted in 1285 (Dripps 1992, p. 1780, n. 1, citing Maitland and Pollock 1968, pp. 490–491).
15. Shockingly, this exception survives to this day in many states, albeit in a diluted form: in many states, a husband cannot be liable for third degree rape of his wife.
16. Rape law, in essence, 'struck a balance between the interests of males-in-possession and their predatory counterparts' (Dripps 1992, p. 1783). Like the law of property dealing with wild animals,

    the theft of a woman already reduced to possession was a serious crime; but if a woman broke the man's possession as an animal might escape a pen, his interest in her lapsed. Thus, the notorious common-law procedural rules requiring prompt complaint, resistance to the utmost, corroboration, and good reputation, – worked a compromise between competing *male* interest. (Dripps 1992, p. 1783, citing Hale 1664, pp. 633–635)

17. It has, however, been argued that, properly recast, a property theory of rape may not be objectionable (Wald 1997, p. 462). Without 'advocating a literal treatment of rape as theft,' Wald argues that properly 'understanding the relationship between property and rights of sexual control would contribute to a fuller understanding of why rape is so prevalent and why it is so injurious to women.'
18. The model of such efforts is the Michigan 'Criminal Sexual Conduct' statute. See, for example, Dressler (1987, p. 535), who discusses *Michigan Compensation Laws Annotated* §§750.520a – .5201 (West Supp. 1986).
19. Dripps (1992, p. 1783) states that 'the substantive law has not changed much. Consistent with the reformers' concern for [sexual] autonomy, the gravamen of rape remains' as it was at common law 'the conjunction of force and nonconsent.' Indeed, many states continue to fail to punish husbands for some categories of rape.
20. For the proposition that such a market is fundamental to an economic analysis of rape, see, for example, Posner (1985a, pp. 1193, 1199). Posner (1992b, p. 218) assumes the existence of 'marriage and sex markets' comparable to 'explicit markets in goods and services.' Elsewhere, Posner (1992b, p. 218), discusses the relationship between rape and a 'market in sexual relations' and he expounds the concept of a 'marriage market.' Schwartz (1979, p. 805) notes that 'economic analysis asks us to consider the possibility of transactions – contracts – between rapists and victims' in a 'market [that] can provide the appropriate sexual encounter.'
21. Given the magnitude of the debate, a large number of works could be cited here, but the two most prominent, pro and con respectively, are probably Posner (1992a) and Calabresi and Melamed (1972).
22. Under KHZ, a good is anything that people care about, whether or not it is tangible (Chapter 2). Thus economics can explain any interaction in which a person sacrifices a portion of something that he or she cares about in order to acquire something else that he or she cares about even more, at least at the margin. For example, there probably are not any literal 'friendship markets,' but friendship is susceptible to economic analysis (Chapter 2). People sacrifice time (something they undoubtedly care about) in order to be with another person and enjoy their company (something else most people care about). This is not to say that we view our friends as mere instruments for maximizing our own wealth, or that we approach the 'friendship market' with the same attitude that we approach markets for tangible goods. Indeed, part of the value of friendship would disappear if we viewed it from a reductionist perspective. However, by spending time with one friend instead of another, we are demonstrating a preference for that friendship, whether we consciously realize it or not. Similarly, the fact that we spend time with a friend instead of spending our time on a 'nonfriendship good' (such as extra work on a professional project), demonstrates the relative value we attach to 'friendship goods' (such as companionship and intimacy) as opposed to 'nonfriendship goods' (such as our professional reputation and money).
23. For example, Dripps (1992, p. 1786) dubs the theory of a market for sexual services 'the commodity theory.' West (1993, pp. 2413, 2430) calls the sexual market theory presented by Posner (1992a), a 'commodification theory of sex.'
24. There are several distinct versions of what is here termed the market for sexual services. Chamallas (1988, pp. 777, 839–841) argues that 'ideal sex' clearly 'exclude[s] sexual encounters in which money, power, prestige or financial security is traded for sexual pleasure and emotional intimacy,' while West (1993, p. 2430) describes Posner's version of the market for sexual services as one in which the commodity of sex may be traded for an unrestricted 'bundle of goods.' Dripps (1992, p. 1790) argues that Chamallas' objection 'to any bargaining in which one party offers sexual cooperation in exchange for goods that are distributed unjustly according to gender ... is both incongruous and morally problematic.' And compare both the Chamallas and West–Posner–Dripps versions with Schwartz (1979, p. 805), who discusses the possibility of contracts for 'consensual' rape.

    Indeed, perhaps the debate should start here, for the viability of a market for sexual services would seem to depend heavily on the form of market considered.

25. Locke (1962) argues that '[t]hough the earth and all inferior creatures be common to all men, yet every man has a property in his own person.' West (1993, p. 2430) describes Posner's theory of sex markets.
26. Zelder (1993, pp. 1584, 1601), in his review of Posner's (1992a), concludes that Posner is 'to be applauded ... for some worthy attempts to bring economic analysis to bear on the question of rape.' Wohl (1997, pp. 68, 69) notes that Posner 'is the person most closely associated with the school of law and economics.'
27. There is a vast feminist literature on the topic of rape. Among the most influential works are Brownmiller (1975) and Estrich (1987). Dripps (1992, pp. 1780–1783) provides a brief summary of the literature. However, it should be noted that one need not be a feminist to maintain this perspective.
28. Posner (1992a, p. 384) holds that contrary 'to the view held by many feminists, rape appears to be primarily a substitute for consensual sexual intercourse rather than a manifestation of male hostility toward women or a method of establishing or maintaining male domination.' It may, however, be more precise to state, with respect to rapists for whom 'the pleasure of' rape 'vitally depends on' their 'forcible subjugation' of their victims (Schwartz 1979, p. 806), that there is no market substitute for rape. Schwartz (1979, p. 806) states that 'even if prostitution [and thus, "contracts for coerced sex"] were legal, it would not provide an adequate substitute for rape,' for the vital 'element of pleasure [to these rapists] is automatically lacking when [their] sexual partner[s are] willing, whether this willingness has been achieved by purchase or otherwise.' Landes and Posner (1987, pp. 1193, 1199) insist that 'there are market substitutes for coercive sexual acts.'
29. Zelder (1993, pp. 1601–1602) discusses the empirical evidence supporting this proposition, noting that Posner presents 'two primary pieces of evidence concerning the economic rationality of rapists: [1] Isaac Ehrlich's finding that rape incidence is deterred by higher penalties and [2] anthropological data showing that rape incidence rises with bride price.' He argues that '[o]nly the former is logically defensible evidence [because] bride price data obviously do not control for the intellectual, emotional, and physical attributes of women in the sample' (Zelder 1993, pp. 1601–1602).
30. Calabresi and Melamed (1972, p. 1126) note that 'in the majority of cases we cannot be sure of the economic efficiency of' market bypassing transfers such as transfers by theft. They realize that rape may, in essence, be considered theft (ibid.).
31. West (1993, p. 2430) notes that the commodity theory 'implies a particular conception of the wrongness of rape: to take the asset of sex by force instead of by consensual transaction short-circuits the standard market mechanism – a-face-to-face consensual bargain – for ensuring that wealth is maximized.'

    Schwartz (1979, p. 805) notes that '[t]he crime of rape, by further preventing the circumvention of the market process, bolsters the protection against inefficiency.' But see West (1986).
32. Although Duxbury (1995, p. 662, n. 12) was discussing the concept of incommensurability generally, not the feasibility of a market in sexual relations particularly, he did note that 'the representation of women – qua prostitutes, wives, and girlfriends – as a sex market for men' constitutes 'an inappropriate valuation.'
33. It is, however, always possible to attack a conclusion drawn from an economic analysis of law by arguing that the subject of such analysis has been improperly commodified (Duxbury 1995, pp. 677–678). Therefore, a claim of incommensurability is, by itself, unpersuasive. Indeed, the viability of such claims 'depends on whether [they] embody anything more than diverse individual feelings about what ought not to be bought and sold' (Duxbury 1995, p. 678).
34. It is worth noting that Posner's theory could be used to question the efficiency of any criminal law. For example, an efficient murder is theoretically possible if a murderer's pleasure exceeded a victim's disutility at having his or her life taken. Unlike efficient rape, this possibility seems to be more than merely theoretical, since it is easy to imagine a scenario with a sadistic killer and a chronically depressed victim. I will show that

comparing the criminal's utility and the victim's disutility is universally problematic, and ignores the social cost of leaving crimes unpunished.

35. In terms of the Calabresi and Melamed (1972, p. 1092) framework, there are at least 'three types of entitlements – entitlements protected by property rules, entitlements protected by liability rules, and inalienable entitlements.' Furthermore, '[r]ecognition of incommensurability [leads] to the conclusion that certain rights ought to be protected by neither liability nor property rules, but by inalienability rules' (Duxbury 1995, p. 683). An 'inalienable entitlement' is, itself, one the transfer of which 'is not permitted between a willing buyer and a willing seller'(Calabresi and Melamed 1972, p. 1092). And, of course, if transfers are forbidden per se, no values can be assigned to such transfers, and, consequently, interpersonal comparisons of such values become impossible.
36. It should be noted that such valuation can occur only through use of a 'liability rule' which would allow the rapist to 'destroy the initial entitlement [to, in this case, personal integrity] if he or she is willing to pay an objectively determined value for it' (Calabresi and Melamed 1972, p. 1092). Epstein (1997, p. 2091) notes that

    > a liability rule denies the holder of the asset [here, the 'asset' of 'sexual services'] the power to exclude others or, indeed, to keep the asset for [her- or] himself. Rather, [she or] he is helpless to resist the efforts of some other individual to take that thing upon payment for its fair value, as objectively determined by some neutral party.

    See also Calabresi and Melamed (1972, p. 1125) Duxbury (1995, p. 683) and Epstein 1997. Interestingly, Calabresi and Melamed's statement, while perhaps a fair expression of policy preference, is not an accurate account of early law. Instead, it seems that many early legal systems employed liability rules as rape laws. Thus, according to the King James Bible, a 'man' found to have raped a 'virgin,' i.e., an unmarried female, was required to 'give unto the damsel's father fifty shekels of silver, and she shall be his wife' (Deuteronomy 22: 28–29); while among 'aboriginal peoples much customary law was devoted to the payment of compensation to a man whose legal right to control sexual access to his wife or daughter is disregarded [by, inter alia, the rape of his wife or daughter]' (Dripps 1992, p. 1781).
37. Duxbury (1995, p. 678) says, '[t]o pose the question bluntly: how might we ever determine that it is inappropriate to value something as a commodity?'
38. See also Radin's later work (1993). Note that the term 'personal property' (p. 37) is used by Radin to denote property with which one is 'bound up' to such a degree 'that its loss would cause' a cost 'which could not be relieved by replacement of the object with other goods of equal market value.' 'Fungible property' refers to anything 'which is held for purely instrumental reasons'.
39. For example, Radin (1987, pp. 1921–1925) concludes that '[b]odily integrity is an attribute and not an object.'
40. Note, however, that even this proposition is false, for not everything 'personal' is, in fact, deemed 'incommensurable' (Duxbury 1995, p. 678). Duxbury (ibid.), notes that

    > the argument that the peculiarly personal nature of certain things may determine that they ought not to be traded … is unconvincing for the single reason that there are plenty of things with a distinctively personal dimension such as our favourite literature, music, restaurants, holiday locations and the like which are very obviously and very naturally commodified.
41. Radin (1993, p. 198) attempts to answer this question by suggesting the possibility of 'a theory of the good and well developed person … to tell when objects [should be] treated as personal' but fails to develop such a theory (Duxbury 1995, p. 666).
42. Dripps (1992, p. 1786, n. 27) and Duxbury (1995, p. 670) note that these theories are inadequate.
43. By use of the word 'woman' in lieu of 'person' or some comparable gender-neutral term, West (1993, 1986) seems to imply that only women can be prompted to 'consent' to sex, which results in personal disutility. The theory underlying this proposition seems to be that such goods as 'money, power, prestige [and] financial security' are distributed

unequally such that men have greater access to them than women (Chamallas 1988, p. 839); and that men desire sex and women power, and, thus, that immoral sex-for-power trades are induced. Thus West (1993, 1986), among others, argues that at least some women are forced to consent to sex to obtain power. A prominent problem with this argument is that it demeans women and assumes a tremendous degree of immorality on the part of both genders. It demeans women because it presumes that many are incapable of obtaining power or money by any other means than trades of their sexual services. It assumes the immorality of men by presuming that they would allow, if not force, women to trade such services for power; and, yes, it assumes a similar immorality on the part of women by presuming that they would consent to such trades. On the other hand, Dripps (1992, p. 1791) argues that '[b]ecause there is no heterosexual reason to suppose that the ex ante distribution of sexual assets is any less arbitrary than the ex ante distribution of other assets' people should be able to 'trade their (arbitrarily distributed) attractiveness to improve their holdings of other (arbitrarily distributed) goods.' One cannot help but wonder how a *reason* can be heterosexual or homosexual.

44. If heterosexual practices are morally problematic because they are, in essence, immoral exchanges in which women trade sexual services for money, power, and prestige, then homosexual practices are undoubtedly plagued by the same moral difficulties. It is generally accepted that older people of both genders tend to have more money, power, and prestige than their younger counterparts (Ehrenburg and Smith 1994, pp. 295–299). Thus, assuming, as does West (1993, 1986), that sex-for-power trades are induced by unequal distributions of wealth, it seems likely that younger homosexuals will trade sexual services for the money, power, and prestige of older homosexuals, making homosexual practices as morally problematic as their heterosexual counterparts.
45. Landes and Posner (1987, p. 9) conclude that, although critics 'have argued that a system of law designed to promote efficiency is immoral,' such criticisms are 'largely misplaced when directed at a positive theory' such as that at issue here 'for such a theory is interested in explaining, rather than defending, the common law.'
46. Current scholars generally agree that sexual conduct contrary to commonly accepted moral or religious standards 'should not be punished criminally' (Malamut 1993, pp. 45, 47) (citing *Model Penal Code* 213.2, Comment 2, and 213.6 note on adultery and fornication (1980)). Kadish and Schulhofer (1995, pp. 155–167) state that 'Perhaps the best illustration of the trend in various parts of the U.S. toward removing criminal sanctions from "immoral" conduct is the decriminalization of fornication and cohabitation' (1995, p. 111). For the proposition that fornication remains immoral to many people see, for example, Exodus 22:16 and Leviticus 19:20 (King James Bible). However, Hill (1985, p. 123) notes that the fact that many people find fornication immoral does not, by itself, justify punishing those who commit it.
47. For example, Mansfield (1994, p. 14) notes that '[t]he purpose of a model is to make predictions concerning phenomena in the real world, and in many respects the most important test of a model is how well it predicts these phenomena.'
48. It is true that '[l]aw and social morality will constrain much of the same behavior' but '[t]his does not mean … that the law will enforce every aspect of morality that concerns preventing harm to others.' In fact, '[m]any immoral acts that hurt others are unregulated by the law' (Greenawalt 1995, pp. 710, 711). Indeed, 'there must remain a realm of private morality and immorality which is, in brief and crude terms, not the law's business. To say this is not to condone or encourage private immorality' (Hill 1985, p. 123, quoting Home Office, Scottish Home Department, 'Report of the Committee on Homosexual Offenses and Prostitution' (Wolfenden Report)).
49. Duxbury (1995, p. 6789, citing Buchanan 1985, pp. 101–103) raises the possibility that 'a market valuation is inept when it degrades that which is being valued.' West (1993, p. 2424) argues that 'regarding the commodification … of sexual and reproductive services as morally problematic sounds not just stylistically odd, but morally deaf.' However, Wald (1997, p. 459) argues that properly 'understanding the relationship between property and rights of sexual control would contribute to a fuller understanding of why rape is so prevalent and why it is so injurious to women.'

50. Critics of Posner who misunderstand the implications of using economics to study sexuality include West (1993) and Radin (1987).
51. Far from being rhetoric which justifies a tolerant attitude towards rape, any reasonably conducted economic study of rape concludes that the harm to society as a whole and the victim greatly exceeds the gain experienced by the rapist.
52. It is, of course, entirely possible that a community's view of sex degrades one of the participants. The solution, however, is to attempt to change the norm, not to pretend that it does not exist.
53. See also West (1993, p. 2430).
54. A transfer of wealth may be deemed either coercive or voluntary. A coercive transfer is one that occurs involuntarily outside of the market; a voluntary transfer is one that occurs voluntarily within the market.
55. Although rape may often be a pure coercive transfer, it may, however, assuming a market for sexual services, also be an impure coercive transfer. This raises the dilemma of efficient rape. West (1993, p. 2430) discusses Posner's analysis. Note, however, that it is not invariably true that efficiency demands that coercive transfers be criminally forbidden.
56. Within American society, 'rape is now a felony in every state and is universally regarded as a tort as well' (Schwartz 1979, p. 805). See also Dressler §213.1 (1987), Williams (1983), and *Model Penal Code* § 213.1 (1962), Restatement (Second) Of Torts § (1964).
57. Posner (1992b, p. 218) defines an efficient rape as a rape in which 'the satisfactions of the rapist ... exceed the victim's pain and distress.' Thus, such rapes are arguably efficient and, as Posner (1992b, p. 218) notes, it can be argued that the rapist 'ought to be permitted to rape, provided only that he derives more pleasure from the act, over and above all substitutes ... than the pain suffered by his victim.' Thus, in terms of the framework developed above, efficient rape may be considered an impure coercive transfer with a positive net change in social welfare. Hence, even Posner (1985b, p. 1198) concludes that rape is a 'seemingly more problematic example of the concept of crime as pure coercive transfer.' There may be other difficulties as well. For example, Schwartz (1979, p. 806) argues that the theory is deficient for two reasons. First, it seems to hold that rape law is designed to protect prostitution. Since prostitution is, of course, illegal in itself, the traditional theory is 'descriptively defective', a view shared by Coleman (1988, pp. 153, 162). Second, Schwartz argues that even presuming the legality of prostitution, prostitution could not provide an adequate substitute for rape for often the pleasure of the rapist depends on his forcible subjugation of the victim. Thus, Schwartz seems to argue that rape laws are economically inexplicable because there is no acceptable market transaction they could be designed to promote. Conversely, Landes and Posner (1987, p. 158, citing Posner 1985b, pp. 1198–1199) argue that 'there are market substitutes for coercive sexual acts – substitutes presumptively more efficient than using the legal system to direct the allocation of resources to sex.'
58. Posner's position on the subject of efficient rape, however, seems to have fluctuated in its tenacity. At one point he calls 'the prohibition against rape ... not only consistent with but entailed by a normative economic analysis of sex' (Posner 1992a, p. 182). At another, Posner (1992b, p. 218) says only that 'there are practical objections' to 'a rape license,' but does not compare the strength of these objections with the theoretical gains that might flow from legalizing efficient rape. For other arguments supporting the inefficiency of rape and/or the efficiency of rape law, see Zelder (1993, pp. 1601–1602), Ellis (1983), and Fried (1978, pp. 92–93).
59. However, Posner (1992a, p. 386) stresses that this argument is utilitarian, not economic. See also Posner (1985b, p. 1197).
60. It is undoubtedly true that fear of future rape is both prevalent and costly, for '[m]ost women experience fear of rape as a nagging, gnawing sense that something awful could happen, an angst that keeps them from doing things they want or need to do, or from doing them at the time or in the way they might otherwise do' (Gordon and Riger 1991, p. 2). However, just as Nietzsche's murderer 'thirsted after the bliss of the knife' a rapist

may experience equally intense pleasure in anticipating an assault (Nietzsche 1968, pp. 150–151).

61. For example, one could conduct a survey of rape victims, asking them how much they would have demanded before 'consenting' to rape (that is, by not pressing charges) and the second group how much they would pay. It would be profoundly insensitive to ask a rape victim such a question, but it seems highly likely that the number a victim would accept would be high, approaching infinity. WTP_r could be roughly estimated by considering the value rapists attach to their freedom (which they sacrifice by comitting a crime) multiplied by their estimate of the probability of arrest and conviction. Given low conviction rates for rape, WTP_r is likely low, at least compared with WTA_v.
62. Note that while there is a wealth of anecdotal support for this conclusion, no empirical evidence can be found. Such evidence would, of course, be necessary for a proper KHZ analysis. Nevertheless, the lack of any empirical studies probably indicates that rape is so obviously unacceptable that no such study is thought necessary. Indeed, the mere suggestion that such a study into the acceptability of rape be conducted would undoubtedly be objectionable to many.
63. Schwartz (1979, p. 808) states that 'our real judgment is that the act of rape is plainly wrong in any moral sense'; and he notes (p. 807) that 'the obvious truth is that rape is morally offensive, and deeply so.' West (1993, p. 2424) notes that 'rape evidences ... a malignant impulse toward women' and that as 'common intuition holds, rape is a violation of personhood in the deepest sense imaginable.' She also says (1986, p. 1449) 'I would guess that the average reader, unlike Posner, views rape and prostitution as manifestations of what is wrong with sexual relations in this society and would not view the legal availability of prostitution (along with other sex markets such as dating and marriage) as a reason for the wrongness of rape.' Posner (1992b, p. 386) himself recognizes that the prohibition against rape is founded in 'unshakable moral institutions.' See also *Coker* v. *Georgia*, 433 U.S. 584 (1977).
64. Both Louisiana and Georgia have recently passed 'capital-rape laws' (Higgins 1997, p. 30). In upholding the former, the Louisiana Supreme Court noted that similar laws passed (though subsequently invalidated) in Florida and Mississippi may indicate a trend in public opinion 'favoring such penalties' (Higgins 1997, p. 30, citing *State* v. *Wilson*, 685 So. 2d 1063 (La. 1996)). Note that such laws may be construed as a reasonable judgment that society is willing to pay more to deny standing to rapists than to grant it. If so, then a positive WTA on the part of the victim would be sufficient to find rape KHZ inefficient and, thus, properly illegal.
65. Posner (1992a, pp. 386–387) himself says that rape is 'not really utility maximizing,' but insists that this is a 'utilitarian' rather than 'economic' argument. Under KHZ, a community's sense of outrage and grief at rape is both 'economic' and 'utilitarian,' since the community's regard for others is an economic concern (Chapter 2).
66. For a discussion of the strength of opinions surrounding the issue of rape, see, for example, Kadish and Schulhofer (1995, p. 315).
67. More precisely, *men* during the Middle Ages regarded a women's sexuality as the property of her husband or father. It is hard, if not impossible, to say whether women ever believed this, even during the Middle Ages, since the writers of the age were almost all men.
68. The lingering, partial exemption of husbands from rape liability may be explained by lingering sexist attitudes, or it may be an example of the written law changing more slowly than social attitudes.
69. Assuming that women did consent to such a grisly exchange, such an exchange can only be explained by a grotesque difference in bargaining power. This demonstrates that actual consent does not necessarily legitimate a legal rule.
70. Posner's (1992b, p. 218) suggestion that marital rape was legal because the 'felt impropriety' was 'dilute[d]' is interesting, because it implicitly recognizes the role of the regard for others in determining legal rules. However, Posner likely regards the 'dilute[d]' sense of impropriety towards marital rape as a non-economic factor in determining the law.
71. Posner's definition of wealth maximization has fluctuated. Although he has said that

wealth maximization is equivalent to KH efficiency (Posner 1987a, p. 16; 1986, pp. 12–13; 1992b, pp. 88–89) he has also said that wealth maximization is equivalent to GNP (Posner 1987a, pp. 19–20). At one point he implies that wealth maximization is equivalent to utility (1987a, p. 18), but at other points he has said that they are different (1981a, p. 60). (That Posner cannot be always assuming equivalence between wealth maximization and KH is shown by his statement; 'The wealth-maximizing society does not set contentment as its goal' (Posner 1987a, p. 19).

72. See also *Russ* v. *Woodside Homes, Inc.*, 905 P.2d 901, 905 (Utah Ct. App. 1995) (stating that exculpatory clauses 'relieve one party from risk of loss or injury in a particular transaction or occurrence and deprive the other of the right to recover damages from loss or injury.'). Eisenberg (1993) defines an exculpatory clause as a contract clause which purports to release a party from liability for injury caused by that party's actions.
73. See also Restatement of the Law, Second, of Contracts §79. See also *Batsakis* v. *Demotsis*, 226 S.W.2d 673 (Tex. Civ. App. 1949), which states that 'mere inadequacy of consideration will not void a contract.' Farnsworth (1982) concludes that parties are free to make agreements as they wish, and courts will usually enforce any bargained-for exchange without passing on its substance. Note, however, that 'the broad prohibition against review of "adequacy" hasn't meant that fairness of an exchange is not a legal concern' (Dawson, Harvey and Henderson 1993). However, Farnsworth (1982, pp. 40, 66–67) insists that courts' sole inquiry is whether the parties went through a bargaining process, and that unfair terms are relevant only as evidence of coercion, fraud, or sarcasm, or evidence that the 'exchange' was really a gift.
74. See also Farnsworth (1982, p. 326). Schell (1993, p. 441) states that despite 'the general need to enforce contracts as written, the law recognizes a number of occasions when judicial review of agreements is warranted. Defenses based on public policy are among the most ancient of these exceptions.'
75. See, for example, Farnsworth (1990, pp. 353–356, 1982, p. 333) and Schell (1993, p. 463). Schell (1993, p. 463) states that 'contractual risk-shifting may reduce the incentives of parties performing important services to the public at large to take reasonable care in the performance of their contractual duties.' See also *Bisso* v. *Inland Waterways Corp.*, 349 U.S. 85 (1955), which notes that holding exculpatory clauses unenforceable 'discourage[s] negligence.' An alternative ground of unenforceability is unconscionability (Dawson, Harvey and Henderson 1993, pp. 700–726).
76. Exculpatory clauses may purport to excuse (1) liability for intentional torts, (2) strict liability, and (3) liability for negligence. Exculpatory clauses which purport to excuse liability for intentional torts are clearly unenforceable (Farnsworth 1990, p. 353, 1982, p. 333). See *Alack* v. *Vic Tanny Intl. of Missouri, Inc.*, 923 S.W.2d 330 (Mo. 1996) (stating that 'there is no question that one may never exonerate oneself from future liability for intentional torts or for gross negligence'). With respect to clauses purportedly excusing strict liability of a seller of a product, the majority rule is that 'a seller of a product can't exempt himself from the strict liability imposed for physical harm caused by its unreasonably dangerous condition' (Farnsworth 1982, p. 334). See also Restatement of the Law, Second, of Contracts §195(3). Talbott (1988, p. 30) notes that although 'courts have permitted a contractual waiver of a seller's strict liability for product defects only in cases not involving personal injury' that nonetheless 'an exception may be made in cases of a fairly negotiated contract between two merchants for the sale of an experimental product' (Restatement of the Law (Second) of Contracts §195, Comment c). Talbott (1988, p. 30) states that courts have 'uniformly limited such waivers to agreements between commercial entities for commercial losses.'
77. See also *Tunkl* v. *Regents of University of California*, 60 Cal. 2d 92 (1963). Farnsworth (1982, pp. 333–334) states that 'courts have held such an agreement unenforceable because the agreement affects the public interest and the other party is a member of a protected class.' See also Farnsworth (1990, pp. 353–354).
78. However, Farnsworth (1990, p. 354, 1982, p. 334) disagrees.
79. See *Garretson* v. *United* 456 F.2d 1017 (9th Cir. 1972).

80. For some relevant work, see, for example, Talbott (1988), Schell (1993), and Posner (1992b, pp. 113–115).
81. Cooter and Ulen (1997, p. 167) state that '[i]n general, economic efficiency requires enforcing a promise if the promisor and promisee both wanted enforceability when it was made.'
82. See *Tunkl*, 60 Cal. 2d. 92 (1963) (stating that because a 'hospital–patient contract falls within the category of agreements affecting the public interest' a standardized release from liability for negligence imposed as a condition for admission to a charitable research hospital having superior bargaining power is unenforceable). Talbott (1988, p. 31) notes that 'the paternalistic defense argues that the person granting the waiver is for all intents and purposes at the mercy of the corporate or institutional party ... and any such agreements would almost inevitably rebound to the gain of th[at party] and to the individual's and ultimately the public's loss.' Talbott (1988, p. 28) also notes that '[i]n the development of these now well-established principles of law, the quasi-coercive nature of the bargaining – in order to buy the car or gain admission to the hospital, you must sign the waiver – has played a decisive role.'
83. Although Posner is here discussing the efficiency of standard contracts, the analysis is similar. Consider also Talbott (1988, p. 31, 47 n, 16).
84. The *Tunkl* opinion makes this argument. See *Tunkl*, 60 Cal. 2d. 92. 306. The exculpatory clause itself could be valued as the probability of an injury to the promisor due to the promisee's negligence times the probability of a successful suit on that injury times the present value of the expected judgment.
85. Talbott (1988, pp. 25, 30) states that 'post-*Tunkl* cases generally consider [inter alia] whether there existed disparity of bargaining power' (*Tunkl*, 60 Cal. 2d 92).
86. That is, in cases involving exculpatory clauses executed by an individual promisor in favor of a monopolist promisee.
87. With respect to (1) competition between common carriers consider 'fare wars' between airlines; (2) competition between hospitals and doctors consider recent developments in the health care industry; (3) competition among 'public warehousemen' consider the abundance of private mini-storage companies; and (4) competition among public utilities (see The Telecommunications Act of 1996), providing for competition among telecommunications providers ranging from traditional cable companies to municipal electric utilities.
88. Here, as elsewhere in this section, the term 'price' is defined broadly to include not only the monetary price of the good or service, but also the value of the exculpatory clause.
89. Posner (1992b, p. 114) notes that 'all the firms in the industry may find it economical to use standard contracts and refuse to negotiate with purchasers. But what is important is not whether there is haggling in every transaction but whether competition forces sellers to incorporate in their standard contracts terms that protect the purchasers.' A similar statement could be made with respect to exculpatory clauses.
90. Talbott (1988, p. 26) states that '[w]here the population of potential accident victims is very large and the probability of injury is very small, it may well be rational for each potential victim to sell her right to compensation at a price that would not begin to compensate her if she were unlucky enough to be injured.'
91. Talbott (1988, p. 40) concludes that 'none of the well-known normative political theories explains this result,' including 'Posner's theory of Wealth Maximization.'
92. Given the regard for others upon which KHZ efficiency is premised, the allocative change will quite possibly be integratively efficient as well.
93. Note, however, that strictly construed, such 'benefits' are actually compensation for previous losses. See, for example, Wade *et al.* (1994) and Cooter and Ulen (1997, pp. 306–311).
94. See also Aristotle (*Ethics*) and our discussion in part (II). Again, in the absence of proper empirical evidence, anecdotal references and common sense must be the twin pole stars of decision.
95. Landes and Posner (1987, pp. 27–28, 315–316) note that the movement toward contribution among negligent tortfeasors is one of the areas of 'greatest divergence between

efficient and actual rules of tort law.' Posner (1992b, pp. 188–189) is among those who state that no-contribution rules are more efficient than contribution. Keeton *et al.* (1984) are among those who note the movement towards contribution.

96. However, Landes and Posner (1987, p. 24) argue that the only way to invalidate an existing theory is by presenting evidence that an alternative theory better explains the subject phenomena than does the existing theory.

97. Landes and Posner (1987, p. 91) state that cases 'in which the victim's injury is caused by more than one injurer are of two different types: the simultaneous joint tort and the successive joint tort.' In a simultaneous joint tort, the victim 'suffers a single or indivisible injury as a result of the tortious activity of two or more persons'; and in a successive joint tort 'one tortfeasor aggravates an injury inflicted by the other.' Only simultaneous joint torts are at issue here.

98. The common law recognized two circumstances in which joint and several liability would hold: (1) if the defendants acted together to cause the victim's harm, or (2) if the fault for the victim's harm was considered indivisible between multiple tortfeasors (Cooter and Ulen 1997). And see for example, Restatement (Second) of Torts §§875, 881. The term '[j]oint tortfeasor' has been defined as two or more persons jointly and severally liable in tort for the same injury to persons or property, whether or not judgment has been recovered against them' (Schwartz *et al.* 1979, pp. 779, 781, n. 9). *Black's Law Dictionary* (1990) states that the term 'joint tortfeasors' 'refers to two or more persons jointly and severally liable in tort for the same injury to person or property.'

99. The efficiency of joint and several liability, itself, will not be considered here; but for insightful economic analyses in support of such liability consider Cooter and Ulen (1997, p. 302) who conclude that '[t]here are several economic reasons for joint and several liability' and Kornhauser and Revesz (1989, pp. 832–833), who set forth an analysis of 'the properties of several classes of apportionment rules not predicated on a finding of joint and several liability' which attempts to 'provide [some] normative guidance as to when such liability is desirable from an efficiency prospective.' However, Manzer (1988, pp. 628, 648–649) argues that joint and several liability induces overdeterrence. Nonetheless, Kornhauser and Revesz (1989, pp. 856–858) do conclude that '[a]lthough rules of joint and several liability are efficient under negligence, they will not produce efficient results under strict liability.'

100. For an early treatment of the effect of contribution on pretrial settlement, see James (1941).

101. 'Indemnity,' according to Keeton *et al.* (1984), is 'an order requiring another to reimburse in full one who has discharged a common liability.' The Restatement of the Law of Restitution §77 (1937) states that 'a person who has discharged a duty that is owed by him but which as between himself and another, should have been discharged by the other is entitled to indemnification' (see also Restatement (Second) of the Law of Torts §886B). 'Although it was occasionally said that contribution "is but pro tanto indemnity" ... contribution and indemnity were traditionally distinguished in [three] respects': (1) indemnity is based upon contract, contribution upon principles of equity, (2) indemnity shifts the entire loss to another party, and (3) only in cases of contribution are both parties jointly liable (Higgenbotham and Wiggins 1990, p. 698). But see *American Motorcycle Ass'n* v. *Superior Court* 578 P.2d 899, 907 (Cal. 1978) (stating that 'the dichotomy between the two concepts [of indemnity and contribution] is more formalistic than substantive, and [that] the common goal of both doctrines, the equitable distribution of loss among multiple tortfeasors, suggests a need for reexamination of the relationship between these twin concepts') (superseded by statute as stated in *Miller* v. *Stouffer*, 11 Cal Rptr. 2d 454 (1992)). Indeed, *American Motorcycle*'s recognition of the need for reexamination proved prophetic, in that California subsequently repealed joint and several liability through Proposition 51. See *Miller* v. *Stouffer*, 11 Cal. Rptr. 2d 454 (1992).

102. Di Cola (1992, pp. 1543, 1544, n. 5, quoting 18 Am. Jur. 2d Contribution §1 (1985)) defines 'contribution' as 'a payment made by each person, or by any of several persons, having a common interest or liability, of his share in the loss suffered or in the money necessarily paid by one of the parties in behalf of all the others.' Gregory (1938) adopts a

similar definition. See *Vickers Petroleum Co.* v. *Biffle*, 239 F.2d 602, 606 (10th Cir. 1956). See *Roberts* v. *Robert V. Rohrman, Inc.*, 909 F. Supp. 545, 553 (N.D. Ill. 1995) (defining 'contribution' as the 'principle whereby a tort-feasor against whom judgment is rendered is entitled to recover proportional shares of the judgment from other joint tort-feasors whose negligence contributed to the injury and who are also liable to the plaintiff'); *Avnet, Inc.* v. *Allied Signal, Inc.*, 825 F. Supp. 1132, 1138 (D.R.I. 1992) (stating that '[a] claim for contribution is a claim in which one liable party seeks to recover from another liable party for the latter party's share of common liability'); *United States* v. *Conservation Chemical Co.*, 619 F. Supp. 162, 224 (W.D. Mo. 1985)(claim dismissed by *United States* v. *Conservation Chemical Co.* 1988 U.S. Dist. Lexis 18283 (W.D. Mo. 1988)). See also *Blomgren* v. *Marshall Management Services, Inc.*, 483 N.W.2d 504, 506 (Minn. Ct. App.1992) (defining 'contribution' as a 'remedy for one who has discharged more than his fair share of common liability for a burden, allowing one to recover a proportionate share from the other liable party'); *Somer* v. *Federal Signal Corp.*, 593 N.E.2d 1365, 1372 (N.Y. 1992) (noting that '[c]ontribution enables a joint tort-feasor that has paid more than its equitable share of damages to recover the excess from other tort-feasors').

103. See *Palmer* v. *Wick and Pultneytown Steam Shipping Co.*, A.C. 318 (1894).
104. Keeton *et al.* (1984, p. 337) argue that 'the better English view, even before their statute, appears clearly to have been that contribution is not denied in cases of mere vicarious liability, negligence, accident, mistake, or other unintentional breaches of the law.'
105. Keeton *et al.* (1984, pp. 336–337) argue that 'the origin of the rule' allowing contribution among negligent joint tortfeasors 'and the reason for it were' ultimately 'lost to sight.'
106. Higgenbotham and Wiggins (1990, pp. 700–701) note that '[t]he English case of *Merrywether* v. *Nixan* ... is generally cited as the beginning or early restatement of the common law rule [that] there could be no contribution among joint tortfeasors, whether negligent or intentional.' See *Merrywether* v. *Nixan*, 101 Eng. Rep. 1337 (K.B. 1898).
107. 'Although the record is sparse, it is believed that the injuries' in *Merrywether* 'were intentionally inflicted' (Schwartz *et al.* 1979, p. 782). Indeed, the case involved 'the intentional tort of trover' (ibid.). See *Merrywether*, 101 Eng. Rep. 1337 (stating that one 'Starkey brought an action on the case against plaintiff and defendant for an injury done by them to his reversionary estate in a mill, in which was included a count of trover, for the machinery belonging to the mill'). This was also Keeton's (1984, pp. 336–337) conclusion.
108. This holding was apparently founded upon the maxim '*ex turpi causa non oritur actio*,' which Leflar (1932) defines as '[o]ut of a base [illegal or immoral] consideration, an action does ... not arise' *Black's Law Dictionary* 589 (6th edn 1990). Thus, the 'traditional justification for the common law rule was that a tortfeasor should not be able to use the judicial system to recover for his own wrongs'(Comment 1968, p. 730). Consider also Schwartz *et al.* (1979, p. 782, n. 19).
109. For some examples, see Higgenbotham and Wiggins (1990, p. 701), Schwartz *et al.* (1979, p. 782) and Stanley (1994, p. 4). Indeed, Lord Kenyon (in *Merrywether*) explicitly states that the decision 'would not affect cases of indemnity where one man employed another to do acts, not unlawful in themselves' (Keeton *et al.* 1984, pp. 336–337). *Merrywether*, 101 Eng. Rep. 1337.
110. Keeton *et al.* (1984, p. 337) note that '[l]ater [English] cases seized upon th[e] limitation [of *Merrywether* to intentional torts], and held that the rule against contribution did not apply unless the defendant was a willful and conscious wrongdoer.' Higgenbotham and Wiggins (1990, p. 701) note that 'English cases after *Merrywether*, and early American cases, noted the distinction between negligent and intentional torts, and allowed contribution in the former.' See also Schwartz *et al.* (1979, p. 729). *Merrywether*, 101 Eng. Rep. 1337.
111. Schwartz *et al.* (1979, p. 782) note that '[t]he earlier American cases also seemed to draw the distinction between intentional and negligent torts, allowing contribution in negligence actions only.'
112. In commenting on the phenomenon, Reath (1898, p. 177) notes that '[i]t is singularly

unfortunate, and has led to misunderstanding, that *Merrywether* v. *Nixan* should have been continually treated as stating the "general rule." As a matter of fact that case states not the general rule, but the exception.' *Merrywether*, 101 Eng. Rep. 1337.

113. Federal common law also denied contribution in tort cases, absent some express statutory provision in favor of contribution or some indication of Congressional intent to allow such a right (Higgenbotham and Wiggins 1990, pp. 725–726; Easterbrook, Landes, and Posner 1980, pp. 332–333).
114. Jurisdictions allowing contribution were the District of Columbia, see *Knell* v. *Feltman*, 174 F.2d 662 (D.C. Cir. 1949); Nevada, see *Weiner* v. *United Air Lines*, 216 F. Supp. 701 (S.D. Cal. 1962) (applying Nevada law); Iowa, see *Best* v. *Yerkes*, 77 N.W.2d 23 (Iowa 1956); Louisiana, see *Quatray* v. *Wicker*, 178 La. 289 (1933)(superseded on other grounds by statute as recognized in *Cole* v. *Celotex Corp.*, 599 So. 2d 1058, 1070 (La. 1992); Maine, see *Bedell* v. *Reagan*, 192 A.2d 24 (Me. 1963); Minnesota, see *Grothe* v. *Shaffer*, 305 Minn. 17 (1975); Pennsylvania, see *Goldman* v. *Mitchell-Fletcher Co.*, 292 Pa. 354 (1928); Tennessee, see *Davis* v. *Broad St. Garage*, 191 Tenn. 320 (1950); and Wisconsin, see *Ellis* v. *Chicago and N.W. Ry.*, 167 Wis. 392 (1918).
115. The unpopularity of the no contribution rule is noted by Landes and Posner (1987, p. 192), Keeton *et al.* (1984, p. 338), and Schwartz *et al.* (1979, pp. 783–784).
116. See also Keeton *et al.* (1984, p. 338); Higgenbotham and Wiggins (1990, p. 702).
117. Higgenbotham and Wiggins (1990, pp. 701–702) note that to 'evade the inequitable results occasioned by applying the no-contribution rule, some courts fashioned exceptions,' while other courts either 'applied a rule that distinguished "active" from "passive" negligence' or 'recognized a right to contribution in favor of a tortfeasor to whom another tortfeasor had violated a duty.'
118. Kornhauser and Revesz (1989, p. 841, n. 48) note that '[b]eginning in the nineteenth century … common law courts began to recognize… a right [to contribution].'
119. This legislative trend is discussed by Higgenbotham and Wiggins (1990, p. 702), Fleming (1983, p. 233), Cavanaugh (1987, p.1285–1286) and Cooter and Ulen (1997, pp. 301–302). Apparently, the 'movement toward comparative fault has accelerated the movement toward contribution, since comparative fault statutes commonly provide also for contribution' (Keeton *et al.* 1984, p. 338, n. 17).
120. 'Law Reform (Married Women Tortfeasors) Act' §6 (1935) provides that 'where damage is suffered by any person as a result of a tort … any tortfeasor liable in respect of that damage, may recover contribution from any other tortfeasor who is, or would if sued have been, liable in respect of the same damage, whether as joint tortfeasor or otherwise; so, however, that no person shall be entitled to be indemnified by him in respect of the liability of which contribution is sought.'
121. 'This trend, however, [has] not change[d] the rule that always existed that contribution could not be enforced between willful or intentional tortfeasors' (Schwartz *et al.* 1979, p. 784). See also Restatement (Second) of Torts §886A(3), comment j, which provides that there 'is no right to contribution in favor of any tortfeasor who has intentionally caused the harm'; the Uniform Contribution Among Tortfeasors Act, §1(c) U.L.A. (1955); and Higgenbotham and Wiggins (1990, p. 702).
122. The Uniform Contribution Among Tortfeasors Act §1 U.L.A. (1955), provides that 'where two or more persons become jointly and severally liable in tort for the same injury to person or property or the same wrongful death, there is a right to contribution among them even though judgment has not been recovered against all or any of them.' By 1979, 15 jurisdictions had adopted some version of this uniform act (Schwartz *et al.* 1979, p. 786). By 1990, that number had risen to at least 20 (Higgenbotham and Wiggins 1990, p. 702).
123. Unif. Comparative Fault Act, §4, 12 U.L.A. 47 (1979).
124. Restatement (Second) of Torts §886A(1) holds that, except as otherwise stated, 'when two or more persons become liable in tort to the same person for the same harm, there is a right of contribution among them, even though judgment has not been recovered against all or any of them.'
125. Restatement of Restitution §81 (1937) provides that '[a] person who has discharged

more than his proportionate share of a joint duty is entitled to contribution from the other or others except where the payor is barred by the wrongful nature of his conduct.'

126. Eggen (1995, pp. 1701–1702), notes that '[n]ot only are the uniform laws inconsistent with one another, but inconsistent applications of identical provisions exist among states adopting the same uniform act.'
127. 'The requirement that the [contribution] claimant be "liable" in respect of the plaintiff's damages may be satisfied not only when he has been actually held liable but also when he has settled' (Fleming 1983, p. 236).
128. See also Higgenbotham and Wiggins (1990, p. 714).
129. Interestingly, some careless plaintiffs have signed a 'release of one joint tortfeasor' which 'discharged the liability of all joint tortfeasors.' Therefore, 'a settlement with one tortfeasor in which a release was given would prevent the plaintiff from going after other joint tortfeasors' (Easterbrook, Landes and Posner 1980, p. 333). Conversely, if a settling defendant pays more than that defendant's share of the liability, that defendant may not seek contribution from the non-settling defendant. See the Uniform Contribution Among Tortfeasors Act §1(d), U.L.A. (1955).
130. Higgenbotham and Wiggins 1990, p. 714). But see Comment (1968, pp. 730–731) which concludes that the 'pitfalls' inherent in a rule permitting contribution can be easily avoided. Di Cola (1992, pp. 1555–1556) states that law and economics 'scholars have acknowledged … that contribution rules can be structured in a way that avoids the negative impact on settlement.' However, Easterbrook, Landes and Posner (1980, pp. 363–364, 365–366) argue that such rules 'would probably be very costly to administer.'
131. The Restatement notes that a rule prohibiting contribution from the settling defendant would both be 'very unfair to the other tortfeasors' and would provide 'a clear incentive to collusion between the settling parties' (Restatement (Second) of the Law of Torts, comment m). Keeton *et al.* (1984, p. 338, note 13) argue that *Penn. Co.* v. *West Penn. Ry.*, 144 N.E. 51 (Ohio 1924) is an example of such collusion.
132. The Restatement (Torts Second, comment m) notes that there 'are three possible solutions for the situation' but there are important policy reasons which weigh against each of them.
133. The current (1977) version of the Uniform Act provides that when 'a release or a covenant not to sue or not to enforce judgment is given in good faith to one of two or more persons liable in tort for the same injury or the same wrongful death …[i]t discharges the tortfeasor to whom it is given from all liability for contribution to any other tortfeasor' (Uniform Contribution Among Tortfeasors Act' §1, U.Law A (1955)). Thus, the 'Uniform Act favors settlements' (Higgenbotham and Wiggins 1990, p. 714).
134. Restatement (Second) of the Law of Torts §886, Caveat and Comment m, states that the 'Institute takes no position on the effect of a release of one tortfeasor from liability for the harm or a covenant not to sue him for it upon the right of other tortfeasors to contribution from him.'
135. In the words of Kornhauser and Revesz (1989, p. 831), the 'apportionment of … losses among the various responsible parties raises difficult and controversial questions.' Indeed, Di Cola (1992, p. 1546) notes that the 'literature discussing contribution [in such areas as] securities, antitrust, and environmental law is extensive.' In the securities area see, for example, Sachs (1994) and Adamski (1981). In the antitrust field, see, for example, Easterbrook, Landes and Posner (1980), and Polinsky and Shavell (1981). In the environmental law sphere, see, for example, Hernandez (1997).
136. However, the trend towards contribution is not universal, and indeed California has abandoned joint and several liability. See *Miller* v. *Stouffer*, 11 Cal. Rptr. 2d 454 (1992).
137. This chapter concerns only the efficiency of contribution where liability is founded upon simple tort negligence. For an efficiency analysis of contribution where liability is strict, see Kornhauser and Revesz (1989, pp. 834, 858–861), who conclude that 'while no-contribution rules will not lead to the efficient result under strict liability, rules of contribution, if properly designed, can do so.' And, for an efficiency analysis of cases in which liability is based upon an intentional tort see Landes and Posner (1987, p. 204),

who note that 'economic analysis of no contribution in the intentional case is symmetrical with that in the unintentional.'

138. According to most commentators, a rule of contribution among negligent joint tortfeasors is traditionally KH inefficient, when compared to a rule of no-contribution (Landes and Posner, 1987; Easterbrook, Landes and Posner, 1980; Polinsky and Shavell, 1981; Shavell 1987, pp. 164–167; Cooter and Ulen 1997; Stanley 1994). Posner (1992b, p. 1553) notes that the 'primary objection to contribution is that it is economically inefficient.' The commentary is not, however, unanimous. Comment (1968, pp. 730, 735) argues that '[c]ontribution... increases deterrence [over a rule of no-contribution] by the certainty that each tortfeasor will incur some liability ... rather than by the existence of a chance that some tortfeasors will escape all compensation responsibility.' Landes and Posner (1987, pp. 192–193) counter that this 'criticism rest[s] on a confusion between ex ante and ex post' for '[i]f, ex ante, each defendant bears a [sufficient expected] cost ... of liability, each defendant will be deterred, even if ex post all but one pay nothing.' See also Arrow (1973).

139. With respect to incentives for efficient accident avoidance see, for example, Kornhauser and Revesz (1989, p. 837), who state that from 'an efficiency perspective, the objective of the liability and apportionment rules is to induce rational actors to produce the socially efficient amount' of harm and who describe and analyze 'eight categories of apportionment rules under negligence and two ... under strict liability.'

140. For a given allocative change to be KH efficient, the gainers from the change must 'gain more than the losers lose' (Katz 1996, p. 2240). See, for example, Cooter and Ulen (1997, pp. 41–42). A movement from no-contribution to contribution results is traditionally KH-irrelevant 'ex post distributional consequences' (Easterbrook, Landes and Posner 1980, pp. 349–359). For example, a movement from no-contribution to contribution could result in a transfer of wealth from defendants who could have sought contribution to those from whom such contribution would have been procured, and the movement could result in a loss of judicial economy. It, therefore, fails to satisfy traditional conceptions of KH efficiency.

141. For example, Di Cola (1992, pp. 1556–1558) argues that, while the 'reliability of the efficiency model as an accurate predictor of result ... depends on the validity of the assumptions embedded in the analysis ... Several recent commentators ... have undermined the validity of some of those assumptions.'

142. For example, see Easterbrook, Landes and Posner (1980, p. 350). Di Cola (1992, pp. 1557–1558) notes the 'model's assumption that all litigants have perfect information.' Moreover, in Stanley's (1994, p. 6) view, both Easterbrook, Landes and Posner (1980) and Polinsky and Shavell (1981) assume 'symmetric information and beliefs in reaching their conclusions and recommendations.'

143. Di Cola (1992, pp. 1557–1558, citing Yi 1990, pp. 18–20) notes the assumption and states that '[w]hen some defendants are insolvent ... the positive effects of a no-contribution rule on settlement will be less than predicted.'

144. For example, see Kornhauser and Revesz (1989, p. 832). Easterbrook, Landes and Posner (1980, p. 351) note that our 'conclusion that no-contribution and contribution rules yield the same deterrence assumes that' the actors are risk neutral. Note that Easterbrook, Landes and Posner (1980, p. 351) define risk neutrality as indifference 'between paying (receiving) a certain sum and paying its uncertain actuarial equivalent.' Cooter and Ulen (1997, p. 47) define risk neutrality as 'constant marginal utility of income' by which one is 'indifferent between a certain prospect of income and an uncertain prospect of equal expected monetary value.'

145. Kornhauser and Revesz (1989, pp. 847–850) explore the effects of assuming that all actors are irrational on the analysis of contribution. Cooter and Ulen (1997, pp. 296–297) discuss the ramifications of assuming actor rationality for a microeconomic analysis of law generally.

146. While this assumption is by no means universal, it was made by Landes and Posner (1987, p. 204) for a portion of their work. For example, Kornhauser and Revesz (1989, p. 832) note that 'these commentators considered the choice between apportionment and

contribution only under negligence.' However, Landes and Posner (1987, p. 204) analyze the effects of contribution and no-contribution rules for intentional torts as well. The assumption of negligence liability is also made throughout this chapter.

147. Kornhauser and Revesz (1989, pp. 846–847) assume that 'the standards of care are set at the socially optimal level.'

148. Ibid. (pp. 832–833) note that 'because there can be no right to contribution without joint and several liability, [several] commentators [have] assumed, without much discussion that rules of joint and several liability would govern.' A similar assumption is made throughout this chapter. Joint and several liability has been found to induce efficient outcomes (ibid., pp. 847–851).

149. Although this assumption may be unrealistic (see, for example, Keeton *et al.* 1984, pp. 469–471), it is probably not vital to the analysis (Cooter and Ulen 1997, pp. 259–292).

150. This is what Kornhauser and Revesz (1989, p. 837) call a 'full liability rule.' Kornhauser and Revesz (pp. 837–839), describe the rule and note that although commentators 'are split on whether courts apply a full liability of a partial liability rule' by which a liable actor is 'liable only for those losses that ... are caused by the actor's negligence ... most economic models have assumed that' a full liability rule is in force.

151. The assumption is made here as well.

152. Easterbrook, Landes and Posner (1980, p. 353) note that they assume 'that the antitrust system operates without error' in that 'the substantive principles are correctly assessed, where what is meant by correctly is given by economic analysis.' See also Landes and Posner (1987, pp. 197–198).

153. Cooter and Ulen (1997, p. 302) note that in an analysis of contribution versus no-contribution, 'the critical distinction is between situations in which the optimal precaution is unilateral by one of the defendants and those in which it is joint among all of them.' Landes and Posner (1987, p. 190) note that a 'simultaneous joint tort... can involve either joint care or alternative care.'

154. Refer to Cooter and Ulen (1997) for a definition of 'bilateral care.' Landes and Posner (1987, pp. 60, 190–191) note that 'in a case of joint care optimal accident avoidance requires both parties (here, both injurers) to take care.' See also Posner (1992b, pp. 170–171).

155. Landes and Posner (1987, pp. 60, 191, 198) provide a definition of 'alternative care.' Cooter and Ulen (1997, p. 275) note that 'unilateral precaution' cases require only 'one party to an accident to take precaution against it.' For more details, refer to Posner (1992b, pp. 170–171).

156. Posner (1992b, p. 188) notes that '[a]t common law ... the rule in alternative care cases [is] indemnity.'

157. Landes and Posner (1987, pp. 198–201) conduct an efficiency analysis of the rule of indemnity in alternative care cases.

158. Again, it is here assumed that liability is founded upon negligence (Easterbrook, Landes and Posner 1980). Legally, negligence may be defined as conduct 'which falls below the standard established by law for the protection of others against unreasonable risk of harm' (*Black's Law Dictionary* 1990). Kornhauser and Revesz (1989, p. 836) note that '[n]egligence rules define a standard of care' and that 'if a[n actor] meets her standard of care, she will bear no portion of the social loss.' Economically, that standard may be said to be equal to that level of precaution, x^*, which minimizes the expected social cost of an accident, C_s, where that cost is defined as the cost of precaution, Cx, plus the cost of expected harm from an accident, $p(x)L$; that is, $C_s = Cx + p(x)L$. The level of precaution which minimizes the expected social cost of an accident is that at which the marginal cost of an additional unit of precaution equals the marginal benefit of the resulting reduction in the cost of expected harm; thus, the efficient level of precaution is that value of x, x^*, for which $C = -p'(x^*)L$. Consequently, a potential injurer is negligent if it employs precaution $x < x^*$ (Cooter and Ulen 1997, pp. 273–274; Posner 1992b, pp. 163–167).

159. Compare this statement with Kornhauser and Revesz's (1989, p. 871) analysis. Kornhauser

and Revesz (1989, p. 836) note that '[t]he efficient amount of [harm] is that which maximizes the social objective function: the sum of the benefits derived by the actors minus the social loss.'

160. For ease of exposition it is here assumed that there are only two potential injurers. This analysis is, however, adaptable to cases of more than two potential injurers (Landes and Posner 1987).
161. It is, of course, also necessary that the victim not be negligent (Wade *et al.* 1994, pp. 566–581).
162. Kornhauser and Revesz (1989, p. 842) call this a 'unitary share rule' which, in their 'taxonomy' 'correspond[s] to rules of joint and several liability.' Kornhauser and Revesz (1989, pp. 841–842) explain that, under a unitary share rule 'the negligent actors pay not only for the damages attributable to their own actions but also for the damages attributable to non-negligent actors' and thus, that 'the victim recovers the maximum loss allowable whenever at least one actor is negligent, regardless of how much of the damage is caused by non-negligent actors.' Kornhauser and Revesz (1989, p. 841) suggest a 'fractional share rule' under which 'the negligent actors do not pay for the damages attributable to non-negligent actors.' Di Cola (1992, pp. 1556–1558) notes that use of that rule could 'shift' the 'contribution/no-contribution efficiency calculus.'
163. Specifically, given that $C_s = Cx + p(x)L$, the cost of compliance with the legal standard, Cx, is $C_s - p(x)$; and, thus, $Cx < C_s$ (Cooter and Ulen 1997, pp. 270–272).
164. Kornhauser and Revesz (1989, pp. 847–848). Kornhauser and Revesz (1989, pp. 847–848) conclude that '[i]f all but one of the actors are non-negligent, it would not be rational for the remaining actor to be negligent.'
165. Again, to simplify the analysis, it is assumed that there are only two potential injurers. This analysis may easily be expanded to account for more than two potential injurers by including additional terms.
166. For example, Easterbrook, Landes and Posner (1980, p. 345) note that an actor 'will choose to comply with or violate the antitrust laws depending on whether its anticipated gain from the violation is greater or less than its expected liability.' Kornhauser and Revesz (1989, p. 836) state that '[a]n economically rational [actor] … seeks to maximize her private objective function: the benefit that she derives from the activity that leads to the production of the [harm] minus whatever share of the social loss the legal regime allocates to her.'
167. Note that it is assumed here that the victim C has an incentive to behave non-negligently by employing precaution z^*; this is indeed the case under either rule of allocation, contribution or no-contribution.
168. 'Under negligence… [f]or a no-contribution rule to be efficient … the sum of the probabilities that the actors attach to the risks of being held responsible for the … damage must be equal to one' (Kornhauser and Revesz 1989, p. 861). See also Landes and Posner (1987, p. 203). This, in turn, requires that each actor have perfect knowledge for without such knowledge, 'different actors may attach inaccurate probabilities to their risk of liability and the probabilities may not sum to one' (Di Cola 1992, pp. 1557–1558). Thus, it has been argued that, because '[u]nder a rule of no contribution, each prospective tortfeasor is uncertain what share of the accident cost he will bear … misallocations can result' (Landes and Posner 1987, p. 203). Landes and Posner (1987, p. 203) analyze and refute this argument.
169. Specifically, the total expected loss of injurer A′ (or injurer B′) depends on whether the other potential injurer is negligent, $x(y) < x^* (y^*)$ or non-negligent, $x (y) = x^* (y^*)$ (Landes and Posner 1987, p. 195).
170. To say that B is non-negligent is to say that B chooses precaution y^* (Landes and Posner 1987, p. 194).
171. If B employs precaution y, B is negligent (Landes and Posner, 1987, p. 194).
172. $s^A p(x, y, z^*)D + A(x)$ will be less than $A(x^*)$ whenever (1) C chooses only to sue B or (2) C chooses to sue both A and B but A's share of the collective damages is sufficiently small.

173. This is true because, as discussed above, B will seek to minimize its total expected loss (Kornhauser and Revesz 1989, p. 836).
174. In the antitrust context, see Easterbrook, Landes and Posner (1980, pp. 344–353).
175. For example, Posner (1992b, p. 189) concludes that 'a rule of contribution, which allows a joint tortfeasor made to pay more than his [or her] "fair" share of the plaintiff's damages to require contribution from the other joint tortfeasors, will also create the right safety incentives for all joint tortfeasors – and this regardless of how the contribution shares are determined (pro rata, relative fault, etc.).'
176. Easterbrook, Landes and Posner (1980, p. 344) note that 'any rule apportioning damages produces adequate deterrence if the aggregate damages are properly selected.'
177. Pro rata contribution admits some equitable exceptions, however; thus, equity sometimes requires (1) treating two joint tortfeasors as liable for a single share, or (2) that 'the share of a tortfeasor who is insolvent or absent from a jurisdiction be borne by others' (Keeton *et al.* 1984, pp. 340–341). In addition, in other jurisdictions 'the distribution of the liability is in proportion to the comparative fault of the defendants' (Keeton *et al.* 1984, pp. 340–341). The effect of both the exceptions to the pro rata rule and the proportional fault rule itself is to alter the values of the 'individual liability shares', s^A and s^B (Easterbrook, Landes and Posner 1980, p. 350). Such an effect is inconsequential to the analysis presented here. Easterbrook, Landes and Posner (1980, p. 350) note that 'the specific values of the individual liability shares ... have no bearing on the analysis (which is the reason no contribution and contribution yield identical effects).'
178. Again, this is true because, as discussed above, B will seek to minimize its total expected loss (Kornhauser and Revesz 1989, p. 836).
179. Easterbrook, Landes and Posner (1980, p. 349) employ a similar analysis in the antitrust setting.
180. Easterbrook, Landes and Posner (1980, p. 357, n. 59) conclude that 'in the multiple-defendant case, it will always be possible to find positive settlement values ... that make the plaintiff and at least n–1 defendants better off compared to their expected trial outcomes.'
181. By assumption, $k < n$ (Easterbrook, Landes and Posner 1980, p. 357, n. 60).
182. After settlement with n–1 defendants, the expected value of C's claim against defendant n has been expressed as

$$V_{ECn}{}^{C} = p^{C}(D - ?S_i),$$

where i equals 1 to n–1 and hence, $?S_i$ equals the total settlement received from the settling n–1 defendants. Whether C settles with n depends on whether n's offer is greater than $V_{ECn}{}^{c}$ (Easterbrook, Landes and Posner 1980, pp. 354, 355, 357).
183. Di Cola (1992, p. 1555, citing Yi 1990, pp. 18–20) notes further that '[a] no-contribution rule can also create a "prisoner's dilemma" which tends to increase settlement amounts,' whereas 'the presence of contribution has a negative effect on the plaintiff's recovery.' For a more formal proof, see Easterbrook, Landes and Posner (1980, pp. 359–360, 365), who conclude that a 'rule of no contribution creates competition among defendants to settle rather than litigate.'
184. Landes and Posner (1987, pp. 202–203) note that a rule of contribution will 'discourage defendants from settling.'
185. Di Cola (1992, pp. 1555–1556) notes that 'contribution rules can be structured in a way that avoids the negative impact on settlement.'
186. A third contribution rule, a 'carve-out' rule, would 'reduce[] the potential liability of a non-settling defendant by [the] settling defendants' share of damages (instead of by total settlements)' (Di Cola 1992, p. 1556). See also Easterbrook, Landes and Posner (1980, pp. 363–368).
187. Landes and Posner (1987, pp. 202–203) note that 'the traditional rule in cases where contribution is allowed' is to allow a joint tortfeasor who loses at trial 'to get contribution from the [settling defendant].' Keeton *et al.* (1984, p. 340) note that the 'usual holding has been that the [settling] defendant ... is not released from contribution' despite the

fact that there 'has been much dissatisfaction with this [rule] because it becomes impossible for a defendant to settle the case.'

188. Easterbrook, Landes and Posner (1980, p. 361) note that what are here termed the traditional rule and the settlement bar rule 'correspond roughly to the original [1933] and amended [1957] versions of the Uniform Contribution Among Tortfeasors Act' (see also Di Cola 1992, p. 1556).
189. Here it is assumed that a pro rata contribution rule is employed (Easterbrook, Landes and Posner 1980, p. 362).
190. Di Cola (1992, p. 1555) notes that '[i]f [traditional] contribution from settling defendants is allowed, settlement does note bar further liability and … each defendant's incentive to settle decreases.'
191. It seems that a carve-out rule also 'produces the same incentive to settle as a no-contribution rule' (Di Cola 1992, p. 1556).
192. Landes and Posner note that 'the settlers may have settled for tiny sums, leaving the non-settlers to bear the lion's share of the liability.' See also Di Cola (1992, p. 1556). Similarly, with respect to the carve-out rule, it is argued that (1) although those which equally apportion liability are easy to administer, they 'negatively affect contribution's fairness objectives'; and (2) although those which apportion liability according to fault would be fair, they would be 'very expensive to administer' (Landes and Posner 1987, p. 201–203).
193. Indeed, the two carve-out rules may be included in this list as well. However, Stanley (1994, p. 6) notes that '[w]hen the analysis is expanded to allow for asymmetric information, previous conclusions do not always hold.'
194. In the federal system and in those state systems modeled after it, this would be accomplished via a cross-claim.
195. Landes and Posner (1987, p. 201) conclude that no contribution is 'undoubtedly the cheapest to administer.'
196. Di Cola (1992, p. 1553) notes that contribution is generally thought to both increase the cost of litigation and discourage settlement 'without a concomitant increase in deterrence.'
197. Landes and Posner (1987, pp. 219–222) hypothesized that contribution would 'be found more often in states that do not weight [traditional] efficiency heavily … than in states that do weight it heavily' but they found only 'limited support' for their hypothesis.
198. For more details, see Zerbe (1998a, Chapters 2, 3).
199. Again, given the regard for others upon which KHZ efficiency is premised, the allocative change will quite possibly be integratively efficient as well.
200. Recall that the *(G–L)* term is intended to represent the traditional KH efficiency calculation and the *(WTP – WTA)* term the additional distributional component of KHZ efficiency – that is, the valuation of the change in the distribution of wealth caused by the underlying allocative change.
201. For example, Landes and Posner (1987, pp. 315–316) note that it might be desirable to embed 'the positive economic theory of tort law' in 'a broader economic theory of judicial and legislative action' because under such a theory 'apparent anomalies' as the movement to contribution 'may disappear.' We argue that the KHZ efficiency theory is just such a 'broader theory' (Landes and Posner 1987, p. 315).
202. Easterbrook, Landes and Posner (1980, pp. 349–350) describe this transfer as only an 'ex post distributional' consequence with 'no offsetting gains in allocative efficiency.' This is, however, a change in the distribution of wealth that is relevant in a calculation of KHZ efficiency.
203. We discussed the increase in administrative cost above. It is here assumed that there is no liability insurance. On the role of such insurance in the contribution/no-contribution debate see Keeton *et al.* (1984, p. 338). Inclusion of insurance in the KHZ analysis would probably have the effect of increasing the magnitude of *L*. *L*, however, would remain positive (Keeton *et al.* 1984, p. 338).
204. I suggested in Chapter 2 that the value of distributional changes can be measured in principle as other non-market goods are measured, which is by contingent valuation

surveys and by observed behavior. In the absence of contingent valuation surveys, this subsection will rely on anecdotal evidence, which, of course, is simply one form of observed behavior, and, in the present circumstances, the only available form.

205. Landes and Posner (1987, p. 192) note that 'the rule of no contribution has been denounced by most commentators.'
206. Di Cola (1992, p. 1563) notes that the 'impetus behind abrogating the common law proscription of contribution in negligence actions has been a sense that it is unfair and unjust for one tortfeasor to bear the burden for all wrongdoers.' A vast literature details the inequity of no-contribution (Keeton *et al.* 1984, pp. 337–338). DiCola (1992, p. 1562) notes that perhaps 'the strongest and most frequent objection to the no-contribution rule is that it is unfair to defendants.' Conversely, contribution is a rule which evolved in equity. See *Gomes* v. *Brodhurst* 394 F.2d 465, 467 (3d Cir. 1967) (describing contribution as 'a rule of reasoned fairness'). Schwartz *et al.* (1979, p. 780) note that because 'contribution traces its origin to equity, rather than contract, it serves as a means of assisting in the fair distribution of loss thereby preventing injustice, and which is designed to do justice.' Di Cola (1992, p. 1563) notes that fairness 'considerations have weighted heavily in instances where the courts or Congress have granted a right to contribution.' Comment (1968, p. 736) notes that the 'values underlying the notion of equal protection or fairness may also support contribution.' Cavanaugh (1987, p. 1287) states that the 'principal rationale for adopting a rule of contribution in antitrust cases is fairness.' Easterbrook, Landes and Posner (1980, p. 340) note that a 'fairness argument from the mouth of the intentional wrongdoer is unappealing because the wrongdoer can avoid his predicament by conforming his conduct to the law's demands.' However, Higgenbotham and Wiggins (1990, p. 744) hold a contrary view.
207. This, of course, suggests that, contrary to the suggestions of Di Cola and many other commentators, there is no need to 'balance anti-contribution efficiency arguments' against fairness considerations' (Di Cola 1992, p. 1562). Rather, fairness considerations will, by virtue of the distributional component of KHZ efficiency, often be incorporated into the efficiency analysis itself.
208. For example, Keeton *et al.* (1984, p. 338) note that the 'only kind words said by any writer over the last century for the rule denying contribution have been addressed to the proposition that contribution will be used chiefly to permit liability insurance companies to shift a part of the loss.'

9. The efficiency of the common law: An economic analysis of dueling, cannibalism, the gold rush, racism, and antitrust law

9.1 INTRODUCTION

Chapters 2 and 3 introduced a concept of economic efficiency that rests on the axioms. In particular, my definition of efficiency requires (1) a recognition that benefits and costs are psychological and subjective, (2) a recognition that one must point to a superior rule or practice in order to say that some existing practice or rule is inefficient, (3) the inclusion of the transactions costs of operating the rule or practice as a part of the determination of efficiency, and (4) the inclusion of the value of all goods for which there is a WTP or WTA in determining inefficiency. This chapter applies these concepts to perhaps the major puzzle in law and economics, the efficiency of the common law.

The common law[1] has been found to tend toward economic efficiency[2] in important instances (Posner 1986, p. 19f).[3] This is an important claim, for it is not only a broadly descriptive assertion but a predictive one about the nature of common law. If this claim is true, why is it true?

Though various evolutionary models have been offered to explain it (Rubin 1977; Priest 1977; Goodman 1978) none of these explanations is wholly satisfactory (Cooter and Ulen 1988, pp. 492f; Posner 1990, p. 372). Although I agree with those who have said that the common law tends towards efficiency, I offer a novel explanation as to why it tends to be efficient. Second, and equally important, the explanation suggests the conditions under which a particular common law rule is likely to be inefficient.[4] The chapter illustrates these ideas through a series of examples.

The central idea is straightforward: the common law is generally efficient because it usually incorporates well-accepted social norms, which correspond to psychological rights or ownership. I will show that laws adopting uncontentious social norms are not simply efficient, but necessarily efficient. I argue, further, that judges adopt social norms because they are acting in accord with a social norm – the norm that judges dispense justice. It follows that it will be efficient to change a norm, or to change the common law, only when conditions change. By a change in conditions, I mean a change in technology, in institutions, in sentiments, or in knowledge. When conditions change, norms are no longer uncontentious, and thus are no longer norms. Furthermore, the fact that conditions are changing may increase the transactions cost of applying a norm, even if the norm has popular support in the community.

Finally I show, through a series of examples, that when conditions change, uncontentious norms may not exist. In such a circumstance, neither the existing common law nor its new development may be efficient. One of the examples raises the issue of the moral justification of economic efficiency. I show that Posner's justification of actual consent fails, but that a justification is nevertheless to be found in the sentiments of the community when the definition of efficiency incorporates certain features.

9.2 THE COMMON LAW TENDS TO EMBODY SOCIAL NORMS

The idea that the common law tends to embody social norms is solidly embedded in scholarship on the common law (*Black's Law Dictionary* 1999, p. 270; Devlin 1965).[5] This body of judicially derived rules is seen by Hogue (1966, p. 3) as 'social rules' that 'continue to reflect the character of the social order.'[6] Hogue (1966, pp. 9–10) notes that the medieval judges did not believe that they were making new laws – rather, they were recognizing the customs of a certain territory and giving those customs legal effect.[7]

The great medieval jurist Henry de Bracton, who died in 1268, noted that in England legal right is based on an unwritten law that usage had approved (Hogue 1966, p. 10, citing Bracton 1915, p. 41). Before incorporating custom, especially particular or local custom, into common law, royal judges were careful in determining the validity of custom (Hogue 1966, p. 196).[8]

According to Blackstone (1900, p. 46), before a custom was included in the common law, tests of both general and particular custom were applied. These criteria were clearly formulated by the late eighteenth century (Blackstone 1900, pp. 53–54). Good custom, according to Blackstone (pp. 56–57) is (1) ancient,[9] arising from a 'time whereof the memory of no man runneth not to the contrary,' (2) continuous, since 'revival gives it a new beginning which will be within time of memory,' (3) peaceful, in that it is 'not subject to contention and dispute,' (4) reasonable, in the light of legal reasoning – that is, not absurd or unjust, (5) certain, in the sense of being ascertainable, (6) compulsory, 'not left to the option of every man,' and (7) consistent. An alleged custom which does not satisfy all seven criteria is not really a custom.[10]

The eminent legal scholar Maitland 'noted a three-stage progression from customs originating in the "common wisdom and experience of society," through the stage of becoming "established customs," to the point at which they receive "judicial sanction in courts of last resort"' (Maitland and Montagu 1915, p. 213; Hogue 1966, p. 190, note 213) (see also Hogue 1966, p. 190). This reliance on custom is noted by Pollock (1929, p. 254). Plucknett (1956, p. 307), in his highly regarded treatise on the history of the common law, notes that laws created by legislation, and expressed in authoritative texts, cover but a very small period of our legal history. Before they existed, the principal element in most legal systems was custom. He notes that there were, of course, other factors as well in many cases, but, 'the great mass of the law into which these exceptional elements had to be fitted was custom. Our earliest Anglo-Saxon "laws" are modifications of detail and obviously assume that the legal fabric is essentially customary' (Plucknett 1956, p. 307).

The customs that came to make up the common law, then, tended to be old customs, about which there was little disagreement or contention, and important customs, in the sense that there was social sanction for failure to conform to them. The modern rediscovery by Ellickson (1991), and others such as Anderson and Hill (1975, p. 163) and Zerbe and Anderson (1999), of 'order without law' was both well known and the basis for an important part of English law.

There are also more recent examples of courts adopting custom to govern the legal decision. For example, the courts relied on norms in the whaling industry in the nineteenth century (Ellickson 1991). Ellickson (1991, p. 92) notes, 'in fact whalers' norms not only did not mimic law; they *created* law.' In the dozen reported Anglo-American cases in which ownership of a whale carcass was contested, judges regarded themselves as bound to honor whalers' usages that had been proved at trial (Ellickson 1991, p. 92). In the antitrust context, courts continue to adopt the law to reflect real-world business practices and current economic theory, in order to ensure that the antitrust law actually promotes competition.[11]

9.3 WHY ADOPTING NORMS IS EFFICIENT

A norm is, of course, simply a set of rights – psychological ownership – established by custom. Psychological ownership consists of the belief of an entitlement to ownership, which may differ from legal ownership, which is an enforceable right to ownership. I shall say that a norm that is uncontentious is one in which the aggregate WTP to change the norm is less than the aggregate WTA. Otherwise the norm is said to be contentious.

A rule-setting institution that adopts uncontentious norms is then establishing property rights where they did not exist legally before and also making sure that these legal rights correspond with psychological rights. This is necessarily an efficient activity, as was shown in Chapter 3. Thus a rule which adopts uncontentious norms is necessarily efficient.

Consider an example in which the norm might be inefficient, and consider the question whether or not the court should recognize the norm. Even where norms are contentious, their adoption may be efficient. Suppose, for example, that the norm in a community is that group A has the right to collect driftwood along a certain beach, but that the other group in the community, group B, has no such right. That is, psychological ownership in driftwood among group A has been established. Suppose, however, that members of group B might be the more efficient collectors of driftwood. Were group B to have the right to collect driftwood, the national product might be greater and the existing norm inefficient. Suppose the court adopts the existing norm as a law, giving the right to collect driftwood exclusively to A. If the members of group B are more efficient collectors, group A will sell the right to group B, so that at most the loss from adopting the norm is the transactions costs of the sale; if no sale takes place, the loss is non-existent, or in any event less than the transactions costs of the sale. In the absence of other information, the assignment of rights to A is more likely to be efficient. A's loss – were the right to be assigned to B – would be measured by its WTA, but B's gain would be measured by its WTP. In addition, to assign the right to B when it has psychologically belonged to A will be seen as unfair by others, and that perception would be part of the efficiency loss from an assignment to B. Unless there is other information about the value to the two groups, the efficient assignment is to A. When the rule-making institution adopts the existing norm, it specifies property rights and thus lowers the transactions costs of A selling the right to B, so that the right is more likely to transfer. But the transfer would be one in which group A was compensated, and thus it is more likely to be seen as fair than one in which no compensation is given. For the court to determine that it was more efficient to assign the right to B would require the court to determine that the right was worth more to B than to A, and this determination would be both expensive and error prone. The court knows, moreover, that the amount by which B's WTP exceeds A's WTA cannot exceed the transactions costs of selling the right to driftwood once property rights are established. So granting the right to A rather than to B – that is, following the norm – is more likely than not to result in efficiency. These transactions costs are likely to be less than the costs of having the courts attempt to determine whether or not B is the efficient holder of the right. Thus, the general rule of adopting norms, especially uncontentious norms, is an efficient rule where conditions are not changing.

Where there is sentiment for change of a norm, however, the norm is not 'peaceful' but is contentious. The requirement that norms incorporated into common law be well established and uncontentious helped ensure that the willingness to accept them was less than the willingness to have them changed (Blackstone 1900, pp. 43f). The requirement of a social sanction for failure to obey a norm suggests that only important custom became enshrined into law. Thus, Blackstone's (pp. 56–57) criterion guarantees the incorporation of only true norms, which are norms that are efficient.[12]

I have shown that in a static world and even in a world of modest change, enforcing a norm will generally be efficient, since it embodies existing rights. That is, a norm is efficient if it corresponds with or embodies psychological reference points – as it must if it is uncontentious and of long duration. Plucknett (1956, p. 44) gives some idea of the force of these rights when he notes that lawyers were entrenched within '*feudal learning, which, moreover, had become the basis of every family fortune in the land*' [emphasis added].[13] Since the common law historically adopted uncontentious norms of long standing, it tended to be efficient.

Thus, Ellickson's (1991) discussion of the conditions under which norms are efficient, and his discussion of why norms in whaling and norms with respect to wandering cattle are more efficient than other, hypothetical norms, misses the point. Norms are efficient if they are stable and uncontentious, because they could be no other way. Ellickson's own examples, if read from the perspective illustrated here, demonstrate just this point. His interesting discussion indicates why norms of closely knit groups may be different from those of more diverse groups, and why it might to better to belong to a closely knit group than not; but it does not explain why norms are efficient.

The syllogism then goes like this. To establish rights that correspond to psychological rights when conditions are unchanging is by definition efficient. Norms that are uncontentious, and of long standing, involve the establishment of psychological rights. When legal ownership corresponds to or sanctifies psychological ownership, it will be efficient. When norms are law there is such a correspondence, and the law is efficient, assuming that it does not produce unreasonable transactions costs.[14] A wide variety of common law codifies just such a scenario (Cohen and Knetsch 1992).

9.4 WHY JUDGES ADOPT NORMS AS COMMON LAW

The argument here is that judges act according to a social norm, a norm of justice.[15] What empirical evidence there is suggests that judges actually do seek to do justice in deciding cases (Glick 1990, pp. 261–302). I will say that justice occurs when decisions meet one's reasonable expectations. Reasonable expectations are, in turn, formed by social norms. Justice therefore occurs when social norms are followed. I shall say, then, that judges adopt norms because they dispense justice. To do this is also KHZ efficient.

As John Chipman Gray (1909, p. 114) points out, 'the essence of a judge's office is that he shall be impartial.' A similar sentiment was expressed by the commission of four bishops, two earls and six other barons who were appointed after the triumph of Henry III over the baronial faction: 'Furthermore, we ask the same lord king ... that, for doing and rendering justice, he will nominate such men as, seeking not their own interests, but of those of God and the right, shall justly settle the affairs of subjects according to the praise-worthy laws and customs of the kingdom' (Hogue 1966, p. 67, citing *Dictum of Kenilworth*).

Posner's (1990, pp. 359f) view of judges is not apparently at variance with the one expressed here. Posner (1981b, p. 17) notes that Holmes's *The Common Law* (1881) is an extended paean to judges' skill in adapting common law doctrines to durable public opinion. Durable public opinion, of course, is what we mean when we speak of norms. This opinion then helps to define efficiency, so that the efficiency of the common law, far from being unusual, should be expected. Judges act according to a norm – a norm that expects them to dispense justice;[16] they use the language of justice. I will cite one example among almost endless possibilities because, first, it uses the language of justice, second, it illustrates the regard for others, third, it shows concern for the income distribution, and, fourth, it fits with my custom here of using historical references.

In *Gilmore* v. *M'Kelvey* (MacDevitt 1884, p. 10) a case arising out of the Irish land law of 1881, the court says, 'With respect to the question of value, the court is perfectly unanimous. One cannot help having a certain feeling with respect to a gentleman who having in 1878 voluntarily and without coercion taken a couple of fields outside the town from a lady, not very wealthy, at a rent of £30 a year, comes in the year 1882, and seeks to get a perpetuity in that land as against her at a rent of £12 15s. I have no doubt Mr. Gilmore reconciled himself to the transaction, *but there are many people who would not*' [emphasis added].

Attempts such as those of Landes and Posner (1975) to explain judicial behavior from an interest group perspective are 'simply unconvincing' as North (1981, p. 57) and Buchanan (1975) have pointed out. As Hogue (1966, p. 253) points out, 'when judges in medieval England failed to maintain the high standards of learning and disinterested action expected of them, English feudal barons, churchmen, and merchants insisted on reform.'

Efficiency itself is such an important norm that we should not be surprised when impartial judges advance changes in rules that are efficient. Gray (1909, p. 3) thought that judges and jurists approached the law from the side of public welfare, and sought to adopt it to the common good. Holmes (1881) pointed out that when revenge was the prevailing sentiment, the law provided a remedy for a wrong that approximated what would have been considered necessary to give victims their traditional vengeance. Later, when revenge became less important relative to the values of deterrence and compensation, the old doctrines were ingeniously adapted to the new sentiments.

In the more modern era, when the pace of changes in conditions has been more rapid, greater reliance undoubtedly has been placed on judicial judgment of what is efficient, as compared with well-established custom in the development of efficient common law. As Friedman (1959, p. 26) notes, 'since the First World War the tempo of social change has accelerated beyond all imagination. With it the challenge to the law has become more powerful and urgent.'[17]

A full explanation of the origin of the norm that judges should dispense justice would require a treatise on English history, which I do not provide.[18] The relationship between the British king and the judiciary may explain the norm in part. Efficient norms that promote the wealth of a nation are likely to increase the sovereign's wealth as well, and will in general then be left undisturbed. Thus, norms such as those requiring that debts be paid or that contracts be honored among citizens are wealth increasing, and will not be disturbed by the sovereign. The sovereign's judges have, then, an incentive to see that those norms are enforced. We will note, finally, that in some cases the sovereign may gain from violating an efficient norm – for example, that the sovereign may not confiscate property without compensation.[19] So I do not argue that not all efficient norms will be represented by the common law. Instead, I claim that the common law is generally efficient, when there is a relevant, uncontentious norm. I note then the outline of a story of the norm of justice, but I will not explore further the complex question here of the origin of the norm of the rule of law.

9.5 WHEN NORMS ARE INEFFICIENT: EFFICIENCY WHEN CONDITIONS CHANGE

Inefficiency, then, arises from changing conditions. The world is, of course, not static, nor wholly efficient. Changes in sentiments, technology, or knowledge that create a dynamic world also create inefficiencies. A social change may render a previously efficient rule inefficient when the change results in ambiguous ownership, as with a new valuable resource, a shift in psychological ownership, a change in sentiments reflected in the regard for others, or a shift in transactions costs. Thus, it is efficient to change the status quo only when conditions change. A change in conditions implies, as North (1981) noted, a change in relative prices. As relative prices change, behavior will change in response, and so, also, will the efficient equilibrium change. North has attempted to explain historical change on the basis of just such responses to changes in relative prices. This sort of historical change represents KH-efficient changes.

The efficient law changes in response to changes in technology, institutions, sentiments, and knowledge. The slower the pace of change, the easier it is for changes in custom to precede law. The slower the pace of change, the easier it is for judges to accurately determine the social standards of the age and adopt custom into law. Thus, I would expect common law to be more efficient in a quieter age.[20]

But, even in the Middle Ages, common law was attuned to changes in custom. Azo, the civilian jurist who was according to Plucknett (1956, p. 308) held in high esteem by Bracton, noted that 'a custom can be called long if it was introduced within ten or twenty years, very long if it dates from thirty years, and ancient if it dates from forty years.' Hogue (1966, p. 8) notes that in every generation both lawyers and laymen seem to have been drawn toward two desirable – but separate and contradictory – goals. The first of these is the goal of permanence, stability, and certainty in legal doctrines. The second is the goal of flexibility and adaptability, permitting adjustment of the law to social necessity.[21]

Custom has changed over time, and the law has changed with it. Plucknett (1956, p. 308) notes, 'the Middle Ages seem to show us bodies of custom of every description, developing and adapting themselves to constantly changing conditions.' He continues, 'indeed nothing is more evident than that custom in the Middle Ages could be made and changed, bought and sold, developing rapidly because it proceeded from the people, expressed their legal thought, and regulated their civil, commercial and family life.'

Judges have historically sought out custom to incorporate into common law. No better example of this may be found than in the achievement of Lord Mansfield. Mansfield was the Chief Justice of the court of King's Bench from 1756 to 1788. It was his achievement to incorporate the merchant law into the common law, and to fashion what had been a body of special customary law into general rules within the common law. Hogue (1966, pp. 248–249) notes of Mansfield, 'When a case touched commercial law, he saw to it that reputable merchants of the city of London formed the jury. Thus he secured in his court the participation of jurors who presumably understood every detail of material evidence. Outside court, on social occasions, he cultivated the acquaintance of merchants to acquire for himself a precise knowledge of their ways of doing business.'[22]

The more rapid the pace of change, the more likely is inefficiency to be created. This is because the more rapidly conditions change, the less chance there is for uncontentious norms to develop and the more difficult it is for judges to determine what is in fact efficient. When conditions change more rapidly, there may be no particular custom or particular norm that the common law can incorporate. There may be, however, reasonable generalizations from existing particular custom that represent the reasonable expectations of rights-holders and which are thus efficient. There will also be general norms or general custom that can be applied, although it may be doubtful that a general norm will be superior if a particular norm exists. By general custom, I mean general norms that may be regarded as principles. Such norms may include an expectation that one is entitled to what one earns, that promises should be honored, or that equals should be treated equally. But the more rapidly conditions change, the less likely it may be that even general custom will apply.

When social conditions change, the analogy between past cases and the current issue may become strained, which may make it difficult for the parties to predict how the law will be applied to a current dispute. The harder it is to predict how a law will be interpreted, the higher transactions costs will be, as hordes of lawyers and experts are enlisted as consultants (in the hopes of avoiding a lawsuit) or litigators (once a lawsuit occurs).

Thus the KHZ theory of common law efficiency suggests that when conditions change more rapidly – when there is no uncontentious norm – it becomes more difficult to determine the efficient outcome or rule so that common law decisions are less likely to be efficient.

Today, courts recognize that the law must change in response to changes in sentiments, knowledge, and custom. For example, the United States Supreme Court noted in 1997 that antitrust law must change to reflect 'new circumstances and new wisdom,' and that the common law cannot remain 'forever fixed where it was' in a previous era.[23] The problem is that in a period of rapid change it is more difficult for a judge to determine whether sentiments, knowledge, or customs are changing, and to determine the course of their change (Friedman 1959).

9.6 LAW AND NORMS UNDER CONDITIONS OF CHANGE

It is easy to find examples for which the common law is efficient.[24] But it is almost as easy to find examples for which it is not.[25] The following five examples discuss the difficult formation of common law under changing conditions. The first, dealing with the law of dueling, shows the relationship between changes in sentiments and changes in law.[26] The second, dealing with the law of necessity in the context of cannibalism, shows judges attempting to impose their own moral standards in the face of weak or changing social norms. This second example is also used to demonstrate that the justification furnished by Posner for wealth maximization, actual 'ex ante' consent, does not work well. The third example, dealing with the history of American mining law, demonstrates that in eras of rapid social change the transactions costs of using a law can make the law inefficient, even when the law is consistent with psychological ownership and the regard for others. The fourth example, dealing with the development and demise of the 'separate but equal' standard in school segregation, demonstrates the relationship between changing sentiments, shifts in the regard for others, and changes in law. The fifth example, dealing with developments in antitrust law, illustrates the relationship between changes in knowledge, shifts in efficiency, and changes in law.

9.7 DUELING AND ECONOMIC EFFICIENCY

The social convention of dueling in the ante-bellum South has been held by Schwartz, Baxter and Ryan (1984) to have been an efficient norm. The offered proof, which consists of pointing out elements of efficiency in the practice, cannot, however, be accepted, because its definition of efficiency does not take into account the regard of others. The problem which Schwartz, Baxter and Ryan do not overcome is that dueling, even in the ante-bellum South, was a contentious norm. Its efficiency can not therefore be proved without a closer examination of the regard for others. That is, the sentiments of the general population would need to be determined more closely.

The evidence suggests that the sentiments against dueling were considerable. Schwartz, Baxter and Ryan (1984, p. 326) note that 'one other important feature of the larger social context was that the duel was explicitly made illegal and subjected to severe penalties.' The laws were, in fact, carefully designed to eliminate the practice. This contention was not confined to the ante-bellum South. In England, for example, there was never a time when private dueling was legal, according to William Bothwick (1776, p. 19).[27] From a KHZ perspective, what is of interest is why the practice of dueling arose, and why it waned.

Trial by combat was a part of the legal system in England only after William the Conqueror (Neilson 1891, pp. 31f). It arose, in large part, in response to widespread perjury, and from reasoning apparently by the elite that it was better to risk one's body than one's soul (Neilson 1891, p. 6). Possibly, in a more Christian period, it was felt that God gave victory to the right, although – somewhat ironically – the Christian church was actually attempting to abolish dueling. As Gibbon (1899, p. 552) noted, 'Is it not true that the event both of national wars and of private combat is directed by the judgment of God? And does not Providence award the victory to the juster cause.' From the Crown's point of view, dueling was narrowly efficient, in that it seems to have brought more money into the treasury than the costs of holding the combat (Neilson 1891, p. 39). In England, probably from the time after Henry I, there was no battle in civil cases unless the property in dispute was worth at least ten shillings (ibid., p. 33). In Scotland, however, which England considered to be a more primitive country, parties had recourse to 'cold iron' even in disputes concerning the most trivial property (Bothwick 1776). 'In a rude age, this method of preceding was exceedingly natural' (ibid., p. 8, n. 157).

A change in sentiments played a role in the decline of dueling.[28] The practice was never universal (Neilson 1891, p. 2). It was not practiced by the Greeks, nor the Egyptians, nor was it part of the Roman codes or the treatises of their jurists. In Europe, from its earliest days, the influence of the Christian church was directed against trial by combat, and seems to have been in the main directed against it during succeeding centuries (ibid., p. 12). Clearly, by Bothwick's time (the late eighteenth century) the practice was regarded with repugnance (ibid., pp. 2–3). Neilson notes that 'its roots must be sought in lands inhabited by a people not yet advanced beyond the barbarian stage' (ibid., p. 3). There was a steady process of restriction of trial by battle to the writ and the appeal of felony. By 1219, a rigid line had formed around the duel which it could not pass: 'in burgh after burgh it passed away … in the other courts in which it was competent, the judges more and more found reasons and made them, for disallowing a mode of trial in which they could have little faith, and in which the people at large by no means loved … When the century ended, trial by battle was far advanced on the high road to extinction. It had become uncommon before the close of the reign of Henry VI' (ibid., p. 72).

In the South after the Civil War, the value of honor probably declined. A similar explanation may apply to England and Scotland. Bothwick (1776, p. 8) notes that 'expressions which go for nothing in the year 1776 would not have gone for nothing in the year 1400. In proportion as honesty is become rare, a sense of personal honour is become less delicate.'

9.8 THE LAW AND ECONOMICS OF CANNIBALISM

Introduction

Abandonment, murder, and cannibalism were of more than abstract interest in nineteenth-century Britain. In 1884 alone, 561 British-registered ships, along with nearly 5,000 lives, were lost on the high seas.[29] One of those lives was Richard Parker's. The case arising from his death, *Regina* v. *Dudley and Stephens*,[30] one of the most famous cases in Anglo-American common law, has been a staple of criminal law textbooks and is cited to this day (Toole and Levy 1981, p. 80). What does the economic theory of value have to say about this case? That is, what is the efficient disposition?

The facts of the case are clear (see, generally, Simpson 1984). On July 5, 1884, four crewmen set out from England on a small yacht, the *Mignonette*, intending to sail to Australia. A violent storm sank their boat 1,600 miles from the Cape of Good Hope, and through the forceful and resourceful action of Captain Thomas Dudley they escaped in a small dinghy with no water and two tins of turnips. They were able to collect and drink rain water, but this soon ran out. On about the fifteenth day, the cabin boy Richard Parker became violently ill from drinking seawater. The common belief at the time, shared by the crew of the *Mignonette*, was that drinking sea water would cause certain death. On the twentieth day, July 25, after nine days in a row with no food and seven with no water, and fearing that the whole crew would die of starvation and dehydration, Dudley, with the assent of Stephens but not of Parker, slit Parker's throat. Dudley and Stephens shared another common, but erroneous, belief of their time; that blood could be safely drunk only from a body not yet dead.[31] Brooks, the third seaman, remained passive concerning the murder, but did use Parker's flesh as food. Four days later the men were rescued, 'still alive but in the lowest state of prostration.'[32]

Upon return to England, Dudley and Parker, showing no shame over their actions and making no secret of what had occurred, relied upon well-established 'custom of the seas' and precedent for their defense.[33] They were nonetheless charged with murder. The jury who tried Dudley and Stephens found 'that if the men had not fed upon the body of the boy they would probably not have survived. That the boy, being in a much weaker condition, was likely to have died before them' (Clark and Marshall 1967).

The Actual Practice of Necessity

Simpson (1984, Chapters 5 and 6) provides data on 31 wrecks in which questions of necessity arose in practice, if not in law. Some form of sacrifice or homicide is involved in each case, but they do not all involve cannibalism (Simpson 1984). Like Simpson, I use the term 'necessity' to describe any situation in which one person's life was sacrificed in order to preserve the lives of others, whether or not any criminal charges were ever filed. In Table 9.1 I have organized the necessity incidents into five categories, depending on the method that was used to select the victim: 'wait until dead,' 'tough guy,' 'strictly utilitarian,' 'altruism' and 'by lots.' The category 'wait until dead' represents those cases in which there was no murder but there was cannibalism after death. This choice, which was the most frequent, is less compelling in a situation such as Dudley and Stephens', since they feared that waiting would result in the death of all, and in which it was believed that ingesting the blood of a victim allowed to die of natural causes would not be safe. The 'tough guy' procedure resulted in exemptions for tough guys, with the least tough guys being chosen. The tough guy was usually defined by belonging to a definite group, so that, for example, passengers were sacrificed before sailors, because the sailors were a more cohesive group. The third method is the 'altruistic' method, under which the 'victim' voluntarily goes to his death so that the others, especially women and children, might be saved. The fourth category is 'strictly utilitarian': in this category, choice was made on the basis of considerations such as whether or not the victim was married.

Table 9.1 Methods of choice

Wait until dead	**Egalitarian**
Anna Morse, Date unknown	No name, 1641
Nottingham Galley, 1710	Dolphin, 1759
Nautilus, 1807	Peggy, 1765
George, 1822	Essex, 1820
Francis Mary, 1826	Spaight, 1835
Eliz. Rashleigh, 1835	Euxine, 1874
Home, 1936	
Hannah, 1836	**Altruism**
Earl Morris, 1838	Birkenhead, 1852**
Blake, 1851	
Sally Steelman, 1878	**Strictly utilitarian**
	Spaight, 1835
Tough guy	Caledonia, 1839
Mary, 1737	Mignonette, 1884
Tiger, 1766	William Brown, 1892
Medusa, 1816	*(See Tough guy)*
Granious, 1828	
William Brown, 1892*	

Notes:

* The William Brown is listed in two categories because the various defendants engaged in very different behavior.

** Birkenhead is classified as altruistic because 'the men of the 74th Highland Regiment stood at attention on deck, the band playing, while the women and children were saved, the captain very properly went down with his ship' (Simpson 1984, p. 97).

I place the *Mignonette* in this category because a major consideration in the choice of the victim Parker was his closeness to death and the likelihood of his dying naturally before the others. The fifth method, 'egalitarian,' involved the drawing of lots.

The *Dudley and Stephens* Decision

The issue of fundamental rights or duties is raised by *Dudley and Stephens*. According to Simpson (1984), the general standard prior to *Dudley and Stephens* was that the necessity of sacrificing one to save the rest was a viable defense against a change of murder. This necessity defense was accepted in the leading case of the time, *United States* v. *Holmes*, 26 F. Cas. 360, 1 Wall Jr. 1 (C.C.E.D. Pa. 1842) in which it was said that the drawing of lots was justified. Although the law was hardly well defined, the custom known as 'the law of the sea' was well established. Simpson (1984, Chapter 5) provides a discussion of the standards of the time in regard to the sort of choice that faced Dudley and Stephens. In the period before the arrest of Dudley and Stephens it appears fair to say that all five of the categories in Table 9.1 were more or less consistent with these standards except for 'tough guy.' That is, in 84 percent of the cases the standard of conduct actually observed appeared to be in reasonable accord with general social standards of the time.[34] Even in the 'tough guy' cases there were no prosecutions except in the instance of the William Brown (*United States* v. *Holmes*).[35]

Opinion of what was acceptable behavior in extreme circumstances was in the process of changing at the time the *Mignonette* met with misfortune. Although the behavior of Dudley and Stephens may have been in reasonable accord with previous social standards, it was no longer acceptable to the upper end of the judiciary. The legal establishment conspired (to use Dershowitz's term) to circumvent the possibility of a jury acquittal (Simpson 1984). Judge Baron Horace Huddleston sat as trial judge, and arranged for the jury to return a special verdict, a device that had not been used for a hundred years, that left the ultimate decision to a special court of review (the Queen's Bench). Baron Huddleston sat on the special court of review convened through this highly irregular procedural gambit, and examined a trial record which he himself had actually doctored. Dudley and Stephens were sentenced to be hanged. In reaching this sentence, however, the Court knew 'that the lives of Dudley and Stephens were not at stake' (Mallin 1967, p. 396), since the Crown had already announced that it would commute the sentence if they were sentenced to death.[36] Their sentence was, in fact, commuted by the Crown to six months.

Judge Huddleston and the Review Court were determined in advance to send a message about acceptable British behavior.[37] *Dudley and Stephens* is described as a 'clarion call' (ibid., p. 20). The Court was attempting to set a new standard of behavior. Chief Justice Coleridge gave the opinion of the Court:[38]

> To preserve one's life is generally speaking a duty, but it may be the plainest and the highest duty to sacrifice it … these duties impose on men the moral necessity, not of the preservation, but of the sacrifice of their lives for others, from which in no country, least of all, it is to be hoped, in England, will men ever shrink, as indeed they have not shrunk.

He stated that it was impossible to measure the comparative value of lives, and that necessity could be no excuse for murder in any circumstances. Coleridge concluded that Dudley and Stevens had a duty to sacrifice their lives even though this would not have saved Parker's life (of course, it would have saved Parker from murder and cannibalism). Coleridge and his fellow justices did not believe that they were forsaking their duty to preserve life when they sentenced Dudley and Stephens to death by hanging. This decision represents a shift in the moral paradigm.[39] This standard set by the Court was at variance with the custom of the times, and set stricter requirements than the mass of people felt to be warranted. But it was a standard apparently accepted by the aristocracy, endorsed by leading newspapers, and by Joseph Conrad (Boyer 1986) through his literature. The judgment itself helped to mold opinion. Once Dudley and Stephens had been ruled murderers, public opinion moved against them (Simpson 1984, p. 242).[40]

Actual, Ex Ante Consent and Hypothetical Consent

The moral justification Posner attempts to provide for wealth maximization is actual, ex ante consent. Posner explains that a purchaser of a lottery ticket has consented to the loss that will occur if the ticket does not win. The justification fails, since actual consent, desirable though it may be, is not normally available for government decisions, and does not exist even in the examples Posner (1981a, pp. 94f) suggests. Actual consent has the same flaw as Pareto efficiency – it does not apply to most decisions.

Even if actual consent exists in particular cases, it may be repugnant to social norms. That is, circumstances may render actual consent inferior to a different decision based on hypothetical consent. In short, the regard for others must be introduced into the discussion.

Suppose it turns out that the four men in the boat had been asked to purchase lottery tickets as a sort of insurance policy that determined their relative standing as victims in case of 'necessity.' The higher the premium that was paid, the further removed he would be from potential victim status.[41] Suppose further that an advocate of Posner's (1981a, pp. 94f) justification for wealth maximization, actual consent, purchased the lowest priority number, being relatively poor, and figuring that the probability it would be used was negligible. He was then consumed in accord with actual consent.

Although we have provided here what Posner (1981a, pp. 94f) has not provided in his examples, *actual, ex ante consent*, its use seems neither relevant nor desirable. The purchaser of the cheapest ticket will be said by Posner to have consented, but this is not the relevant consent. The relevant consent is determined by social norms. The procedure itself is one that some societies are likely to find repugnant, notwithstanding that their members voluntarily purchase such 'insurance.' Two characteristics of this example would lead to its social unacceptability: the choice of actual death in case necessity arose, and the difference between the willingness to pay, WTP, and the willingness to accept, WTA, in the case of a life.

This example differs from one in which construction workers at risk show ex ante choice by accepting a higher wage. In the latter case, the selection of the victim is by an 'act of God.' In the cannibalism case, people choose a victim. The difference between the WTP and the WTA will be enormous in the cannibalism case, first, because of income effects: a rich man will pay more for a ticket than a poor one, other things being equal. Second, and more important, substitution effects increase the difference, probably to infinity. One's life is a unique good, and the substitutes for it are poor. The lottery approach does not recognize a right to life, in the sense that in a decision concretely involving life and death one's life should only be sacrificed for justifiable cause. The lottery reflects no such cause. Both the WTP and the WTA reflect the income distribution and the value placed on money, not just on life.[42] That the rich may live longer because they can afford better health care does not seem unreasonable in a society in which there is social support for the way wealth is acquired. Where a known life is to be sacrificed with certainty, however, one must inquire as to the value of life to society, not just the value of money. It seems doubtful that the level of priority of the ticket purchased would be found an acceptable method of victim allocation by a court, or by society. Nor should it. The scheme is repugnant. One is unlikely to feel that his position in this grisly queue should depend on how much he paid, or was able to pay, for the ticket.

Consider now the application of wealth maximization where no lottery has taken place. Posner (1972, pp. 323–324) points out that it is often necessary to substitute market values for the WTA payment by the bearer of costs:

> The second consequence of the law's inability to ascertain preferences accurately is a tendency of the legal process to suppress variance in value. Many people place a value on their homes that exceeds its market price. Yet a standard of subjective

value, while economically correct, would be virtually impossible to administer due to the difficulty of proving that the house was worth more to the owner than the market price.

The justification for the substitution of market values for real values is similar to that we provided for Kaldor–Hicks; this would reasonably be a method chosen in an initial position where the costs of determining subjective value are larger than the gains to be generally made.

In the cannibalism example, one similarly has an incentive to over-report the value of one's life. The subjective value of one's life to oneself and to others might be efficiently ignored where it is costly to determine. The value of life would, then be its net human capital. The narrow or wealth-maximization efficiency rule that emerges from this rule, in the context of the cannibalism example, is to eat the person with the lowest present value of future earnings compared with his value as nourishment, or, more pithily, *eat the person who has the lowest price per pound.*[43] Dudley and Stephens improved on this rule to the extent that they considered the fact that they picked Parker because it was believed that he was already doomed to die.

Smart and Williams (1973) consider a traveler in a Latin country who discovers a group of Indians about to be executed by a military officer, for no particularly good reason. He protests, and is told that the Indians will go free if the traveler kills one of them. Suppose the traveler then decides to kill the one who pays him the least to live. That is, he sell tickets to avoid execution. There is actual ex ante consent, in the sense that the loser 'chose' to pay less than any one else, but the scheme is not an acceptable method of making a decision in our society. Furthermore, the loser probably would not have 'chosen' to pay the least amount of money, if he had possessed more money to offer to the traveler. Smart and Williams note that in deciding whether or not to kill one of the Indians, the traveler must confront the difference that a death by his own hand makes, and that such consideration is relevant to the decision. We can imagine a rights-based analyst working with the Indians themselves, to provide an answer for the selection of the victim (even if their answer is that all should die) that would give greater legitimacy to the decision of the traveler, whatever it is.

We can imagine also that if the crew of the *Mignonette* had discussed what the survivors should do if they found themselves in trouble at sea, they would have all agreed to the proposition that if one seemed certain to die – and to die before the others – that person would be sacrificed for the others. Such, in fact, seemed like the implicit understanding among seamen, and probably helps to explain, along with difficulties of prosecution, the absence of prosecutions in other cases in which men at sea were victims, the public support of Dudley and Stephens at the time, their commuted sentence, and Simpson's support of their actions a hundred years later. Simpson's strongest distaste is for the trial procedure, as well it should be. Rights and duties are acceptable when chosen by fair procedures; the Court here failed such a reasonable test of fair procedure. The behavior reasonably based on hypothetical consent (fair procedure) would then be likely to be usually accepted and upheld. The actual consent that Posner (1981a, p. 94) suggested would not be.

The issue of consent did indeed arise for the crew of the *Mignonette*. Dudley initiated several discussions about the possibility that lots should be drawn if it came to that, but the others argued variously that this was premature. The possibility of lots was again raised by Dudley on the day before Parker was killed. By then, however, Parker's consent was probably impossible, as he was probably comatose (Simpson, 1984, pp. 60–62). In addition, Brooks refused to draw lots at this time (he was the strongest of the three at that point). In other words, it was impossible for all four men to reach a unanimous agreement as to any decision, and therefore no action would have had actual consent from the affected parties. A standard that the courts could apply is that used in contract cases in which hypothetical consent is used. The standard used is to determine what sort of agreement the parties would have come to if they had foreseen the contingencies that did arise. This standard, of course, is consistent with efficiency, as well as with the sort of basic hypothetical consent we consider here as the justification for economists' normative analyses. This same standard seems appropriate in the case of Dudley and Stevens, and, if it was used, we would probably conclude that their behavior was consistent with the agreement that the crew of the *Mignonette* would have reached *if* they had discussed it before the problems occurred. Presumably, even Parker would have agreed to such an arrangement, so long as he did not know that he was the one who would actually be eaten.

The point is that even actual consent may provide an inferior moral defense to ex ante hypothetical consent. For example, there may exist a morally superior non-Pareto alternative to even an apparent Pareto action. The life of Sir Richard Burton furnishes an example (Brodie 1967, pp. 63–64):

> Richard Burton, while working as a civil servant in Kind, Pakistan, discovered the practice in which wealthy criminals condemned to death by British justice would buy replacements to be hung in their stead. This replacement buying was purely voluntary. Burton interviewed one pauper 'baudal' who had agreed to be executed for a murder he had not committed and asked him why he had agreed to do this. 'Sain,' came the answer, 'I have been a pauper all my life. My belly is empty. My wife and children are half starved. This is fate, but it is beyond my patience. I got two hundred fifty rupees. With fifty I will buy rich food and fill myself before going out of the world. The rest I will leave to my family. What better can I do, Sain?'

One might imagine a morally superior alternative to this voluntary market exchange, one that might be made by a chooser in an initial position. Notice that once the existence of a morally preferred alternative is made known, the original seemingly Pareto superior alternative is no longer Pareto superior, since those who prefer the morally superior alternative would not consent, and would be harmed by the choice of the original alternative.

9.9 TRANSACTIONS COSTS AND INEFFICIENCY: THE LAW OF GOLD MINING

Introduction

A glaring example of a law which created excessive transactions costs is the mining law, especially after the California gold rush. During the gold rush, the thousands who had come to California in search of gold had organized themselves into mining districts; each district adopted a series of mining rules, and appointed a body to settle disputes between prospectors (Davis 1902, p. 14). On the whole, these rules proved remarkably efficient during the early days of the gold rush (Zerbe and Anderson 1999, p. 24).

In 1851, California's legislature (with the support of the courts)[44] gave legal effect to these mining district rules (Miller 1991, p. 35). However, by 1851, almost every aspect of mining in California had changed dramatically from its beginnings in 1848: the nature of the typical mining claim, the technology of mining, the startup costs and entry barriers, and the social values of the prospectors themselves (Jackson 1980, pp. 313–315). By giving legal force to the mining rules of 1848–1850, the courts were adopting the values of an earlier – and in many ways simpler – time, and ignoring the dramatic social changes that had occurred in the mining industry (Jackson 1980, pp. 313–315). Moreover, when new geological knowledge became available which suggested that Congress's original understanding of mining was flawed, the courts limited the applicability of the new knowledge by insisting on giving the terms in the mining statute their original understanding.[45] The mining district rules did not provide answers to many of the most important questions facing litigants and the courts after 1851, forcing the courts to make ad hoc decisions that provided little or no guidance to the mining industry (Leshy 1987, p. 89).

Because the outcome of a mining dispute was difficult to predict, the mining laws led to the imposition of grotesque transaction costs, in the form of excessive litigation expenses and wasteful (but legally necessary) mining industry practices (ibid., pp. 21, 94, 110).[46] Judge Beatty noted in his report that after seventeen years of experience in Nevada, 'I cannot at this moment recall a single instance in which the owners of really valuable mining ground have escaped expensive litigation, except by paying a heavy blackmail' (Davis 1902, p. 70).

In 1866 Congress compounded the problem by giving federal approval to the mining district rules (ibid., p. 36). The new federal law shared the vices of California's 1851 statute: it ignored the dramatic changes in the mining industry, and it failed to define most of the key concepts that judges and prospectors needed to interpret (Leshy 1987, pp. 93–94). The final version of the law was adopted in 1872, and it has been amended only in minor ways since then (ibid., p. 270).

Historical Background

Those who flocked to California in pursuit of gold found themselves in a legal vacuum (Davis 1902, pp. 10–12). The gold rush began in January 1848, but California was not a state until 1850, and it had not even officially become a part of the union until Mexico signed the treaty of Guadalupe Hidalgo on July 4, 1848. The only US governmental presence in California at the start of the gold rush was Colonel Mason and his small outfit of soldiers. Mason himself concluded that he had insufficient forces to stop the prospectors from extracting gold from public land, and therefore 'resolved' not to interfere. Mason's only action, interestingly enough, was to declare the laws of Mexico inapplicable to the Californian prospectors.

Given the chaos of the situation, the prospectors acted with remarkable orderliness. They formed mining districts of varying sizes (ultimately over 500 were formed), and each district appointed an individual or a group to adopt rules and settle disputes (Snyder 1902, p. 58; Zerbe and Anderson 1999, pp. 10–11). The leader of a district was variously described as an Alcalde, a chairman, an arbitrator, or a recorder (Zerbe and Anderson 1999, p. 10). The rules were usually adopted through democratic procedures, and were posted publicly in well-known places (Davis 1902, p. 30–34). The rules provided simple criminal laws (with harsh penalties) and regulated every aspect of mining.[47] The mining rules varied from district to district, but each provided that a prospector gained an enforceable right (a mining claim) to the land he worked by being the first to discover gold there (ibid., p. 16). To maintain this right, a prospector had to post notice over the claim itself (such as a sign describing his claim) and begin working the claim within a fairly short time. In some districts, it was also necessary to file a claim with the Alcalde. A prospector could buy or sell a claim to another (ibid., pp. 19–20). Most districts imposed a limit on how many claims a prospector could hold at one time by virtue of discovery, but some allowed a prospector to purchase as many claims as he wished.[48]

On the whole, these rules – both criminal and mining – were obeyed with a regularity that astounded observers from other states (Zerbe and Anderson 1999, p. 24). The speed with which the prospectors formed rules which everybody was willing to enforce was particularly surprising, since, in the absence of a police force, the prospectors could enforce their rules only by temporarily abandoning their own claims (ibid., p. 10).[49]

Although the prospectors came from a variety of states and regions in America, they overwhelmingly shared two cultural values, which I have previously called 'Jacksonian democracy' and 'Lockean fairness' (ibid., p. 4). Jacksonian democracy is characterized by a belief in universal (white male) suffrage, and a desire for local autonomy (ibid., p. 6). The Americans of the nineteenth century had a remarkable propensity for solving problems in their communities by forming grass-roots organizations to address them (ibid.; Steffen 1983, p. 248). The value of Jacksonian democracy and local autonomy also helps explain why the prospectors formed a fairly large number of districts, and adopted rules through democratic and public procedures (Zerbe and Anderson 1999, p. 6).

Lockean fairness holds that one gains a moral entitlement to property by adding one's own labor to it (ibid., pp. 7–8). Under Lockean fairness, neither employees nor employers have this entitlement: the employee has surrendered his right to property by becoming a wage slave, while the employer has no right to the fruits of another's labor. The value of Lockean fairness explains why prospectors restricted themselves to relatively small claims, on a first come, first served basis. A first come, first served basis rule was consistent with the value that the first person to add labor to property acquires an entitlement to it. Relatively small claims were consistent with the value that idealized the autonomous producer, because a small claim was the most that an individual laborer could efficiently work.

It was these shared cultural values that allowed the prospectors to coordinate their efforts (ibid., p. 5). Cultural values reduce the information costs involved in coordination; they reduce the cost of knowing whether one's partner is cheating, and provide certainty that a cheater will be punished. They also provide an internal motivation to refrain from cheating, in that cheaters feel guilt and shame. In other words, culture informs one's regard for others, and regard for others leads one to count the guilt stemming from cheating as a loss. Umbeck (1981) is undoubtedly right that a mining group's willingness to fight determined whether their rules would be observed by potential claim jumpers, but it was the prospectors' shared cultural values which allowed them to coordinate their efforts and rely on their companions to punish defectors (Zerbe and Anderson 1999, p. 5). Because of their cultural values, the prospectors regarded their rules as fair, and attached value to the stability of the rules as an end in itself, even when a cheater had not attempted to harm them personally (ibid., p. 9). The prospectors expressed this value in their WTP, which in this case is both a 'willingness to purchase' stability and a 'willingness to punish' defectors.

One example which dramatically demonstrates the power of shared cultural values to effect coordination involves Sim's mistreatment of Sprenger:

> Two mining partners, (Sim and Sprenger) worked a claim together. Sprenger met with an accident and was crippled and helpless. Against the custom of the camp, Sim ejected Sprenger from the claim. Sprenger took the matter to the local Alcalde or mayor. Sim, it later transpired, bribed the Alcalde to support him. Without knowing of the bribe, the prospectors refused to accept the Alcalde's support of Sim, and 'over a thousand miners threw down their picks and shovels – and came to the main camp.' The miners formed a new court, reinstalled Sprenger as half owner of the claim; Sim was ordered to pay the costs of his partner, the Alcalde was deposed, and the prospectors, learning of the bribe, exacted the bribe from the Alcalde, and a new organization was set up to settle disputes, 'The Hayden Court.' (Zerbe and Anderson 1999, p. 11; Shinn 1947, pp. 190–198)

This example demonstrates four key points. First, the prospectors learned of the unfair decision with remarkable speed, and responded with an extremely large force. Clearly, this was a close knit society with low coordination costs, given the speed and size of the response. Second, the mere fact that the Alcalde's decision was inconsistent with the rules of the camp was enough to outrage the prospectors and spur them to action, even without the added fact of the bribe. This shows that the prospectors placed a high value on the fairness of their rules in the abstract, and on the stability that the rules offered. Third, the Alcalde escaped with his life, despite being surrounded by a thousand armed prospectors who could have killed him without any probable punishment by the US government (Shinn 1947, pp. 190–198). Finally, the prospectors' rule against ejecting injured partners acted as a low-cost form of insurance in a dangerous occupation. It is unlikely that an equilibrium reached through violence would produce such a humanitarian rule (particularly since the injured partner would be unable to protect himself), but this rule is consistent with efficiency (Zerbe and Anderson 1999, pp. 11–12).

Another fascinating example is that of Doughtery:

> William Doughtery and a companion found gold in a canyon on the Yuba River. They were doing well when, after several days, they were visited by a delegation of miners from a neighboring camp. The visitors, six or eight in number, proposed to share the find. A meeting was held and it was decided that each miner should be allowed to own a strip of land ten feet wide on the river and three hundred feet deep. Doughtery and his companion were in the minority, and could not have objected even had they wished; but the plan was so entirely in accordance with the usual custom – the unwritten law of older camps – that they yielded a ready and

> cheerful acquiescence. In view of the fact that they were discoverers, it was unanimously agreed that they should have first choice of ground. (Zerbe and Anderson 1999, p. 14; Shinn 1947, pp. 165–166)

Again, the restraint that the new group used was remarkable, in that they demanded no more than they were entitled to by the custom of the camp. They even went so far as to let Doughtery and his partner claim the best spots. Clearly, this is not a case in which a stronger group settled into a point of equilibrium with Doughtery's group that reflected the two groups' relative abilities to fight. The compromise may indeed have reflected their relative *willingness* to fight, but the new group's willingness to fight reflected its cultural values, and not simply the probable outcome of a fight. What is also interesting is Doughtery's 'cheerful' compliance, which may reflect an overly romanticized view of the incident, but which may have stemmed from Doughtery's recognition that the new group's proposal was fair. Indeed, given the rules of the camp, Doughtery would have been a cheater had he insisted on more.

A final piece of evidence of the importance of shared cultural norms is the fact that most of the instances in which mining disputes led to violence involved intercultural exchanges between white Americans and Chinese and Latin work gangs (Zerbe and Anderson 1999, pp. 22–23). The white prospectors felt they had little in common with Chinese or Latin work gangs, partly because of racial prejudice (the ugly side of Jacksonian democracy) but partly because they had different work ethics. The Chinese and, to some extent, the Latin prospectors were employees working for large financial ventures (from New York, Europe, Latin America, or Asia), and in this role were anathema to the Lockean fairness principle of the white prospectors (ibid., p. 23).

Mining After 1851

By 1851, the nature of mining had changed. One of the key differences was the change in the nature of the typical claim from placer claims to lode claims. From 1848 to 1850, most prospectors came to California in search of placer claims, which were relatively pure deposits of gold lying on or near the surface (Jackson 1980, p. 314). Placer claims were often found in rivers or in dry riverbeds, and were worked with a pan and shovel. A placer claim could be effectively mined by a single prospector, with no specialized experience, working on a small claim (Miller 1991, p. 18).

Lode claims, in contrast, consisted of one or more veins of gold within a single fissure of rock, often in an impure form, and often several hundred feet below the surface.[50] Lode claims could be worked only by large groups of men with specialized training and expensive equipment (Miller 1991, p. 44). Where placer claims had low financial entry barriers, most lode claims could be worked for profit only by firms with capital backing. By 1851, most of the placer claims and shallow lode claims had been extracted (Jackson 1980, pp. 313–315). Furthermore, the technology for working placer claims had evolved as well, from a simple shovel and pan, to a two-to-three man 'rocker,' to a five-to-six man 'long tom,' to the sluice box. A sluice box was a succession of cleat-lined wooden troughs, continued almost indefinitely until the prospectors ran out of wood or the terrain no longer allowed a straight line. Some sluice boxes were over a thousand feet long, and worked by more than two dozen men. In effect, by 1851 an individual prospector – or even a group of friends who decided to go into the mining business together – had little hope of mining a claim for profit. This explains the seeming paradox of the fact that the gold rush was considered 'over' by 1850, even though the volume of gold extracted from California was actually higher – far higher – in 1850 and 1851 than it was in 1848 and 1849 (ibid, p. 314).[51] The gold was not gone, but the 'rush' was.[52]

Given the impracticality of being an independent prospector after 1851, it is not surprising that Lockean fairness and its contempt for capitalists and their wage slaves declined. Two examples, taken from the life of the miner, mining lawyer, and mining-state Senator William Stewart show this change in the social values of prospectors. The first is the fact that Stewart once lost $1.5 million overnight, when one of his mines was flooded (Miller 1991, pp. 52–53). In 1849, a single mine would not have been worth $1.5 million in the first place (Jackson 1980, p. 314). Clearly, the amount of capital involved in working a claim had skyrocketed from the halcyon days of 1849. The second is the fact that Stewart's only political stumble was an incident in which he was almost lynched by a group of outraged prospectors when he suggested lowering their wage rate from $4.00 to $3.50 an hour (soon after this incident, he convinced the mining companies to maintain high wages) (Miller 1991, p. 53). In 1849, most prospectors were outraged whenever capitalists brought employees to mines in the first place. By the early 1850s, it was expected that a mining company would have employees, and therefore wage rates were a sensitive issue (Jackson 1980, p. 314).

Lode vs. Placer Claims

The most troublesome feature of the mining rules for courts after 1851 were the rules for lode claims (Snyder 1902, p. 62). A placer claim consisted of a strip of land, and gave the prospector the right to extract all gold on or beneath that land (Davis 1902, pp. 20–22). A lode claim, in contrast, gave the prospector the right to all gold or minerals that were part of the same vein, even if the twists and turns of the vein led it underneath another person's property or mining claim.[53] Interestingly enough, the rule for lode claims parallels an ancient Prussian statute, which had been abandoned because it produced too many lawsuits (Snyder 1902, p. 62). After 1872, a prospector gained a protectable interest in a lode claim only if he discovered the apex – the portion of the lode closest to the surface. Therefore, mining companies lived in terror that even if they were the first to discover some portion of a vein, another prospector would claim that he had actually discovered the apex (Davis 1902, p. 61).

Historians are divided on whether the special rule for lode claims was efficient in 1848 to 1850 or was a mere historical accident (compare Davis 1902, p. 73, with Leshy 1987, pp. 93–94). Since the prospectors were only concerned with the vein, it may have made sense to treat the vein as the claim and the land as a mere easement which followed the vein (Davis 1902, p. 73). Since even a shallow lode claim was likely more expensive to develop than a placer claim, the right to follow the vein might have been a necessary inducement to undertake the expense of lode mining (Miller 1991, p. 44). Since the course of a vein was difficult to predict from the apex, being entitled to follow the course of the vein might have been the only way to ensure that one received a large enough portion of the vein to offset the cost of lode mining.

In any event, the worst that can be said about the lode claim rule is that it was relatively harmless in 1848–1850, since placer claims were predominant, and the lode claims in those years tended to be small and relatively close to the surface (Jackson 1980, p. 314). Furthermore, most mining rules sharply restricted the total length of a vein claim, which may have reduced the volume of legal headaches stemming from extra-lateral rights (Davis 1902, p. 23).[54]

By 1851, lode claims were predominant, and changes in technology allowed prospectors to extract gold and silver that lay buried deep beneath the earth. These changes led to legal quandaries to which the mining rules did not provide cogent answers, because they involved disputes over lodes with characteristics that the early prospectors had never encountered (Davis 1902, p. 37). When the mining rules were unclear, the courts were not able to find clear criteria for resolving the dispute (Leshy 1987, p. 89).[55]

What was especially ironic was that the courts were giving litigants unclear answers at the precise moment when the industry needed clarity. One advantage of the mining rules to the prospectors of 1849 was that they were flexible and subject to change – for example, a rule could often be revised after ten days' notice (Davis 1902, pp. 30–31). Precisely what placer size was efficient depended on the conditions of the land. In general, the richer the land, the smaller the claim should be (Zerbe and Anderson 1999, pp. 16–17). If a rule was adopted when holdings were rich, it would be desirable to quickly change it when the holdings became poor, and vice versa. Because the camps of 1849 were close-knit societies (as evidenced by the Sprenger and Sims example) and because the rules were posted publicly (when they were written at all), all of the members of a camp would usually be aware of changed rules immediately (Shinn 1947, pp. 190–198).

The changes in the mining industry after 1851 aggravated the problems inherent in the lode rule, and rendered its advantages largely irrelevant. Because lode claims involved investments of thousands or even millions of dollars, by 1851 a company desired predictability over flexibility (Davis 1902, p. 37).[56] A company often had to invest millions of dollars before it saw any profit from a mine, and most of that investment would be useless for any purpose other than mining that claim (Leshy 1987, p. 160). In order to make a return on its investment, a mining company had to work a claim without interruption for a considerable period of time. Because the mining rules were flexible, a sudden rule change could divest a mining company of a claim before it had made any profit on its investment (Davis 1902, p. 37). Furthermore, the mining companies were not close-knit societies with shared values of Jacksonian democracy and Lockean fairness, and may not have always been aware of sudden changes in the mining rules, especially if they simultaneously worked claims in several different districts (ibid., p. 66). Thus it is particularly ironic that lode claims, which by their nature demanded predictability to ensure a return on a million-dollar investment, were governed by convoluted and unpredictable rules.[57]

Brown v. *'49 and '56 Quartz Mining Co.* involved a dispute over whether a deposit of 'washed gold' lying at the bottom of a quartz gold vein belonged to the discoverer of the vein (Quartz Mining Company) or to the first party to discover the deposit of washed gold itself (Brown).[58] There was conflicting evidence as to whether the custom of the prospectors was to award the gold to the discoverer of the vein or to award it to the discoverer of the deposit itself.[59] The fight was all the more contentious since the washed gold was both purer and easier to extract than the vein, and was therefore more valuable. The judge concluded that the weight of evidence was that the custom was to award the deposit to the finder of the vein, since the deposit had originally been part of the same ledge. Therefore, the judge awarded the washed gold to the Quartz Mining Company.[60]

Brown, noting that the 'originally part of the same ledge' test could give the initial discoverer of a vein a monopoly on all of the gold in a large area, objected to the broadness of this grant.[61] He pointed out that by this reasoning the Quartz Mining Company could claim all of the gold along the entire area of the ravine, a distance of 500 feet. The judge responded, without explanation, 'I think the reasoning could hardly reach to that extent.' Why the judge thought so is not clear; perhaps he meant that a geologist could not trace the origin of gold with sufficient certainty when the gold was more than 500 feet away from the vein, or perhaps he simply felt, intuitively, that one's legal entitlement to gold more than 500 feet from the vein was too attenuated to be enforceable. However, at no point did he lay down a test – or even a rule of thumb – as to what degree of geological certainty as to common origin (or what degree of moral entitlement to a profit) is necessary to make out a claim.

Ironically, the judge defended his decision on the grounds that it was 'clearly stated and limited' and would avoid vexatious litigation and 'fine distinctions.'[62] In fact, the reasoning for his decision was vaguely stated and its ramifications were uncertain, and his decision invited litigation in that every discoverer of a deposit could argue that a particular deposit was so far away from the vein that the rule 'could hardly reach to that extent.' The only way to find out how far the rule extended would be to bring a suit which involved slightly different facts, and see at what point the judge decided that the claim no longer reached that extent. Unfortunately, that is what appears to have happened. Millions of dollars in litigation costs were expended to see just how far the claims of the original veins extended (Davis 1902, p. 71; Leshy 1987, p. 21). It is hard to imagine a greater invitation to litigation than an infinitely broad grant of rights qualified by an undefined caveat.

The legal difficulties caused by *Brown* are even greater than one might suppose, because of the byzantine rules regarding the patenting of placer and lode claims.[63] Under these rules, seemingly conservative steps can lead to the surrender of one's legal rights. If the washed gold deposit had been more distant from the vein, at some point the court probably would have concluded that it was a separate placer claim, rather than part of the lode claim.[64] Had the Quartz Mining Co. taken the seemingly conservative route of filing a *placer* claim to the deposit of washed gold, in addition to filing a lode claim to the vein, it might have been construed as abandoning its lode claim and might have lost its rights to both the vein and the deposit (Leshy 1987, p. 94). On the other hand, if Quartz had first filed a placer claim to the deposit, and then filed a lode claim to the vein, the subsequent *lode* claim would not be viewed as an abandonment of the placer claim. The most obvious problem with this rule is that it seems arbitrarily confusing. The other problem with this is that Quartz actually found the vein (which was clearly a lode claim) *before* it found the washed gold deposit. It is hardly sensible to pressure prospectors into delaying filing lode claims until they are certain that there are no potential placer claims nearby. To make matters worse, it was not always clear whether a particular deposit of gold was a placer or a lode claim (ibid.), as *Brown* itself demonstrated.

Eureka Consolidated Mining Co. v. *Richmond Mining Co.* involved a dispute as to whether the discoverer of a lode of silver gains a right to every vein and spur emanating from the same lode, or whether each vein in a multiple-vein lode is a separate claim.[65] The court concluded that the first discoverer of a vein is entitled to every vein and spur that is part of the same lode.[66] The court noted that 'lode,' 'vein,' and 'spur' – concepts of enormous legal significance – were used by prospectors before they were used by geologists, and that geologists were therefore only of limited use in defining these terms.[67] The term 'lode' was a derivative of 'lead,' and was used generically by prospectors to refer to any set of conditions which indicated a high probability of a valuable vein of mineral being discovered. Most often, a lode was a fissure of rock which contained one or more veins, but any other 'well-defined area' could also be referred to as a lode, if it was likely to contain one or more veins.[68] Therefore, a vein did not have to be a continuous strip of mineral, and could be (and often was) 'choked off' for several feet in several places.

Eureka insisted that a lode should refer broadly to any 'well-defined area' which contained one or more veins, provided all of the veins had been produced by the same creative forces.[69] Richmond insisted, in contrast, that each vein was a separate lode, especially if the veins were contained in separate fissures or if one of the veins lay within a fissure and the other(s) did not. The court concluded that a lode encompassed all of the veins which lay within well-defined areas, if produced by the same creative force.

Although *Eureka* was a carefully considered opinion, written by a judge with considerable experience in mining law and mining, it proved even more contentious than *Brown* (Miller 1991, p. 155). The irony of *Eureka* is that the term 'well-defined area' is itself not defined at all. Geologists – often those of national reputation – differed as to how perfectly an area had to be defined from its surroundings to constitute a lode.[70] Some identifying characteristics of a 'lode' are universal to any lode claim, while others are rare.[71] The Court admitted in *Iron Silver Mining* v. *Cheesman* that any attempt at a universal definition of 'lode' or 'vein' was doomed to failure.[72] The 'same creative forces' test is even broader than the 'originally part of the same ledge' test of *Brown*, and encouraged litigants to dig up geological evidence (literally) as to whether two veins had been produced by the 'same creative force,' when it is highly unlikely that a prospector would take such evidence into account in guessing whether a claim contained valuable ore.[73] Only painstakingly, over the course of more than a century, did courts cobble up – on a case-by-case basis – a set of rules which determined when multiple veins were products of the 'same creative force,' and what degree of clarity of surroundings led to the definition 'well defined area' (Leshy 1987, pp. 21, 89).[74] The outcome of a dispute was so difficult to predict that mining companies would develop the claim or portion of a claim that they felt was the least likely to be contentious, even when it was not the most profitable claim to work (Davis 1902, p. 71).

The difficulty of determining the scope of a mining claim was exacerbated by the fact that one who discovered a deposit of minerals had an incredibly short grace period in which to file a claim. Although the legal rule was that one who discovers a deposit must file a claim within a 'reasonable time,' in practice the term 'reasonable time' was construed narrowly (ibid., pp. 65–66). Given the complexity of mining law, a company frequently did not have sufficient time to make more than an educated guess about the size and nature of the deposit that it had discovered, while its rivals could file a suit the moment they discovered that it had made a mistake.

The *Eureka* and *Brown* tests also had the ironic consequence of being an additional factor which prevented independent prospectors from entering the market.[75] To litigate a dispute under *Eureka* or *Brown* required not only an excellent mining lawyer but a staff of geological experts, a staff of mining-custom experts, and an array of glass models and diagrams, all of which were out of the reach of a poor litigant (ibid., p. 53).[76]

The Alcalde Was No Longer the Efficient Rule Maker

The social changes that had occurred in California by the 1850s not only rendered the rules of the mining districts inefficient, they also rendered the reliance on the Alcaldes as rulemakers inefficient (Davis 1902, p. 66). As I mentioned earlier, the Alcaldes were generally able to change their rules within a ten-day period, whereas California's legislature was almost certainly much slower to adopt new rules (ibid., p. 30). This flexibility was desirable in 1849, but became an impediment in the 1850s (ibid., pp. 37, 66–72). Dr. Raymond Rossiter, the commissioner of mining statistics for the western states and territories, even suggested in his report to Congress that some Alcaldes would deliberately change rules after providing minimal notice with the express purpose of cheating a claimant (ibid., p. 56, quoting Raymond 1869, p. 221). In any event, the difficulties in figuring out which district had jurisdiction over a claim, combined with the fact that districts were constantly amending their rules, created a logistical nightmare for mining companies (Davis 1902, p. 69).

One problem was that neither the California statute of 1851 nor the federal statutes of 1866 and 1872 provided any penalties for Alcaldes who accepted bribes, or otherwise abused the power of their office (ibid., p. 56, citing Raymond 1869, p. 221). In 1849, an Alcalde accepted a bribe at his peril: at any moment, a thousand armed prospectors could march into his office and demand justice (Shinn 1947, pp. 190–198). By the time California had become a state, it was much less likely that angry prospectors would resort to this sort of confrontation, which significantly reduced an Alcalde's incentive to refuse bribes.

Unfortunately, Congress trusted the mining districts to play a major role in shaping mining law, and expected them to account for changes in technology and mining practices (Leshy 1987, p. 107–108). For example, Congress allowed mining districts to set more stringent rules limiting the size of a claim, increasing the requirements for posting claims and giving notice to other miners, and increasing the amount of work necessary to maintain a claim (Davis 1902, pp. 66–72). In fact, the districts sometimes reduced the maximum claim which could be made as a result of discovery (with no limits on the amount which could be purchased) but rarely, if ever, set higher working requirements or required more extensive posting (ibid., pp. 66–72).[77] Prospectors and mining companies who already had claims desired the ability to retain their claims with as little work as possible, while those who did not have claims wanted to make it easy to acquire a claim (ibid., pp. 66–72). In any event, the districts disappeared relatively quickly (Leshy 1987, p. 108).

One puzzle is why the mining districts never repealed the lode rule, given how quickly the rule created problems. One possibility is that the mining districts themselves knew very little about geology, and therefore could not create a more sensible rule (Davis 1902, p. 51). Another reason may be that the mining districts did not realize that the rule was inefficient and refused to listen to the critics who suggested that it was (ibid., p. 67).

The Efficiency of Court Enforcement of Mining Rules

Conversely, other problems with using the mining district rules stemmed from the fact that they were being enforced by judges and juries, instead of Alcaldes and juries of prospectors. One of the chief arguments in favor of the federal statute which adopted the mining district rules was that prospectors had 'made it, knew it, and trusted it' (Davis 1902, p. 44, citing Connes Report). However, the mining district's rules were being *interpreted* by courts and juries who often *did not* know the intricacies of mining, let alone the intricacies of the mining laws, which in turn meant that even a prospector who was familiar with his mining district rules could not predict how a *court* would apply it.

California treated the state of the mining rules at the time of the dispute as a question of fact, to be decided by juries on the basis of evidence, rather than as a question of law.[78] Given the rapidly changing nature of the mining rules, this may have been a sensible decision (ibid., p. 30). Furthermore, it had always been the case that what an Alcalde or the rule book *said* was the rule in that district was far less important than whether the prospectors were willing to *enforce* it, as was demonstrated graphically in the Sprenger and Sim example (Shinn 1947, pp. 190–198). However, treating the mining district rules as evidence led to some bizarre results, since it meant that the mining district rules acquired the baggage of the laws of evidence.

In *English* v. *Johnson*, there was a dispute as to which of two prospectors had the right to a claim of land.[79] English was the first to discover the vein and post a sign over his claim, but Johnson insisted that English had not acquired an enforceable right to the claim because he had not filed a record with the district as required by the rules.[80] Johnson offered a portion of the mining district rules as evidence.[81] English argued that Johnson should not be able to offer only a part of the rules, and should offer the entire rule book or none of it. The court sided with English, and excluded the mining district rule. It apparently concluded that neither Johnson nor English had complied with the mining district rules; therefore it used the older common law doctrine that, as between two trespassers on public land, the first in time had a superior right, and sided with English.[82]

At first glance, the court's decision seems imminently sensible. It is undoubtedly suspicious that neither Johnson nor English was willing to submit to the rules in their entirety, and so it is likely that neither had complied with all of the rules.[83] The puzzle, though, is why the court did not compel the disclosure of all of the rules, rather than giving the parties an 'all or nothing' option. The court itself noted that its imposition of the 'first in time' doctrine in a situation where neither party had complied with the mining rules would not apply if the mining rules had specified a different outcome.[84] This statement is baffling, however, because in *English* we do not know what the mining district rule was when neither party complied, because the rules were never accepted into evidence.[85] Thus, because courts used the laws of evidence to determine whether a mining district rule would be considered, two adverse claimants could not be certain whether the mining district rules would actually be consulted by the court.

Another problem with having courts apply mining rules was that because courts tended to prefer more familiar common law doctrines to the mining rules, they jealously restricted the scope of the mining rules. For example, while courts recognized that mining rules created special rules for the abandonment or forfeiture of property (namely, that a mining claim was lost if it was not worked adequately) they held that mining laws did not have any effect on the common law doctrine of estoppel – a puzzling distinction since estoppel and forfeiture are related concepts, and the work requirements of the mining rules do not fit neatly into either doctrine.[86] One court reversed the jury verdict, since it was not certain whether the jury had *correctly* concluded that the rule of *abandonment* was different in mining claim cases than in other species of property, or whether it had *incorrectly* believed that the rules for *estoppel* were different for mining claims.[87]

Similarly, *Waring* v. *Crow* recognized that under the mining rules a claim was lost if it was not developed, but held that one tenant's non-compliance could not extinguish the claim of another tenant, even if the mining rules provided otherwise.[88] Apparently, *Waring* concluded that the law of forfeiture was subject to change by the mining rules, but that the law of tenancy and the rights of co-tenants were sacrosanct, and could not be upset by a 'mere neighborhood custom or regulation.'[89]

These cases show that the judges did not regard the mining rules as fair and that therefore they attempted to restrict their application. The rules had been efficient for the prospectors in 1849, because the prospectors endorsed the moral values implicit in the rules, and would have viewed a disposition of property contrary to the rules as a loss. The judges did not trust these 'mere neighborhood' customs, and viewed any disposition of property inconsistent with the older English–American common law as a loss.[90] Non-Californian judges were even more contemptuous of the mining rules, perhaps because they found the mining rules even more alien than the Californian judges did.[91]

However, the judges could not ignore the California statute of 1851, and therefore could only curtail the law indirectly. Because they limited the law indirectly, they limited its application in inconsistent and surprising ways. For example, a prospector of 1849 would have been baffled by the statement that his camp's mining rules changed the law of abandonment but did not change the law of estoppel, or that the mining rules affected the rights of one holder but could not change the rights of his co-tenants.

Mining Claims Used to Gain Land for Non-Mining Uses

From their inception, mining district rules required the discoverer of a mining claim to actively work the claim, and prospectors were contemptuous of those who would be a dog in the manger (Davis 1902, p. 21). The early rules, particularly in areas with rich claims, were often very harsh (Zerbe and Anderson 1999, p. 18). For example, in some districts a prospector was judged to have abandoned his claim unless he worked it within ten days of discovery (Davis 1902, p. 21). The Mining Law statute set a requirement of $100 a year per claim on 'assessment work,' which was a significant incentive in 1850 (it represented up to seven weeks' wages for the typical laborer), but which quickly became almost ludicrously inadequate (Leshy 1987, p. 109).[92] Furthermore, there was no time limit within the year in which the work had to begin. Part of why Congress set a low work limit was that it entrusted the mining districts to set more restrictive rules as changes in technology and mining practices took place (ibid., p. 108). In fact, this did not happen, and the mining districts no longer exist.

Ironically enough, while Congress has refused to adjust the labor expenditure requirement, the courts have interpreted 'assessment work' somewhat narrowly, forcing some companies to set up token 'tunnel sites' and other devices and machinery just to meet the statutory requirements (ibid., p. 94, 110). Most critically, exploratory drills and other devices are considered discovery costs rather than assessment work, and cannot be used to meet the federal requirement, even though they are necessary tools for any mining company today and are often quite expensive (ibid., p. 102, 110). Thus, the rules require both too much and too little: they require expenditures which are totally unnecessary, but they do not require enough of an expenditure to deter claimants who have no real interest in mining and who merely wish to use the mining laws to acquire property (ibid., p. 110).[93]

This is demonstrated by the experiences of one Ralph Cameron, who used a trumped up mining claim to gain land near the most popular tourist spots on the Grand Canyon shortly before it was turned into a National Forest reserve (Leshy 1987, p. 58). Cameron operated a resort there, and in fact never actively prospected the claim. Not surprisingly, Cameron was eventually booted off the land, and it was allowed to become a National Forest (ibid., pp. 57–60).[94] What is surprising is that Cameron managed to operate the resort for nearly 35 years while his case was digested in the federal courts, ultimately reaching the Supreme Court. It is estimated that Cameron made a healthy profit from his resort even after paying his substantial legal fees. And though there are few cases of abuse as obvious as Cameron's, there are many people who abuse the mining laws in similar ways. In fact, the Bureau of Land Management once estimated that *over 80 percent* of all mining claims are made 'without a serious intent of mining development' (ibid., p. 72, quoting Marion Clawson of the BLM).

In 1849, Cameron never would have managed to pull off a stunt of this sort, and probably would not have had the gall to attempt it. There is nothing new about an entrepreneur profiting off prospectors by providing a hotel or some other valuable service to them (Jackson 1980, p. 260). However, the hotel owners of 1849 did not use the mining laws themselves to gain prime real estate for free. A prospector who had attempted this sort of chicanery in 1849 would have found a thousand armed and ill-tempered prospectors on his doorstep within the week (Shinn 1947, pp. 190–198). Furthermore, in 1849 there would have been no incentive to manipulate the mining law in this way, since the land that was subject to gold prospecting was little more than sand and sagebrush, useless for any purpose other than mining (Davis 1902, p. 14).[95] Moreover, in the 1850s a farmer or any other landowner who improved public land in California gained an enforceable interest in it, without resorting to characterizing his use as a mining claim.[96] The mining district rules and the federal statute were unable to deal effectively with Cameron, since the sort of manipulation he engaged in would never have been attempted in the first place in the years when the mining district rules were originally formed.

Perhaps more significant than the problem of scoundrels like Cameron is the problem of speculators. A speculator is an individual who learns that a mining company is interested in a parcel of land (perhaps because the mining company has begun investigating the land but has not done anything that would clearly trigger a legally protectable interest in the land) and who then locates a mining claim without any intention of turning a single 'spadeful of dirt' (Leshy 1987, p. 78). The speculator then offers to sell his or her right to the land to the mining company. If the law requires the mining companies to buy claims from speculators, is the mining law inefficient?

Whether it is inefficient to require a mining company to buy a claim from a speculator depends on whether we grant standing to speculators. If we deny speculators standing, then requiring mining companies to pay speculators results in a net loss – it reduces the profits of mining companies without increasing the wealth of anybody who 'counts.' If we grant speculators standing, then requiring mining companies to pay them does not necessarily result in a net loss.

There are two reasons why we might deny speculators standing. First, the regard for others might view it as unfair to require mining companies to pay speculators, so society might experience a loss whenever mining companies pay speculators for claims. Second, we might deny speculators standing in order to reduce transactions costs. If the law requires mining companies to pay speculators, it also requires mining companies to undertake a set of transactions (and therefore incur additional transactions costs).

It might seem to be a tautological truth that requiring mining companies to pay prospectors will always result in higher transactions costs. However, it is not. It is true that if a prospector discovers a valuable mineral deposit and offers to sell it to a mining company, the mining company must negotiate a deal, and will incur transactions costs. However, the prospector has saved the mining company the difficulty of discovering the mineral deposit. In some cases, the search costs of locating a mineral deposit might be considerably higher than the transactions costs of negotiating a deal with a speculator. In such a case, the prospector is actually *reducing* the transactions costs of the mining company. Furthermore, the regard for others would not be opposed to requiring mining companies to pay prospectors in such cases; if any thing, most people would probably feel that it would be unfair for the mining company to refuse to pay the prospector. Therefore, it is efficient to require mining companies to pay prospectors in these circumstances.

However, it is possible to be the first person to satisfy the legal requirements for 'discovery' of a mineral deposit even if another person was the first to actually *learn* that there was a deposit there (Leshy 1987, p. 178). In fact, it is only in such cases that a prospector is given the derogatory label 'speculator.' If a speculator is the first person to satisfy the legal requirements of discovery, but a mining company already knew that there was a mineral deposit in the vicinity then the speculator is not reducing the mining company's search costs; he or she is simply increasing transactions costs. Furthermore, the regard for others is probably opposed to requiring mining companies to pay speculators whose 'discovery' of a mineral deposit is really just a technicality. Therefore, it is inefficient to require a mining company to pay a speculator when the speculator 'discovered' a mineral deposit that the mining company actually knew about.

Furthermore, it is possible that a mining company actually did 'discover' a mineral deposit in both the legal and the actual sense, but that the mining company is still willing to pay a speculator since the mining company knows that the cost of proving that it discovered the mineral would be prohibitive. In such a case, it is even more inefficient to require the mining company to pay the speculator. However, the cost of litigating a mining dispute is so high that many companies pay speculators even when they know that the speculators' legal arguments are completely groundless.

9.10 SOLUTIONS

It is important to note that, although the mining law statute is almost universally condemned by those who have studied it, the mining law does not appear to be inconsistent with either psychological ownership (Davis 1902, p. 73) or the regard for others (Leshy 1987, p. 25). In fact, psychological ownership may not be relevant to mining law, since mining claims are most likely commercial goods.[97] The reason why it is inefficient to disrupt psychological ownership is the disparity between the loser's WTA and the gainer's WTP. With a commercial good, WTA and WTP are nearly identical, so psychological ownership is irrelevant. If psychological ownership of mining claims does exist, any attempt to amend the mining law would probably disrupt psychological ownership. For example, while extra-lateral rights almost inevitably lead to a large amount of litigation (Davis 1902, p. 70), eliminating them would probably cause people with a vested interest in extra-lateral rights to suffer a WTA loss, while the party that received these minerals would receive a windfall in WTP terms (Davis 1902, p. 73).[98]

As far as the regard for others is concerned, while there are many who regard the mining law as 'a hopeless anachronism,' those who oppose the law are opposed to it for completely inconsistent reasons, and want to change it in contradictory ways (Leshy 1987, p. 25). The key controversy is the mining law's grant of free access to federal land, as opposed to a system of federal leasing. Some who want to change the law want to strengthen mining companies' free access to mining land, by helping them avoid payments to speculators, and, in general, by streamlining the procedures for acquiring a mining claim and expelling others from it (ibid., p. 288). On the other hand, many want a system of federal leasing, either to generate revenue or to improve the government's ability to enforce environmental regulations (ibid., pp. 49, 67). Since neither side is willing to accept the changes the other proposes, the current, anachronistic law remains a compromise that nobody really likes (indeed, virtually every government agency that has studied the law has recommended either substantial modifications or its complete abolition) but which all sides are willing to live with (ibid., p. 287). Therefore, changing the law would not make it more consistent with the regard for others. Indeed, the difficulty faced by those who have attempted to change the law suggests that the current compromise is the position with the most support.

The problem with the mining law is that it results in gross transactions costs.[99] The mining law increases transactions costs, and thus the cost of mining, in at least four ways. First, the application of the mining law is frequently uncertain, in the sense that even one who is familiar with the mining law may have trouble predicting the outcome of a mining dispute (Davis 1902, p. 70). The uncertainty of the mining laws increases the risk of investing in a mining claim, since even a company which has discovered a valuable mineral deposit may not make a profit from it, if a court concludes that the deposit was 'really' discovered by somebody else. Second, mining law disputes are expensive to litigate, even in situations in which the mining law *does* provide a clear answer (ibid., p. 53). In order to litigate a mining dispute, one must hire a small army of geological experts and lawyers, all of whom expect to be paid a hefty fee. Third, the mining law is antiquated, in the sense that it requires mining companies to engage in mining practices which serve no useful purpose other than satisfying the statutory requirements (Leshy 1987, p. 89). These unnecessary practices are often expensive. Fourth, the mining laws are lax, in the sense that they do not discourage claimants from filing frivolous claims (ibid., p. 77). The lax nature of the mining law is an invitation to free riders, who file claims solely to elicit a settlement from the companies that actually discovered the mineral deposits. The danger of nuisance claims is exacerbated by the first and second problems, since the high cost of litigating a mining claim and the uncertainty of a favorable outcome both increase a mining company's incentive to settle.

The high transactions costs associated with mining have decreased the wealth of America in two ways. First, they have deterred investment in mining, and have driven people out of the mining industry. Leshy notes that the American mining industry is on the verge of collapse, and that a major source of its decline is the mining law itself. Second, transactions costs have decreased the profits of those who have decided to remain in the mining industry (ibid., pp. 4–6). Leshy notes that the mining law has both 'thwarted' the development of mineral resources and made it more expensive.

However, showing that the mining law results in transactions costs is hardly evidence that the mining law is inefficient, since transactions costs are ubiquitous. To say that the mining law is inefficient, it is necessary to show that an alternative law would have resulted in lower transactions costs. I do not have the data to prove, with certainty, that an alternative rule would be more efficient. However, I suggest that the following amendments would increase the efficiency of the law:

1. The dichotomy between lode and placer claims should either be eliminated or be replaced with a distinction which reflects current geological science, not the understanding of Congress in 1872. Note that the first group of experts whom Congress appointed to study the mining law recommended abolishing extra-lateral rights (ibid., p. 288).
2. The law should provide penalties for those who file frivolous mining claims, or provide streamlined procedures for cases in which one party's claim appears to have little justification.
3. The law should eliminate all anachronisms, such as requiring the creation of token tunnel sites.
4. The minimum expenditure to maintain a mining claim should be increased, but the definition of assessment work should be broadened to cover costs that are currently considered 'discovery' costs, such as seismic tests.

Of course, it may be that the solutions I suggest would create unanticipated problems, and new definitional uncertainties. However, the widespread evidence that the mining law results in transactions costs far greater than the costs associated with other industries suggests that new solutions should be considered.

9.11 *PLESSY* V. *FERGUSON*: A MISAPPLICATION OF THE COMMON LAW TRADITION

The common law tradition of using social norms to create law is not invariably efficient, and it is particularly likely to be inefficient if the norm is contentious. As Blackstone (1900, pp. 56–57) noted, a norm is an efficient tool in creating law only when the norm is uncontentious. When social conditions are rapidly shifting, there may be no norm which has a sufficient grip on public opinion to be uncontentious. To the extent that a contentious norm appears to be predominant, its popularity may decline rapidly, making it hazardous to rely on norms during an era of social change. One of the clearest examples of a court attempting to use social norms to create law is *Plessy* v. *Ferguson*.[100] *Plessy* is, however, one of the clearest examples of a court bungling the common law tradition. *Plessy* bungled the common law tradition in three ways: (1) it adopted a 'norm' which lacked economic standing; (2) it adopted a 'norm' when a competing norm existed; and (3) it adopted a 'norm' which ultimately lost out to a competing norm.

Plessy upheld a Louisiana statute that provided for 'separate but equal' accommodations for white and African-American train passengers, and which provided for fines and imprisonment of passengers and train employees who refused to comply with the rules.[101] Contrary to popular belief, *Plessy* did *not* require that the facilities for whites and African-Americans be equal; it held that a racially discriminatory law is constitutional if it is 'reasonable' in light of the 'established usages, customs, and traditions of the people.'[102] Because the statute was consistent with Louisiana's 'social conventions,' the statute was held constitutional.[103]

Justice Harlan argued in dissent that the 'reasonableness' of the statute in light of Louisiana's 'social conventions' was irrelevant.[104] At first glance, this appears to be a rejection of the common law tradition; if so, his dissent would be of little use in determining the efficiency of *Plessy*. However, Harlan's opinion makes it clear that it is not Louisiana's social conventions that are relevant, but those of the United States.[105] Thus, the Fourteenth Amendment renders Louisiana's policies unconstitutional.[106] Using the language of KHZ, Harlan is arguing that Louisiana's custom of segregation lacks standing, because the United States had made a reasonable social judgment that the costs of governmental racial discrimination outweigh any benefits the citizens of the state would receive from it.[107] Just as a thief lacks standing to argue that his WTP for stolen goods is higher than his victim's WTA, Louisiana lacks standing to argue that its statute is efficient because of its consistency with Louisiana's norms.

The majority in *Plessy* at least partially recognizes the legitimacy of Harlan's argument, in that it attempts to formulate a norm which justifies Louisiana's statute but which is consistent with the spirit of the Fourteenth Amendment.[108] The majority argues that racial integration is only appropriate when it is 'voluntary' and a product of 'a mutual appreciation of each other's merits.' This argument was incoherent, however, because Louisiana's statute provided for fines and imprisonment if a white and an African-American passenger decided to sit together because they had a 'mutual appreciation of each other's merits.' The majority's incoherence was inevitable, because there *was* no norm which justified Louisiana's statute, but which was consistent with the Fourteenth Amendment.[109]

Furthermore, *Plessy* improperly applied a norm which lacked the uncontentiousness that Blackstone (1900, pp. 56–57) required.[110] At the time of *Plessy*, there were competing norms of racial integration and racial segregation, and it is likely that neither norm was sufficiently 'uncontentious' to guarantee efficiency.[111]

Furthermore, the norm *Plessy* established did not become uncontentious over time. In fact, over time, support for *Plessy*'s norm evaporated, leading the Supreme Court to back away from its holding.[112] In *Ex Rel Gaines* v. *Canada*, the Supreme Court held that it was unconstitutional for Missouri to provide for a legal education for African-Americans by paying their tuition to attend law school in an adjacent state.[113] In *Gaines*, the majority demanded that the privilege of education be extended to all races on an 'equal' basis, while the dissent insisted that the question was merely whether the state had made a 'reasonable' effort to provide 'specialized education' to African-Americans.[114] The dissent's approach was probably more consistent with *Plessy*'s 'reasonableness' standard than the majority's approach was, but after *Gaines* 'reasonableness' was not enough.[115]

Sweatt v. *Painter* involved an attempt by Texas to maintain the University of Texas as an all-white law school by creating a smaller, adjacent law school for African-Americans, with many of the same faculty and textbooks.[116] The majority held that this 'separate' school was not 'equal.' While *Sweatt* could have relied on the tangible inferiority of the African-American law school, it instead focused on the 'intangible' factors such as 'reputation of the faculty, experience of the administration, position and influence of the alumni, standing in the community, traditions and prestige.' While *Sweatt* recognized the theoretical possibility of a separate law school which was equal to the white one, it is hard to imagine how any non-white school – which in Texas would necessarily be a *new* law school – could have alumni of equal 'influence,' or comparable community standing and 'prestige.'

McLaurin v. *Oklahoma State Regents for Higher Education* held that a graduate school of education had violated the Fourteenth Amendment, even though it had admitted an African-American into its department, because it forced him to sit in a designated row in the classrooms, and in a designated table in the cafeteria and in the library.[117] McLaurin's education would have been as 'equal' to that received by the white students as any separate education could have been, considering that he would have heard the same lectures from the same professors and studied the same books in the same library. However, the court recognized that interaction with other students is an essential aspect of education, and that McLaurin would be unfairly (and unconstitutionally) denied this interaction.[118] Any theoretical possibility of a segregated school's passing constitutional muster which was left open by *Sweatt* was closed by *McLaurin*.[119] If interaction with other students is an essential part of education, such that denying an equal opportunity to interact means denying an equal education, then segregation is inherently unconstitutional, since the effect (indeed, the *purpose*) of segregation is to stop students of different races from interacting. When we consider *Sweatt's* recognition that the 'position and influence' of a school's alumni are an essential element of its quality, it becomes clear that segregated schools disadvantaged African-American students.[120] After *McLaurin*, *Brown* v. *The Board of Education* seems like a short conceptual step.[121]

Brown formally declared that segregated schools are inherently unequal.[122] *Brown* justified its departure from *Plessy* on the grounds that social conditions had changed.[123] First, *Brown* noted that public education was far more important in 1954 than it had been at the time of the Fourteenth Amendment's passing (1868) or even at the time of *Plessy* (1896). Compulsory education, which dramatically increased the importance of high-quality public education, was not adopted by every state until 1918.[124] Second, *Brown* cites a series of psychological studies arguing that segregation harmed the self-esteem of African-American students.[125] The validity of those studies has been vigorously attacked,[126] but what is more important for our purposes is the implicit recognition that society's willingness to tolerate attacks on the self-esteem of African-Americans had changed: in other words, the regard for others had changed. As the regard for others shifted, *Plessy*, which had probably never been efficient, became ever more palpably inefficient.[127] *Plessy* responded to the argument that segregation was intended to degrade African-Americans with a callous statement that it was only insulting 'if the colored race chooses that construction' – implicitly stating, 'That's your problem: deal with it.'[128] *Brown* recognized that the regard for others had shifted, such that the possibility that African-American students' self-esteem suffered from segregation was counted as a loss.[129]

9.12 ANTITRUST LAW AND CHANGES IN KNOWLEDGE

I noted earlier that changes in knowledge, as well as changes in technology and sentiments, may necessitate a change in law in order for the common law to be efficient. One area of law in which changes in knowledge have had a dramatic effect on the common law is antitrust law. Even though antitrust law is governed by a federal statute, it is generally accepted that Congress intended for courts to supply the content of the antitrust law by creating an antitrust 'common law.'[130] In deciding antitrust cases, courts recognize that the law should change to reflect new economic theory and data.

In particular, changes in knowledge have made it efficient to change the law of vertical restraints. In antitrust vernacular, a 'vertical restraint' is an attempt by a manufacturer to control the activities of wholesalers, distributors, or retailers. There are two basic categories of vertical restraints. First, there are price restraints, in which the manufacturer sets either a minimum or a maximum price at which a retailer may sell its products to customers. Second, there are non-price restraints, in which the manufacturer limits the customers to whom a retailer may sell its products. Non-price restraints usually take the form of territorial restraints, in which a retailer is given an exclusive right to sell the manufacturer's product within a certain area, in return for promising not to sell the product to any customers outside of the area.

Horizontal restraints, on the other hand, refer to agreements between firms at the same level – that is, two or more manufacturers *or* two or more retailers – not to compete. Like vertical restraints, horizontal restraints usually involve either price-fixing or territorial market divisions.

Although the Sherman Act prohibits 'every contract, combination, or conspiracy' to suppress competition, the courts quickly realized that every contract suppresses competition in some sense (since an agreement to sell 100 widgets to one person is an implicit agreement not to sell those particular widgets to anybody else) and that Congress could not have intended to outlaw every business agreement, or even every agreement between competitors.[131] Therefore, courts developed a 'rule of reason' in which only 'unreasonable' restraints – those which harm competition more than they benefit it – are violations of the antitrust laws.[132] On the other hand, the courts realized that some types of agreements – such as horizontal price-fixing – were so likely to harm competition that an in-depth analysis of each one was not justified.[133] Such agreements are unlawful 'per se.' If it is proved that a defendant engaged in an agreement that is subject to the per se rule, the defendant will be punished, and cannot escape liability by arguing that his agreement had procompetitive effects. In holding that a type of agreement is unlawful per se, the court is essentially making an economic *prediction* that the probability that an agreement of that type would injure competition is so much greater than its probability of benefiting competition that it is not worth the court's time to analyze the competitive consequences of a particular agreement of that type.[134] Therefore, economics is of great aid to judges who must decide whether to hold a type of agreement unlawful per se.[135] In characterizing an agreement as unlawful per se, the court is denying the defendant economic standing: indeed, Harlan once noted in dissent that the per se rule is a 'no trial rule.'[136]

Surprisingly enough, the first case involving a vertical restraint was *White Motor Co.* v. *United States*, which was decided in 1963.[137] In *White Motor Co.*, a truck and auto parts manufacturer placed both price and non-price restraints on distributors.[138] The Justice Department argued that both the price and non-price restraints should be subjected to the per se rule, and the lower court agreed. White Motor Co. did not contest the ruling that vertical price-fixing was illegal per se, but it did argue that vertical non-price restraints should be governed by the rule of reason. The Supreme Court agreed with White Motor Co. Specifically, it held that because the application of the per se rule is a prediction that agreements of a certain type are almost always profoundly anticompetitive, the per se rule should not be applied to a type of agreement that the courts did not have enough experience with to make a reliable prediction.[139] In other words, the court decided that too little was known 'about the economic and business stuff out of which [non-price restraints] emerge' to say, with certainty, that vertical non-price agreements would almost always harm competition. Therefore, the court remanded the case to the district court, to determine whether White Motor Co.'s non-price restraints could be justified under the rule of reason. Specifically, the court speculated that vertical non-price restraints, unlike horizontal territorial restraints, might benefit competition by allowing small companies to break into a business, and such restraints might be necessary to save a failing manufacturing company.

Four years later, in *United States* v. *Arnold, Schwinn & Co.*, the court imposed the per se rule on vertical, non-price restraints, unless the restraint was part of a consignment contract.[140] Schwinn manufactured bikes and sold them through retailers. About 75 percent of the sales to retailers were characterized as 'consignment contracts' while the other 25 percent were described as 'sales contracts.' Both the consignment and sales contracts with retailers placed territorial restraints on the sellers' ability to sell the bikes. The court apparently felt that it had become familiar enough with vertical non-price restraints to make a reliable economic prediction about their competitive effect.[141] It began its analysis by interpreting *White Motor Co.* narrowly, stating that *White Motor Co.* extended the rule of reason to non-price restraints only when the manufacturer was a new, small company or a failing business, and noted that Schwinn was neither.[142]

In analyzing the competitive effect of vertical non-price restraints, *Arnold, Schwinn & Co.* concluded that some small companies could compete with manufacturing giants only if they could offer dealers exclusive sales contracts which involved vertical non-price restraints.[143] On the other hand, the court felt that 'prudence' dictates that it would be foolish to allow a company to give a dealer an exclusive contract while retaining 'title' to and 'dominion' over the goods.[144] Therefore, the court compromised by applying the rule of reason to non-price restraints in consignment contracts, but applied the per se rule to restraints in sales contracts. The court justified this compromise by arguing that it was consistent with the '*ancient* rule against restraints on alienation.'[145] The court dismissed Schwinn's argument that its exclusive dealerships enabled it to compete more effectively with larger competitors, since Schwinn was not a failing business.[146]

Justice Stewart, in a forceful dissent, argued that the majority's reliance on an '*ancient*' rule to resolve a difficult antitrust issue was misplaced, since the fact that there was an '*ancient*' rule against restraints on alienation is of little help in predicting whether a vertical restraint will benefit or harm competition today.[147] He noted that, in any event, the '*ancient*' rule against restraints on alienation outlawed only unreasonable restraints, and therefore operated much more like the rule of reason than the per se rule.[148] He agreed with the majority – and Schwinn – that being able to offer exclusive dealerships was necessary if a company was to attract quality retailers and distributors, but he felt that whether a transaction with a retailer was characterized as a consignment or a sales agreement made little practical difference to the manufacturer's ability to restrict competition, and therefore should not determine whether an agreement violates the antitrust laws.[149]

One year later, the Supreme Court extended the per se rule to vertical price-fixing agreements, in *Albrecht* v. *Herald Co.*[150] *Albrecht* involved a newspaper company that terminated a paperboy's route when he charged more than the maximum price specified in its contract with him.[151] Although the price the *Herald* set was not predatory, and the *Herald*'s low prices would obviously benefit its consumers, the court applied the per se rule,[152] offering three justifications. First, the court noted that part of the purpose of the antitrust law is to preserve entrepreneur's independent business judgment, and that an entrepreneur's judgment was restricted regardless of whether he was forced to offer low prices or forced to offer high prices.[153] The court insisted that a firm should not be able to substitute 'the perhaps erroneous judgment of the seller for that of the competitive forces of the market.' Specifically, a manufacturer might set prices so low that the dealer was unable to make a profit, or it might set prices that would prevent the dealer from offering essential services to customers.[154] Second, the court argued that the *Herald* could not justify its maximum price-setting rule on the grounds that it protected consumers from paper boys who themselves enjoyed a monopoly, since it was the *Herald* that granted the paperboys a monopoly in the first place.[155] In other words, if the Herald believed that an exclusive paper route gave a paperboy monopoly power which he could use to demand supercompetitive prices, the correct solution was to refuse to give him an exclusive paper route in the first place, not to grant it and then take the additional anticompetitive act of price-fixing. Third, the court noted that a maximum price-setting agreement might actually be a minimum price-setting agreement in disguise.[156] That is, a manufacturer might characterize something as a maximum price in a contract, but the dealers might realize that the manufacturer *really* wants them to charge that price at a minimum.

Justice Harlan and Justice Stewart, in dissent, argued that all three of the court's justifications for the per se rule were economically naive. First, Stewart pointed out that the antitrust laws are not concerned with protecting the independent business judgment of an entrepreneur when the entrepreneur is exercising monopoly power.[157] In fact, the paperboy's 'business judgment' is less likely to be consistent with the needs of the market than the *Herald*'s, since a paperboy will complain about a reasonable maximum price only when it prevents him from charging a supercompetitive price to consumers. Harlan pointed out that, in any event, a company could completely eliminate independent entrepreneurs by hiring its own sales employees, and while such an act would not violate the antitrust laws in any way, it would be more destructive to competition than the *Herald*'s modest price-ceiling rule.[158] Second, Stewart argued that a paperboy's exclusive territory was most likely a natural monopoly, which was a product of the market's inability to support more than one paperboy per territory, rather than a grant of monopolistic power by the Herald.[159] Third, Harlan pointed out that while it might be true that some maximum-price agreements are disguised minimum-price agreements, many maximum-price agreements are not.[160] In deciding whether or not to apply the per se rule to maximum-price agreements, he noted that the question 'is not whether dictation of maximum price is ever illegal, but whether it is always illegal.'

Continental T.V., Inc. v. *GTE Sylvania, Inc.*[161] reversed *Arnold, Schwinn & Co.*,[162] and held that vertical, non-price restraints should be subjected to the rule of reason. *Sylvania* noted that *Arnold, Schwinn & Co.*, had been wrongly decided for a number of reasons.[163] First, *Arnold, Schwinn & Co.* ignored *White Motor Co.*'s warning that a per se rule was justified only when a court had sufficient experience with a business practice to make a reliable economic prediction about its consequences.[164] The majority in *Arnold, Schwinn & Co.* did not identify any piece of data that had not been available to *White Motor Co.*, yet it changed the rule.[165] Instead, *Arnold, Schwinn & Co.* attempted to resolve its difficulties by turning to 'ancient' common law distinctions.[166] Second, to the extent that there were data that were available to *Arnold Schwinn & Co.* which had not been available to *White Motor Co.*, those data strongly indicated that a per se rule against vertical non-price restraints would be inefficient, and even disastrous.[167] Third, developments in economic theory after *Arnold, Schwinn & Co.* strengthened the case that a per se rule against vertical non-price agreements was a mistake, and that a rule which distinguished between consignment and sales contracts was wrongheaded.[168] In fact, it was the large companies with little legitimate need for exclusive dealerships that were the most likely to be able to characterize their transactions as consignment contracts, and the small companies with a strong need to offer exclusive dealerships that were the least likely to be able to do so.[169]

In general, most economists became convinced that because interbrand competition was more important in protecting consumers than intrabrand competition, a manufacturer's interests were more likely to be consistent with the public's interest than a distributor's or a retailer's interests were likely to be.[170] For example, vigorous interbrand competition ensured that a dealer with an exclusive territory could not exploit his monopoly power, since a consumer would turn to a different brand name rather than pay supercompetitive prices. Additionally, economists noted that exclusive dealerships allowed a manufacturer to eliminate 'free riders' who might dissuade retailers from offering vital services and repairs, or from marketing the manufacturer's products.[171] As the economic evidence mounted that *Arnold, Schwinn & Co.* had been wrongly decided, and as more and more scholars advocated its reversal, it became increasingly efficient to reverse the decision.[172] Because *Sylvania* explicitly relied on the expertise of economists, and recognized that it is desirable to change a common law rule when new knowledge suggests that the old rule is inefficient, *Sylvania* has been haled by many writers as a turning point in antitrust legal history, and the beginning of modern antitrust analysis (Calkins 1997, p. 417).[173]

The recent case of *State Oil Co.* v. *Khan* reversed *Albrecht*.[174] *Khan* noted that none of *Albrecht*'s 'dire predictions' of what would happen if vertical price maximums were legal were founded in fact, and that *Albrecht* had created additional problems.[175] In essence, Harlan's predictions about the probable effects of *Albrecht* were borne out by the court's subsequent experience.[176] *Albrecht* actually contributed to the elimination of independent entrepreneurs, since it encouraged manufacturers to replace dealers with sales employees.[177] Further, many economists concluded that *Albrecht* had hurt consumers, since a dealer was considerably more likely to set a supercompetitive price than a manufacturer was likely to set a subcompetitive price, since the latter either prevented dealers from making a reasonable profit or prevented them from offering services that consumers desired.[178] Also, *Albrecht*'s logical underpinning was undercut by *Sylvania*: since it was now lawful, in many circumstances, to give a dealer an exclusive territory, it seemed foolish to prevent the manufacturer from protecting consumers by setting a maximum price.[179] Finally, the court agreed with Harlan that the possibility that a maximum price was a disguised minimum price was hardly an excuse for outlawing all maximum-price agreements.[180] Under the rule of reason, the court could identify any alleged maximum-price agreement that was actually a minimum-price agreement.[181]

In conclusion, when one surveys the line of antitrust cases dealing with vertical restraints, one sees two changes. First, there is a shift in the court's attitude towards the significance of new economic knowledge.[182] *Arnold, Schwinn & Co.* quite consciously chose an 'ancient' rule to draw a line on a difficult economic issue, and turned its back on recent economic knowledge.[183] *Albrecht* similarly cited a 'non-economic' concern with protecting the independent business judgment of dealers.[184] *Sylvania* and *Khan*, in contrast, recognized the importance of new economic knowledge, since the decision of whether to apply the per se rule is an economic prediction about an activity's impact on the marketplace.[185] Second, there was an increase in the availability and prominence of economic literature discussing antitrust law. In fairness to *Arnold, Schwinn & Co.*, the volume of economic literature which was available to assist courts in deciding whether or not to extend the per se rule was much greater than it was at the time of *Sylvania*.[186] Indeed, *Arnold, Schwinn & Co.* itself provoked a great deal of the economic literature that *Sylvania* relied on.[187]

9.13 SUMMARY

This chapter has advanced a thesis about why the common law can be efficient. I have shown, first, that custom is necessarily efficient in a static world because it establishes psychological ownership. Even in a non-static world, uncontentious and long-standing custom is likely to be efficient when legal rights correspond with psychological ownership and the pace of change is not too rapid. The common law was historically efficient, as it adopted uncontentious and long-standing norms. When judges adopted these social norms, they were complying with the social norm that their role was to dispense justice.

But the common law is not always efficient. The greater the pace of change – in technology, knowledge, or sentiments – the less likely it is that there are relevant, uncontentious norms. In periods of great change, then, the efficient resolution of legal problems is less clear, and the less likely it will be that the common law is efficient. The law of dueling changed as sentiments changed and the law moved from one probably efficient equilibrium to another. In the case of cannibalism, the law ran into difficulty when it attempted to cope with the necessity defense in a situation in which sentiments were not clear. When technology of gold mining changed, not only did the previous law become inefficient, but the evolving common law failed to find a path to efficiency, as this path became obscure in the absence of new relevant norms. The court's difficulty in crafting an efficient rule in *Plessy* v. *Ferguson* was a direct reflection of changing social conditions and changing sentiments about segregation. Finally, new knowledge allowed the courts to move from inefficient legal antitrust restraints on vertical business arrangements to a more efficient law of vertical restraints.

When efficiency is seen as a branch of moral theory, the definition of efficiency itself takes on an ethical and moral component. Posner attempts to justify KH on the grounds of actual ex ante consent. This does not work because such actual consent does not generally exist. The KH efficiency hypothesis as a positive prediction of the common law must be deficient, since KH efficiency is considered without recourse to its ethical and moral context. Efficiency, as defined in economics, will carry moral weight in those instances in which the efficient decision is also seen as fair.[188]

The KHZ efficiency hypothesis better reflects the actual sentiments of the community because it explicitly includes considerations of fairness, the distribution of income, and in general what I have called the regard for others, and it does not disregard transactions costs, as KH does. Thus it has a firmer moral grounding than the KH hypothesis. In the end, says Dershowitz of the *Mignonette* case, necessity is a jury defense, a recourse to the conscience of the community (Simpson 1990).[189] Economic efficiency analysis must also reside in the conscience of the community, through an explicit reliance upon the structure of rights, not only to ensure that a model for efficiency has support, but to even give the model meaning. The common law tends not towards efficiency, but towards fairness and justice.[190] And it is efficient because, properly considered, fairness and justice are part of economic efficiency, and therefore are part of KHZ efficiency.

NOTES

1. The common law is used here and throughout this article to mean that body of law developed by judges through case decisions (Posner 1992b, p. 31; *Black's Law Dictionary* 1999, p. 270).
2. The name of this sort of efficiency is KH efficiency. Kaldor (1939) developed a theory of efficiency, which Hicks (1939) modified. A change in wealth is KH efficient if the value of the gains to one party exceeds the value of the losses to the other (Zerbe and Dively 1994).
3. The list of scholars who suggest that the common law tends towards efficiency includes Coase (1960), Calabresi (1961), Bruce (1984), Shavell (1987), Landes and Posner (1987), Polinsky (1989), and Cooter and Ulen (1988).
4. It is important to note that the fact that a common law rule is inefficient means only that it would be efficient to change that rule – *not* that it would be efficient to abandon the common law approach itself in favor of a system in which judges merely interpreted statutes.
5. The ideal is so well accepted that the term 'common law' has been defined as 'the body of those principles and rules of action … which derive their authority solely from usages and customs of immemorial antiquity' *Black's Law Dictionary* (1999).
6. Thus, when the law says that this or that is a legally protected interest it is putting into authoritative form the ideas that are acceptable to society at one time or another about the comparative value of different kinds of activity (Hurst 1950, p. 12) . The law moves with the main currents of American thought.
7. Hogue (1966, p. 10) notes that according 'to an old principle in jurisprudence, judges cannot make law except when they find a social norm worthy of enforcement by the state.' See also Cooter (1996, p. 1649) and Blackstone (1900, p. 67).
8. Lawrence Friedman (1973, p. 17) notes that the 'common law is an unwritten law' and

that its 'ultimate highest source … [i]s not an enactment but general custom, as reflected in the decisions of common law judges.'

9. Blackstone (1900, p. 46) notes 'indeed these judicial decisions are the principal and most authoritative evidence, that can be given, of the existence of such a custom as shall form part of the common law.'
10. A literal application of Blackstone's (1900, p. 43) criteria would make it virtually impossible to incorporate norms into the common law. KHZ views Blackstone's criteria as an ideal along a continuum. The more contentious a norm is, the less the likelihood that making it into law will be efficient. Conversely, the closer a norm is to Blackstone's (1900, p. 43) ideal (by being uncontentious, ancient, continuous, etc.), the more likely it is to be efficient to adopt it into the law.
11. See *State Oil Co.* v. *Khan*, 522 U.S. 3, 21 (1997). The appointment of Posner as a mediator in the recent Microsoft case is an example of the courts' recognition of the importance of economic analysis to the development of antitrust law, since Posner is well known as a proponent of the economic analysis of the law (Grimaldi 1999).
12. Again, Blackstone's (1900, pp. 56–57) norms represent the ideal along a continuum, not a rigid requirement.
13. A full appreciation of this point, for example, is sufficient to show that the concepts of market failure and of externality are incoherent for policy purposes (Zerbe and McCurdy 1999).
14. Underlying this proof is a notion that preferences are to be taken as given. And it is true that in benefit–cost analysis preferences are usually taken to be given. However, efforts to change the law to accord with preferences may themselves be KH efficient. Underlying this proof is the notion that changing preferences to be in accord with the law cannot be described as efficient.
15. This view is not universal. See, for example, Everson (1919) and Blanck (1996).
16. The trickier question, of course, is what it means to say that a judge should 'do justice.' Under the jurisprudential doctrine of positivism, a judge does justice (especially in a democratic country) by following the 'plain meaning' of statutes (Allen 1992, p. 692). Under the natural law and legal realist theories of law, a judge does justice by recognizing either transcendent moral values (natural law) (Pennington 1997, p. 1097) or public policy and common sense (legal realism) (Allen 1992, p. 692).
17. Friedman (1959, pp. 26f) notes the law's response to some of these changes. Examples of common law adapting to change may be found in *McPherson* v. *Buick*, 217 N.Y. 382, 111 N.E. 1050 (1916); *Donoghue* v. *Stevenson*, (1932) at 562. A host of similar examples are mentioned by Wolfgang Friedman (1959).
18. I will, however, note that a straightforward extension of the work of Weingast (1997) and of Calvert (1995) suggests that a norm of justice arises as an equilibrium condition in a 'game' that produces stable democracies. The equilibrium condition requires that citizens agree on the boundary of the state and that those boundaries be self enforcing (Weingast 1997). In a game-theory setting, this occurs when constitutional or other provisions are held in sufficiently high esteem that citizens are willing to defend them. We will note also that disturbing a norm is costly because it fuels opposition.
19. Myers (1971, p. 1) notes the puzzle that England produced a more stable democracy earlier than other European countries but had an earlier stronger monarch. This puzzle may be resolved by considering the role of norms. A stronger monarch produces a more uniform system of norms. This more uniform system will make it more difficult for the monarch to play off some groups against others.
20. It does not follow, however, that the common law should not be used in eras of rapid social change – simply that we should recognize that using it imposes certain costs. Just as the common law runs into trouble during eras of rapid social change, so too would any other system of law which attempted to create a match between norms and laws. In a civil law country judges are simply administrators, and play little or no role in creating law. In such a country, it is the legislature that would run into trouble, as it attempted to find an uncontentious norm when no uncontentious norm existed. If a common law or civil law country attempted to ignore norms, this would create inefficiency, by definition.

21. Hogue (1966, p. 8) also notes that 'the result of the pull in these two directions has been an unresolved tension between factions, parties, or groups of men; not always a tug-of-war between conservatives and radicals. The dual objectives can exist in the legal thought of a single jurist.'
22. See also Plucknett (1956, pp. 350, 664).
23. See *State Oil* v. *Khan*, 522 U.S. 3, 21 (1997).
24. For example, the general common law rule that a landowner is not liable for negligently harming a trespasser is probably efficient. The exceptions in which a landowner is liable to a trespasser are probably efficient as well.
25. The law of mining and significant pieces of labor law come to mind (Lande and Zerbe 1996).
26. An ongoing change in sentiments is happily reflected in Sen's (1999, pp. 20, 104–107) criticism of values that have lead to the phenomenon of 'missing women,' that is, women in developing countries whose survival has not been given proper weight.
27. William Bothwick (1776, p. 19) notes 'That although, in times of ignorance, our ancestors had recourse to a blind method of trial by duels, yet there never was a period in the annals of Britain, when duels could be lawfully engaged in by private parties.'
28. A similar experience may be seen in the history of flogging in the British Navy. 'Flogging around the fleet disappeared by the mid eighteen hundreds, and by 1870 a captain's right to order flogging was severely restricted. In 1879 it was abolished', according to Robert Massie (1991).
29. The known count was 4,632 (see Simpson, 1984, p. 98). I am indebted to Judge Frank Easterbrook for bringing Simpson's book to my attention.
30. *Regina* v. *Dudley and Stephens* 14 Q. B. D. 273 (1884). See also 14 Q.B.D. 560 (1885) for discussion of the special verdict and *Queen* v. *Dudley*, 1 T.L.R. 29 (1984) for the report of the trial at Exeter Assizes.
31. John Bolen, pathologist, tells me that there is no magical quality of edibility that depends on whether the body is living or not. The simple rule is the healthier the body, the better.
32 *Regina* v. *Dudley and Stephens* Q.B.D., pp. 273–275.
33. A modern statement of the necessity defense is given by Clark and Marshall (1967, pp. 360–361) as 'an act which would otherwise be a crime may be excused if the person accused can show that it was done only in order to avoid consequences which could not otherwise be avoided, and which, if they had followed, would have inflicted upon him, or upon others whom he was bound to protect, inevitable and irreparable evil; that no more was done than was reasonably necessary for that purpose; and that the evil inflicted by it was not disproportionate to the evil avoided.'
34. These cases could also be reasonably classified as strictly utilitarian as well.
35. The behavior of Dudley and Stevens does not suffer from a comparison with the behavior in these other cases. It is true that in about 41 percent of the cases cannibalism followed natural death, though in some instances it followed very, perhaps suspiciously, close. Dudley and Stephens, however, were faced with a situation unlike the others, since waiting until natural death occurred was likely to have led to the death of all. In addition, as mentioned they labored under the belief that the use for food and drink of a body dead of natural causes was not safe. About 22 percent of cases involved a choice of murder victim (and often of executioner) by drawing lots, though in several of the cases the results strained credulity in the choice of victim. In 19 percent of the instances, the 'tough guys' spared themselves. Fifteen percent of the cases were utilitarian. Behavior in one instance, about 4 percent, was altruistic. It might, however, be anti-utilitarian to kill the person nearest death if that person held sufficient value (the young Mozart, for example).
36. For a discussion of the procedural irregularities, see Mallin (1967).
37. An instance in which accepted principles were not followed also resulted in one of the few cases to reach the courts besides the *Regina* v. *Dudley* and *United States* v. *Holmes* cases. This involved the Donner party and Frank Packer, a Colorado gold hunter, who committed murder and subsequent cannibalism. Packer was tried before Judge Gerry in 1887. Gene Fowler's account is classic:

> Although Judge Gerry delivered what was considered the most eloquent hanging speech in Western court history, an apocryphal sentence is the one that persists, and by which this scholarly gentleman's name still lives. Larry Dolan, who had a grudge against Packer, attended every session of the trial. Between times, Larry filled himself to the larynx with 'Taos Lightning.' Just as the fluent Judge Gerry began a classical pronouncement of doom, Larry let out a cheer and fell from a bench. Then he rose, and ran drunkenly to his favorite saloon, bellowing like ten Apis bulls of Egypt: 'Well, boys, ut's all over; Packer's to hang. The judge, God bless him. p'intin' his tremblin' fingers at Packer, so ragin' mad as he was, he said, 'They was siven Dimmycrats in Hinsdale County, but you, yuh voracious man-eatin' son of a bitch, yuh eat five of thim! I sintince ye t' be hanged by th' neck until y're dead, dead, dead; as a warnin' ag'n reducin' the Dimmycratic populashun of th' State.' (Perkins 1959, p. 345)

38. The change in law introduced by *Regina* v. *Dudley* may be interpreted as reflecting a change in 'tastes' (in more than one sense!) – a change in tastes primarily on the part of members of the ruling class to be sure – but such changes in law are probably not wholly divorced from the sentiments of the general population. Certainly the tastes that are appropriate to one age or situation may be inappropriate in another. A vegetarian philosophy in a hunter–gatherer society might be ridiculous and inappropriate, but not so inappropriate in a materially wealthy society with a sufficient supply of vegetarian food (Clarke 1957).
39. Posner (1990) develops a concept of the law with which I agree. Posner notes that the law is better, though not fully, described as the activity of judges, whose scope of license is limited by the outer bounds of professional propriety and moral consensus (pp. 456–457).
40. The decision in *Dudley and Stephens* and its consequences has been (sarcastically) described as Pareto optimal: 'The judges obtained their precedent. Dudley and Stephens their freedom, Harcourt (the Home Secretary who reluctantly commuted their sentence to six months instead of life) his continued reputation for humanity, and society its inconsistent ends' (Mallin 1967, p 407). Simpson (1984), however, believes that the procedural irregularities, and the apparent determination of the Court to come to a predetermined verdict to make a moral point, are less acceptable than the straightforward behavior of Dudley and Stephens. He apparently believes that a decision was available to Dudley and Stevens that was morally superior to the one that was made. Surely it is not unreasonable to argue that allowance for murder might be properly made in the situation given in *Dudley and Stephens*; i.e., that the death of one is inevitable in the near future, regardless of the sacrifice of another, and is more likely to be earlier than other deaths which can possibly be avoided by the sacrifice of the one death.
41. Judge Frank Easterbrook suggested this example to me as representing Posner's wealth-maximizing approach in these circumstances.
42. The WTA would be superior to the WTP because it is less subject to income constraints.
43. I think I am indebted to Ben Hu for this succinct rule. Note that failure to eat Parker would be a clear deadweight loss.
44. See *Hicks* v. *Bell*, 3 Cal. 219 (1853).
45. See *Eureka Consol. Mining Co.* v. *Richmond Mining Co.*, 8 F. Cas. 819, 822 (D. Nevada 1877). More recently, courts have departed from Congress' original understanding when interpreting the mining statute (Leshy 1987, pp. 22–23).
46. For example, it is estimated that one-fifth of the fabulous wealth of the Comstock lode was consumed in litigation (Leshy 1987, p. 21). Interestingly enough, the lead counsel of the victor of the Comstock Lode cases was William Stewart, the chief proponent of the federal mining statute of 1866 (Miller 1991, p. 50).
47. Historians disagree as to whether the mining district rules were a spontaneous creation of the miners or were taken from the laws of Mexico, from Cornish mining practices, or even from an ancient Prussian statute (Davis 1902, pp. 9, 16–18). The Cornish miners' 'rake veins' rules and the rules of an ancient Prussian statutes bore vague similarities to

the miners' rules for lode claims, discussed below (Snyder 1902, p. 62). The Prussians repealed the statute in question when it led to too many lawsuits (Snyder 1902, p. 62).

48. See, for example, *Prosser* v. *Parks*, 18 Cal. 47 (1861).
49. Umbeck (1981) argues that the miners behavior should be viewed as a series of violent or potentially violent confrontations which settled into an equilibrium when each group of miners occupied a set of claims that they were willing to fight for, and which no other group was willing to challenge. This equilibrium was then codified into mining rules (Umbeck 1981). However, Umbeck (1981) fails to explain how the miners coordinated themselves into groups that were willing to fight to protect each member's claims. Moreover, it does not appear to be the case that the miners first engaged in violence, then reached a stable equilibrium, and then drafted rules to enforce the status quo. Rather, the miners formed rules before any mining or violence over mining claims commenced, and their cultural values determined whether they were willing to fight to enforce their rules (Zerbe and Anderson 1999, p. 3).
50. See *Eureka Consol. Mining Co.* v. *Richmond Mining Co.*, 8 F. Cas. 819 (D. Nevada 1877).
51. The total amount of gold produced in California rose from $3.7 million in 1848, to $10.6 million in 1849, to $45.3 million in 1850, and peaked in 1853 at $63.8 million (Jackson 1980, 314).
52. The 'rush' was also over in the sense that the flood of immigration to California had slowed to a trickle by 1851 (Jackson 1980, p. 314).
53. Eventually the rule for lode claims was modified so that a miner could only follow the dip on to another person's property if the vein continued in a more or less straight line on to the other claim (Davis 1902, pp. 54–55).
54. An 'extra-lateral' right is the right to follow a vein on to another person's property (Davis 1902, p. 70).
55. See *Iron Silver Mining Co.*v. *Cheesman*, 2 McCrary 196.
56. See *Merced Mining Co.* v. *Fremont*, 7 Cal. 317, 320 (1857).
57. See *Merced*, 7 Cal. at 320.
58. See *Brown*, 15 Cal. 152 (1860).
59. See ibid. at 161.
60. See ibid. at 159–160.
61. See ibid. at 160.
62. See ibid. at 160–161.
63. Under the mining laws, one who discovered and began extracting gold gained an enforceable interest against other claimants without filing anything with the federal Land Department (Leshy 1987, p. 266). If the patent was approved by the Land Department, the holder received limited protection from collateral challenges (Leshy 1987, p. 266).
64. See *Brown*, 15 Cal. 152 (1860), 160–161.
65. See *Eureka*, 8 F. Cas. 819.
66. See ibid. at 823, 825.
67. See ibid. at 822.
68. See ibid. at 822–823.
69. See ibid. at 822–825.
70. See ibid. at 824–826.
71. See also *Hyman* v. *Wheeler*, 29 Fed. Rep. 347.
72. See *Cheesman*, 2 McCrary 196.
73. *Eureka*, 9 F. Cas. 819. *Brown*, 15 Cal. 152.
74. *Eureka*, 9 F. Cas. 819.
75. *Eureka*, 9 F. Cas. 819. *Brown*, 15 Cal. 152.
76. See *Eureka*, 9 F. Cas. 819. See *Brown*, 15 Cal. 152.
77. See ibid.
78. See *Morton* v. *Solambo Copper Mining Co.*, 26 Cal. 527, 532 (1864).
79. See *English* v. *Johnson*, 17 Cal. 107 (1860).
80. See ibid. at 116.
81. See ibid. at 119.

82. See ibid. at 115.
83. See ibid. at 119.
84. See ibid. at 118.
85. See ibid. at 119.
86. See *Kelley* v. *Taylor*, 23 Cal. 11 (1863). Under abandonment, a landowner loses property by leaving it with no intention of returning. Under estoppel in pais, a land owner loses property by fraudulently encouraging another person to build expensive improvements on the owner's land and then claiming the improvements as his. It seems clear that the mining law rules requiring the active working of a claim are related to both of these doctrines, but do not match either perfectly. Under most mining district rules, a miner could lose his claim even if he had not defrauded another miner to lose his claim, and he could lose his claim if he left, even if he left with the intention of returning, so long as he was actually absent for a sufficient period of time.
87. See ibid.
88. See *Waring* v. *Crow*, 11 Cal. 366 (1858). The court hedged by noting that it did not really believe that such a mining rule existed, but it nonetheless made it clear that it would not follow the alleged mining rule even if it existed. Ibid. at 372.
89. See ibid.
90. See ibid.
91. See *Leonard* v. *Peeples*, 30 Ga. 61, 64 (1860) (saying of an alleged mining rule 'if there be such a custom, it is so unreasonable, that it was probably enforced with a bowie-knife'). *Leonard* was a Georgia case which involved a dispute over a sale of a mining claim to land in California.
92. The reader may wonder what constitutes 'assessment' work. This seemingly simple question has no easy answer. Indeed, some of the most heated legal battles of the twentieth century concern which expenses constitutes 'assessment' work. I direct the interested reader to Snyder (1902).
93. Prior to discovering valuable minerals, a miner can gain a limited right of exclusive possession called Pedis Possessio, which is enforceable against other miners but not against the federal government (Leshy 1987, pp. 97–102). See *Union Oil Co.* v. *Smith*, 249 U.S. 337 (1919). Unfortunately, exploratory drilling does not even give a miner a Pedis Possessio right (Leshy 1987, p. 102).
94. Cameron's legal challenges were all rejected by the Supreme Court in 1920. See *Cameron* v. *United States*, 252 U.S. 450 (1920). Cameron was not actually ejected for another four years, after four more lawsuits and two contempt proceedings (Leshy 1987, p. 60).
95. See also *Merced*, 7 Cal. at 322.
96. See *Rogers* v. *Soggs*, 22 Cal. 444 (1863).
97. Davis (1902, p. 73) notes: 'The prospector and the discoverer feels in his every fibre, no matter what fictitious sacredness judicial construction has thrown about the idea of the surface, that the lode itself is the only real property, as it is the only thing that he has been hunting, and when he finds the lode his desire "to stay with it till it reaches hell" is a passion that cannot be understood by one who has never owned a lode mine and worked in it, or who has never lived in a mining company.' To the extent that this describes a mining company's attitude towards a mining claim, the claim is clearly not a commercial good, since there is a psychological attachment to the mine apart from its financial value.
98. Of course, Davis (1902, p. 73) does not refer to WTA and WTP, but he notes that the miner 'feels in his every fibre' that he is entitled to follow the course of a vein.
99. Insofar as there is a universal sentiment about the mining law, the sentiment is that it is inefficient, in the sense that it results in too much litigation (Leshy 1987, p. 287).
100. See *Plessy* v. *Ferguson*, 163 U.S. 537 (1896).
101. See ibid. at 541, 550–551.
102. See ibid. at 550–551.
103. See ibid. Harlan points out, in dissent, that racial *segregation* was not Louisiana's social convention in any event, since it prevented an African-American servant from waiting on a white patron during the ride, something that Louisiana's social conventions not only allowed but demanded of African-Americans. See ibid. at 553. The point is not that a

norm of servitude is morally superior to a norm of segregation, but merely that the alleged norm of segregation was not even historically accurate.

104. See ibid. at 550–551, 557.
105. See ibid. at 554. Harlan notes '(T)he Constitution of the United States does not, I think, permit any public authority to know the race of those entitled to be protected in the enjoyment of [constitutional] rights.' Saying that a public authority may not 'know' a certain fact when making a decision is an apt description of what it means to deny economic standing.
106. See ibid.
107. See ibid. at 555.
108. See ibid. at 550–551.
109. See ibid. at 551, 557.
110. *Plessy*, 163 U.S. 537.
111. See ibid. At a minimum, Harlan's eloquent dissent provides an example of one competing norm. See ibid. at 552–564.
112. Ibid. See *McLaurin* v. *Oklahoma State Regents for Higher Education*, 339 U.S. 637 (1950); *Sweatt* v. *Painter*, 339 U.S. 629 (1950); *Missourri Ex Rel Gaines* v. *Canada*, 305 U.S. 337 (1938).
113. See *Gaines*, 305 U.S. at 342, 349–352.
114. See ibid. at 349, 353.
115. Compare *Plessy*, 163 U.S. at 550–551 with *Gaines*, 305 U.S. at 349, 353
116. See *Sweatt*, 339 U.S. at 632–636.
117. See *McLaurin*, 339 U.S. at 638–642.
118. See ibid. at 640–641.
119. See *McLaurin*, 339 U.S. 637; *Sweatt*, 339 U.S. 629.
120. See *Sweatt*, 339 U.S. at 634.
121. *McLaurin*, 339 U.S. 637; *Brown* v. *The Board of Education of Topeka*, 347 U.S. 483 (1954).
122. See *Brown*, 347 U.S. at 493.
123. See ibid. at 492–493.
124. See ibid. at 490.
125. See ibid. at 494–495.
126. Indeed, many of the authors of these studies retracted their findings.
127. See *Plessy*, 163 U.S. 537.
128. See ibid. Harlan, in contrast, recognized that 'everyone knows' that the purpose of the Louisiana statute was to degrade African-Americans. See ibid. at 556–557.
129. See *Brown*, 347 U.S. 483.
130. See *Khan*, 522 U.S. at 20, 21.
131. See *Chicago Board of Trade* v. *United States*, 246 U. S. 231, 238 (1918).
132. See *United States* v. *Standard Oil Co. of New Jersey*, 221 U.S. 1, 59–60 (1911).
133. See *Northern Pacific Railroad Co.* v. *United States*, 356 U.S. 1, 5–6 (1958).
134. See *Khan*, 522 U.S. at 10.
135. See *Khan*, 522 U.S. at 10.
136. See *Albrecht* v. *Herald Co.*, 390 U.S. 145, 159 (1968)
137. See *White Motor Co.* v. *United States*, 372 U.S. 253 (1963).
138. See ibid. at 257–259.
139. See ibid. at 263.
140. See *United States* v. *Arnold, Schwinn & Co.*, 388 U.S. 365, 379 (1963). In a consignment contract, a manufacturer delivers a product to a distributor, but retains title to the product until it is actually sold to a customer. The distributor keeps some of the sales money for itself, and sends the rest to the manufacturer, at a previously agreed upon ratio. See ibid.
141. See ibid. at 373–374.
142. See *Arnold, Schwinn & Co.*, 388 U.S. at 374–375; *White Motor Co.*, 372 U.S. at 263.
143. See *Arnold, Schwinn & Co.*, 388 U.S. at 379. This is almost certainly a misreading of *White Motor Co.*, since there is no evidence that White Motor Co. itself was a new company or a failing business. See *White Motor Co.*, 372 U.S. at 263. The references to

new companies and failing businesses were intended to be *examples* of situations in which the rule of reason might be satisfied, not to constitute an *exclusive* list.
144. See ibid. at 378–379.
145. See ibid. (emphasis added).
146. See ibid. at 374–375.
147. See ibid. at 392.
148. See ibid. at 391.
149. See ibid. at 388, 391.
150. See *Albrecht*, 390 U.S. 145 (1968).
151. See ibid. at 147–148.
152. See ibid. at 154.
153. See ibid. at 152.
154. See ibid. at 152–153.
155. See ibid. at 154.
156. See ibid. at 153.
157. See ibid. at 169.
158. See ibid. at 160–161.
159. See ibid. at 169.
160. See ibid. at 165–166.
161. See *Continental T.V., Inc.* v. *GTE Sylvania, Inc.*, 433 U.S. 36 (1977).
162. *Arnold, Schwinn & Co.*, 388 U.S. 365.
163. See *Sylvania*, 433 U.S. at 59. *Arnold, Schwinn & Co.*, 388 U.S. 365.
164. See *Sylvania*, 433 U.S. at 47–48; *White Motor Co.*, 372 U.S. at 263. *Arnold, Schwinn & Co.*, 388 U.S. 365.
165. See *Sylvania*, 433 U.S. at 47–48. *Arnold, Schwinn & Co.*, 388 U.S. 365; *White Motor Co.*, 372 U.S. 253.
166. See *Sylvania*, 433 U.S. at 53. *Arnold, Schwinn & Co.*, 388 U.S. at 380.
167. See *Sylvania*, 433 U.S. at 53; *Arnold, Schwinn & Co.*, 388 U.S. at 382–394.
168. See *Sylvania*, 433 U.S. at 48–49. *Arnold, Schwinn & Co.*, 388 U.S. 365.
169. See *Sylvania*, 433 U.S. at 56.
170. See ibid. at 52.
171. See ibid. at 55.
172. *Arnold, Schwinn & Co.*, 388 U.S. 365.
173. *Sylvania*, 433 U.S. at 47–48.
174. See *Khan*, 522 U.S. 3. *Albrecht*, 390 U.S. 145.
175. See *Khan*, 522 U.S. at 19. *Albrecht*, 390 U.S. 145.
176. See *Khan*, 522 U.S. at 19. *Albrecht*, 390 U.S. 145.
177. See *Khan*, 522 U.S. at 16–17. *Albrecht*, 390 U.S. 145.
178. See *Khan*, 522 U.S. at 17–18. *Albrecht*, 390 U.S. 145.
179. See *Khan*, 522 U.S. at 14. *Sylvania*, 433 U.S. 36; *Albrecht*, 390 U.S. 145.
180. See *Khan*, 522 U.S. at 17; *Albrecht*, 390 U.S. at 165–166.
181. See *Khan*, 522 U.S. at 17.
182. It is worth noting that in the early cases there are virtually no references to the economic literature, while the later cases are peppered with them.
183. See *Arnold, Schwinn & Co.*, 388 U.S. at 380.
184. See *Albrecht*, 522 U.S. at 152, 158. In fact, the existence value of independent business people is an 'economic' good, but *Albrecht* does not discuss the value of independent business judgment in economic terms.
185. See *Khan*, 522 U.S. at 21; *Sylvania*, 433 U.S. at 54.
186. *Sylvania*, 433 U.S. 36; *Arnold, Schwinn & Co.*, 388 U.S. 365.
187. See *Sylvania*, 433 U.S. at 47–48. *Arnold, Schwinn & Co.*, 388 U.S. 365.
188. See Zerbe (1998a, 1998b)
189. The *Migonnette* gave us an example in which the court would have preferred the destruction of four lives through starvation to the destruction of one life through cannibalism. This is clearly 'inefficient' in the sense of the destruction of greater human capital, but it is not necessarily inefficient in a KHZ sense. Whether or not this outcome is inefficient

in a KHZ sense depends on where rights and sentiments lie. In other words, if the regard for others finds cannibalism sufficiently appalling, it might be more efficient to sacrifice four lives to starvation than to sacrifice one life to cannibalism.

190. See Easterling (1992) for an analysis in which efficiency contributes to fairness.

10. A Recapitulation

10.1 THE KHZ CRITERION

The standard criteria used to judge whether or not a public investment or a new law or regulation is desirable are referred to as the Kaldor–Hicks (KH) criteria. These represent two different potential compensation tests, one of which – Kaldor – is that a new investment or new law is desirable if the winners could compensate the losers for the loss. The Hicks test is that a project is worthwhile if the potential losers could not bribe the potential winners not to undertake the project. These criteria explicitly leave out distributional effects on two grounds: that their omission is necessary if a measure is to be scientific, and that whether compensation should take place 'is a political question on which the economist, qua economist, could hardly pronounce an opinion' (Kaldor 1939).

However, the relationship between the various measures to actually be used (CVs, or compensating variations, and EVs, equivalent variations, and the WTP and the WTA) for welfare analysis and the compensation criteria is not straightforward, as Boadway and Bruce (1984) show and as I discuss in Chapter 3. The CV measures the value of a price change using final prices while the EV uses original prices. It was long thought that the CV measure was identical to the Kaldor compensation test and that the EV measure was identical to the Hicks test, but this is not in fact the case (Boadway and Bruce 1984).

The use of the KH criteria has been subject to a barrage of criticisms, both ethical and technical. Technical objections include reversibility (the Scitovsky paradox), status quo bias and indeterminacy, the failure to include transaction costs as costs, and, finally, the fact that the use of the CV alone may result in recommendations that would not pass a potential compensation test.

In addition there are important ethical criticisms. Of these the most compelling are those that note that the income distribution and the fact of compensation or its absence are omitted as values in KH analysis. Other important values are said to be missing as well (Anderson 1993; Fried 1978; Kelman 1981; Sagoff 1988). For example, a criticism is that the use of the discount rate to evaluate projects – which is normally justified by the KH criteria – is immoral because it gives insufficient weight to the values of the future. Additional criticisms concern the results of applications of efficiency analysis; for example, efficiency analysis is held by Dworkin to be defective because it fails to condemn slavery.

In this book I have introduced a new set of assumptions – which I modestly call the KHZ criterion – that build on the KH criteria, but that are not subject to the criticisms noted above. Three assumptions are essential: first, I define efficiency in terms of the willingness to pay (WTP) and the willingness to accept (WTA) payment for a change. The WTP and WTA are to be grounded in psychological reference points so that losses (to be measured by the WTA) and gains (to be measured by the WTP) are to be based on changes from the psychological reference points. These psychological reference points will in general be determined by property rights (defining 'property' broadly) and therefore by the law. Second, all goods for which there is a WTP must be included in efficiency analysis. Third, transaction costs of operation but not of rule enactment are to be included in costs.

These assumptions lead to several additional foundational points and a variety of results. Among the foundational points are that (1) one must point to a superior rule or practice in order to say that some existing rule or practice is inefficient; (2) one should include the regard of others (those not directly affected) for those directly affected by a project; (3) one may cease to speak of utility as if it were a thing that can be measured. Finally, I specify that KHZ is not *the* decision, but an aid to decision, and that its language is not always the best for determining 'the right thing to do.' The major burden of the book is to show that these suggestions are advances in scope and utility and that they can be applied in practice.[1]

KHZ eliminates the technical criticisms that have been made and obviates most of the ethical criticisms (it is impossible to eliminate all ethical criticisms on any decision scheme). This is its justification. More broadly the justification for using KHZ has two parts and is spelled out in Chapter 2. The first argument is that it has the best chance among any competing criteria of making *all* of the people in a society better off 'at the end of the day' (that is, over a substantial set of projects or decisions) if the government uses KHZ as general criterion for evaluating each decision *instead of using some other criteria such as KH*. A particular person is better off 'at the end of the day' if his gains from the projects that help him outweigh his losses from the projects that hurt him. If the government uses KHZ to evaluate each project, and approves a project only if it is KHZ efficient, the net social gain will be higher than it would be if the government used any other basis for evaluating each project. This first argument will be used as the basis for a social-contract justification. The second argument for KHZ is that it is superior to KH because KH is less useful, in that it can lead to absurd results because it excludes certain important values, such as the income distribution, and is therefore less acceptable to society. This argument too can find a social-contract justification.

The most severe critics of normative economic analysis have been lawyers and philosophers who have unfortunately taken Richard Posner as the standard to be attacked. But Posner has proved to be too easy a mark. This is because he fails to understand economic efficiency well and fails to provide a well-grounded defense for its use. That is, wealth maximization is not KH as the term is usually used, let alone KHZ. Posner's contribution, rather, has been to show that even his incompletely formulated version of KH is useful – a fact which his critics have mainly failed to address. Indeed, critics such as Coleman and Dworkin have failed to provide any compelling alternative. Rather their contribution has been to drive home the important fact – which should have been obvious – that any decision criterion must seek its justification in moral theory. But moral theory, to be useful, must in turn be grounded in the workable, the practicable, and the acceptable. In general, neither KH's advocates nor its critics have thus grounded it. The more thoughtful critics, such as Michelman, have recognized this and have sought to build on the usefulness of KH. That, of course, is also what I have attempted to do here. But I maintain further that if KH is to be most useful, some reformulation of it is necessary, and it is in this spirit that I have offered the KHZ criterion.

10.2 APPLICATIONS

The importance of specifying the psychological reference point is shown in Chapter 3 in a discussion of *Vincent* v. *Lake Erie Transportation Co.*[2] Here it is shown that Coleman's discussion of efficiency is ungrounded because he fails to specify the psychological reference point. Finally, in Chapter 3, I consider the technical objections that have been raised to economic efficiency analysis. I show that the problems of reversibility, (the Scitovsky paradox), failures to pass compensation tests, and status quo bias are not problems for KHZ. In Chapter 4, I show that there is no problem of indeterminacy for KHZ.

What must be shown to prove a legal rule efficient is discussed in Chapter 4 in the context of a decision by Judge Posner, the *Lorenzen* case.[3] Here I show that although some people, including a dissenting judge, view this as a decision based on considerations of economic efficiency, it is in fact not such a decision although it uses in part the language of efficiency.

In Chapter 4, I use Waldfogel's assertion that Christmas giving results in deadweight as a not untypical example in which deadweight loss is discovered without having a superior alternative to offer. This is an example of the failure to include transactions costs. When we say that a tax has deadweight loss in partial equilibrium analysis, we can compare this to deadweight losses for other taxes, and we know that we can actually eliminate the deadweight loss by eliminating the tax. This is useful information. In many cases, as in the case of Christmas giving, inefficiency calculations or estimates of deadweight loss find inefficiency by comparing the actual world with a hypothetical world in which there are no transactions costs. In other cases, economic efficiency is subject to criticism on the grounds that it fails to consider important values. And, in still other cases, inefficiency is declared without the writer's having in mind any superior alternative. KHZ does not make the mistake of failing to include transactions costs, nor does it make the mistake of failing to consider all goods for which there is a WTP or a WTA. Although Christmas giving may be KH inefficient, it is KHZ efficient, and KHZ's analysis of Christmas giving is more consistent with social reality.

Chapter 5 considers the role of rights in efficiency analysis. I show, first, that even the efficiency part of the Coase Theorem applies only to commercial goods, and that otherwise it is both technically wrong and misspecified, since it fails to take into account the divergence between WTP and WTA. I show that where no psychological ownership exists (that is where ownership is unspecified), rights should be assigned to the highest bidder, subject to the regard for others. This result solves the indeterminacy problem noted by Posner, Kennedy, and others.

I show further that Baker's objection to the use of potential compensation tests as a guide to settle the assignment of rights in dispute fails to consider the right argument and that his objection is misplaced. Baker notes that when the sum of two or more parties' psychological expectations of ownership of a good is greater that 100 per cent, it would be impossible to satisfy a potential compensation test. This is true, but it is irrelevant. Whenever two or more people have a total psychological ownership of 100 percent, there will be a net loss no matter what criteria are used to decide how to distribute the goods. The question is whether or not the use of the KH or KHZ measures, rather than some third set of measures, can satisfy a potential compensation test *with respect to the other measures*. That is, could the losers according to the other test be compensated by the winners determined by the use of a KH test? The answer is yes, since using KH will result in a lower net loss than any other rule (except for KHZ). Since the answer is yes, Baker's case for not using economic efficiency measures for rights in dispute fails. The issue is similar in considering whether to use KHZ or KH. KHZ is even more efficient than KH in the WTP–WTA context, so it is superior to KH for the same reason that KH is superior to other rules.

Finally where rights are partly but incompletely specified, it turns out that both the WTP and the WTA should be considered in the assignment of rights and that the weight that should be given to each depends on the degree of psychological ownership of the parties.

Chapter 5 introduces and illustrates the important issue of economic standing – that is, who has standing to have his or her values counted in a benefit–cost context. Examples are found in the criminal law of theft, in abortion rights, and in determining whether harm can occur when it is unknown by those injured. The analysis of abortion rights illustrates particularly the important role that the regard for others often plays in determining efficiency. The case examples from the law discuss the efficiency of allowing an injured trespasser to sue the owner of the land where he was injured, and the efficiency of allowing parties to recover the sentimental value of property as part of their damages under the law of remedies.

In Chapter 6 I consider missing values and the regard for others. Examples of values thought to be missing from economic efficiency, such as personal integrity, are instead found to reside in KHZ. The discount-rate paradox, by which economic efficiency is thought to ignore harm (or benefits) to those experiencing it far into the future, and which is used to argue against the use of discount rates, is found to be better understood as arising from a failure to include the moral sentiments of present generations for those in the future.

Of course, the most important missing value in most economic studies is the value of fair income distribution and the fact of compensation. In KHZ these are included as economic goods. A technique developed by Harberger is presented as a method for valuing income distribution changes. The argument for inclusion of these goods lies in the regard for others. Others (those not directly affected) will have a WTP or WTA for these goods. In part this regard arises from what is felt to be fair. An application of the role of fairness is made in the form of the Happyville example created by Portney.

In Chapter 6 I also return to the issue of whether sentimental value is a missing value and provide some empirical estimates of its importance and its nature, in the context of Christmas giving. Another example of the application of missing values and the regard for others is found by commenting on the debate about KH between Dworkin and Posner, in which the test of the moral value of the theory is held to be (at least by Dworkin) whether or not the test condemns slavery. It is shown that the discussion misdefines efficiency as well as misunderstands the basis for the justification for an efficiency example.

Chapter 7 is a modification and extension of an article of Howard McCurdy and myself published in the *Journal of Policy Analysis and Management*. It shows that when transactions costs are included in a test for efficiency – as they must be in KHZ – the concepts of market failure and of externalities are rendered incoherent. Rather, there is no general rule for determining proper government intervention other than the general KHZ rule of comparing the benefits and costs of government intervention. The emphasis should be instead on the government's advantage of using coercion to reduce transactions costs. The examples provided there include those of the lighthouse, the use of bees for pollination, and land tenancy, all derived from the work of Coase, Cheung and Samuelson. The use of salt to de-ice roads is presented as an example of government non-market failure, as a result of the transactions costs of intra-agency coordination. Protection against theft is suggested as an example of efficient government intervention.

Chapters 8 and 9 deal with common law efficiency. Chapter 8 attempts to showed that the common law is better explained as a system to promote KHZ efficiency than as a system to promote KH efficiency. It considers examples from criminal law (rape), from contract law (exculpatory clause jurisprudence), and from the law of torts (contribution among negligent tortfeasors). It should be no surprise to hear the KHZ does a better job of explaining the direction and rationale of the common law.

Chapter 9 considers the questions of when and why the common law is efficient. This chapter was the most fun to write. Look at the range of topics considered: economic analysis of dueling; cannibalism; the California Gold Rush; racism; and antitrust law. The argument is that when conditions are static, the admission into law of uncontentious norms is necessarily efficient. Because a big part of the common law is the process of giving legal force to social customs, this admission explains common law efficiency. When conditions change – and by conditions I mean technology, institutions or sentiments – then the common law has to change as well in order to be efficient. When the pace of change in conditions is sufficiently rapid, however, there are no uncontentious norms, so the question of when changes in the common law would be efficient may be unclear. The examples mainly illustrate inefficient law under changing conditions, but the antitrust example also shows how academic knowledge can help determine what is efficient.

So this is what I have done. My hope is that I have convinced the reader who has been patient enough to go through the arguments and demonstrations that the approach here is superior to the existing one. Of course, even if the virtues of the KHZ approach are as apparent to others as they are to me, and they may not be, it will take some time for them to be realized and for KHZ to become the new standard for project evaluation. I thank the reader for having given them a hearing.

NOTES

1. Zerbe and Graham (1999). This is an example of an application to an important environmental issue, the proposed removal of the dams on the lower Snake River.

2. *Vincent* v. *Lake Erie Transportation Co.*, 109 Minn. 456, 124 N.W. 221 (1910).
3. *Lorenzen* v. *Employees Retirement Plan of the Sperry & Hutchinson Co.*, 699 F. Supp. 1367 (E.D. Wis. 1988), rev'd 896 F.2d 228 (7th Cir. 1990).

References

Abbott, Frederick M. (1996), 'Review of "Product Standards for Internationally Integrated Goods Markets", by Alan O. Sykes', *American Journal of International Law* 90(January): 162–165.

Adamski, M. Patricia (1981), 'Contribution and Settlement in Multiparty Actions Under Rule 10b–5', *Iowa Law Review* 66: 533–573.

Alchain, Armen (1965), 'Some Economics of Property Rights', *Il Politico* 30: 816–829.

Allen, Anita (1992), 'Autonomy's Magic Wand: Abortion and Constitutional Interpretation', *Boston University Law Review* 72: 683.

Allen, Douglas (1991), 'What are Transaction Costs?' in Richard O. Zerbe and Victor P. Goldberg (eds), *Research in Law and Economics*, Greenwich: JAI Press, 14, pp. 1–18.

Allen, Douglas (1996), 'Transaction Costs', *Encyclopedia of Economics* 1: 893–926.

Allen, Douglas and D. Lueck (1992), 'Contract Choice in Modern Agriculture: Cash Rent versus Cropshare', *Journal of Law and Economics* 35(2): 397–426.

Anderson, Elizabeth (1993), *Value in Ethics and Economics*, Cambridge, MA: Harvard University Press.

Anderson, C. Leigh and Eugene Swimmer (1997), 'Some Empirical Evidence on Property Rights of First Peoples', *The Journal of Economic Behavior and Organization* 33(1): 1–22.

Anderson, Terry and P. J. Hill (1975), 'The Evolution of Property Rights: A Study of the American West', *Journal of Law and Economics* 18: 163.

Anderson, Terry and D. Leuck (1992), 'Land Tenure and Agriculture Productivity on Indian Reservations', *Journal of Law and Economics* 35(2): 427–455.

Armitage, Thomas (1985), 'Economic Efficiency as a Legal Norm', in Richard Zerbe (ed.), *Research in Law and Economics*, Greenwich: Jai Press, 7, pp. 1–27.

Aristotle (1949), 'The Nicomachean Ethics', in Lon Fuller (ed.), *The Problems of Jurisprudence*, Brooklyn: Foundation Press.

Aristotle (1949), 'Politics', in Lon Fuller (ed.), *The Problems of Jurisprudence*, Brooklyn: Foundation Press.

Arrow, Kenneth (1951), 'Little's Critique of Welfare Economics', *American Economic Review* 41(5): 923–934.

Arrow, Kenneth J. (1969), 'The Organization of Economic Activity: Issues Pertinent to the Choice of Market versus Nonmarket Allocation', in *Joint Economic Committee, The Analysis and Evaluation of Public Expenditures: The PPB System*, 91st Congress, 1st session.

Arrow, Kenneth J. (1973), 'Social Responsibility and Economic Efficiency', *Public Policy* 21: 303–317.

Arrow, Kenneth J., M. Cropper, G. Eads, R. Hahn, L. Lave, R. Noll, P. Portney, M. Russell, R. Schmalensee, V. Smith and R. Stavins (1996), *Benefit–Cost Analysis in Environmental, Health, and Safety Regulation: A Statement of Principles*, Washington, DC: American Enterprise Institute.

Arrow, Kenneth J., R. Solow, P. Portney, E. E. Leamer, R. Radner and H. Schuman (1993), *Report on the National Panel on Contingent Valuation*, Federal Regulations, January 15, 58(10): 4603, 4601–4614.

Atiyah, P. S. (1979), *The Rise and Fall of Freedom of Contract*, New York: Oxford University Press.

Babbie, Earl (1989), *The Practice of Social Research*, 5th edition, Belmont: Wadsworth Publishing.

Baker, Edwin C. (1980), 'Starting Points in the Economic Analysis of Law', *Hofstra Law Review* 8: 939.

Balkin, J. M. (1987), 'Too Good to be True: The Positive Economic Theory of Law', *Columbia Law Review* 87: 1447–1489.

Baron, Jane and J. Dunoff (1996), 'Against Market Rationality: Moral Critiques of Economic Analysis in Legal Theory', *Cardozo Law Review* 17(January): 431–496.

Barzel, Yoram (1985), 'Transaction Costs: Are They Just Costs?', *Journal of Institutional and Theoretical Economics* 141(March): 4–16.

Baumol, William J. (1979), 'Quasi Optimality: The Price We Must Pay for a Price System', *Journal of Political Economy* 87(June): 578–599.

Baumol, William J. and W. E. Oates (1975), *The Theory of Environmental Policy*, Englewood Cliffs, NJ: Prentice Hall.

Beck, Robert J. (1995), *Refugees in Inter-War Europe: The Emergence of a Regime*, Oxford: Clarendon Press.

Becker, Gary (1968), 'Crime and Punishment: An Economic Approach', *Journal of Political Economy* 76(2): 169–217.

Becker, Gary (1976), *The Economic Approach to Human Behavior*, Chicago: University of Chicago.

Beutel, F. (1957), *Some Potentialities of Experimental Jurisprudence as a New Branch of Social Science*, Lincoln: University of Nebraska.

Black, Duncan (1969), 'On Arrow's Impossibility Theorem', *The Journal of Law and Economics* 12(2): 227–248.

Black's Law Dictionary (1990), Bryan A. Garner (ed.), Minneapolis: West Group.

Blackman, Sean G. (1995), 'An Analysis of Aider and Abettor Liability under Section 10 (b) of the Securities Exchange Act of 1934: *Central Bank of Denver* v. *First Interstate Bank of Denver*', *Connecticut Law Review* 27(Summer): 1323–1376.

Blackstone, William (1900), *Commentaries on the Laws of England*, Christian, Chitty, Lee, Hovenlew and Ryland (eds), vol. I. 19th edition, Philadelphia: J. B. Lippincott.

Blanck, David (1996), 'The Appearance of Justice Revisited', *Journal of Criminal Law and Criminology* 86: 887–927.

Blum, Walter and H. Kalven, Jr. (1965), *Public Law Perspectives on a Private Law Problem: Auto Compensation Plans*, Boston: Little, Brown.

Boadway, Robin W. and N. Bruce (1984), *Welfare Economics*, New York: Basil Blackwell.

Boadway, Robin W. and D. W. Wildasin (1984), *Public Sector Economics*, 2nd edition, Oxford: Basil Blackwell.

Boardman, Anthony E., D. H. Greenberg, A. R. Vining and D. L. Weimer (1996), *Cost–Benefit Analysis: Concepts and Practice*, Upper Saddle River: Prentice Hall.

Bothwick, William (1776), *Remarks on British Antiquities*, Edinburgh: William Gordon.

Boyer, Allen D. (1986), 'Crime, Cannibalism and Joseph Conrad: The Influence of *Regima* v. *Dudley and Stephens* on Lord Jim', *Loyola of Los Angeles Law Review* 20(1): 9–34.

Bracton, Henry de (1915–1941), *De Legibus Et Consuetudinbus Angliae*, G. E. Woodbine (ed.), 4 vols, Cambridge, MA: Harvard University Press.

Brodie, Fawn M. (1967), *The Devil Drives*, New York: W. W. Norton.

Broome, John (1991), 'Utility', *Economics and Philosophy* 7(1): 1–12.

Browning, Edgar K. and J. M. Browning (1992), *Microeconomic Theory and Applications*, 4th edition, New York: Harper Collins.

Brownmiller, Susan (1975), *Against Our Will: Men, Women, and Rape*, New York: Simon & Schuster.

Bruce, Christopher J. (1984), 'Testing the Hypothesis of Common Law Efficiency: The Doctrine of Informed Consent', *Research in Law and Economics* 6: 227–265.

Bruce, Neil and R. G. Harris (1982), 'Cost–Benefit Criteria and the Compensation Principle in Evaluating Small Projects', *Journal of Political Economy* 90: 755–775.

Buchanan, Allen (1985), *Ethics, Efficiency, and the Market*, Totowa: Rowman & Allanheld.

Buchanan, James (1974), 'Good Economics – Bad Law', *Virginia Law Review* 60: 483–492.

Buchanan, James (1975), 'Comments on the Independent Judiciary in an Interest Group Perspective', *The Journal of Law and Economics* 18(3): 903.

Byrns, Ralph T. and G. W. Stone (1992), *Microeconomics*, vol. XVI, 5th edition, Glenview: Scott.

Calabresi, Guido (1961), 'Some Thoughts on Risk Distribution and the Law of Torts', *Yale Law Journal* 70: 499–553.

Calabresi, Guido (1968), 'Transaction Costs, Resource Allocation, and Liability Rules: A Comment', *Journal of Law and Economics* 11: 67–73.

Calabresi, Guido (1983), *Tragic Choices*, Cambridge, MA: Harvard University Press.

Calabresi, Guido and D. Melamed (1972), 'Property Rules, Liability Rules, and Inalienability: One View of the Cathedral', *Harvard Law Review* 85(April): 1089–1128.

Calkins, Stephen (1997), 'An Enforcement Official's Reflections on Antitrust Class Actions', *Arizona Law Review* 39: 413.

Calleros, Charles (1994), *Legal Method and Writing*, vol. XII, 2nd edition, Boston: Little, Brown.

Calnan, Alan (1997), *Justice and Tort Law*, Durhan: Carolina Academic Press.

Calvert, Randall L. (1995), 'A Rational Choice Theory of Social Institutions: Cooperation, Coordination, and Communication', in Jeffrey Banks and Eric Hanushek (eds), *Modern Political Economy*, New York: Cambridge University Press.

Cavanaugh, Edward D. (1987), 'Contribution, Claim Reduction, and Individual Treble Damage Responsibility: Which Path to Reform of Antitrust Remedies?', *Vanderbilt Law Review* 40: 1277–1336.

Chamallas, Martha (1988), 'Consent, Equality, and the Legal Control of Sexual Conduct', *Southern California Law Review* 61: 777–862.

Cheal, David (1988), 'The Ritualization of Family Ties', *American Behavioural Scientist* 31(6, July–August): 632–644.

Cheung, Steven N. S. (1969), *The Theory of Share Tenancy*, Chicago: University of Chicago Press.

Cheung, Steven N. S. (1973), 'The Fable of the Bees: An Economic Investigation', *Journal of Law and Economics* 16(1): 11–33.

Cheung, Steven N. S. (1980), *The Myth of Social Cost*, San Francisco: Cato Institute.

Chichilnisky, Graciela (1997), 'What is Sustainable Development', *Land Economics* 73(4): 467–492.

Chipman, John (1987), 'Compensation Principle', in John Eatwell, Murrary Milgate and Peter Newman (eds), The New Palgrave: A Dictionary of Economics, vol. I, pp. 524–531.

Chipman, John and James C. Moore (1978), 'The New Welfare Economics 1939–1974', *International Economic Review* 19(3): 547–583.

Clark, William L. and W. L. Marshall (1967), *A Treatise on the Law of Crimes*, 7th edition, Mundelein: Callaghan.

Clarke, Arthur C. (1957), *The Deep Range*, New York: Harcourt Brace.

Coase, Ronald H. (1937), 'The Nature of the Firm', reprinted in R. Coase, *The Firm, the Market, and the Law*, Chicago: The University of Chicago Press, 1988.

Coase, Ronald H. (1960), 'The Problem of Social Cost', *Journal of Law and Economics* 3 (October): 1–44.

Coase, Ronald H. (1964), 'Discussion of "Direct Regulation and Market Performance in the American Economy", by Richard E. Caves, and "The Effectiveness of Economic Regulation: A Legal View", by Roger C. Cramton', *American Economic Review* 54(May): 194–197.

Coase, Ronald H. (1974), 'The Lighthouse in Economics', *Journal of Law and Economics* 17(October): 357–376.

Coase, Ronald H. (1988), *The Firm, the Market, and the Law*, Chicago: The University of Chicago Press.

Cohen, David and J. L. Knetsch (1992), 'Judicial Choice and Disparities Between Measures of Economic Values', *Osgoode Hall Law Journal* 30: 737.

Coleman, Jules (1980), 'Efficiency, Utility, and Wealth Maximization', *Hofstra Law Review* 8(3): 509–551.

Coleman, Jules (1982), 'The Economic Analysis of Law', in J. Ronald Pennock and John W. Chapman (eds), *Ethics, Economics, and the Law*, New York: New York University Press.

Coleman, Jules (1988), 'Crimes, Kickers and Transaction Structures', *Markets, Morals and the Law*, New York: Cambridge University Press.

Comment (1968), 'The Allocation of Loss Among Tortfeasors', *Southern California Law Review* 41: 728.

Confucius (1993), *The Analects of Confucius*, Raymond Dawson (trans.) New York: Oxford University Press.

Cook, Fay (1979), *Who Should Be Helped: Public Support for Social Services*, Beverly Hills: Sage Publications.

Cook, Fay and E. Barrett (1992), *Support for the American Welfare State: The Views of Congress and the Public*, New York: Columbia University Press.

Cooter, Robert D. (1996), 'Decentralized Law for a Complex Economy', *University of Pennsylvania Law Review* 144: 1643.

Cooter, Robert D. and T. Ulen (1988), *Law and Economics*, New York: Harper Collins.

Cooter, Robert D. and T. Ulen (1997), *Law and Economics*, 2nd edition, New York: Harper Collins.

Coursey, Donald, J., L. Hovis and W. D. Schulze (1987), 'The Disparity between Willingness to Accept and Willingness to Pay Measures of Value', *The Quarterly Journal of Economics* 102(3): 679–690.

Coursey, Donald and R. D. Roberts (1992), 'Aggregation and the Contingent Valuation Method for Evaluating Environmental Amenities', Working Paper, Olin School of Business, Washington University, St. Louis, Missouri.

Cunningham, Whitney (1992), 'Testing Posner's Strong Theory of Wealth Maximization', *Georgetown Law Journal* 81: 141–166.

Dahlman, Carl J. (1979), 'The Problem of Externality', *Journal of Law and Economics* 22(1): 141–162.

Davis, John (1902), *Historical Sketch of the Mining Law in California*, Los Angeles: Commercial Printing House.

Dawson, John P., W. B. Harvey and S. Henderson (1993), *Cases and Comment on Contracts*, 6th edition, Westbury: Foundation Press.

De Alessi, Louis (1996), 'Error and Bias in Benefit–Cost Analysis: HUD's Case for the Wind Rule', *Cato Journal* 16(Spring/Summer): 129–147.

Demsetz, Harold (1967), 'Toward a Theory of Property Rights', *American Economic Review* 62(May): 347.

Des Jarlais, Don, S. Deren and D. Lipton (1981), 'Cost-Effectiveness Studies in the Evaluation of Substance Abuse Treatment', in J. Lowinson and P. Ruiz (eds), *Substance Abuse: Clinical Problems and Perspectives*, Baltimore: Williams and Wilkins, pp. 806–816.

Devlin, Patrick (1965), *The Enforcement of Morals*, New York: Oxford University Press.

Di Cola, Elisabeth A. (1992), 'Fairness and Efficiency: Allowing Contribution under ERISA', *California Law Review* 80(6): 1543–1594.

Dressler, Joshua (1987), *Understanding Criminal Law*, New York: M. Bender.

Dripps, Donald A. (1992), 'Beyond Rape: An Essay on the Difference Between the Presence of Force and the Absence of Consent', *Columbia Law Review* 92: 1780–1809.

Dunford, Richard W., F. R. Johnson, R.A. Sandefur and E. S. West (1997), 'Whose Losses Count in Natural Resources Damages?', *Contemporary Economic Policy* 15(4): 77(11).

Duxbury, Neil (1995), 'Law Markets and Valuation', *Brooklyn Law Review* 61: 657–701.

Dworkin, Ronald (1980), 'Is Wealth a Value?', *Journal of Legal Studies* 9: 191.

Dworkin, Ronald (1986), *Law's Empire*, Cambridge: Belknap Press.

Easterbrook, Frank H., W. M. Landes and Richard A. Posner (1980), 'Contribution Among Antitrust Defendants: A Legal and Economic Analysis', *Journal of Law and Economics* 23(2): 331–370.

Easterling, Douglas (1992), 'Fair Rules for Siting a High-Level Nuclear Waste Repository', *Journal of Policy Analysis and Management* 11: 442.

Eatwell, John, M. Murray and P. Newman (ed.) (1987), *The New Palgrave: A Dictionary of Economics*, London: Macmillan.

Eggen, Jean Macchiaroli (1995), 'Understanding State Contribution Laws and Their Effect on the Settlement of Mass Tort Actions', *Texas Law Review* 73: 1701–1777.

Eggertsson, Thrainn (1990), *Economic Behavior and Institutions*, Cambridge: Cambridge University Press.

Ehrenburg, Ronald G. and R. S. Smith (1994), *Modern Labor Economics*, Glenview: Scott.

Eisenberg, Melvin A. (1993), *Gilbert Law Summaries: Contracts*, Gardena: Harcourt Brace Jovanovich Legal and Professional Publications.

Ellickson, Robert (1987), 'A Critique of Economic and Sociological Theories of Social Control', *Journal of Legal Studies* 16: 67.

Ellickson, Robert (1991), *Order Without Law: How Neighbors Settle Disputes*, Cambridge, MA: Harvard University Press.

Ellis, Dorsey D., Jr. (1983), 'An Economic Theory of Intentional Torts: A Comment', *International Review of Law and Economics* 3: 45–57.

Englard, Izhaz (1993), *The Philosophy of Tort Law*, Brookfield: Dartmouth.

Epstein, Richard A. (1997), 'A Clear View of the Cathedral: The Dominance of Property Rights', *Yale Law Journal* 106: 2091–2120.

Estin, Ann Laquer (1995), 'Economics and the Problems of Divorce', *University of Chicago Law School Roundtable* 2: 517–597.

Estrich, Susan (1987), *Real Rape*, Cambridge, MA: Harvard University Press.

Everson, George (1919), 'The Human Element of Justice', *Journal of Criminal Law and Criminology* 10: 90.

Faith, Roger L. and Robert D. Tollison (1983), 'The Pricing of Surrogate Crime and Law Enforcement', *Journal of Legal Studies* 12: 401–411.

Farnsworth, E. Allen (1982), *Contracts*, 1st edition, Boston: Little, Brown.

Farnsworth, E. Allen (1990), *Contracts*, 2nd edition, Boston: Little, Brown.

Farrell, Joseph (1987), 'Information and the Coase Theorem', *Journal of Economic Perspectives* 1(1): 113–129.

Faulhaber, Gerald R. (1987), 'Comment, The Role of Government in a Mixed Economy: Reprise', *Journal of Policy Analysis and Management* 6(Summer): 557–561.

Feeny, David, S. Hanna and A. F. McEvoy (1996), 'Questioning the Assumptions of the Tragedy of the Commons: Model of Fisheries', *Land Economics* 72(2): 187–205.

Fischel, William (1996), *Regulatory Takings: Law, Economics and Politics*, Cambridge, MA: Harvard University Press.

Flatt, Victor (1994), 'The Human Environment of the Mind: Correcting NEPA Implementation by Treating Environmental Philosophy and Environmental Risk Allocation as Environmental Values under NEPA, *Hastings Law Journal* 46(1): 85–123.

Fleming, John G. (1983), *The Law of Torts*, 6th edition, Sydney: Law Book Co.

Fogel, Robert and S. Engerman (1974), *Time on the Cross: The Economics of America Negro Slavery*, Boston: Little, Brown.

Ford, Rebecca L. (1993), 'The Lawyer's Bookshelf', *New York Law Journal* 209: 108.

Frank, Robert H. (2000), *Microeconomics and Behavior*, 4th edition, Boston: Irwin McGraw-Hill.

Frankel, Tamar (1995), 'Foreword, Symposium, A Recipe for Effecting Institutional Changes to Achieve Privatization', *Boston University International Law Journal* 13(Fall): 295–311.

Fried, Charles (1978), *Right and Wrong*, Cambridge, MA: Harvard University Press.

Friedman, Lawrence (1973), *A History of American Law*, New York: Simon & Schuster.

Friedman, Lee (1984), *Microeconomic Policy Analysis*, New York: McGraw-Hill.

Friedman, Milton (1953), The Methodology of Positive Economics', *Essays in Positive Economics*, Chicago: University of Chicago Press.

Friedman, Wolfgang (1959), *Law in a Changing Society*, London: Stevens & Sons, Limited.

Gaulding, Jill (1995), 'Race, Sex, and Genetic Discrimination in Insurance Markets: What's Fair?', *Cornell Law Review* 80(September): 1646–1694.

Giancoli, Douglass (1991), *Physics*, 3rd edition, Englewood Cliffs: Prentice Hall.

Gibbon, Edward (1899), *Decline and Fall of the Roman Empire*, New York: P. F. Collier & Son.

Ginsburg, Jane C. (1995), 'Putting Cars on the "Information Superhighway": Authors, Exploiters, and Copyright in Cyberspace', *Columbia Law Review* 95(October): 1466–1499.

Glick, Henry R. (1990), *Courts in American Politics*, New York: McGraw-Hill.

Goldberg, Victor (1979), 'Protecting the Right to be Served by Public Utilities', *Research in Law and Economics* 1: 145–156.

Goodman, John (1978), 'An Economic Theory of the Evolution of the Common Law', *Journal of Legal Studies* 7: 393.

Gordon, H. S. (1954), 'The Economic Theory of a Common Property Resource: The Fishery', *Journal of Political Economy* 62(April): 124–142.

Gordon, Margaret T. and Stephanie Riger (1991), *The Female Fear: The Social Cost of Rape*, New York: Free Press.

Gorman, W. M. (1953), 'Community Preference Fields', *Econometrica* 21(1): 63–80.

Gray, John Chipman (1909), *The Nature and Sources of the Law*, New York: Columbia University Press.

Gregory, Charles (1938), 'Contribution Among Tortfeasors: A Uniform Practice', *Wisconsin Law Review*: 364–401.

Greenawalt, Kent (1995), 'Legal Enforcement of Morality', *Journal of Criminal Law and Criminology* 85: 710–725.

Grimaldi, James (1999), 'Microsoft Trial: Mediator, Lawyers Work Out Details for Next Meeting', *Seattle Times*, December 1, p. F1.

Hammond, Peter (1985), 'Welfare Economics', in George Feiwel (ed.), *Issues in Contemporary Microeconomics and Welfare*, New York: Macmillan.

Hanneman, Michael W. (1991), 'Willingness to Pay and Willingness to Accept: How Much Can They Differ?', *American Economic Review* 61: 635.

Harberger, Arnold (1971), 'Three Basic Postulates For Applied Welfare Economics: An Interpretative Essay', *Journal of Economic Literature* 9: 785.

Harberger, Arnold (1978), 'On the Use of Distributional Weights in Social Cost–Benefit Analysis', *Journal of Political Economy* 86: 87.

Hardin, Garrett (1968), 'The Tragedy of the Commons', *Science* 162 (December 13): 1243–1248.

Hardin, Garrett (1978), 'Political Requirements for Preserving Our Common Heritage', in H. P. Bokaw (ed.), *Wildlife and America*, Washington, DC: Council on Environmental Quality, pp. 310–317.

Harrod, Roy F. (1938), 'Scope and Method of Economics', *Economic Journal* 48: 383.

Heal, Geoffrey H. (1998), *Valuing the Future: Economic Theory and Sustainability*, New York: Columbia University Press.

Hernandez, Michael V. (1997), 'Cost Recovery or Contribution', *Harvard Environmental Law Review* 21(1): 83–136.

Hewins, W. A. S. (1911), 'Economy', *Encyclopedia Britannica* 11: 898–900.

Heyne, Paul (1988), 'The Foundations of Law and Economics', in Richard O. Zerbe, Jr. (ed.), *Research in Law and Economics*, Greenwich: Jai Press, 11, pp. 53–71.

Hicks, John R. (1939), 'The Foundations of Welfare Economics', *Economic Journal* 49: 696.

Hicks, John R. (1943), 'The Four Consumer Surpluses', *Review of Economic Studies* 11(1): 31–41.

Higgenbotham, Ernest R. and K. B. Wiggins (1990), 'Contribution and

Indemnity', *ALI-ABA Course of Study, Trial Evidence, Civil Practice and Effective Litigation Techniques* C491: 697.

Higgins, M. (1997), 'Is Capital Punishment for Killers Only', *ABA Journal* 83: 30.

Hill, Candace Grant (1985), 'Note, Public Employees and Private Conduct: Cohabitation and the Vagueness of Immortality', *Journal of Family Law* 23: 111–132.

Hogue, Arthur (1966), *Origins of the Common Law*, Indianapolis: Liberty Press.

Holmes, Oliver Wendell (1881), *The Common Law*, Boston: Little, Brown.

Honoré, A. M. (1984), 'Property Title and Redistribution' in John Arthur and William Shaw (eds), *Readings In Philosophy of Law*, Englewood Cliffs: Prentice Hall.

Hotelling, H. (1938), 'The General Welfare in Relation to Problems of Taxation and of Railway and Utility Rates', *Econometrica* 6(July): 242–269.

Hovenkamp, Herbert (1991), 'Legal Policy and The Endowment Effect', *Journal of Legal Studies* 20: 225–234.

Hurst, James Willard (1950), *The Growth of American Law*, Boston: Little, Brown.

Hyman, David N. (1990), *Public Finance: A Contemporary Application of Theory to Policy*, Chicago: Dryden Press.

Jackson, Donald (1980), *Gold Dust*, New York: Alfred A. Knopf.

James, Fleming (1941), 'Contribution Among Joint Tortfeasors: A Pragmatic Criticism', *Harvard Law Review* 54: 1156–1183.

Johnsen, D. Bruce (1986), 'Wealth is Value', *Journal of Legal Studies* 15: 263–288.

Jordon, Karen (1995), 'Managed Competition and Limited Choice of Providers', *Arizona State Law Journal* 27(Fall): 875–952.

Jost, Timothy S. (1995), 'Oversight of the Quality of Medical Care: Regulation, Management, or the Market?', *Arizona Law Review* 37(3): 825–68.

Just, Richard, Darrell Hueth and Andrew Schmitz (1982), *Applied Welfare Economics and Public Policy*, Englewood Cliffs: Prentice Hall.

Kadish, Sanford H. and Stephen J. Schulhofer (1995), *Criminal Law and Its Processes*, 6th edition, Boston: Little, Brown.

Kahneman, Daniel and Amos Tversky (1979), 'Prospect Theory: An Analysis of Decision under Uncertainty', *Econometrica* 47(2): 263–291.

Kahneman, Daniel, J. Knetsch, and R. Thaler (1991), 'Anomalies: The Endowment Effect, Loss Aversion, and Status Quo Bias', *Journal of Economic Perspectives* 5(1): 193–206.

Kahneman, Daniel and C. Varey (1991), 'Notes on the Psychology of Utility', in Jon Elster and John Roemer (eds), *Interpersonal Comparisons of Well-Being*. New York: Cambridge University Press.

Kaldor, Nicholas (1939), 'Welfare Propositions in Economics and Inter-Personal Comparisons of Utility', *Economic Journal* 49: 549.

Kang, John (1995), 'Perpetuating Market Misallocations in Health Care Through Employer Health Insurance Mandates', *The American Journal of Tax Policy* 12(Fall): 513–547.

Kanigel, Robert (1997), *The One Best Way: Frederick Winslow Taylor and the Enigma of Efficiency*, New York: Viking.

Katz, Avery (1996), 'Positivism and the Separation of Law and Economics', *Michigan Law Review* 94(7): 2229–2269.

Katz, Michael and Harvey S. Rosen (1998), *Microeconomics*, 3rd edition, Boston: McGraw Hill.

Kaufman, C. (1980), 'The Scientific Method in Legal Thought: Legal Realism and the Fourteen Principles of Justice', *St. Mary's Law Journal* 12: 77–112.

Keeton *et al.* (1984), *Prosser and Keaton on the Law of Torts*, 5th edition, St. Paul: West Publishing Co.

Kelman, Steven (1981), 'Cost–Benefit Analysis: An Ethical Critique', *Regulation* 5(1): 33–40.

Kennedy, Duncan (1981), 'Cost–Benefit Analysis of Entitlement Problems: A Critique', *Stanford Law Review* 33: 387–446.

Kitch, Edmund W. (1995), 'The Theory and Practice of Securities Disclosure', *Brooklyn Law Review* 61(Fall): 763–888.

Knetsch, Jack L. (1994), 'Environmental Valuation: Some Problems of Wrong Questions and Misleading Answers', *Environmental Values* 3: 351.

Knetsch, Jack L. (1995), 'Assumptions, Behavior Findings, and Policy Analysis', *Journal of Policy Analysis and Management* 14(1): 68–78.

Knetsch, Jack L. (1997), 'Reference States, Fairness, and Choice of Measure to Value Environmental Changes', in Max H. Bazeman *et al.* (eds), *Environment, Ethics and Behavior: The Psychology of Environmental Valuation and Degradation*, San Francisco: The New Lexington Press.

Kornhauser, Lewis A. and Richard L. Revesz (1989), 'Sharing Damages Among Multiple Tortfeasors', *Yale Law Journal* 98: 831–884.

Kovacic, William (1995), 'Designing and Implementing Competition and Consumer Protection Reforms in Transitional Economics', *DePaul Law Review* 44(Summer): 1197–1224.

Krepps, David (1990), *A Course in Microeconomic Theory*, Princeton: Princeton University.

Kuhn, Thomas K. (1970), *The Structure of Scientific Revolutions*, 2nd edition, Chicago: University of Chicago Press.

Kunreuther, Howard and Douglas Easterling (1992), 'Are Risk–Benefit Tradeoffs Possible in Siting Hazardous Facilities?', *American Economic Review* 80(2): 252–256.

Kuperberg, Mark and C. Beitz (eds) (1983), *Law, Economics, and Philosophy*, vol. III, Totowa: Rowman & Allanheld.

Kuznets, C. (1948), 'On the Valuation of Social Income – Reflections on Professor Hicks' Article', *Economic*, N.S. 15(February): 1–16.

Landa, Janet, T. (1994), *Trust, Ethnicity, and Identity: Beyond the New Institutional Economics of Ethnic Trading Networks, Contract Law, and Gift-Exchange*, Ann Arbor: University of Michigan Press.

Lande, Robert H. and R. O. Zerbe, Jr. (1996), 'Anticonsumer Effects of Union Mergers: An Antitrust Solution', *Duke Law Journal* 46(2): 197–239.

Landes, William and R. Posner (1975), 'The Independent Judiciary in an Interest Group Perspective', *The Journal of Law and Economics* 18: 875.

Landes, William and R. Posner (1980), 'Joint and Multiple Tortfeasors, an Economic Analysis', *Journal of Legal Studies* 9(3): 517–555.

Landes, William and R. Posner (1987), *The Economic Structure of Tort Law*, Cambridge, MA: Harvard University Press.

Langbein, John (1977), *Torture and the Law of Proof: Europe and England in the Ancien Regime*, Chicago: University of Chicago Press.

Larson, Jane E. (1995), 'Free Markets Deep in the Heart of Texas', *Georgetown Law Journal* 84(December): 179–260.

Lec, Stanislaw J. (1962), *Unkempt Thoughts*, Jacek Galazka (trans.), New York: St Martin's Press.

Leffler, Keith (1978), 'Physician Licensure: Competition and Monopoly in American Medicine', *Journal of Law and Economics* 21(1): 165–186.

Leflar, Robert A. (1932), 'Contribution and Indemnity between Tortfeasors', *University of Pennsylvania Law Review* 81: 130.

Lerner, Abba (1944), *The Economics of Control*, New York: Macmillan.

Leshy, John D. (1987), *The Mining Law: A Study in Perpetual Motion*, Washington, DC: Resources for the Future.

Lesser, Jonathan and Richard O. Zerbe (1995), 'What Economics Can Contribute to the Sustainability Debate', *Contemporary Economic Problems* 13(3): 88–100.

Lesser, Jonathan, D. Dodds and Richard O. Zerbe (1997), *Environmental Economics and Policy*, Reading: Addison-Wesley.

Lesser, Jon and R. O. Zerbe Jr. (1998), 'A Practitioner's Guide to Benefit Cost Analysis', in Fred Thompson and Mark Green (eds), *The Handbook of Public Finance*, New York: Marcel Drekker.

Levmore, Saul (1992), 'Irreversibility and the Law: The Size of Firms and Other Organizations', *Journal of Corporate Law* 18: 333.

Letsou, Peter (1996), 'The Scope of Section 12(2) of the Securities Act of 1933: A Legal and Economic Analysis', *Emory Law Journal* 45(Winter): 95–152.

Levy, Daniel and D. Friedman (1994), 'The Revenge of the Redwoods? Reconsidering Property Rights and the Economic Allocation of Natural Resources', *University of Chicago Law Review* 61: 493.

Lind, Robert (1999), 'Analysis for Intergenerational Decisionmaking', in Paul Portney and John P. Weyant (eds), *Discounting and Intergenerational Equity*, Washington, DC: Resources for the Future, pp. 173–180.

Linder, Marc (1995), 'I Gave My Employer a Chicken that Had No Bone: Joint Firm–State Responsibility for Line-Speed-Related Occupational Injuries', *Case Western Reserve Law Review* 46(1): 33–143.

List, John A. and Shogren, Jason F. (1988), 'The Deadweight Loss of Christmas: Comment', *American Economics Review* 88(5): 1350–1355.

Little, Ian M. A. (1957[1950]), *A Critique of Welfare Economics*, 2nd edition, Oxford: Oxford University Press.

Locke, John (1962), 'Two Treaties of Government', in Ernest Baker (ed.), *Social Contract*, New York: Oxford University Press.

Loomes, G. and R. Sugden (1983), 'A Rationale for Preference Reversals', *American Economic Review*, 73(3): 428–432.

Loomis, John (1995), 'Measuring the Benefits of Removing Dams and Restoring the Elwha River: Results of a Contingent Valuation Survey', Working Paper, Department of Agricultural Resource Economics, Colorado State University, Fort Collins, Co.

Lothrup, Robert C. (1986), 'The Misplaced Role of Cost–Benefit Analysis in Columbia Basin Fishery', *Environmental Law* 16: 517.

Lowi, Theodore J. (1992), 'The State in Political Science: How We Become What We Study', *American Political Science Review* 86(March): 1–7.

Lumley, Sarah (1997), 'The Environment and the Ethics of Discounting: An Empirical Analysis', *Ecological Economics* 20: 71–82.

MacDevitt, E. O. (1884), *Land Cases, Being a Collection of Reports of Decisions Under the Irish Land Acts since the Passing of the Land Law (Ireland) Act, 1881 With Other Cases Now Reported For the First Time*, Dublin: Alex. Thom & Co.

MacRae, Duncan and J. A. Wilde (1985), *Policy Analysis for Public Decisions*, Lanham: University Press of America.

Maitland, F. W. and F. C. Montagu (1915), *Sketch Of English Legal History*, J. F. Colby (ed.), NewYork: Putnam.

Maitland, F. W. and F. Pollock (1968), *The History of English Law Before the Time of Edward I*, London: Cambridge University Press.

Malamut, Michael (1993), 'Proposal for Revision of Archaic Statutes Implicating Private Consensual Noncommercial Adult Sexual Conduct', *Law and Sexuality* 3: 45–126.

Mallin, George (1967), 'In Warm Blood: Some Historical and Procedural

Aspects of *Regina* v. *Dudley and Stephens*', *University of Chicago Law Review* 34: 387–407.

Malloy, Robin (1992), 'Letters From The Longhouse: Law, Economics and Native American Values', *Wisconsin Law Review* 5: 1569.

Mansfield, Edwin (1994), *Microeconomics*, vol. XIII, 8th edition, New York: W. W. Norton.

Manzer, Nancy L. (1988), '1986 Tort Reform Legislation: A Systematic Evaluation of Caps on Damages and Limitations on Joint and Several Liability', *Cornell Law Review* 73(3): 628–652.

Marshall, A. (1890), *Principles of Economics*, 8th edition 1920, London: Macmillan.

Mas-Colell, Andreu, M. Whinston and J. Green (1995), *Microeconomic Theory*, New York: Oxford University Press.

Massie, Robert (1991), *Dreadnought: Britain, Germany and the Coming of the Great War*, New York: Random House.

Mayr, Ernst (1997), *This Is Biology*, Cambridge, MA: Harvard University Press.

McCloskey, Donald (1982), *The Applied Theory of Price*, New York: Macmillan Publishing Company.

Meade, J. E. (1952), 'External Economies and Diseconomies in a Competitive Situation', *Economic Journal* 62(1): 54–67.

Medema, Steven G. (1994), 'Ronald Coase's Contributions and Major Themes', *History of Economic Ideas* 3: 15–60.

Medema, Steven G. and R. O. Zerbe, Jr. (1999a), 'The Coase Theorem', in S. Medema, G. Bouckaert and G. DeGeest (eds), *The Encyclopedia of Law and Economics*, Aldershot: Edward Elgar.

Medema, Steven G. and Richard O. Zerbe, Jr. (1999b), 'Educating Alice: Lessons from the Coase Theorem', forthcoming in *Research in Law and Economics* 19: 69–112.

Meeks, Thomas J. (1990), 'The Economics Efficiency and Equity of Abortion', *Economics and Philosophy* 6: 95.

Michelman, Frank (1967), 'Property, Utility and Fairness: Comments on the Ethical Foundations of "Just Compensation" Law', *Harvard Law Review* 80(6): 1165–1258.

Michelman, Frank (1979), 'A Comment on some Uses and Abuses of Economics in Law', *University of Chicago Law Review* (46): 307.

Miller, Charles W. (1991), *Stake Your Claim! The Tale of America's Enduring Mining Laws*, Tucson: Western Lore Press.

Minkler, Linse (1998), 'Government and The Willingness-to-Accept Measure pf Value', Working Paper, Center for Real Estate and Urban Economic Studies, University of Connecticut.

Mishan, Ezra J. (1952), 'The Principle of Compensation Reconsidered', *The Journal of Political Economy* 60(4): 312–322.

Mishan, Ezra J. (1971), *Cost–Benefit Analysis*, London: George Allen Unwin.

Mishan, Ezra J. (1981), *Introduction to Normative Economics*, New York: Oxford University Press.

Mishan, Ezra J. (1982), *Cost–Benefit Analysis*, 3rd edition, London: George Allen & Unwin.

Morrison, E. R. (1998), 'Judicial Review of Discount Rates used in Regulatory Cost–Benefit Analysis', *University of Chicago Law Review*, Fall, 65(4): 1333–1369.

Myers, A. R. (1971), *England in the Late Middle Ages*, Baltimore: Penguin Books.

Neilson, George (1891), *Trial By Combat*, New York: Macmillan.

Nelson, Julie (1993), 'Persuasion and Economic Efficiency', *Economics and Philosophy* 9: 229.

Nelson, Richard (1987), 'Roles of Government in a Mixed Economy', *Journal of Policy Analysis and Management* 6(Summer): 541–557.

Nietzsche, Friederich (1968), 'Thus Spoke Zarathustra', in Walter Kaufmann (ed.), New York: Viking.

North, Douglas (1981), *Structure and Change in Economic History*, New York: W. W. Norton & Co.

North, Douglas and R. P. Thomas (1973), *The Rise of the Western World: A New Economic History*, Cambridge: Cambridge University Press.

Nozick, Robert (1974), *Anarchy, State and Utopia*, New York: Basic Books.

Okun, A. (1975), *Equality and Efficiency: The Big Tradeoff*, Washington, DC: The Brookings Institute.

Ostrom, Elinor (1990), *Governing the Commons*, Cambridge: Cambridge University Press.

Owen, David (1996), 'Interfaces and Interoperability in *Lotis* v. *Borland*: A Market-Oriented Approach to the Fair Use Doctrine', *Fordham Law Review* 64(April) 2381–2423.

Page, Talbot (1992), 'Environmental Existentialism', in Robert Contanza, Bryan Norton and Benjamin D. Haskell (eds), *Ecosystem Health*, Washington, DC: Island Press.

Pareto, Vilfredo (1896), *Cours D'Economie Politique*, vol. II, Lausanne: F. Rouge.

Parfit, Derek (1992), 'An Attack on the Social Discount Rate', in Claudia Mills (ed.), *Values and Public Policy*, Fort Worth: Harcourt Brace Jovanovich.

Parfit, Derek (1994), 'The Social Discount Rate', in R. E. Goodwin (ed.), *Politics of the Environment*, Aldershot: Edward Elgar.

Parsons, Wes (1983), 'Note: The Inefficient Common Law', *Yale Law Journal* 92(5): 862–887.

Pashigian, Peter (1995), *Price Theory and Applications*, New York: McGraw Hill.

Pearce, David, A. Markandya and E. Barbier (1989), *Blueprint for a Green Economy*, London: Earthscan Publications.

Pearce, David and R. Kerry Turner (1989), *Economics of Natural Resources and the Environment*, Baltimore: Johns Hopkins Press.

Pennington, Kenneth (1997), 'The Spirit of Legal History', *University of Chicago Law Review* 64: 1097.

Perkins, Robert L. (1959), *The First Hundred Years: An Informal History of Denver and the Rocky Mountain News*, Garden City: Doubleday.

Pigou, A. C. (1932[1920]), *The Economics of Welfare*, 4th edition, London: Macmillan.

Plater, Zgymunt, J. B. Robert, H. Abrams, W. Goldfarb and R. L. Graham (1998), *Environmental Law and Policy: Nature, Law, and Society*. St Paul: West Publishing.

Plucknett, Theodore (1956), *A Concise History of the Common Law*, 5th edition, London: Butterworth.

Polinsky, A. Mitchell (1974), 'Economic Analysis as a Potentially Defective Product: A Buyer's Guide to Posner's Economic Analysis of Law', *Harvard Law Review* 87(June): 1655–1681.

Polinsky, A. Mitchell (1980), 'Resolving Nuisance Disputes: The Simple Economics of Injunctive and Damage Remedies', *Stanford Law Review* 33: 1075–1112.

Polinsky, A. Mitchell (1983), *An Introduction to Law and Economics*, Boston: Little, Brown.

Polinsky, A. Mitchell (1989), *An Introduction to Law and Economics*, 2nd edition, Boston: Little, Brown.

Polinsky, A. Mitchell and Stephen Shavell (1979), 'The Optimal Tradeoff between Probability and Magnitude of Fines', *American Economic Review* 69(5): 880–891.

Polinsky, A. Mitchell and Stephen Shavell (1981), 'Contribution and Claim Reduction among Antitrust Defendants: An Economic Analysis', *Stanford Law Review* 33: 447–471.

Pollock, F. (1929), *First Book of Jurisprudence*, 6th edition, London: Macmillan.

Portney, Paul (1992), 'Trouble in Happyville', *Journal of Policy Analysis and Management* 11: 131–132.

Posner, Richard (1972), *Economic Analysis of Law*, 1st edition, Boston: Little, Brown.

Posner, Richard (1977), *Economic Analysis of Law*, 2nd edition, Boston: Little, Brown.

Posner, Richard (1979), 'Utilitarianism, Economics, and Judicial Theory', *Journal of Legal Studies* 8: 103.

Posner, Richard (1980), 'Ethical and Political Basis of Efficiency', *Hofstra Law Review* 8: 501.

Posner, Richard (1981a), *The Economics of Justice*, Cambridge, MA: Harvard University Press.

Posner, Richard (1981b), 'A Reply to some Recent Criticisms of the Efficiency Theory of the Common Law', *Hofstra Law Review* 9: 775.

Posner, Richard (1984), 'Wealth Maximazation and Judicial Decision Making', *International Review of Law and Economics* 4(2): 131–135.

Posner, Richard (1985a), 'Wealth Maximization Revisited', *Notre Dame Journal of Law, Ethics and Public Policy* 2: 85.

Posner, Richard (1985b), 'An Economic Theory of the Criminal Law', *Columbia Law Review* 85: 1193.

Posner, Richard (1986), *Economic Analysis of Law*, 3rd edition, Boston: Little, Brown.

Posner, Richard (1987a), 'The Justice of Economics', *Economic Delle Schelte Pubbliche* 1: 1.

Posner, Richard (1987b), 'The Justice of Economics', *Journal of Public Finance and Public Choice* 15: 23–24.

Posner, Richard (1990), *The Problems of Jurisprudence*, Cambridge, MA: Harvard University Press.

Posner, Richard (1992a), *Sex and Reason*, Cambridge, MA: Harvard University Press.

Posner, Richard (1992b), *Economic Analysis of Law*, 4th edition, Boston: Little, Brown & Company.

Post, Joseph (1995), 'A Lawyer's Ramble Down the Information Superhighway', *Fordham Law Review* 64(December) 782–793.

Priest, George (1977), 'The Common Law Process and the Selection of Efficient Rules', *Journal of Legal Studies* 6: 65.

Procaccia, Uriel (1996), 'Crafting a Corporate Code from Scratch', *Cardozo Law Review* 17(January): 629–645.

Purdy, Jedediah (1998), 'The Chicago Acid Bath: The Impoverished Logic of "Law and Economics"', *American Prospect* 0(36): 88.

Radin, Margaret J. (1987), 'Market Inalienability', *Harvard Law Review* 100: 1849–1937.

Radin, Margaret J. (1993), *Reinterpreting Property*, Chicago: University of Chicago Press.

Randall, Alan (1983), 'The Problem of Market Failure', *Natural Resources Journal* 23(1): 131–148.

Rawls, John (1971), *A Theory of Justice*, Cambridge: Belknap Press.

Raymond, Rossiter W. (1869), *The Mines of the West: A Report to the Secretary of the Treasury*, New York: J. B. Ford.

Reath, Theodore W. (1898), 'Contribution Between Persons Jointly Charged For Negligence – *Merrywether* v. *Nixan*', *Harvard Law Review* 12: 176.

Regan, Donald H. (1972), 'The Problem of Social Cost Revisited', *Journal of Law and Economics* 15: 427–437.

Robbins, Lionel (1932), *An Essay on the Nature and Significance of Economic Science*, London: Macmillan.

Robbins, Lionel (1938), 'Interpersonal Comparisons of Utility: A Comment', *Economic Journal* 48: 635.

Rose, Carol (1992), 'Giving, Trading, Thieving, and Trusting', *Florida Law Review* 44: 295.

Rose, Jonathan (1980), 'Contributions in Antitrust: Some Policy Considerations', *Antitrust Law Journal* 48: 1605–1607.

Roth, Theodore (1991), 'Law and Economics', *University of Chicago Magazine* 83(6): 28.

Rougeau, Vincent D. (1996), 'Rediscovering Usury: An Argument for Legal Controls on Credit Card Interest Rates', *University of Colorado Law Review* 67(Winter): 1–46.

Rubin, Paul (1977), 'Why is the Common Law Efficient?' *Journal of Legal Studies* 6: 51.

Ryan, John P. *et al.* (1980), *American Trial Judges: Their Work Styles and Performance*, New York: Free Press.

Sachs, Margaret V. (1994), 'Freedom of Contract: The Trojan Horse of Rule 10b–5', *Washington and Lee Law Review* 51: 879–924.

Sagoff, Mark (1988), *The Economy of the Earth*, New York: Cambridge University Press.

Salanie, Bernard (1997), *The Economics of Contract*, Cambridge, MA: MIT Press.

Samuelson, Paul A. (1950), 'Evaluations of Real Income', *Oxford Economic Papers* 2(1): 1.

Samuelson, Paul A. (1954), 'The Pure Theory of Public Expenditure', *Review of Economics and Statistics* 36(November): 386–389.

Samuelson, Paul A. (1964), *Economics: An Introductory Analysis*, 6th edition, New York: McGraw Hill.

Schell, G. Richard (1993), 'Contracts in the Modern Supreme Court', *California Law Review* 81: 431–529.

Schultze, William D., D. S. Brookshire and T. Sandler (1981), 'The Social Rate of Discount for Nuclear Waste Storage: Economics of Ethics', *Natural Resources Journal* 21: 811–832.

Schwartz, Gary T. (1979), 'Economics, Wealth Distribution, and Justice', *Wisconsin Law Review*: 799–813.

Schwartz, Stuart R. *et al.* (1979), 'Contribution in Private Actions under the Federal Antitrust Laws', *Southwestern Law Journal* 33: 779–822.

Schwartz, W., K. Baxter and D. Ryan (1984), 'The Duel: Can these Gentlemen be Acting Efficiently?', *Journal of Legal Studies* 13: 321.

Scitovszky, Tibor (1941), 'A Note on Welfare Propositions in Economics', *Review of Economic Studies* 9: 77–88.

Scott, Anthony (1955), 'The Fishery: The Objectives of Sole Ownership', *Journal of Political Economy* 63(April): 116–124.

Sen, Amartya (1982), 'Rights and Agency', *Philosophy and Public Affairs* 11(1): 1.

Sen, Amartya (1987), *The Standard of Living*, Cambridge: Cambridge University Press.

Sen, Amartya (1995), 'Rationality and Social Choice', *American Economic Review* 85(1): 1–24.

Sen, Amartya (1999), *Development as Freedom*, New York: Alfred Knopf.

Shavell, Steven (1981), 'A Note on Efficiency vs. Distributional Equity in Legal Rulemaking: Should Distributional Equity Matter Given Optimal Income Taxation?', *American Economic Review, Papers and Proceedings* 71: 414.

Shavell, Steven (1985), 'Criminal Law and the Optimal Use of Nonmonetary Sanctions as a Deterrent', *Columbia Law Review* 85: 1232–1262.

Shavell, Steven (1987), *Economic Analysis of Accident Law*, Cambridge, MA: Harvard University Press.

Shinn, Charles Howard (1947), *Mining Camps: A Study in American Frontier Government*, New York: Alfred Knopf.

Simpson, A. W. Brian (1984), *Cannibalism and the Common Law: The Story of the Tragic Last Voyage of the Mignonette and the Strange Legal Proceedings to which it gave Rise*, Chicago: University of Chicago Press.

Simpson, A.W. Brian (1990), *Cannibalism and the Common Law: The Story of the Tragic Last Voyage of the Mignonette and the Strange Legal Proceedings to which it gave Rise*, special edition, Birmingham, Alabama: Notable Trials Library.

Singher, Thomas C. (1995), 'Regulatory Derivatives: Does Transnational Regulatory Cooperation offer a Viable Alternative to Congressional Action?', *Fordham International Law Journal* 18(April): 1397–1474.

Skaggs, Neil T. and J. Lon Carlson (1996), *Microeconomics: Individual Choice and Its Consequences*, 2nd edition, Cambridge: Blackwell.

Slesnick, Daniel T. (1998), 'Empirical Approaches to the Measurement of Welfare', *Journal of Economic Literature* 36(4): 2108.

Smart, John C. and Bernard Williams (1973), *Utilitarianism – For and Against*, Cambridge: Cambridge University Press.

Snyder,Wilson I. (1902), *Mines and Mining*, Chicago: T. H. Flood.

Solnick, Sara and D. Hemenway (1996), 'The Deadweight Loss of Christmas: Comment', *American Economic Review* 86(5): 1328–1336.

Spohn, Cassia and J. Horney (1992), *Rape Law Reform: A Grassroots Revolution and Its Impact*, New York: Plenum Press.

Sprenkel, S. Vander (1962), 'Legal Institutions in Manchu China', in *London School of Economics, Monographs on Social Anthropology*, 24. London: Athlone.

Stanley, Timothy James (1994), 'An Analysis of the Rules of Contribution and No-Contribution for Joint and Several Liability in Conspiracy Cases', *Santa Clara Law Review* 35: 1–122.

Starrett, David A. (1972), 'Fundamental Nonconvexities in the Theory of Externalities', *Journal of Economic Theory* 4: 180–199.

Steffen, Jerome (1983), 'The Mining Frontiers of California and Australia: A Study in Comparative Political Change and Continuity', *Pacific Historical Quarterly* 52(4): 428.

Stigler, George J. (1966), *The Theory of Price*, 3rd edition, New York: Macmillan.

Stigler, George J. (1970), 'The Optimal Enforcement of Law', *Journal of Political Economy* 78: 526–536.

Stigler, George J. (1982), *Economists and Public Policy*, Washington, DC: American Institute for Public Policy Research.

Stowe, Harriet Beecher (1981), *Uncle Tom's Cabin*, introduction by Alfred Kazin, New York: Bantam Books.

Sunstein, Cass (1994), 'Incommensurability and Valuation in Law', *Michigan Law Review* 92(4): 779–861.

Sunstein, Cass (1997), *Free Markets and Social Justice*, New York: Oxford Press.

Svenson, Ola and G. Karlsson (1989), 'Decision-Making, Time Horizons, and Risk in the Very Long Term Perspective', *Risk Analysis* 9: 385–398.

Talbott, William (1988), 'Cost Spreading and Benefit Spreading in Tort Law', *Research in Law and Economics* 11: 25–51.

Talbott, William (2000), 'Are there Universal Human Rights?', Working Paper, Department of Philosophy, University of Washington, Seattle.

Thaler, Richard (1985), 'Mental Accounting and Consumer Choice', *Marketing Science*, 4.

Thaler, Richard (1991), *Quasi Rational Economics*, New York: Russel Sage Foundation.

Thomas, Lewis (1992), *The Fragile Species*, New York: Charles Scribner's Sons.

Titmuss, Richard (1971), *The Gift Relationship: From Human Blood to Social Policy*, New York: Pantheon Books.

Toole, Caleb and R. Levy (1981), *Criminal Law: Cases and Materials*, Boston: Little, Brown.

Trumbull, William (1990), 'Who has Standing in Cost–Benefit Analysis?', *Journal of Policy Analysis and Management* 9(2): 201–218.

Tullock, Gordon (1980), 'Two Kinds of Efficiency', *Hofstra Law Review* 8: 659–669.

Umbeck, John R. (1981), *A Theory of Property Rights: With an Application to the California Gold Rush*, Ames: Iowa State University Press.

United States, National Park Service (1995), *Final Environmental Impact Statement: Elwha River Ecosystem Restoration*, Denver, CO: United States Department of Interior, National Park Service, Denver Service Center.

Utset, Manuel (1995), 'Emerging Markets in the Age of Mechanical Reproduction', *Boston University International Law Journal* 13(Fall): 351–365.

Wade, John W. *et al.* (1994), *Cases and Materials on Torts*, 9th edition, Westbury: Foundation Press.

Wald, Alexandra (1997), 'What's Rightfully Ours: Toward a Property Theory of Rape', *Columbia Journal of Law and Social Problems* 30: 459–502.

Waldfogel, Joel (1993), 'The Deadweight Loss of Christmas', *American Economic Review* 83(5–6): 1328–1336.

Weber, Max (1958), *From Max Weber: Essay in Sociology*, Trans. and ed. with an introduction by Hans. H. Gerth and C. Wright Mills, New York: Oxford University Press.

Weimer, David L. and A. R. Vining (1992), *Policy Analysis: Concepts and Practice*, 2nd edition, Englewood Cliffs: Prentice Hall.

Weingast, Barry R. (1997), 'The Political Foundations of Democracy and the Rule of Law', *American Political Science Review* 91(2): 245.

West, Robin (1986), 'Submission, Choice, and Ethics: A Rejoinder to Judge Posner', *Harvard Law Review* 99: 1449–1456.

West, Robin (1993), 'Sex, Reason, and a Taste for the Absurd', *Georgetown Law Journal* 81: 2413–2430.

Whittington, Dale and Duncan MacRae, Jr. (1986), 'The Issue of Standing in Cost–Benefit Analysis', *Journal of Policy Analysis and Management* 5: 665.

Whittington, Dale and Duncan MacRae, Jr. (1990), 'Judgements about Who has Standing in Cost–Benefit Analysis: A Comment', *Journal of Policy Analysis and Management*, 9(4): 536–547.

Williams, Glanville (1983), *Textbook of Criminal Law*, London: Stevens.

Willig, Robert (1976), 'Consumer Surplus Without Apology', *American Economic Review* 66(4): 589–597.

Wilson, Edward O. (1998), *Consilience: The Unity of Knowledge*, New York: Alfred Knopf.

Wittgenstein, Ludwig (1921), *Tractatus Logico-Philosophicus*, in Proposi-

tions 6.4–7: D. Pears and B. Mcguiness, Trans. London: Routledge and Kegan Paul, pp. 145–151.
Wodehouse, Pelham G. (1943), *Big Money*, New York: Penguin.
Wohl, Alexander (1997), 'Paper Trailblazer', *ABA Journal* 83: 68–73.
Wolcher, Louis (1997), 'Ronald Dworkin's Right Answers Thesis through the Lens of Wittgenstein', *Rutgers Law Journal* 29(1): 43–65.
Wolf, Charles (1979), 'A Theory of Nonmarket Failure: Framework for Implementation Analysis', *Journal of Law and Economics* 22(1): 107–139.
Yi, Jong G. (1990), 'Litigations with Multiple Defendants: How to Settle under Different Apportionment Rules', *Stanford University Center for Economic Policy Research*, Publication No. 255.
Zelder, Martin (1993), 'Incompletely Reasoned Sex: A Review of Posner's Somewhat Misleading Guide to the Economic Analysis of Sex and Family Law', *Michigan Law Review* 91: 1584–1608.
Zerbe, Richard O., Jr. (1976), 'The Problem of Social Cost: Fifteen Years Later', in Steven A. Y. Lin (ed.), *Theory and Measurement of Externalities*: New York: Academic Press, pp. 29–36.
Zerbe, Richard O., Jr. (1980), 'The Problem of Social Cost in Retrospect', *Research in Law and Economics* 2: 83–102.
Zerbe, Richard O., Jr. (1991), 'Comment: Does Benefit–Cost Analysis Stand Alone? Rights and Standing', *Journal of Policy Analysis and Management* 10(1): 96–105.
Zerbe, Richard O., Jr. (1998a), 'An Integration of Equity and Efficiency', *Washington Law Review* 73(April): 349–361.
Zerbe, Richard O., Jr. (1998b), 'Is Cost–Benefit Analysis Legal? Three Rules', *Journal of Policy Analysis and Management* 17(3): 419–456.
Zerbe, Richard O., Jr. (2001), 'What is Economic Efficiency? A New Paradigm', Working Paper, The Evans School of Public Policy.
Zerbe, Richard O., Jr. and C. L. Anderson (1999), 'Fairness and Efficiency in the California Gold Fields', Working Paper, Evans School of Public Affairs, University of Washington.
Zerbe, Richard O., Jr. and D. Dively (1994), *Benefit Cost Analysis in Theory and Practice*, New York: Harper Collins.
Zerbe, Richard O., Jr. and L. Graham (1999), 'The Role of Rights in Benefit–Cost Methodology: The Example of Salmon and Hydroelectric Dams', *Washington Law Review* 74(3): 763–797.
Zerbe, Richard O., Jr. and H. McCurdy (1999), 'The Failure of Market Failure', *Journal of Policy Analysis and Management* 18(4): 558–578.
Zerbe, Richard O., Jr. and H. McCurdy (2000), 'The End of Market Failure', *Regulations* 23(2): 10–14.
Zerbe, Richard O., Jr. and S. G. Medema (1997), 'Ronald Coase, The

British Tradition, and the Future of Economic Method', in Steven G. Medema (ed.), *Coasean Economics: Law and Economics and the New Institutional Economics*, Boston: Kluwer Academic Publishers, pp. 209–238.

Zerbe, Richard O., Jr. and Nicole Urban (1988), 'Towards a Public Interest Theory of Regulation', *Research in Law and Economics*. 11: 1–23.

Zupan, Mark A. (1996), 'Are Public Goods Good for the Public?', working paper, University of Southern California Business School, Los Angeles, California.

Name index

Subject index